Ready-to-Use
AMERICA...
HISTORY
ACTIVITIE...

FOR GRADES 5-12

Lessons & Skillsheets from...
Pre-Columbus to the Space ...

JAMES F. SILVER

**THE CENTER FOR APPLIED
RESEARCH IN EDUCATION**
West Nyack, New York 10994

Library of Congress Cataloging-in-Publication Data

Silver, James F.
    Ready-to-use American history activities for grades 5–12 : lessons and skill sheets from pre-Columbus to the Space Age / James F. Silver
        p. cm.
    ISBN 0-87628-142-0 : Spiral   ISBN 0-87628-756-9 : Paper
    1. United States—History—Study and Teaching (Elementary)— Problems, exercises, etc. [1.
    United States—History—Study and teaching (Secondary)—Problems, exercises, etc.] 1. Title.
    LB1582.U6S55   1995   95-13220
    973'.071—dc20   CIP

©1995 by The Center for Applied Research in Education, West Nyack, NY

Printed in the United States of America

10 9 8 7 6 5 4 3 2 (S)   10 9 8 7 6 5 4 3 2 1 (P)

ISBN 0-87628-142-0 (S)   ISBN 0-87628-756-9 (P)

 THE CENTER FOR APPLIED RESEARCH IN EDUCATION
West Nyack, NY 10994
A Simon & Schuster Company

On the World Wide Web at http://www.phdirect.com

Prentice-Hall International (UK) Limited, *London*
Prentice-Hall of Australia Pty. Limited, *Sydney*
Prentice-Hall Canada Inc., *Toronto*
Prentice-Hall Hispanoamericana, S.A., *Mexico*
Prentice-Hall of India Private Limited, *New Delhi*
Prentice-Hall of Japan, Inc., *Tokyo*
Simon & Schuster Asia Pte. Ltd., *Singapore*
Editora Prentice-Hall do Brasil, Ltda., *Rio de Janeiro*

Dedication

American History Activities is dedicated to those Trenton State College colleagues—administrators, librarians, instructors, staff— who have in various and numerous ways enabled me to write this book for in-service teachers. Special thanks and appreciation are given to Vice-President for Academic Affairs, Claire Hardgrove; Dean of the School of Education, Suzanne Pasch; and Chairperson of the Elementary/Early Education Department, Larry Marcus, for their help and support.

ACKNOWLEDGMENTS

Several individuals and publishing houses have been of immeasurable help in the creation of *American History Activities*.

Mary Salerno, a graduate of Trenton State College's School of Business, who is now a free-lance computer and word processing expert, processed and made camera-ready the complete narrative, including all of the charts, graphs, tables, diagrams, and many of the maps and illustrations. She applied both technical skill and resourcefulness to all that she did.

Steve Busti, a Trenton State college graduate who majored in the graphic arts, drew most of the illustrations and many of the maps in the book. He did more than simply follow instructions; creativity and resourcefulness are evident in everything he produced.

David Evanetz's drawings are the epitome of clarity, as may be seen in the illustrations on pages 178, 201, 216, 218, 219, 220, 227, 232, and 251. Two of artist Evanetz's illustrations grace the cover of *American History Activities*.

Sheila Sweeney of Fair Haven, Massachusetts, as her first venture into textbook illustration, made the drawings that appear on pages 32, 56, 58 (fig. 1), and 226.

Lorna Jean Elliot, a graduate of Susquehanna University, PA, and the Bread Loaf School of English, Middlebury College, Middlebury, VT, copy-edited the entire manuscript and answer key. Her ability to find and address matters needing correction or clarification was remarkable.

Thanks are also given to Silver Burdett Company, and Ginn and Company for their kind permission to reprint illustrations and maps the author used in books he authored for them, including the two volume *The United States Yesterday and Today* (Ginn), and the *Skillbook for the Changing New World* (Silver Burdett).

Permission to adapt some material from *Quaint Idioms and Expressions of the Pennsylvania Germans*, published by the Aurand Press, Lancaster, PA, is greatly appreciated.

ABOUT THE AUTHOR

James F. Silver received his B.A. in Social Studies from Montclair (New Jersey) State College, his M.A. in History from Boston University, his M.A. in Educational Administration from Montclair State College, and his Ed.D. in Curriculum and Instruction from Pacific Western University in Los Angeles. Professor Silver also studied the psychology of reading at Temple University in Philadelphia, which led to his New Jersey state certification as a reading specialist.

Professor Silver's experience includes nine years as an elementary school teacher and principal in Morris County, New Jersey, and more than 35 years in the School of Education at Trenton (New Jersey) State College, where he is now Professor Emeritus in Residence.

During his educational career, Professor Silver has written numerous teachers' manuals, geography and history skill development books, and achievement tests for Silver Burdett Company. He is author of *Geography Skills Activities Kit* and *World Geography Activities* published by the Center for Applied Research in Education. Previous to *American History Activities* he wrote *Environmental Awareness* published by Kendall/Hunt Company. The last four books cited above were written on the professional level for in-service teachers.

ABOUT THIS RESOURCE

Geography and History

"Geography is the mother of all history" is a meaningful phrase. Every event in history took place in a geographical setting. Setting influences events before and during their occurrence, and it influences outcomes. The setting may be a primary cause of an event—as the situation during colonial times when the French, English, seaboard colonists, and Indians all coveted the lush lands between the Appalachian Mountains, Mississippi River, Ohio River, and Great Lakes. The result was the French and Indian War. Or, setting may influence the nature and outcome of an event—as in the D-Day invasion of Normandy, France, during World War II. Normandy's particular geography, the nature of its surrounding waters, even the weather conditions of that particular day—all influenced the tactics employed by the Allies, the casualties they suffered, and the eventual outcome of the event.

Thus, geography is given considerable emphasis in *American History Activities*. The first lesson in the book is concerned with geography, "North America: The Setting for American History." Would it be possible to understand the treks of people across the land bridge, now the Bering Strait, to North America—the reason why all early New World settlements were made on the banks of rivers, or the coasts of oceans, seas, and lakes—without geography and its companion study, climate? Probably not.

Subject Matter and Skills

There is an old saying that applies to teaching: "Give me a fish, and I will eat today; teach me to fish, and I will eat forever." This book treats subject matter as the "fish" and work-study skills as the means of "fishing" well. Every lesson in *American History Activities* is subject-matter centered; simultaneously, every lesson gives special attention to developing reading and work-study skills. Subject matter may naturally be forgotten over a period of time, but well developed work-study skills will improve the quality and quantity of students' retentive powers. Even more important, such skills will facilitate students' abilities to retrieve information and to learn independently.

An example of combining subject matter and skill development is illustrated by the student application activity on page 37. The subject matter concerns the variety of activities carried out by French settlers in the New World. The skills employed to facilitate comprehension and retention of that material are (1) gaining information from pictures by noting details and (2) determining the main idea of a picture by discerning the relationships and patterns of its parts. Both of these skills are clearly related to reading a paragraph for its main idea and supporting details. Every application page in the book could be so analyzed.

Instructor's Pages

Throughout *American History Activities* are numerous pages designed to give help in supplementing instruction. Indicated in the top right margin as "Instructor's Page: Information and Suggestions," these pages may apply to the application page or pages that follow. It will be helpful at times to photocopy an entire instructor's page, or part of it, for distribution among the students.

Instructor's pages will vary according to the nature of the subject being studied. For example, on page 119 two tables of statistics are listed on the topic of land and sea transportation which the instructor may make available to the students so as to develop skill in completing bar graphs. In another example, page 147, the novel *Uncle Tom's Cabin* is synopsized for the instructor to read or tell, while the following page provides an opportunity for students to react to the story.

The kinds of information and suggestions that instructor's pages may include are listed below:

☞ discussion-type questions and points that could be included in the discussions

☞ diagrams, charts, tables, and graphs that may be made into transparencies

☞ suggested activities—for example, an "American History to 1860 Trivia Challenge" game complete with questions, answers, and board diagram

☞ extra information that will enhance topics under study

☞ a complete answer key for all student application pages

Noteworthy Personalities in American History

The persons listed below have made significant contributions to the history of the United States. Each one is featured in a one- or two-page account that is, in most cases, accompanied by illustrations. The personalities represent a cross section of American society: women and men of various ethnic and racial groups, occupations, and specialities. The personalities featured include, in order of presentation in the book, the following:

- Ferdinand Magellan (explorer)
- Sir Francis Drake (adventurer)
- Peter Zenger (newspaper publisher)
- Ben Franklin (patriot)
- Paul Revere (patriot)
- Alexander Hamilton (patriot)
- Sequoia (Indian scholar)
- Thomas Jefferson (patriot, president)
- Meriwether Lewis and William Clark (explorers)
- Sacajawea (Indian guide)
- Narcissa Whitman (pioneer missionary)
- John Fitch (inventor)
- Robert Fulton (inventor)
- Cyrus McCormick (inventor)
- Samuel Morse (inventor)
- Harriet Tubman (slave liberator)
- Frederick Douglass (abolitionist)

- Abraham Lincoln (president)
- John Ericsson (inventor)
- Clara Barton (teacher, nurse)
- Chief Joseph (Indian leader)
- George Washington Carver (inventor)
- George Washington Goethals (canal builder)
- Matthew Henson (explorer)
- Charles Lindbergh (aviator)
- Herbert Hoover (humanitarian, president)
- Jim Thorpe (athlete)
- Mildred "Babe" Didrikson (athlete)
- Jesse Owens (athlete)
- Althea Gibson (athlete)
- Dwight Eisenhower (soldier, president)
- Albert Einstein (mathematician)
- Jack Kennedy (naval officer, president)
- Martin Luther King (civil rights leader)
- Christa McAuliffe (astronaut)

In addition to the above listed persons, more than passing reference has been made to persons who, directly or indirectly, significantly affected the development of the United States. The list includes:

- Ponce de Leon (explorer)
- Hernando Cortes (explorer)
- Hernando De Soto (explorer)
- Francisco Coronado (explorer)
- Giovanni da Verrazano (explorer)
- Jacques Cartier (explorer)
- Samuel de Champlain (explorer)
- Sieur de LaSalle (explorer)
- Estevanico (explorer)
- Francis Marion (guerilla fighter)
- Haym Salomon (financier)
- John Paul Jones (ship captain)

- York (explorer)
- Jim Beckwourth (mountain man)
- George Bush (pioneer)
- James Watt (inventor)
- Eli Whitney (inventor)
- Jan Matzeliger (inventor)
- Sojourner Truth (abolitionist)
- John Brown (abolitionist)
- Carl Schurz (soldier)
- Robert Smalls (ship captain)
- Orville and Wilbur Wright (inventors)

In addition, vignettes of Joseph Stalin, Benito Mussolini, and Adolph Hitler are presented.

Student Application Pages

Some important characteristics of the student application pages throughout this text follow:

☞ There are more than 160 pages designed to bring about active student responses to the narratives and graphics that the pages contain.

☞ All of the student application pages have been designed to be photocopied as needed for student use.

☞ Procedures and suggestions on the instructor's pages directly relate to the student application pages.

☞ Some student application pages are completed independently by students; other pages are completed as the instructor moves through the lesson.

☞ Almost every conceivable graphic is used throughout these pages: maps, illustrations, graphs, charts, tables, and diagrams.

☞ Work-study and reading skill development opportunity abounds throughout the student application pages: locating information, outlining, classifying, map reading, inferential thinking, picture reading, plotting graphs, determining main ideas and supporting details, vocabulary development, listing, listening, speaking, drawing, discussion, and many others.

Relationship of American History Activities to American History Textbooks

Basic American history textbooks must, of necessity, present a sweeping, chronological/topical history of the United States. There are, literally, thousand of topics, personalities, and events to be treated. *American History Activities* does not have that obligation. Its purpose is to extend and enrich selected elements of our history, elements that are worthy of special emphasis. For example, the acquisition of horses by native American Indians had an enormous impact on their ways of living. Yet, it is a rare elementary or secondary textbook that devotes more than a paragraph or two to the topic. *American History Activities* broadens that coverage with four full pages, "Indians and Horses," that contain information for the instructor, illustrations, and student activity pages.

The topics have been selected because of their general appeal, their ability to generate student interest, and their ability to shed light upon historical events. The materials have been arranged to facilitate lessons preparation for the teacher and active participation for the students. Some examples of lessons follow:

☞ "The Mayan Indians and Corn" (pp. 7–8)

☞ "The Voyages of Magellan" (pp. 23–24)

☞ "Minority Explorers and Builders" (pp. 51–52)

☞ "Sacajawea and the Lewis and Clark Expedition" (pp. 102–103)

☞ "Abraham Lincoln: From Log Cabin to White House" (pp. 156–157)

☞ "Building the Panama Canal" (pp. 191–193)

☞ "African-Americans and Others Fight Discrimination" (pp. 240–241)

Table of Contents

Section 5: English Activities in the New World

Section 6: Living in the English Colonies

Section 7: Confrontation Between the French and English

Section 8: England and Its American Colonies Disagree and Separate

Section 9: People, Issues, and Events After the Revolution

Section 10: Interest Grows in the Lands Beyond the Mississippi River

Section 11: Our First War as an Independent Nation

Section 12: A Singular Person and Event

Section 13: Growth in Industry, Agriculture, Transportation and Communication

Section 17: Developing the Great Plains

Section 18: A Singular Person

Section 19: The United States Expands Continentally and Internationally

Section 20: The United States Expands Its Population

Section 21: Beginnings—Automobiles and Airplanes

Section 22: World War I Through the Great Depression

Section 23: American Sports Heroes

Section 24: World War II

Section 25: Post-WWII People and Events

S E C T I O N   1

Pre-Columbus North America

NORTH AMERICA: THE SETTING FOR AMERICAN HISTORY

"Geography," it has been said, "is the 'Mother of All History'." Everything that has happened, is happening, and will happen took place or will take place in a geographical setting. It is virtually impossible to completely understand an event without considering where it took place and the natural and political considerations of the place. Even the people participating in the event were somehow influenced in their thinking and perceptions by the geographical setting in which they were born and lived.

The best way, then, to start the study of American history, is by learning something about where it all happened. Therefore, throughout this book geography will be given considerable emphasis.

Suggestions for Teaching

1. Photocopy for distribution the map on the facing page and the bottom portion of this page.

2. As you mention the number at the beginning of each line below, have your students locate the number on the map and the physical feature it identifies. Then, they should write the name of the feature on the appropriate line.

3. You may also want to make a transparency of the map and the bottom portion of this page to complete as your students complete their page.

4. From time-to-time give additional information about the features. *Example*: Notice that the Mississippi River begins near the Canadian border.

NORTH AMERICA AND ITS MAJOR PHYSICAL FEATURES

Major Rivers

1. _____
2. _____
3. _____
4. _____
5. _____
6. _____
7. _____
8. _____

Major Mountain Chains

9. _____
10. _____
11. _____
12. _____

13. _____
14. _____
15. _____
16. _____

Major Islands/Groups

17. _____
18. _____
19. _____
20. _____
21. _____

Major Surrounding Waters

22. _____
23. _____
24. _____

25. _____
26. _____
27. _____
28. _____
29. _____
30. _____
31. _____
32. _____
33. _____

Major Lakes

34. _____
35. _____
36. _____
37. _____

Name: _____ Date: _____

NORTH AMERICA: THE SETTING FOR AMERICAN HISTORY

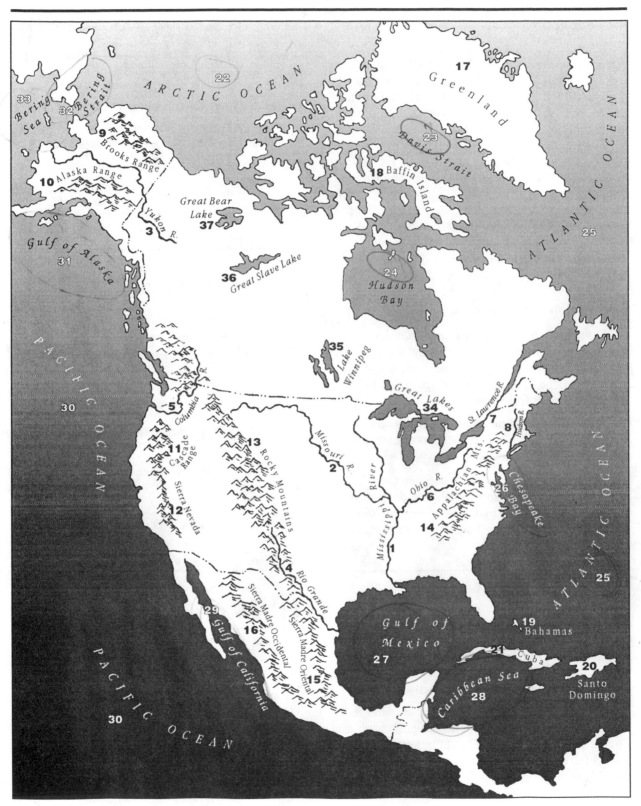

THE EARLIEST AMERICANS

Introduction

Evidence is mounting that indicates North America has been inhabited by people, whom Columbus called "Indians," for at least 20,000, and perhaps 40,000, years. Most historians believe that the earliest of these people came from Asia, most likely Siberian Asia. They carried themselves, their children, and their scanty possessions over a land bridge, since sunken and replaced by the Bering Strait. They had no beasts of burden, and they did not know the use of the wheel. They obtained their food by hunting, fishing, or gathering. Yet, over a period of several thousand years they managed to populate every region of North America and South America—a remarkable people and a remarkable feat.

Suggestions for Teaching

1. Supply your students with photocopies of the map and text on the facing page, and the question page that follows it. Have your students find the answers to the questions from the map and the accompanying information.

After the questions have been answered discussions can take place with supplemental questions and comments made.

2. How many Indians are living in the United States today? The most reliable and up-to-date statistics are furnished by the *Statistical Abstract of the United States* and are listed in the next column.

Make the statistics available to your students via the chalk board. Then, have them show the data on the incomplete graph on page 5. Remind them that each symbol is to represent 20,000 Indians, and that it may be necessary to have a partial symbol at the end of a line of symbols for a particular state.

The Ten States with the Greatest Indian Population	
State	**Indian Population (Rounded)**
Oklahoma (OK)	250,000
California (CA)	240,000
Arizona (AZ)	200,000
New Mexico (NM)	130,000
North Carolina (NC)	80,000
Washington (WA)	80,000
Texas (TX)	60,000
New York (NY)	60,000
Michigan (MI)	60,000
South Dakota (SD)	50,000

Notes:

1. The statistics for each state have been rounded to the nearest 10,000.

2. The term "Indian" does not include Eskimo and Aleut.

3. *National Geographic* (October, 1991) gave a figure of some 2,000,000 Indians in North America at the time of Columbus's landing in 1492.

Indian Sign Language

Even though there were many different Indian languages and dialects spoken in pre- and after-Columbus America, various tribes still were able to communicate effectively through signs. Even today many of the signs used for communicating with the hard-of-hearing resemble Indian signs.

You can bring your students' attentions to some aspects of Indian sign language through the illustrations that follow. It might be amusing to use some of the signs in class, for example, the signs for "Yes" and "No."

YES

Right hand: fingers clenched, facing down, even with shoulder
Index finger: pointing up
Second finger: pressed by thumb

Action: Drop hand quickly downward; index finger closes over thumb

NO

Right hand: facing left; fingers unclenched

Action: Arm swings right, palm up

Return to original position

Name: _____ Date: _____

THE EARLIEST AMERICANS

Early People of North America: The information on this page is about the earliest people, later to be called "Indians," who migrated from Asia to North America. The process took thousands of years. Each group that came into North America either settled in camps abandoned by earlier settlers or moved on and beyond to establish settlements of their own.

Bering Strait - Once a land bridge, now a strip of water about 50 miles long . . .before the land sank could be crossed by walking, later crossed by small boat or by walking on ice in winter . . .

Isthmus of Panama - Land bridge used by early people to enter South America from North America, now the site of the Panama Canal . . .

Food Eaten by Early People - Huge mammoths (now extinct), caribou, and smaller animals; nuts, berries, roots; fish . . .

Clothing of Early People - Made from skins of animals sewn together with leather thongs . . . no knowledge of weaving as a means of making cloth . . .

Shelter of Early People - Caves, tents made of skin, ice houses (igloos) . . .

Weapons - Spears, sticks, stones . . . no bows and arrows in the earliest groups . . .

Method of Travel - Walking and carrying possessions on their backs, some rafting if currents carried them in the desired direction . . .

Routes of Early People in North America

Tribes - Hundreds of tribes scattered all over the American continents, a migration process that took thousands of years . . . regional settlements and some of the tribes that lived in the area:

Region	Tribe Example
• Arctic 1	Eskimo
• Northwest Coast 2	Chinook
• Far North 3	Huron
• California/ Intermountain 4	Hopi, Ute
• Southwest Plains 5	Apache, Pueblo
• Great Plains (west of the Mississippi River) 6	Pawnee, Sioux
• Plains (east of the Mississippi River) 7	Cherokee, Chickasaw
• Southeast 8	Seminole
• Eastern Woodlands 9	Iroquois, Delaware
• Mexico 10	Aztec
• Yucatan 11	Mayan
• West Indies 12	Carib, Arawak

Note: Numbers listed after each region correspond to numbers shown on the map.

Of interest: Before the earliest people came to North America, horses roamed the land. Then, for unknown reasons, the horses either died or wandered north and crossed the land bridge into Asia. They returned with the Spanish explorers in the early 1500's. Eventually the Indians, as they were called, captured some of the horses and learned how to ride them and use them for transporting possessions from place to place . . . Eastern Woodlands Indians began farming about three thousand years ago, but it took many years for farming to become their most important way of obtaining food. When this happened it meant that more time could be spent on developing permanent homes and villages, government, art and other forms of culture . . . All of the Indian tribes scattered over the continent had to adapt to the environment in which they lived. Thus, Indian tribes developed different ways of living. Arctic Indians and Northwest Coast Indians depended on fish and, later, whales for food, but the Great Plains Indians depended upon the buffalo. Southwest Plains Indians built homes on the sides of cliffs; Great Plains Indians built tents of skins or constructed sod houses; Northwest Indians erected homes of wood and bark, and so on . . .

Name: _____ Date: _____

THE EARLIEST AMERICANS

Text Questions

Answer *Yes* or *No* to the following questions:

1. Did the early people find horses when they arrived in North America? _____

2. Did the early people know how to weave cloth? _____

3. Did the Woodlands Indians know how to farm when Columbus came to North America? _____

4. Could mammoths be hunted today? _____

5. Was the land bridge between Asia and North America about 50 miles long? _____

6. Were the Northwest Indians mostly dependent on buffalo for food? _____

7. Did the Southwest Plains Indians build their shelters mostly from skins? _____

Map Questions

1. What two rivers did the early people first follow when they entered North America? _____

_____

2. What river did the early people follow that led them to the Mississippi River? _____

3. What river joins the Mississippi River from the east? _____ In which direction does this river flow, toward the northeast or toward the southwest? _____

4. What were two of the islands that the Carib and the Arawak inhabited? _____

_____

5. What four groups of Indians settled around the Gulf of Mexico? _____

_____

6. *To do:* Lightly color blue all the waters surrounding North America, and the lakes within the continent.

Matching

Write the number of the item in the first column on the line before its matching item in the second column.

1. Mayan	_____ Southeast
2. Iroquois	_____ Far North
3. Apache	_____ Eastern Woodlands
4. Chinook	_____ West Indies
5. Pawnee	_____ Mexico
6. Aztec	_____ Yucatan
7. Carib	_____ Southwest Plains
8. Huron	_____ Northwest Coast
9. Seminole	_____ Great Plains

The Ten States with the Greatest Indian Populations												
State												
OK												
CA												
AZ												
NM												
NC												
WA												
TX												
NY												
MI												
SD												

Ⓘ = 20,000 Indians

Name: _____ Date: _____

INDIAN RUINS OF OLD MEXICO

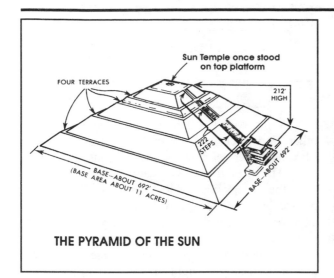

THE PYRAMID OF THE SUN

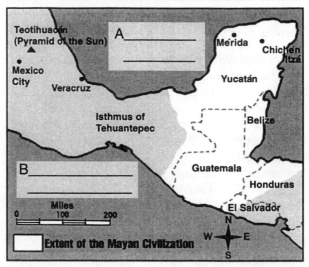

Chichén Itzá, now in ruins, was the holy capital city of the ancient Mayans. It was founded about 1500 years ago near two great wells. One well was used for a water supply. The other, called the Well of Sacrifice, was used in religious ceremonies to please the Mayan's rain-god. It is about 180 feet wide, and the water level is about 70 feet below the rim. In bad (dry) times, pilgrims came from great distances to attend the sacrifices of human beings who were hurled into the well, and to sacrifice valuable personal objects—gold, silver, or jade ornaments, etc.

Chichén Itzá, with its observatory, great temples, and palaces, was at its greatest about A.D. 1200 under foreign rulers, the Toltecs.

The Toltecs came from Teotihuacán (Home of the Gods). They had built there the famous Pyramid of the Sun. Their Aztec conquerors later enlarged this pyramid. It was built of adobe brick, covered with cut stone, and decorated with elaborate, brilliantly colored carved pictures and designs.

Steep steps lead up to the top platform on which the Sun Temple once stood. This pyramid is about as high as a modern 20-story office building. The base covers an area large enough to lay out 51 full-size baseball diamonds with room to spare.

1. Underline the correct choice in each set of parentheses.

Chichén Itzá was built by (*Mayans and Toltecs, Toltecs and Aztecs*). Its location was determined by (*gold, fertile land, wells*). The Well of Sacrifice was about (*70, 100, 180*) feet across. The city was begun about (*500, 1000, 1500*) years ago and was located on the (*Isthmus of Tehuantepec, peninsula of Yucatan*).

2. Parts of what five present-day countries were once part of the Mayan civilization?

_____ _____ _____

_____ _____

3. What are the dimensions of the Pyramid of the Sun?

Height: _____ Length: _____ Area: _____

4. What is the location of the Pyramid of the sun?

Direction from Mexico City: _____

Distance from Mexico City: _____

5. Complete the map labeling. At:

A: *Gulf of Campeche*   B: *Pacific Ocean*

THE MAYAN INDIANS AND CORN

It seems certain that it was the Mayan Indians of Central America who were the first to discover and cultivate corn. At first, thousands of years ago, corn was a wild, slender grass, the seeds of which the Mayans gathered for food. Then, some shrewd Mayan may have had the idea that if some of the seeds were planted, more plants and seeds could be produced. Or, perhaps, it was an accidental discovery: some seeds fell to the ground and an observant and thoughtful Mayan saw the relationship between the seeds and the new plants that sprang up. Regardless of how the Mayans got the idea of planting, this was the probable beginning of agriculture in the Americas. A steady and reliable source of food was now available.

Plants sometimes produce "odd" fruits and seeds; i.e., they are not like the normal yield. So it was with corn grass: a Mayan, most likely, noticed that some of the seeds of the corn grass were in a **cluster** surrounded by a husk or covering. When the seeds from these plants were planted they, in turn, produced **husked** seeds (kernels). This was a wonderful development. Corn grass that produced only a few seeds was replaced by plants that produced many more kernels per plant with less work and less planting space.

1. *Complete the cartoon on the facing page showing a Mayan woman who has noticed a plant with many more corn seeds. In the balloon write the thoughts that might be racing through her head.*

The development of agriculture (planting of seeds to produce food) had tremendous effects throughout all of pre-Columbus America. Now, people did not have to move from place to place to obtain food by hunting and gathering. People could live in one place for a long period of time. This would give them opportunities to develop government, religion, art, sport, recreation, permanent shelters, and in the case of the Mayans, writing, arithmetic, and sciences, including astronomy.

2. *Why would a knowledge of astronomy (the motions and relationships of the sun, moon, stars, earth, etc.) be useful in the cultivation of corn and other crops?*

_____

_____
_____
_____
_____

Along with the benefits of growing corn and other crops there were some harmful results. The Mayans never learned about the conservation of soil. They found that with each planting the yield from their crops became less and less. They didn't realize that by planting crops in the same fields year after year the soil wore out. So, they would move from place to place seeking rich soil. But—and here is a good result of a bad practice—wherever they moved they brought their knowledge of agriculture and all the useful other things they had learned.

3. *What might the Mayans have done to continue to use the same fields and still obtain good crops? Think of what farmers do today.*

_____

_____

_____

_____

_____

Some Mayans, the more adventurous, moved far north into what is now the southwestern United States; others moved into the Mississippi River Valley, and other places. In this way the knowledge of the Mayans spread. Eventually, hundreds of years later, almost all the Indians in the two continents had learned how to grow food. The people who benefited from the Mayan discoveries now had time to develop their own civilizations. It wasn't only the exchange of knowledge and ideas that took place; the trading of *things* also began. For example, volcanic glass used for making sharp knives that could only have come from the Rocky Mountain regions has been found in the graves of mound builders in Ohio. The mound builders probably traded copper for the glass.

THE MAYAN INDIANS AND CORN

4. *The incomplete map can show where the Mayans lived and some of the places mentioned in the story.* **Note**: *The names of the places are modern and did not exist in Mayan times; for example, there was no United States.*

Label the map, as follows:

1. *Yucatan* (site of greatest Mayan development)
2. *Mexico*
3. *Guatemala*
4. *Honduras*
5. *Pacific Ocean*
6. *Caribbean Sea*
7. *Gulf of Mexico*
8. *SW United States*
9. *Mississippi Valley*

What were some of the relationships between the early European settlers and corn? The Europeans learned from the Indians not only about corn, but also about other foods: squash, pumpkins, white potatoes, sweet potatoes, tomatoes, artichokes, beans, peanuts and that sweetest of sweets—maple sugar. If it were not for the Indians—Squanto, in particular—showing the Pilgrims how to grow corn, they may have starved. If that had happened, it seems certain that American history would have been different.

5. Authors use words and phrases called "qualifiers" to indicate to the readers that something they are writing may not be a fact. This is especially true when the narrative is about ancient times. Words such as "about" or "probably so" are examples of qualifiers.

Go back through the story and draw a circle around each qualifier.

Name: _____ Date: _____

THE NEW WORLD AND THE OLD WORLD — FIVE HUNDRED YEARS AGO

1. Study the two illustrations. How are the Europeans and the Eastern Woodlands Indians different? In the chart below list the differences you observe.

ITEM	INDIANS	EUROPEANS
Weapons		
Boats		
Homes		
Ways of transporting goods		
Roads		
Clothing of men		
Clothing of women		
Ways of transporting people		

2. What are two animals that appear in both pictures?

_____   _____

3. Identify three activities that are being carried out as shown in the Indian picture.

_____ _____ _____

4. Wind will furnish the power to drive the European ship. What kind of power will drive the canoe?

_____

5. In the Indian picture what do you notice about the clothing of both the women and men that could serve not only as decorations, but also as a means of keeping flying insects off their arms and legs?

_____

6. From what you can observe in the Indian picture, what would be your guess as to the season of the year it shows? Explain. _____

_____

7. Do you think the European ship is being readied to leave for the New World, or is it returning? Explain your answer. _____

_____

8. Notice the man standing on the paved dock on the left side of the picture. What is there about him that might lead you to think he is a guard? _____

_____

Name: _____ Date: _____

THE NEW WORLD AND THE OLD WORLD — FIVE HUNDRED YEARS AGO

Observing a Picture for Details

How sharp are you at picking out details in a picture? In the Indian camp picture circle the following:

- the baby in the papoose
- the women shelling corn
- the hollow log in which corn is pounded into flour
- the pumpkins
- the corn stalks

In the European port picture circle the following:

- a castle or fort
- the garden tools
- a woman's pocketbook
- a gun
- the crow's nest of a ship
- the feathered cap

INDIANS AND HORSES

The story that follows, "Indians and Horses," may be used in various ways. Here are some suggestion that you may want to utilize:

Completing an Outline

Read and/or narrate the story to your students. As you complete a paragraph, pause and have your listeners complete the partial outline on page 14. If it seems desirable or necessary you can also complete the outline on a transparency as they complete theirs. *Note:* See the completed outline in the answer key.

To supplement the reading make a transparency (or photocopies for distribution) of the illustrations on page 13. As you reach the part of the story where the illustration best applies project it and explain it. Here is some additional information about each illustration:

Picture 1: Spanish Soldiers

The Spaniards' horses were bred for size and strength; they had to carry full-grown soldiers clad in heavy armor. Sometimes, the horse itself had protective armor; this was important because if the horse were wounded it might mean that the rider would be wounded or killed . . . Helmets were often topped with colorful plumes; high boots helped protect soldiers' legs . . .

Picture 2: Indian Travois

The poles for the travois most likely came from trees that grew along stream banks. The original seeds of the trees may have floated down the streams from far away, became lodged, grew and proliferated along moist stream banks . . . Another possibility for obtaining poles for the travois (or for tepees) would be through trade with Indians who lived on the edges of wooded areas to the east or west . . . Horses were able to pull longer and sturdier travois; thus, the Indians were able to have larger tepees and more possessions. Sometimes travois poles were covered with animal skins, sometimes strips of wood were attached to the poles as in a ladder . . .

Picture 3: Buffalo Hunt

Buffalo were killed with either a lance (spear) or arrows. It would be rare that a full-grown buffalo could be killed with one arrow, so the hunter aimed for a hip. This would wound a buffalo, and it would fall down. Then, more arrows could be shot into the wounded animal . . . Often, a hunter's horse would be gored by a buffalo, thus putting the hunter's life in jeopardy . . . For later identification of kills, each arrow carried the special mark of the hunter . . .

Picture 4: Things Made from Buffalo

A joke has it that everything on a hog can be used except the grunt; this remark would be equally true of buffalo. What would you do with a buffalo's tail? Use it as a fly swatter . . . After crossing a stream in a bullboat, the skins were taken off the frame to be used in making a new boat when another stream was encountered . . . A buffalo-hide shield could deflect an arrow, but not a bullet . . . Tepees made from buffalo skins could be easily put up or dismantled, and skins could be easily packed on a travois . . . Buffalo was the mainstay of the plains Indians. After the railroads came and divided the herds, when trains stopped and passengers could have the "pleasure" of shooting buffalo at random, after white hunters killed millions of buffalo for their hides alone, and the herds were decimated almost to extinction, the demise of the plains Indians came about: their source of existence was gone . . .

INDIANS AND HORSES

Some discoveries and inventions are so revolutionary and powerful they change well-established ways of living almost "overnight." Examples of far-reaching creations would include Thomas Edison's incandescent lamp, gun powder and guns, the automobile, and the airplane. For the Indians of North America it was the acquisition of horses that brought about significant changes in the ways that they lived.

Fifty million years before the first humans made their way into North America there were horses on the continent. We know they were here because scientists have found their fossilized remains. Those first horses were no more than 11" tall. Then, through natural selection and adaptation, horses grew in size, and their toes developed into hooves. It was about one million years ago that horses began to look very much like they

INDIANS AND HORSES

are today. In recent centuries modifications in horses have come about as a result of selective breeding; that is, some horses have been bred by humans for strength, others for speed, and so on.

Something happened to horses thousands of years ago that never has been explained satisfactorily—they disappeared from the Western Hemisphere. The most widely accepted explanations for their disappearance are that because of climatic changes they died and/or they travelled over the land bridge, now the Bering Strait, into Asia. When the levels of the oceans rose, as a result of the melting of the continental ice caps, the land bridge became covered with water, thus cutting off possibility of return.

New World Indians had no knowledge of horses before the coming of the Europeans. They carried everything either on their own backs, the backs of dogs, or on *travois*. A travois looked like a stretcher of the kind used to carry wounded soldiers: buffalo skins were laid between two stout poles; two ends of the poles were attached to a dog's back while the other two ends dragged along the ground. Possessions or, perhaps, young children were then strapped to the travois. It was easy to track a travois because the dragging poles left two parallel grooves in the ground. If the Indians had known the use of the wheel and axle, it certainly would have been much easier on the dogs.

In 1519 when Cortes and his men landed on the coast of Mexico the Indians must have been astonished at the sight of men on horses. At first, some of the Indians thought that rider and horse were one being. Fear of the horses was one reason why the Spaniards were able to defeat the Aztec. How does a man on the ground and holding only a spear withstand the charge of a 1,500 pound horse carrying a soldier with armor, gun, and steel sword?

Horses accompanied Spanish explorers—Coronado and others—on their exploratory trips north into what is now the southwestern United States. As the Spaniards moved north they captured Indians and made them slaves. As slaves, the Indians took care of horses and, in so doing, learned how to ride them. Indians of other tribes took note of this and, by trade or by capturing horses that had wandered away or that had become wild, managed to establish their own herds. It took many years, but by 1700 most of the tribes west of the Mississippi River knew about and used horses.

What changes did the introduction of horses bring to Indian ways of living? For one thing, it made the millions of buffalo that roamed the Great Plains more easily and effectively hunted. Indian scouts riding far from their camps could spot buffalo that were on the move. Through a series of signals relayed from one high point to another, word of the buffalo sighting got back to camp. In a matter of minutes from the time buffalo were sighted, Indians on horses could be on their way to the hunt.

The hunt was not a wild every-man-for-himself event. Each hunter had a special task to carry out— a task that had been assigned by the buffalo-hunt leaders. Some hunters were to go after older buffalo; their hides would make tough shields for deflecting arrows in time of war. Other Indians were to kill buffalo cows for their tender meat. Inexperienced young hunters were to kill calves because they were easiest to bring down. It was a rare Indian who would violate the rules of the hunt; if he did, he was sure to be disgraced and punished.

After the hunt, fallen buffalo were processed for their meat, skin, bones, horns, and innards. The meat was either immediately eaten while it was fresh, or it was dried and stored to be used in the winter months. Skins were used for robes, blankets, and tent coverings. Bones were made into needles, arrow heads, and knives. Sinews made excellent thread for sewing skins. Strips of rawhide were used as cord in bows, or they could be stretched over frames resembling tennis rackets—snowshoes, of course—for walking over deep, prairie snow. Horns were hollowed for drinking containers; stomachs were made into water-tight bags. "Bullboats," used for crossing rivers, were made from skins that were stretched over basket-like frames. Nothing gained from the buffalo was wasted.

It was not that the Indians could not hunt and kill buffalo before they had horses. But, horses gave the Great Plains Indians mobility. Horses made it possible for the buffalo to be followed; formerly, the Indians had had to wait for the buffalo to come to them. The buffalo could be followed across the plains for hundreds of miles from east to west or from north to south. With horses the Indians had steady and secure access to food and all the things they needed to live.

That the Indians followed the buffalo for long distances meant that they had to become more efficient in transporting their possessions from place to place. It was horses that were the solution to the problem. Horses could carry people—women, children, older men and women—on their strong, broad backs. Also, horses could carry heavy loads and pull large travois. With increased mobility, Indians from one part of the Great Plains could meet other Indians and exchange ideas and carry on limited trade.

INDIANS AND HORSES

Spanish Soldiers

Buffalo Hunt

Indian Travois

Things Made from the Buffalo

Shield

Tepee

Drum

Bullboat

Name: _____ Date: _____

INDIANS AND HORSES

I.   Important discoveries and inventions
    A. _____
    B. _____
    C. _____
    D. _____
    E. _____

II. The development of horses
    A. Length of time in North America and how
       known
       1. _____
       2. _____
    B. Changes in horses
       1. _____
       2. _____
       3. Breeding
          a. _____
          b. _____

III. Disappearance of horses in North America
    A. Explanations
       1. _____
       2. _____

IV. Pre-horse Indian transportation
    A. Humans
    B. Dogs pulling travois
       1. Description of travois
          a. _____
          b. _____
          c. _____
    C. Items transported
       1. _____
       2. _____

V.   Cortes in Mexico
    A. _____
    B. _____
    C. _____

VI. Indians and horses
    A. Learning about horses

    B. Obtaining horses
       1. _____
       2. _____

VII. Locating buffalo with horses
    A. _____
    B. _____
    C. _____

VIII. Hunting buffalo
    A. Organized by leader
    B. Rules of hunt
       1. _____
       2. _____

IX. Processing buffalo
    A. Items obtained
       1. Meat
       2. Skins
          a. _____
          b. _____
          c. _____
       3. Bones
          a. _____
          b. _____
          c. _____
       4. Sinew for thread
       5. Rawhide
          a. _____
          b. _____
       6. Horns for containers
       7. Stomachs for bags
       8. Skins for boats

X.   Advantages of horses for hunting buffalo
    A. _____
    B. _____

XI. Advantages of horses for transportation
    A. _____
    B. _____

TEPEES: DWELLINGS FOR INDIANS OF THE PLAINS

Interesting Facts about Tepees

• There are two spellings for this type of Indian home: **tipi** and **tepee**. Tipi was the original from the Dakota Sioux. The word meant "place to dwell."

• Indians east of the Mississippi used bark to cover their tepees, but Great Plains Indians found buffalo hide more readily available, more flexible, and more portable.

• The hides of buffalo cows were most often used because they were softer. Buffalo cows killed in the spring were most desirable; their winter hair was already shed making the hides easier to scrape. The smaller tepees may have required less than a dozen hides; the larger tepees—such as a chief's—might have needed twenty to thirty hides.

• A tepee could be erected in less than five minutes if several people worked together. And, it could be dismantled just as quickly, then packed on a travois.

• Entrances, which were about three feet high, usually faced east to catch the morning sun and to avoid the prevailing westerly winds.

• After the basic tepee was erected, inner linings that extended five or six feet above the floor were attached. These linings acted as insulation, stopped drafts, and shed water that may have dripped from the tepee's top opening. Furthermore, up-drafts behind the lining helped clear smoke out of the tepee's smoke opening.

• Sleeping pallets of grass were often arranged around the fire pit as the spokes in a wheel radiate from a hub, thus, the feet of the sleeping occupants were closest to the fire. The Indians had no chairs, but back rests for sitting were erected at the heads of the beds.

• Possessions such as bows, arrow quivers, and axes were hung from the tepee's poles.

• To ensure stability of the tepee a rawhide rope was hung from where the poles met at the top of the tepee to stakes driven into the floor. The rope was tied to the stakes.

• The outer coverings of the tepees were carefully decorated. The men usually drew pictures depicting their exploits in war or hunting; the women were more inclined to draw geometric designs.

• It has been said that Indian tepees may be the best tent-like shelters ever designed. They were wondrously well-adapted to the natural environment and the materials the environment provided.

A completed scene

(5)

How to Build a Model Tepee

Materials:

❏ Styrofoam® board about 10" X 10"
❏ 9 Poles (1/4"–3/8") or straight branches approximately 12" long
❏ 12" length of string
❏ Cloth: rough burlap or canvas; approximately 9" x 24"
❏ Grass cuttings

Procedure: (#'s in ( ) refer to sketches)

1. Lay out three poles on a table. (1)

2. Tightly tie the poles together approximately 1 ½" from one of the ends of the poles. (1)

3. Press the poles—evenly spaced—into the Styrofoam®, thus forming a triangle. (1)

4. Evenly space the remaining 6 poles between the basic three poles. Press the poles into the Styrofoam®, and tie them at the knot. (2)

5. Cut a 3" slit in the long length of the cloth.

6. Decorate the cloth by cutting out and attaching Indian designs, or by drawing directly on the cloth. (3)

7. Attach the cloth to the poles. Fold back the flaps and pin them to the covering. (4)

8. Glue the grass cuttings around the perimeter of the tepee. (5)

9. Make and attach accessories such as a fire pit with a tripod from which a piece of meat is hanging, a rack for drying skins, etc. (5)

knot ⟍ }$1\frac{1}{2}$"

(1)

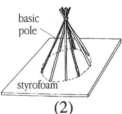

basic pole

styrofoam

(2)

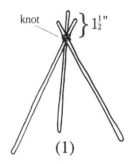

cloth

3" slit

(3) Note that covering is cut with a curved top and bottom, and slanted sides to conform to the conical frame.

(4)

Name: _____ Date: _____

EASTERN WOODLANDS INDIANS

The Indians of North and South America did not all live in the same way. Such things as a dry or wet climate, the presence of forests or deserts, mountains or plains, and nearness to oceans or lakes helped determine how a group of Indians lived. For example, the Indians of the dry areas of what is now Arizona and New Mexico lived very differently from the forest Indians of New York and New Jersey. However, no matter where the Indians lived they learned how to use the things around them to provide food, clothing, and shelter.

The picture at the right shows the homes and some of the activities of the Eastern Woodlands Indians. Read the statements below. Then, *using only what you see in the picture*, decide which statements below are true, which may be true, and which probably are not true. Put checks in the correct boxes on the chart.

Statement	True	May Be True	Probably Not True
1. These Indians knew how to use fire.			
2. The floor of the wigwam is covered with fur rugs.			
3. Fish from the lake were caught and used for food.			
4. The sides of the canoe are made of bark.			
5. These Indians moved frequently from place to place.			
6. Several families lived in the wigwam.			
7. Wood was used for many different things.			
8. An Indian man is making the canoe waterproof.			
9. The illustration shows winter activities.			
10. The canoe can carry only two people.			
11. Hunting was an important occupation.			
12. The lake water was used for drinking and cooking.			

* On a separate sheet of paper, explain why you chose each of the answers above.

16

SECTION 2

Voyages of Discovery in the New World

VIKING SHIPS

① **Mast**: In two sections perhaps 30' high . . . Oak preferred.

② **Sail**: Strips of cloth sewn together . . . Alternating colored stripes . . . As large as 600 sq. ft. (20' x 30').

③ **Symbol**: Designed to strike fear into the enemy . . . Could be removed on peaceful missions . . . Bear, hawk heads sometimes used.

④ **"Clinker-built" sides**: Long boards were lapped over each other (as in some house siding) . . . Fastened to ribs and caulked.

⑤ **Rudder**: Steered ships . . . One man could handle it . . . Sometimes located on the stern (rear) of the ship.

⑥ **Keel**: Ran entire length of ship . . . Made ship easier to steer, kept ship from rolling, increased speed.

⑦ **Shields**: Hung on sides of ship when in harbor . . . Alternating colors, for example yellow and black.

⑧ **Oar holes and oars**: Used when there was little wind or in rivers and harbors . . . Rowers sat on chests . . . Oars up to 17' long, of varying lengths so that all oars would hit water at same moment.

Of added interest: Viking ships sank about 3' into the water when loaded. This meant that they could easily be beached and allowed Vikings to quickly jump in or out. Also, the boats could enter shallow waters where enemy ships could not follow . . . Viking ships were the first landing crafts: horses could easily be loaded and unloaded . . . The men slept in sacks; there was no galley (kitchen); sometimes tents were erected mid-ship for officers . . . Sometimes Viking ships have been referred to as "steeds of the sea."

The ship illustrated above is typical of the kind used by Vikings in their voyages of discovery and in their raids along the coasts and up the rivers of Europe. It was on such a ship that Leif Ericsson sailed to North America.

1. How long were the ships? _____

Compare that length with something you know, for example two average busses laid end to end. _

_____

_____

How wide were the ships? _____

2. When the ships were in the water and fully loaded, how far into the water did they sink? _____

_____

How was this useful for raiding river communities? _____

_____

_____

3. Judging from the number of shields shown on the side of the ship, at least how many Vikings were on the ship? _____

4. What was the main source of power for moving the ship? _____

5. What were the purposes of the keel? _____

_____

_____

6. What is meant by the phrase "clinker-built"? _

_____

7. What was the purpose of the "heads" on the front of the ships? _____

_____

8. What did the sailors use to keep warm when they slept? _____

_____

Name: _____ Date: _____

VIKINGS IN NORTH AMERICA

1. It is well known that Scandinavian adventurers—the Vikings of Norway—explored the islands and coasts of northeastern North America and made at least one settlement. They must have been very brave. To sail across the North Atlantic Ocean in an open boat wasn't easy.

The map at the bottom of the page shows a route taken by some of the Vikings as they sailed west from what is now Norway. Follow the route of travel, and list the places in the order they would have met them.

(1) _____   (5) _____

(2) _____   (6) _____

(3) _____   (7) _____

(4) _____

Why would stops be necessary at the places you have listed? _____

_____

_____

2. It was about the year A.D. 1000 that Leif Ericsson, a Norwegian Viking, is said to have landed in North America. It isn't clear, because there are no written records, whether Ericsson started a settlement or whether it was started by Vikings who came after him. What *is* certain is that a settlement was started; it was called ***Vinland***.

Find Vinland on the map. On what island is it located? _____

3. Archaeologists who uncovered the site found the foundations of a great hall that the Vikings had built. It was about the size of a high school basketball court. They also found evidence that the settlers had dug iron ore from the ground, smelted it, and established a forge in which they made tools.

Then, Vinland was abandoned; no one really knows the reason why. Vinland was all but forgotten in Europe. It wasn't until some 500 years later, in 1492, that Columbus "rediscovered" North America.

Try to think of one or two reasons why the Vikings might have left Vinland.

_____

_____

_____

4. Make your map more colorful and interesting by coloring the waters a light blue, and the land a light brown or green.

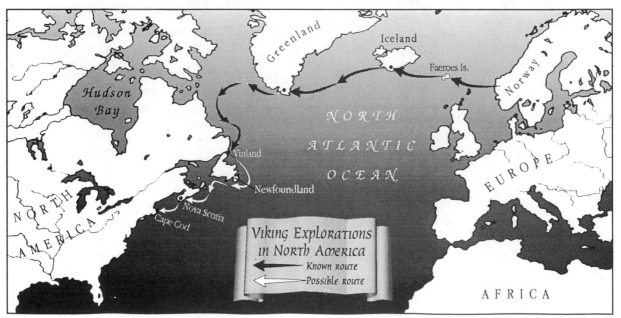

Viking Explorations in North America
→ Known route
→ Possible route

Name: _____ Date: _____

PORTUGAL FINDS AN ALL-WATER ROUTE TO EAST ASIA

Prince Henry of Portugal studied the problem of finding a new route to the Indies. Henry and his advisors decided that it would be a good idea to explore the west coast of Africa. They believed there must be a southern end to Africa. At that end the coast would turn north. A ship following the coast would be led directly to the Far East.

Henry put this idea into action. One ship after another was sent south along the African coast. **According to the map, what river had the Portuguese discovered by 1484?** _____

_____

Each ship's captain made written records and maps of everything he saw. When a captain had sailed as far as he dared, he stopped. Then he would have his men build a marker on the shore. The next captain who came along the coast knew from the marker that he had to sail farther south.

These explorations continued for more than fifty years. Finally, Bartolomeu Diaz found the southern tip of Africa. This happened by accident. A storm had blown Diaz's ship far out to sea. Afterwards, he headed his ship northward towards the land and home. Imagine Diaz's surprise when he realized that during the storm he had passed Africa's southern tip. **According to the map, in what year did he make this discovery?** _____

Ten years later, Vasco da Gama, another Portuguese explorer, followed up Diaz's discovery. Da Gama rounded the southern tip of Africa and then continued northward along the coast. After picking up an Arab guide, he sailed across the Indian Ocean. Da Gama finally sailed into a fine harbor on the coast of India. **In what year did da Gama reach India?** _____ He loaded his ship with spices and other products of the Indies and headed for home. An all-water route to what is now called the East Indies had been found.

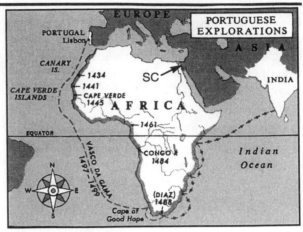

Understanding

1. Answer the following questions by writing *Yes* or *No*. If you answer a question *Yes*, underline once the sentence in the story that proves your answer. If you answer *No*, underline twice the sentence in the story that proves that answer.

a. After the storm did Diaz turn his ship toward the south? _____

b. Did da Gama need help in finding India after he reached the east coast of Africa? _____

c. Did da Gama's ship return to Portugal with a cargo? _____

d. Did Bartolomeu Diaz find the northern tip of Africa? _____

2. As you follow da Gama's sea route, certain places are shown on the map and are listed below. Starting from Lisbon, number them in the order that they are met.

____ Equator   __ Cape of Good Hope

____ Cape Verde Islands   __ Canary Islands

3. There was an almost-all-water route to Asia at the time of Henry—except for one little piece of land in northwestern Africa. Now, a canal—the Suez Canal—crosses that land. The area is shown on the map with the letters "SC." Draw a circle around the area.

COLUMBUS'S FIRST VOYAGE TO THE NEW WORLD

The instructional materials on this page can provide interesting "side lights" on Columbus and his explorations. It is suggested that the graphic materials be put on a transparency; then, the printed information may be used to make the transparency meaningful.

3. _____

5. _____

7. _____

6. _____

2. _____

4. _____

1. _____

Ships Used on the First Voyage

There were three ships: *Niña*, *Pinta*, *Santa Maria*. The *Santa Maria* was the flagship on which Columbus sailed. While sailing through the islands, the *Santa Maria* was wrecked, but Columbus and his men escaped to the *Niña*. . . A sailing ship of the type Columbus used is shown at left; the parts are as follows: 1 - Bow, 2 - Stern, 3 - Main Mast, 4 - Rudder, 5 - Crow's Nest, 6 - Captain's Quarters, 7 - Rigging. . . The *Santa Maria* was about 90' long; the *Niña*, the smallest boat, was about 70' long (by way of comparison, a modern cruise ship can be up to 1,000' long). . . Columbus's ships averaged about 4 mph on the first crossing; a ship such as the U.S.S. *United States* can average 35 mph on a crossing. . . The duties of the sailors were to set sails to catch wind, repair sails, bail out water that spilled or leaked into the ship almost constantly, serve as "look-outs," scrub decks.

DATE		EVENT
A U G	3rd, 1492 12th, 1492	- Columbus departs Palos, Spain - Columbus arrives in the Canary Islands
S E P	6th, 1492 16th, 1492	- Columbus departs Canary Islands - Fleet enters Sarqasso Sea; sailors frightened that they may be stuck there.
O C T	12th, 1492	- Columbus lands in Bahamas; names island San Salvador
N O V	↓ ↓ ↓	EXPLORING THE ISLANDS
D E C	24th, 1492	- *Santa Maria* shipwrecked off north coast of Hispaniola
J A N	16th, 1493	- *Niña* and *Pinta* begin return trip; great storms met; ships become separated
F E B	15th, 1493	- Columbus lands in Azores Islands; taken prisoner but released
M A R	3rd, 1493 15th, 1493	- *Niña* reaches Lisbon, Portugal - *Niña* arrives in Palos; *Pinta* arrives a few hours later

Chronology of Columbus's First Voyage Suggestions for Teaching

1. Point out that the chart on your transparency is a "time line." Time lines list events in chronological order. On some time lines (not this one) the events are spaced proportionately along the line; in a sense, such a time line is a single-line bar graph.

2. Some questions that could be asked:

a. How long was the stay in the Canary Islands? (*26 days including day of arrival and day of departure*)

b. How many days was it from the beginning of the voyage, including the day of departure from Palos, to the day of the landing on San Salvador? *Note*: August has 31 days, September 30. (*71 days*)

c. Your students can complete their route-of-travel maps by adding dates. Encourage them to print small and carefully and to use the abbreviated way to write dates; e.g., below Palos on the map: 8/3/1492 leave and 3/15/1493 return.

Name: _____ Date: _____

COLUMBUS DISCOVERS A NEW WORLD

The map shows the route of Christopher Columbus's first voyage to the New World. The route goes about 5" across the page, but the actual trip was more than 3,000 miles one way.

1. Label the continents shown on the map, as follows:

    A. *Europe*   C. *North America*

    B. *Africa*   D. *South America*

2. The list in the next column includes the names of some of the places he visited on the round trip, but the places are not listed in the order they were met. Study the map, then number the places. The country from which they started, Spain, has already been numbered as 1.

____ Cuba   ____ Palos
____ Azores   ____ Lisbon
_1_ Spain   ____ Hispaniola
____ San Salvador   ____ Canary Islands

3. What was the name of the settlement on Hispaniola?

_____

4. Suppose Columbus had sailed north from San Salvador. What would he have discovered?

_____

5. Why didn't Columbus return to Spain on his flagship, the **Santa Maria**?

_____

_____

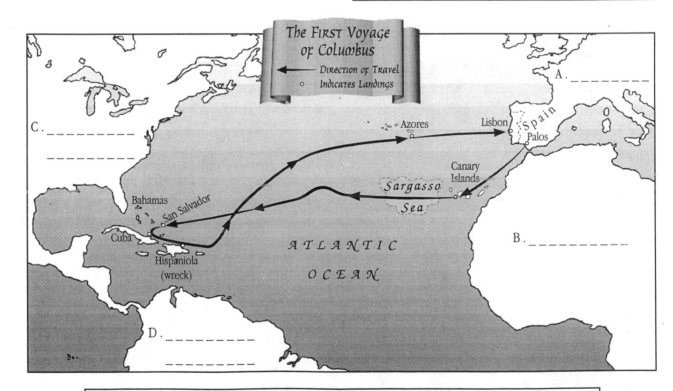

Notes:
1. The Sargasso Sea is not really a "sea". It is a many miles-wide mass of floating seaweed.
2. Columbus's flagship, the *Santa Maria*, was wrecked off the north coast of Hispaniola.
3. Columbus established a fort on Hispaniola called *La Navidad*.

COLUMBUS WRITES HIS IMPRESSIONS OF THE "INDIANS"

1.   Some day, perhaps, Earthlings will meet up with beings from outer space. If that should happen, there is little doubt that each group will observe differences in appearance, mannerisms, weapons, and the like in the other group. Much the same kind of reactions were probably engendered when Columbus and his crew met the "Indians" on the outlying islands off the Atlantic coast of North America.

The two illustrations on the facing page are designed to show some of the surface differences of the two peoples—European and North American. Study and discussion of the illustrations should help your students realize that on the surface, at least, the Europeans had certain advantages in technology. These advantages—weapons, horses, etc.—foreshadowed that in the inevitable conflicts that would come about, the newcomers would prevail and the Indians would be subjugated.

2.   We have no written and printed reactions of the Indians to the Spaniards they met in that fateful autumn of 1492. But, we do have Columbus's reactions as they were recorded in a letter to Queen Isabella and King Ferdinand. The excerpts from his letter, printed below, are revealing of his observations of not only the Indians, but also the land.

Here are some suggestions relative to using the letter as an instructional aid:

a.   Make a transparency of the letter and project it.

b.   Read the entire letter to your students and then ask questions similar to the following: What line (or lines) tells us

- the natives were timid?
- the natives thought the Spaniards were gods?
- the natives helped Columbus?
- the natives were generous?
- how the Indians and Spaniards communicated?

c.   Have your students write reactions to the Spaniards as though they were Indians meeting them for the first time. This could be done in either letter or diary form.

A Letter From Christopher Columbus

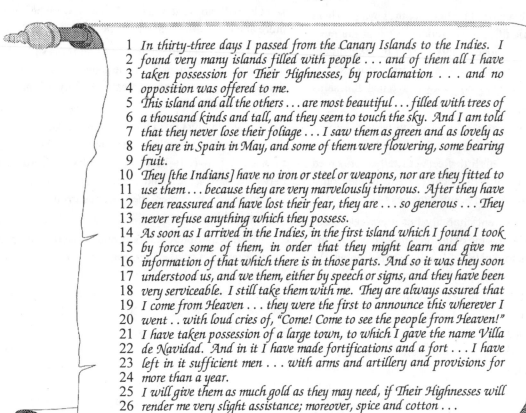

1   In thirty-three days I passed from the Canary Islands to the Indies. I
2   found very many islands filled with people . . . and of them all I have
3   taken possession for Their Highnesses, by proclamation . . . and no
4   opposition was offered to me.
5   This island and all the others . . . are most beautiful . . . filled with trees of
6   a thousand kinds and tall, and they seem to touch the sky. And I am told
7   that they never lose their foliage . . . I saw them as green and as lovely as
8   they are in Spain in May, and some of them were flowering, some bearing
9   fruit.
10 They [the Indians] have no iron or steel or weapons, nor are they fitted to
11 use them . . . because they are very marvelously timorous. After they have
12 been reassured and have lost their fear, they are . . . so generous . . . They
13 never refuse anything which they possess.
14 As soon as I arrived in the Indies, in the first island which I found I took
15 by force some of them, in order that they might learn and give me
16 information of that which there is in those parts. And so it was they soon
17 understood us, and we them, either by speech or signs, and they have been
18 very serviceable. I still take them with me. They are always assured that
19 I come from Heaven . . . they were the first to announce this wherever I
20 went . . with loud cries of, "Come! Come to see the people from Heaven!"
21 I have taken possession of a large town, to which I gave the name Villa
22 de Navidad. And in it I have made fortifications and a fort . . . I have
23 left in it sufficient men . . . with arms and artillery and provisions for
24 more than a year.
25 I will give them as much gold as they may need, if Their Highnesses will
26 render me very slight assistance; moreover, spice and cotton . . .
                                El Almirante

THE VOYAGE OF MAGELLAN

It remained for Ferdinand Magellan, a Portuguese seafarer, to test whether the world was round, if the *real* Indies could be reached by sailing west, and if there was a water passage through North America and South America.

Like Columbus, Magellan found it difficult to convince others to sponsor and finance an expedition. First, King Manuel of Portugal (1) refused to give him the ships, supplies, and men necessary for such a voyage.

Following King Manuel's refusal, Magellan traveled to Spain (2) to make the same request of King Charles. Charles agreed to help Magellan.   _____

When King Manuel heard of the agreement he was very angry; Spain was a bitter rival of Portugal. Manuel realized he had missed an opportunity to get the spices of the Indies and gain possession of new lands. He was also angry with Magellan and called him a traitor.   _____

Magellan began preparations for the voyage. There were many difficulties to overcome. One of the most serious was to convince sailors to join the expedition. King Manuel's spies were spreading stories that Magellan's ships were not seaworthy; that the ships would fall apart.   _____

Magellan was a most determined person; he was also clever at finding solutions to problems. Finally, on September 20, 1519, his little fleet with 250 sailors sailed out of the harbor of San Lucar (3) and headed on a southwest course toward South America (4).

At first things went smoothly, but after weeks at sea with no sight of land some of the men plotted to seize the ship and return to Spain. Magellan heard about the mutiny and successfully put it down.   _____

Magellan kept his fleet sailing ever westward. Finally, the coast of South America was sighted. He followed the coast line southward exploring every bay and river mouth to see if one of them would take him through the continent. Then, a serious event occurred. One of the ships, the *Santiago*, was wrecked while exploring one of the bays.

The sailors thought they would never reach the end of South America. But, one of the openings on the coast proved to be the passage for which they were looking. The passage, which is now called the Straits of Magellan (5), was treacherous and stormy; the sailors prayed for their lives. One of the sights they saw were numerous fires on the slopes that lined the passage. Because of the fires, which were maintained by Indians to keep warm, Magellan called the island "Tierra del Fuego," (6) which in Spanish means "Land of Fires."

A serious setback occurred. The captain of the *San Antonio* did a cowardly thing. He turned his ship around and headed back to Spain.   _____

Finally, the ships broke through the passage. Before them lay a great expanse of calm water, quite different from the stormy passage they had sailed through. The peacefulness of the water led Magellan to name it the Pacific Ocean (7).

On and on sailed the ships, ever westward. Months went by with no sight of land. The men were becoming more and more discouraged and desperate.

Finally, when all seemed lost, land was sighted. It was the island of Guam (8) in the group of islands called the Ladrones. Landing parties were formed, and the sailors replenished their supplies of food and water.

After leaving Guam it was a short sail to the Philippine Islands (9). Magellan landed and made friends with the natives. Unwisely, however, he took sides in a dispute between tribes on the islands. While Magellan was trying to land a force of 49 men, the natives surrounded him in the surf and killed him.   _____

By this time there was only one ship left to complete the journey. It was the *Victoria*, which means victory. The new captain, Juan Sebastian del Cano, obtained a load of spices from one of the islands, and then took off on a southward course for the Cape of Good Hope (10) on the southern tip of Africa (11). After unbelievable hardships in the South Atlantic, including trying to avoid King Manuel's ships, the ragged *Victoria* and its exhausted crew sailed into the harbor of San Lucar on September 4, 1522, almost three years from the time the journey had begun.   _____

Name: _____ Date: _____

THE VOYAGE OF MAGELLAN

1. You will remember that every paragraph should have a main idea and supporting detail. Each of the sentences below contains supporting detail for one of the paragraphs in the story.

After reading the story write on the blank line at the end of each paragraph the number of the sentence below that most naturally completes the paragraph.

1. However, his gallant fight gave some of his men the opportunity to return to the anchored ships.

2. Later, the leader of the mutiny was beheaded and two of the mutineers were left on a lonely strip of South American coast.

3. When the captain and his crew arrived in Spain, King Charles had them imprisoned in dark dungeons.

4. Of the 250 men who began the voyage, only 18 returned to Spain alive.

5. He said that Magellan could have five ships and money to recruit a crew and buy supplies.

6. He tried to have Magellan killed, but Magellan fought off the attackers.

7. Manuel's men started fires on three ships, but they were all put out.

2. Notice that each of the places mentioned in the story is followed by a number in parentheses. Write the names of the places in the corresponding numbered space on the map of Magellan's voyage.

3. What three questions did Magellan hope to answer on his voyage?

a. _____

b. _____

c. _____

4. Who was really the first sea captain to circumnavigate (circle) the world in one complete voyage?

_____

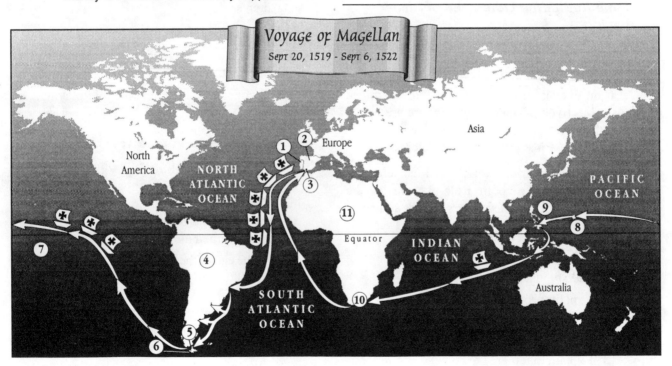

1. _____   5. _____   9. _____

2. _____   6. _____   10. _____

3. _____   7. _____   11. _____

4. _____   8. _____

ROLE-PLAYING HISTORICAL EVENTS

One reason why students may find history difficult is that the events, people, and places seem so remote and far-removed from their lives. It is difficult to fully empathize with characters who lived, perhaps, hundreds of years ago: Indians who trekked across a continent, soldiers who fought at Gettysburg, Peary and Henson as they struggled to reach the North Pole.

It is important that students see historical figures as real people—people who were once children, adolescents, and adults; people who suffered joy, pain, satisfaction, disappointment, success, and failure. The problem for instructors, then, is to help students experience the past in vicarious, but meaningful, ways. Role-playing is one way to accomplish this.

Some Additional Outcomes of Role-Playing

1. Closer identification with historical problems can be gained because the problems seem real.

2. Controversial issues of the past are examined more objectively. Opposing views are presented, more than one solution to a problem may be recognized, and new insights may be developed.

3. Role-playing brings variety and tempered excitement into the classroom. Role-play can rivet the attention of both the role-players and the audience.

Suggested Procedures for Carrying Out Role-Playing

1. Prepare students for the experience:
   - ❑ Explain procedure
   - ❑ Explain the function of both role-players and the audience.
   - ❑ Explain that there are no penalties, recriminations or embarrassments for positions taken. Role-players are as performers in a play; they may not necessarily agree with the positions they represent.

2. Explain the situation to be enacted and the characters involved:
   - ❑ Sometimes situations may be read as in a story.
   - ❑ Time should be allowed for research and preparation.

3. Choose the casts:
   - ❑ Initially, choose those who willingly volunteer.
   - ❑ Sometimes reverse roles. This helps role-players "see" both sides.
   - ❑ Sometimes choose students who might gain the most from the role.
   - ❑ As often as possible have your students work in groups to plan strategy before the enactments.

4. Act out the situation:
   - ❑ Once the role-playing has begun try not to interrupt.
   - ❑ Recognize when to end the role-playing.

5. Follow-up:
   - ❑ It is not necessary to arrive at hard solutions.
   - ❑ Find ways to give specific praise to the participants.
   - ❑ The listeners should be encouraged to ask questions and offer comments about the issues, but their job is not to criticize the acting.
   - ❑ At the end of the experience it would encourage future willingness to participate if the instructor gave both general and specific praise to the group about the enactment, but individuals should not be singled out as the "best," "most convincing," etc.

Adapted from *Environmental Awareness*, James F. Silver, Kendall/Hunt Publishing Co.

ROLE-PLAYING HISTORICAL EVENTS

Columbus and His First Encounters with the Indians

Columbus and some of his men are being met by Indians at the time of the first landing on San Salvador. The Indians are astonished at seeing strangers so differently clothed and armed than themselves. They keep looking at the anchored ships with their great white sails; they grasp the cutting edges of the swords; they wonder about the muskets held in the hands of some of the men. They think the Spaniards are gods; Columbus does nothing to dissuade them.

Columbus and his men are trying to be cordial and authoritative at the same time. He later wrote of the simple, kind, and generous natures of the Indians and of their desire for beads and trinkets. Columbus takes possession of the island in the name of King Ferdinand and Queen Isabella. When he leaves he takes some of the Indians by force.

Magellan Tries the Mutineers

The event takes place on a barren South American coast. Five ships are anchored offshore. Magellan is sitting on an upended cask. Armed sailors surround several mutineers who are standing with their hands tied behind their backs. Three of the mutineers are captains.

Magellan and one of his trusted officers are asking them questions: Where was this plot hatched? (*Spain*) Who were the leaders? Why didn't you come and talk to me if you were bothered?

The men try to defend themselves by answering questions in such ways that their guilt seems less (*If we hadn't joined we would have been killed, etc.*). They also say that they were concerned about their families; they had fears that they would never see Spain again, etc. The three captains are defiant.

Magellan finds the men guilty and pronounces punishment: the ordinary sailors are to be flogged; one captain is to be beheaded; another is to be abandoned on the coast along with another officer; another (*Del Cano*) is to be put to work at hard labor.

26

SECTION 3

Spanish Activities in the New World

EXPLORATIONS OF THE USA'S SOUTH AND SOUTHWEST

The map on the facing page shows the routes of some of the best known Spanish explorers. Some place names have been omitted in the following accounts of their trips. Study the map for the names of the missing places and write them in the spaces provided.

Ponce de Leon

He began his explorations from the island of _____, sailing in a northwest direction through the _____ Islands. From the islands he continued in a northwest direction and landed in what is now _____. He then sailed south along the coast until he reached the south end of the peninsula; then he turned north. His explorations ended in _____ Bay.

Ponce de Leon was searching for the "Fountain of Youth" which he had been told was in Florida. Of course, he never found the "fountain." However, he did learn much about the land, and Spain gained possession of Florida.

Hernando Cortes

Cortes sailed from the island of _____ in 1519. Soon, he reached the _____ Peninsula. He followed the southern coast of the _____ and landed at a site that later became the city of _____. After many difficulties, including a march over rugged mountains, he attacked and conquered the Aztec capital, _____, later to be called _____. Several years after the conquest he explored north and reached the northern end of the _____. Then he returned to Mexico City.

Hernando de Soto

De Soto's mission was to conquer the Indians and secure present-day Southwest United States for Spain. He sailed from Cuba to Tampa Bay, Florida. From Tampa he marched overland to the _____ River, then west over the _____ Mountains. He discovered and crossed the _____ River. He died of fever near the present city of _____. An officer, Luis Alvarado, took over and continued explorations to the _____ River, and then marched overland to Mexico. Of the original 600 soldiers, only 320 survived; however, Spain's claims to the territory explored were strengthened.

Francisco Coronado

Coronado penetrated farther north than any of the other Spanish explorers. He began his explorations in Mexico, traveled north, and discovered, among other things, the _____ of the Colorado River. He crossed the _____ Mountains, the _____ River, and the _____ River.

Coronado was looking for the "Seven Cities of Cibola," which, he had been told by the Indians, held fabulous treasures of gold and silver. He never found the treasures. Disappointed, he returned to Mexico, but his efforts did give Spain another claim to North America's Southwest.

EXPLORATIONS OF THE USA'S SOUTH AND SOUTHWEST

3-1

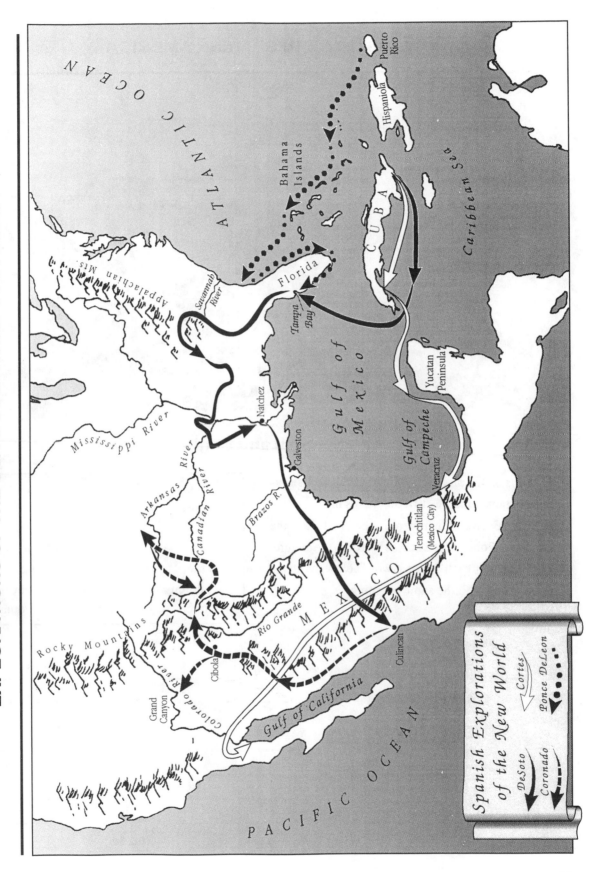

Spanish Explorations
of the New World

DeSoto
Coronado
Cortes
Ponce DeLeon

Name: _____ Date: _____

A VILLAGE IN SPANISH AMERICA

Spanish and English

The words on the picture are Spanish and are used as labels to show what the different items in the picture represent. Each English word in the box means the same thing as one of the Spanish words in the picture. On the line after each Spanish word below, write the English word with the same meaning.

blacksmith	grass	road
cactus	hat	roof
carpenter	horse	sky
cart	house	trees
cattle	man	wall
children	mountain	wheel
church	people	woman

Spanish	English	Spanish	English	Spanish	English
sombrero	_____	cielo	_____	tejado	_____
caballo	_____	gente	_____	pared	_____
mujer	_____	carro	_____	camino	_____
cacto	_____	ganado	_____	árboles	_____
hombre	_____	rueda	_____	carpintero	_____
montaña	_____	templo	_____	herrero	_____
casa	_____	niños	_____	hierba	_____

SPANISH PLACE NAMES IN SOUTHWEST UNITED STATES

From 1519 to 1848, more than 300 years, North America's Southwest was a part of Spain's empire in the New World. Spanish influence on the architecture, religion, literature, and language in the region was enormous. Nowhere is the Spanish influence more noticeable than in the names of natural and political features in what is now California, Arizona, and New Mexico.

Following is an activity that will not only help your students become acquainted with places and locations, but also help them develop an appreciation of the pervasiveness of Spanish culture.

Procedure
1. Photocopy the map of Spanish Place Names in Southwest United States and distribute.
2. Call attention to each of the map features listed in the next column and shown on the map. In the boxes below the names on the map, have your students write the English translation of the Spanish name.

California
San Francisco (St. Francis)
Los Angeles (The Angels)
Sierra Nevada Mountains (Snow-covered Mountains)
Santa Cruz (Holy Cross)
San Diego (St. James)

New Mexico
Las Cruces (The Crosses)
Portales (Gateway)
Sante Fe (Holy Faith)
Tres Piedras (Three Rocks)
Rio Grande (Great River)

Arizona
Casa Grande (Great House)
Sierra Vista (Mountain View)
Colorado River (Colored River)

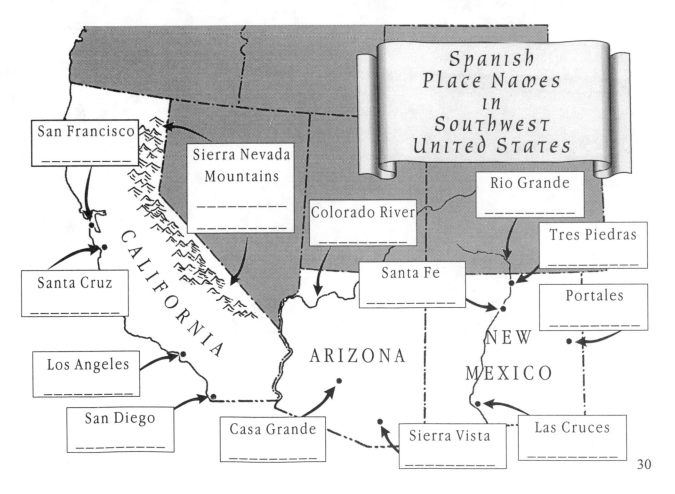

30

SECTION 4

French Activities in the New World

Name: _____ Date: _____

FRENCH LOCATIONS IN THE NEW WORLD

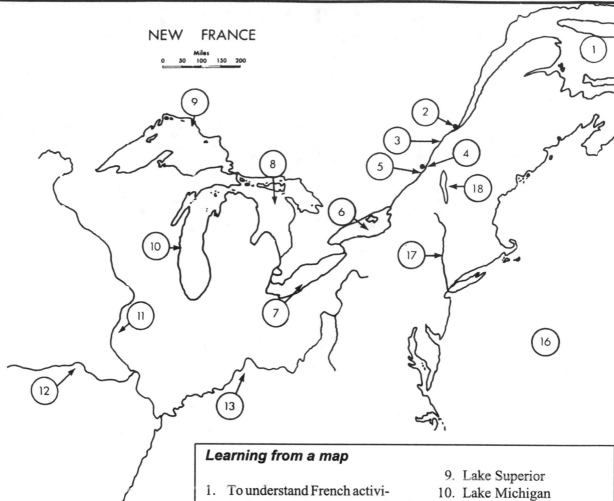

NEW FRANCE

Learning from a map

1. To understand French activities in the New World, you will need to know the location of places listed below. Complete the map above by labeling these places. The numerals on the map show where to write the labels.

   1. Gulf of St. Lawrence
   2. Quebec
   3. St. Lawrence River
   4. Montreal
   5. Lachine Rapids
   6. Lake Ontario
   7. Lake Erie
   8. Lake Huron

   9. Lake Superior
10. Lake Michigan
11. Mississippi River
12. Missouri River
13. Ohio River
14. New Orleans
15. Gulf of Mexico
16. Atlantic Ocean
17. Hudson River
18. Lake Champlain

2. Color the following bodies of water a very light blue: all of the lakes, the ocean, the Gulf of St. Lawrence, and the Gulf of Mexico.

THE VALLEY OF THE ST. LAWRENCE RIVER

The information, questions, and illustration on this page should be helpful in a presentation/question type lesson on the St. Lawrence Valley, especially as concerned with the early French farms along the river.

1. Why was the St. Lawrence Valley an ideal location for colonization? Its assets include the following:

- *An all-water route to the major cities of Europe*

- *Easy transportation up and down the river to communities and farms*

- *A natural moat and barrier for protection from Indian attacks and, later, wars with the British and their American colonies*

- *A gateway to the Great Lakes and waterways of the Mississippi Valley for fur trading*

- *A frozen "highway" over which sleds could be dragged in winter*

2. There were at least two other assets not mentioned above. What might they be?

- *Recreation: boating, swimming, skating*

- *Food: abundance of fish and game*

3. In what way could the river be helpful to enemies?

- *In the winter the river could be crossed on the ice, thus making frontal attack of Quebec possible.*

- *Warships could bombard the town from the river.*

4. The St. Lawrence River Valley is still the dominant region of Canada. Why is this so?

- *Most of the major cities of Canada (Quebec, Montreal, Ottawa, Toronto, Hamilton, Windsor, and others) are located on or near the river.*

- *The St. Lawrence Seaway makes interior North America easily accessible. Note: The Seaway is 2,342 miles long from Duluth, Minnesota, at the western end of Lake Superior, to the Atlantic Ocean.*

- *Proximity to the United States makes for easy trade, transportation, tourism, etc., profitable to both nations.*

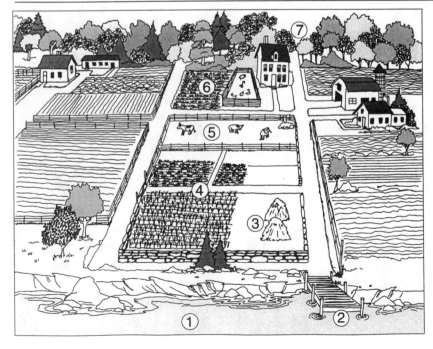

5. The lay-out of the early farms along the St. Lawrence took good advantage of the river, the terrain, and natural features. Many of the farms followed the pattern shown in the illustration and noted below:

① A water front of perhaps one-quarter of a mile

② A dock for boats

③ Hay (winter feed for cattle)

④ Fields of crops (corn, wheat)

⑤ Pasture (for cattle, horses, etc.)

⑥ Vegetable garden (near the house)

⑦ Wooded area in the rear (for fencing, firewood, construction)

THREE FRENCH EXPLORERS

Giovanni da Verrazano (1485?-1527?)

Verrazano, an Italian, was hired by the French to explore the coasts of eastern North America. In January, 1524, he sailed with the west-blowing winds behind his back and reached the coast of North Carolina in forty-nine days. He sailed north along the coast, explored numerous river mouths and bays including New York harbor and the Hudson River beginnings. After exploring the coasts of New England, Nova Scotia, and Newfoundland he returned to France . . . *Of interest:* Before his voyage of discovery the French commissioned him as a privateer. This gave him "license" to raid Spanish shipping. However, from the Spanish point-of-view he was nothing more than a pirate. A few years after his voyage of discovery, he was captured by the Spanish and hanged . . .

Jacques Cartier (1491-1557)

Cartier made three trips to Canada: (1) 1534—to the mouth of the St. Lawrence, (2) 1535—up the St. Lawrence to the present site of Montreal, (3) 1536—to the present site of Quebec, where he tried to start a colony that failed. He did not find the all-water route to China he was looking for, but he did give France a strong claim to Canada . . . *Of interest:* He kidnaped two Indians on his first trip, brought them to France as exhibits of his prowess, and returned them on his second trip . . . It was he that gave Montreal (Mount Royal) its name . . .

Sieur de La Salle (1643-1687)

La Salle completed the exploration of the Mississippi River that Father Marquette (missionary priest) and Louis Joliet (fur trader) had started. From the Great Lakes La Salle followed their route down the Mississippi to the point where the Arkansas River joins the Mississippi. La Salle reached the mouth of the river in 1682, and claimed the entire Mississippi Valley for France. He named the area Louisiana in honor of King Louis XIV . . . *Of interest:* La Salle is credited with the discovery of the Ohio River . . . Five years after his great discovery he was shot by one of his own men while on an exploration of the Mississippi mouth region . . .

Background for the Instructor

The three explorers highlighted on this page were of great importance in bolstering French claims to more than half a continent. Father Jacques Marquette and his companion, fur trader Louis Jean Joliet, also played important parts through their explorations of the upper Mississippi River; however, for the sake of clarity, their explorations are not shown on the map. Samuel de Champlain, who founded the first permanent French settlement, is featured on one of the following pages.

Suggested procedure: Make a transparency of the map, and as it is projected, trace the routes of travel and present supplemental information.

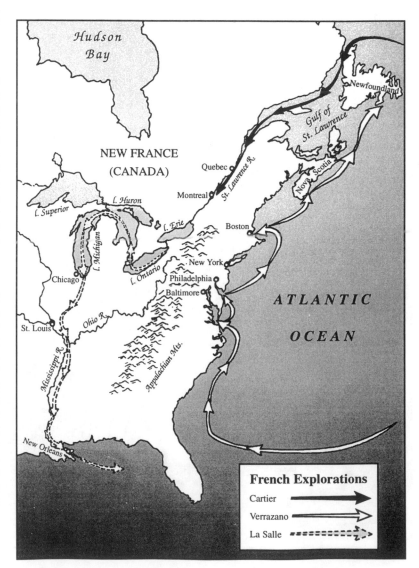

FRANCE'S FIRST PERMANENT NEW WORLD SETTLEMENT

Following are some facts about the life and explorations of Samuel de Champlain, who has been called the "Father of New France." These facts and the accompanying map and illustration can be taught to your students in a presentation-type lesson. Transparencies of the graphics would greatly enhance the presentation.

Facts about Champlain

Early background: He learned navigation from his father, a sea captain, who fished off the coasts of Newfoundland. Later, he was a soldier in the French army and learned about war. His earliest "dream" was to learn about the New World; the dream began to be realized when he sailed to the Spanish colonies in the West Indies between 1599 and 1601. He wrote a book about his voyages (an interesting speculation he made was that a canal should be dug through the Isthmus of Panama) that came to the attention of King Henry IV. He was commissioned by the king to acquire lands in the New World and to seek a "Northwest Passage" through North America to Asia.

Between the years 1603 and 1606 he made attempts to start French colonies in the New World. They all failed, but he gained valuable experience. It was during those years that he also explored the coasts of Nova Scotia and New England.

In the spring of 1608, he made another attempt to establish a permanent settlement. He sailed up the St. Lawrence River to the site of Cartier's failed colony. There were several reasons for the site selection: (1) It was easily reached by water, which was an advantage for trade with Europe and for trade with the Indians of the Great Lakes region to the west; (2) It would be easy to defend as it was located on a flat shelf on the river and was protected in the rear by a high cliff-like slope; (3) The land could be farmed easily, not only at the actual site but also upstream and downstream. He called the settlement "Quebec"—the first permanent French settlement in the New World.

The first winter at Quebec was horrendous; only eight of the original twenty-four settlers survived. Even the survivors may have died without help from a friendly Indian, who told them how to make medicine from the bark of trees. The disease they suffered from was "scurvy," which is caused by a lack of vitamins in diets. Spring brought ships from France with new colonists and supplies.

Champlain made other important explorations after Quebec seemed well established. He journeyed west to Lakes Ontario and Huron, and then south where he discovered the lake that bears his name — Lake Champlain.

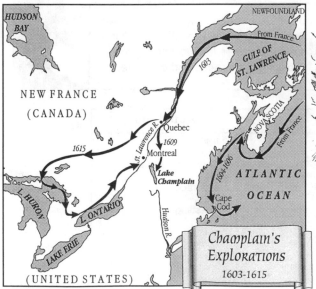

The Fort at Quebec (circa 1615)

FURS AND THE FRENCH

It suited French fur trade objectives well for French colonies to be located on the St. Lawrence River. From their bases on the river the traders could travel by boat, with occasional portages, through the entire Mississippi River Valley, the Great Lakes, and all the rivers that drained into them. They also had easy access to Lake Champlain (more than 100 miles long from north to south), Lake George, the "finger lakes" (Cayuga, Skaneateles, Seneca, Owasco, Canandaigua). Thus, traders were able to gather furs reaped from thousands of square miles.

The water routes also made it possible to have an annual "fur fair" at Montreal, a time when the French and Indians joined in a celebration to not only trade furs, but also have a good time. As the illustration shows there were many diverse activities that took place—a joyful mixture of pleasure and business. The fur fair was an event that helped cement Indian/French relations which, among all the ethnic groups (French, English, Spanish, Dutch, Swedes) that invaded North America, were the most friendly and harmonious.

Suggestions for Using the Illustration

Project the illustration via a transparency and (1) have your students identify and list all the items of trade, and (2) list all of the activities.

The fur trade at Montreal was an opportunity for the French and Indians to join together for fun and trade — a mixing of business and pleasure.

Trade Items			Activities
Indians	**French**		- trading
- furs	- knives	Note: The following are not shown, but probably were traded:	- shooting contests
	- hatchets		- foot races
	- cloth	- iron/copper pots and pans	- wrestling
	- beads	- blankets	- cooking
	- guns	- mirrors	

FISHING BANKS AND THE FRENCH

It was the fish that swarmed over the fishing banks off the coasts of Newfoundland that first attracted the French to the New World. It wasn't the French, however, who discovered the fishing banks. Credit goes to an Italian, John Cabot, who was in the employ of the British. He had been engaged for the purpose of exploring the coasts of North America. He sailed to the North Atlantic just five years after Columbus had journeyed in the warmer latitudes of the Atlantic Ocean.

In Cabot's explorations off Newfoundland his ship plowed through schools of fish so thick they could be scooped up in baskets. His report to the king of England told of this wonder; it wasn't long after the news got around that fishermen of several European countries were attracted to the region.

Why were fish attracted to those northern coasts? The answer to that question lies in an understanding of fishing banks. As the diagram below shows, a "bank" is a kind of underwater plateau. Sunlight is able to penetrate the shallow waters and, in so doing, provides the heat energy upon which tiny plant and animal life—plankton— thrive.

Small fish eat the plankton, larger fish are attracted by the smaller fish, which attracts still larger fish, and so it goes. In the same way, continental shelves attract fish—the shallow waters and the sun provide the conditions that begin the food chain.

Fishing the Grand Banks, as they are called, was not meant for the weak or the timid. Just to get there from England, France, or Spain was dangerous. Upon the ships' arrivals, fog was almost sure to shroud the ships and menacing shores. In winter, the wind shrieked through the rigging of ships which were ice-covered because of the cold. Heavy seas tossed the small ships around as though they were toys; many were the sailors pitched overboard never to be seen again.

The profits to be made from fishing were great, however. Europe needed the protein that fish provided. Another important factor was that much of Europe's population was Catholic, and their customs called for eating fish on Fridays. There was no way that European fisheries could supply all the fish that were needed without tapping these fishing banks.

Suggestions for Teaching

1. As you read or relate the above account, have your students make brief notes under each of the main ideas listed below.

- John Cabot—discoverer of the fishing banks

- Europe's reaction to news of the fishing banks

- Description of fishing banks

- Hardships of fishing off Newfoundland

- Europe's need for fish

2. At the end of the third paragraph present the diagram on the right. Ask questions about the diagram. *Examples:* How deep is the water below the ship to the top of the bank? How deep is the deepest trench?

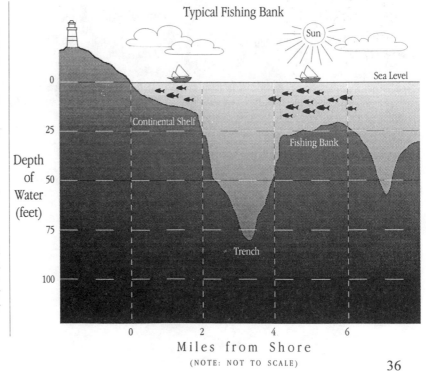

Typical Fishing Bank

Depth of Water (feet)

Miles from Shore
(NOTE: NOT TO SCALE)

Name: _____ Date: _____

FRENCHMEN AT WORK IN THE NEW WORLD

1. Each picture should have a caption. On the line next to each caption below, write the letter of the picture it best describes.

   • Meeting the Indians ___   • Fishing off Newfoundland ___   • Trading with the Indians ___

   • Cooking for the family ___   • Farming along the St. Lawrence ___   • Exploring Lake Champlain ___

2. Each picture offers details that help make the scene more interesting and meaningful. Try to list three details for each picture. One detail has already been provided for each picture to help you get started.

(A) Fishing with hooks _____   (C) Blanket offered _____   (E) Three-masted ship _____

_____   _____   _____

_____   _____   _____

_____   _____   _____

(B) Robed priest _____   (D) Soldier's sword _____   (F) Stew pot _____

_____   _____   _____

_____   _____   _____

_____   _____   _____

Name: _____ Date: _____

VIKING/SPANISH/FRENCH EXPLORERS CROSSWORD PUZZLE

Directions: All of the words in this crossword puzzle relate in some way to the Viking, Spanish, and French explorations in the New World. Most of the words will probably be in your textbook, but in some cases you may have to search in other books.

Across:

1. The ocean Balboa named "The Great South Sea"
3. Viking settlement on an island
6. A peninsula on the south side of the Gulf of St. Lawrence
8. An Indian group that sided with the English against the French
10. The falls that lie between Lake Erie and Lake Ontario
11. Fish caught in great quantities off the coast of Newfoundland
12. One of Columbus's ships on his first voyage
14. The "Father of New France"
16. Islands where Magellan met his death (initials)
18. Columbus sailed from this Spanish port
20. First name of early Viking explorer
21. Aztec ruler defeated by Cortes
22. Place where fish congregate
24. Month Columbus reached the New World

Down:

2. Tierra del _____ , "Land of Fire"
4. A two letter word meaning "of", often found before the last names of Spaniards
5. Famous fishing banks off the coast of Newfoundland
7. Indians who sided with the French against the English
9. Large island met by the Vikings before reaching Greenland
13. French explorer of the Mississippi River to its mouth in the Gulf of Mexico
15. Isthmus connecting North America and South America
17. A sailor on the _____ : first to sight land on Columbus's first voyage
19. Empire in Mexico defeated by Cortes
21. River explored by Marquette and Joliet (initials)
23. City at the mouth of the Mississippi River (initials)

SECTION 5

English Activities in the New World

ENGLISH LOCATIONS IN THE NEW WORLD

The map shows the major coastlines, waters, rivers, and mountains that the English met as they began their period of exploration and colonization. Knowing these locations will serve students well as references to them are made by instructors and/or textbooks.

Suggested Procedure

1.   Make a transparency of the map on this page. Do not write any names on it.

2.   Project the map. Then drill students on the locations. Example of an effective approach: Point to a location and ask: Gulf? (Gulf of Mexico), River? (Hudson), Bay? (Chesapeake), etc.

3.   As you proceed through the English colonial period add "context" to each location. For example, point to the James River. After the student has named the place, ask, "Association?" The student should then give a brief fact about the location such as, "Place where John Smith was leader," or perhaps some other fact.

4.   The list that follows includes basic place names.

Major Waters

Atlantic Ocean
Gulf of Mexico
Delaware Bay
Chesapeake Bay
Massachusetts Bay

Major Rivers

St. Lawrence
Kennebec
Connecticut
Hudson
Delaware
Susquehanna
James
Potomac
Savannah

Miscellaneous

Appalachian Mountains
Cape Cod
Lake Champlain
Lake Erie
Lake Ontario

Name: _____ Date: _____

SETTLERS FROM MANY COUNTRIES

Most of the people in the Northern and Southern Colonies came from England. But, the people of the Middle Colonies came from many different countries of Europe. The differences in the backgrounds of these settlers helped the Middle Colonies to develop. One reason for this was that each of these groups of people had some special skills or knowledge. Another reason was that settlers in the Middle Colonies came to know and respect people who were different from themselves.

People from the **Netherlands**, **Sweden**, and **England** settled in the Delaware and Hudson River valleys. A number of people from **Finland** also settled along the Delaware. The Finns were hardworking people, and many of them were expert woodsmen. They cleared the forests and became excellent farmers.

Other important groups in the Middle Colonies were the Swiss from **Switzerland** and the Germans from **Germany**. These people had heard about Pennsylvania from William Penn's advertisements for settlers. Many of them had been successful farmers in their home country. But, they had suffered from wars and heavy taxes. Some had been punished because they wanted to worship in a way that was different from their rulers' ways of worship.

People from **Scotland**, **Ireland**, and **Wales** also settled in the Middle Colonies. Some of these people were skilled in manufacturing—especially in the weaving of cloth.

The Scottish-Irish people came in great numbers. These were people who had moved to Ireland from Scotland. However, they were unhappy there. Also, they suffered because they followed a different religion from the rest of the people in Ireland. So, many moved across the Atlantic. Often, the Scottish-Irish built homes on the frontier because other people already owned many of the good lands in the east. The land that was left to the east of the frontier was too expensive for poor immigrants to buy.

---

1. Circle the sentences that tell why the Swiss and Germans settled in America.

2. Underline the three two-word phrases in the second paragraph that describe the Finns.

3. What skills were brought to the Middle Colonies by the people from Scotland, Ireland, and Wales? _____

_____

To do:

Nine of the countries mentioned in the story are in bold print. As each country is named, find its name and number in the key on the map on the right. Write the name of each country on the line on the map which has that number.

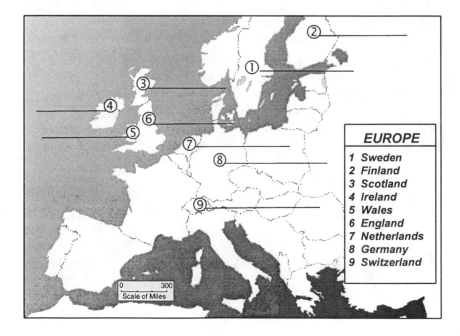

EUROPE

1 Sweden
2 Finland
3 Scotland
4 Ireland
5 Wales
6 England
7 Netherlands
8 Germany
9 Switzerland

0 — 300
Scale of Miles

SIR FRANCIS DRAKE: ENGLISH ADVENTURER

This activity is designed to encourage students to make inferences when the answer to a question is not known.

Suggested procedure: After each paragraph is read orally by the instructor, follow up with immediate questions/discussion.

Francis Drake, later to become "Sir," was a significant factor in helping England to become a world power. The following sequences and incidents will help students to see why this statement is true.

• England, jealous and fearful of the wealth and power Spain was accumulating as results of its exploits in New Spain, resolved to strengthen its own position, but at the expense of Spain. It occurred to the English that one way to accomplish their objective would be to raid and plunder Spanish treasure ships sailing to Spain from South America and Middle America. This decision was justified by the English on the premise that the Spanish had stolen the treasures from the Aztecs and Incas; therefore, England had just as much right to the treasure as Spain.

Were the English correct in their reasoning? Why or why not? This question requires a value judgment. What is the meaning of "stealing?" The following is an operational definition that might be useful: Stealing is taking something that does not belong to you. Does this definition change if one steals something from someone who stole it in the first place?

• Francis Drake was one of the sea captains who was given the "right" by the English queen, Elizabeth, to prey on Spanish ships. So, in 1577 Drake set sail for the New World. His objective? To sail across the Atlantic Ocean, through the Straits of Magellan, north along the west coast of South America, and to take by surprise the Spanish ships as they sailed from Peru, the former empire of the Incas and the source of the stolen treasures. Only one of Drake's ships, the *Golden Hind*, made it all the way to the coasts of Peru.

For what reasons were five ships taken on the mission? Five ships could easily subdue a lone Spanish ship or two; more treasure could be carried back to England; if one or more of the fleet were lost, *there would be others to rescue sailors and to carry on the mission's objectives.*

• One Spanish ship after another was taken by Drake. Soon, he had all the treasure the *Golden Hind* could carry. The problem now became how to get the treasure back to England. The news of Drake's pirating had spread. Every Spanish ship that heard the news was on the lookout for the *Golden Hind*.

Now that the Golden Hind was loaded with loot, why would she be at a disadvantage in battles with other ships? The ship would not be as fast nor as maneuverable. In a battle the Spanish would not want to sink the Golden Hind; if they did the treasure would be lost. This would mean that the ship would be boarded. In all probability the English would be overwhelmed and killed immediately or be killed later by hanging or beheading.

• Drake decided to head north to the coast of North America in the hope that he would find a passage *east* through the continent and then across the Atlantic Ocean to safety. Of course, no such passage existed, as Drake realized when he put into what is now San Francisco Bay. After claiming the land for England, and cleaning and repairing the *Golden Hind* he made a bold decision. He would sail west across the Pacific, cross the Indian Ocean, go around the southern tip of Africa, and then north to England. And he did it! The first Englishman to sail completely around the world.

What mistake of Magellan did Drake avoid in his world-circling voyage? He did not linger on any of the islands and become involved in native wars.

• When news of the *Golden Hind's* return reached Queen Elizabeth, she visited the ship to welcome Drake and his crew and to inspect the treasure. She rewarded Drake by dubbing him a knight, entitling him to be called "Sir."

What were some of the results of Drake's exploits? Drake's success put England on its path to world power (later made more certain by the defeat of the Spanish Armada). Also, England had new claims to territory in North America. The vast treasure Drake brought home helped to pay England's debts, finance new ventures, and increase the strength of its defenses, especially the navy.

41

Name: _____ Date: _____

ROANOKE ISLAND: SITE OF THE "LOST COLONY"

The Lost Colony

The capital of today's state of Virginia is Raleigh—and this name is one of the few evidences of Sir Walter Raleigh's attempt to start an English colony in the New World.

Raleigh, who was a favorite of Queen Elizabeth, obtained her permission to start a colony somewhere along the Atlantic coast in the region which was named Virginia. As a preliminary he had the coast explored for possible sites; the exploring party returned to England with its recommendation: Roanoke Island. Next, Raleigh organized a group of settlers to colonize Roanoke. However, the colony failed; the settlers did not have the knowledge, skills, and willingness to work. When Sir Francis Drake stopped at the settlement with his fleet, the settlers begged him to take them home, and he did.

Raleigh did not give up. In 1587, another colonization group was organized. It consisted of 117 women, men, and children with the equipment and supplies thought necessary for survival. About a month after the settlers were landed, the ships returned to England. The settlers were alone in a vast and unknown world.

For a number of reasons, one of which was a war with Spain, no English ships returned to Roanoke until 1590, three years later. What did they find? Not one person either alive or dead. There was only one clue as to where the people were—a single word, CROATOAN—carved into a tree trunk. This seemed to indicate that the settlers had gone to a nearby island bearing that name. A later search of Croatoan proved fruitless—no trace of the colonists was found. To this day no one knows what happened to the settlers.

The Roanoke colony was abandoned, never to be re-started. As for Raleigh? He fell out of favor and was beheaded by the king who followed Queen Elizabeth. It wasn't until twenty years later, in 1607, that the English made another attempt at colonization—Jamestown.

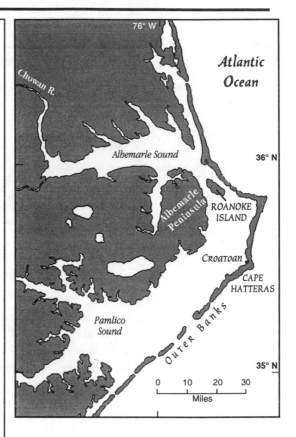

1. Underline the words in the story that tell why the first Roanoke colony failed.

2. What is there about the location of Roanoke that might have influenced its being chosen as a site for the colony?

_____

_____

_____

_____

Reading a Map

Complete the sentences below with information from the map.

Roanoke's latitude is between 35ºN and _____ºN. It is part of a string of long narrow islands called _____. These are barrier islands, which help protect the main coast from storms. To the west of Roanoke is the _____ peninsula; to the east is the _____ Ocean. Croatoan, the place referred to in the story, is about _____ miles south of Roanoke and is very close to Cape _____. The _____ River flows into Albemarle Sound.

JOHN SMITH AND JAMESTOWN'S "STARVING TIME"

Your students should realize that one of the few ways that the events in the history of early America are known is from the writings of those who experienced the event personally or who are reporting the events. One problem that historians have is to decide if the writers are telling the whole truth.

1. Ask your students to think of reasons why what has been written by people writing about events may not be true. Some important considerations follow:

- Was the writer in a good position to see and hear what was happening?
- Could the writer benefit in some way by writing the article with a "slant"?
- Was the writer boasting or trying to appear as a hero?
- Was the article written to protect someone or to hurt someone?
- Does the writer give more emphasis to one thing than to another?
- Was the writer biased or prejudiced toward the people involved in the event?
- Did the writer blend fact and opinion so that it is difficult to separate one from the other?
- Does the writer use the exact words of someone being quoted?
- If the original writing was in a foreign language does its translation into English have exactly the same meaning?
- The words and language usage of English speaking/writing people of several hundred years ago were quite different from those of today. Is the updating of words and expressions conveying the same facts, ideas and opinions that the original writer had in mind?
- How long after the event was the writing done? (Memories can be faulty.)

2. Read the following excerpts from John Smith's account of the speech he gave to the men at Jamestown during the "starving time." Smith wrote the account in 1624, whereas the starving time took place in 1609–1610. Ask your students to consider if any of the questions listed above apply, especially the final three.

As Smith wrote: "Countrymen, the long experiences of our late miseries, I hope is sufficient to persuade everyone to a present correction of himself, and think not that my pains nor the Adventurers' purses, will ever maintain you in idleness and sloth."

Translation: I hope you all realize that as a result of many and long experiences, that you cannot go on forever without working and that neither I nor the company are going to continue to maintain you. *Note*: A reasonably accurate translation, but what about the expression, "my pains?"

As Smith wrote: " . . . the labors of thirty or forty honest and industrious men shall not be consumed to maintain a hundred and fifty idle loiterers."

Translation: Don't think that thirty or forty workers are going to work for one hundred fifty lazy people who are going to sit around all day and do nothing. *Note*: Is "shall not be consumed" fairly translated?

As Smith wrote: " . . . he that gathereth not everyday as much as I do, the next day shall be set beyond the river, and be banished from the fort . . . till he amend his conditions or starve."

Translation: Work as hard as I do, or else you're going to have to leave and starve to death. *Note*: The translation does not mention that there is a chance to come back to the fort if " . . . he amend his conditions. . . ."

43

JAMESTOWN: SOME FACTS AND A CONTRADICTION

• Three ships—*Sara Constant, Goodspeed, Discovery*—furnished by the London Company delivered 105 settlers to Jamestown in May, 1607. Seven months after disembarking, in January, 1608, only 32 had survived. Disease, starvation, and hostile Indians accounted for the deaths.

• John Smith left the colony in October, 1609, never to return. However, on an expedition in 1614 he explored the coast of New England, which he named, and made valuable maps and charts of the coastline. Following his explorations he wrote a book, *A Description of New England*, which did much to excite interest in the newly discovered lands.

• It was tobacco which finally put the Jamestown community and surrounding area on an improved economic foundation. John Rolfe is given credit for this. He managed to obtain superior tobacco seeds from the West Indies; he subsequently planted these at Jamestown. So great was the acceptance of the improved tobacco that in 1620 Virginia colonists exported almost 120,000 pounds to England.

The success of tobacco culture had profound effects on Virginia. First, significant numbers of indentured servants and African slaves were imported to perform the labor. Second, new areas of Virginia were developed for the tobacco culture. *Note*: John Rolfe married Pocahontas, the daughter of Powhattan, the most powerful Indian chief in the Virginia region. This arrangement helped bring a brief cessation of Indian/Virginian warfare. Rolfe brought Pocahontas to England, where she was introduced to the king. Unfortunately, the Indian princess died after only one year's visit. The couple had one child who was only two years old at the time of his mother's death.

• A series of fires, the movement of planters to other parts of Virginia, a dwindling town population, and an unhealthy, lowland, malarial environment all contributed to the eventual abandonment of Jamestown. In 1699, Williamsburg, a few miles to the north, took over as Virginia's seat of government. The site of Jamestown, which was in danger of being eroded away by the action of the James River, survives today through the efforts of Virginia historical societies.

• 1619 was an important date in the history of the Virginia colony. It was the year that the first elected law making body, the House of Burgesses, was created, and it was the year that Africans were brought to Virginia to work in the colony.

The first legislative body

• was composed of 22 members from various "settlements," such as large plantations.

• passed laws for the governance of the colony in such matters as forbidding the sale of guns or gunpowder to the Indians, on the pain of death; required land owners to grow food crops along with tobacco; prohibited gambling and drunkenness.

• was given the exclusive right to tax property and other things.

The first African "servants," as they were called, were brought to America on a Dutch ship. There were twenty of them. They were not referred to as "slaves," but, in fact, they were. It is true that some of the earlier Africans were purchased with the provision that they would work for a specific number of years and then be free; however, most of them were sold to planters with no such provision. A few years after 1619 the overwhelming number of imported African laborers were slaves for life unless they could buy their freedom or were emancipated by their masters.

Most of the earlier imported workers in Virginia were not African. They were white Europeans who agreed to work for a specific number of years in payment for their passage from Europe. They were called "indentured servants." An indenture was a written agreement. At the time of the signing of the agreement, the paper that specified the conditions of the indenture was torn into two pieces—one for the master, one for the worker. At the end of the indenture the servant received the master's half.

It should be realized that the white Europeans volunteered to be indentured, and that eventually they were free. Then, they had the same rights as any other free person: they could own land, they could vote, they could work for wages, and so on.

The irony of all this is that in the same year Virginians gained self-government, the enslavement of Africans also began. It is hard to reconcile how one group that attained freedom could, in the next breath, deny it to others.

44

PILGRIMS PREPARE FOR A VOYAGE AND A NEW WORLD

Let your students imagine that they were Pilgrims in 1620. They are going to sail to the New World on the *Mayflower*. They have to take care of themselves and their families for perhaps eight weeks. There will be nothing that can be bought on the ship, and it is left to each family to provide all the necessities of life.

When they arrive in the New World they will have to supply everything needed to survive in a wilderness.

1. What food would you bring for the sea voyage? Remember that in those times there were no such things as canned food or refrigeration. Here are some suggestions:

- Dried fruit, vegetables, berries, meat
- Nuts
- Flour (for baking bread)
- Water (perhaps wine if the water becomes stagnant)
- Livestock (to be used during and after the voyage: chickens for eggs, cows for milk, etc.; remember that animals need food, too)
- Turtles (fresh meat; kept alive by flipping them on their backs)
- Pickled or salted fish

2. How might you increase your food and water supply while you are on the ship? Suggestions:

- Fish could be caught by hook or net.
- It might be possible to snare birds as they fly around the ship.
- If it rains, water might be collected in pots and pans.

3. What tools and utensils would be needed while on the ship? What other kinds of things might be needed?

- Pots, pans, baskets, plates
- Knives
- Change of clothing
- Soap
- Blankets

- Medicine
- Bible and other books

4. What would you need after you landed?

- Axe, hammer, saw, shovel, nails (for house, barns, etc.)
- Seeds (to plant for future food)
- Plow and other farming tools
- Guns, gunpowder, and shot (for hunting and defense)
- Clothing (weather and seasonal changes)
- Blankets, household utensils, etc.

5. What might you be able to get from the land other than what you might grow?

- Wood for fires, building
- Wax from bayberries or animal fat for candles
- Wild animals for food (deer, turkey, pheasant, etc.)
- Fish from the sea and rivers
- Nuts and berries, some roots

6. What would you do to make sure the colony was properly governed?

- Elect a leader
- Elect a legislative (law-making) body
- Elect, appoint, or designate a judicial body or person
- Enact laws for the good of the colony: procedures for providing the security of the colony from internal and/or external dangers; procedures for apprehending, trying, and punishing those who break laws; provisions for education, marriage, public works, and taxes.

Note: It might be helpful to review the Mayflower Compact, which was an agreement by the signers that they would work together to properly govern the colony. The specifics of governance were left for later. Here is a major quote from the Compact: " . . . in the presence of God and one another, (We) covenant (agree, contract) and combine ourselves into a civil body politic, for our better ordering and preservation. . . ." The signers agreed to obey laws made by the governing body.

Name: _____ Date: ___-_____

PILGRIMS MEET THE NEW WORLD

Reading a map is not unlike reading a book. In both it is necessary to know the meaning of the words and symbols. When reading books readers get deeper meaning when they combine the words into thoughts. The same thing is true when reading maps; that is, it is first necessary to recognize the symbol and what it stands for. So, if you see the symbol for *river* and then see a symbol for *city*, you realize that the city is located on a river. You have combined the two symbols into something more than when you see them alone.

The map on this page contains many bits of information about the Pilgrims' first contacts with the place they were to settle. Try to write two or three paragraphs that tell the story the map tells.

One way to start might be to describe Cape Cod. Here's an example: "Cape Cod looks like an arm bent at the elbow with a hand at the end cocked like a fist . . . "

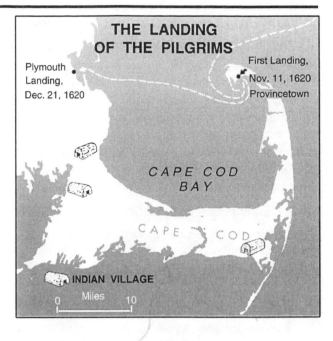

THE LANDING OF THE PILGRIMS

Plymouth Landing, Dec. 21, 1620

First Landing, Nov. 11, 1620 Provincetown

CAPE COD BAY

CAPE COD

INDIAN VILLAGE

0   Miles   10

_____

_____

_____

_____

_____

_____

_____

_____

_____

_____

_____

_____

Note: Use the other side, if necessary.

PENNSYLVANIA AND THE QUAKERS

Basic Facts about the Quakers

The Quakers have been and still are one of the most remarkable minority groups in American history. Cruelly persecuted in both Britain and the colonies, they have consistently worked towards bringing about true equality among people. Quakers were in the forefront of the fight to abolish slavery, often at the risk of personal injury. As early as 1688, Quakers in Germantown, Pennsylvania, issued a strong protest against slavery.

Some Quaker beliefs and practices:

- They do not believe in war. In colonial times they refused to serve in the king's army or navy. Even in modern times they stand by their beliefs; however, many Quakers willingly serve in life-sustaining activities and capacities in war, such as serving as "medics" in combat zones.

- They do not believe in taking a person's life as punishment for committing a crime.

- They believe that all people, even kings and queens, are equal; therefore, they would not call anyone by a title such as "Sir" or "Your Lordship."

- In colonial times they refused to pay taxes to support the king's church. This is one of the major reason they were persecuted. They were said to be against Christianity; whereas, in reality, they were not.

- "Quakers" is a nickname for the religious group; the official name is Society of Friends. It is not clear how the Friends came to be called Quakers. One story has it that they sometimes attained religious fervor to such an extent that they would tremble or quake.

- Presently, there are approximately 120,000 Quakers in the United States. Most Quakers live in the Northeast and the Midwest. Some of our most notable people have been or are Quakers: John Greenleaf Whittier (poet), Herbert Hoover (President). One of the most noted of Quaker women was Mary Dyer, a colonist from England. She was arrested many times for refusing to change her beliefs. Finally, in Boston in 1660, she was tried and hanged. Never once did she change her opinion that she had the right to worship God as she believed. All Americans today are beneficiaries of Mary Dyer, Quaker, and other people who have been willing to die for what they believed was right.

- William Penn, one the earliest Quakers, was the son of Admiral Penn of the British navy. Because of the severe persecution of Quakers in England, William Penn decided to start a colony in North America. He was greatly aided in this objective by King Charles II, who owed him a large sum of money that had been originally borrowed from his father. The debt was paid by a grant of land west of the Delaware; the grant was larger than England itself. An indication of the philosophy of the Quakers was that their first settlement was called Philadelphia, which means in Greek "brotherly love"; thus, Philadelphia is known even today as the "City of Brotherly Love." Sometimes, Philadelphia is called the "Quaker City."

Discussion questions:

1. Are dissenting groups such as the Quakers things of the past? (*No. The example set by the Quakers and others still lives today. In fact, the Bill of Rights (first ten amendments to the Constitution) was deliberately added because the people and their representatives believed strongly in the right to disagree without fear of intimidation or persecution. Here are some examples of modern dissenters: prohibitionists, various abortion groups, Martin Luther King and his followers, women's rights advocates, and so on.*)

2. Are such dissenting groups and individuals sometimes, even today in the 1990's, persecuted for their beliefs? (*Yes. They often face ridicule, bodily harm, job discrimination, and harassment.*)

3. Do dissenters contribute to the development of the country? (*Yes. They force the vast majority to think. They upset complacency and the status quo. Although they may not completely achieve their ends, they often bring about modification and reform.*)

4. Are there harmful effects of dissension? (*Yes. Sometimes groups are so zealous in promoting their beliefs they take the law into their own hands, and, sometimes, the rights of others are violated.*)

SECTION 6

Living in the English Colonies

1619: First Africans imported

... and this is the land of the free?

AFRICAN-AMERICANS IN EARLY AMERICAN HISTORY

This page of facts points out some significant aspects of the status and treatment of the people of African descent in early American history. The facts may be read to your students in their entirety or on occasion as your class travels through American history.

• It seems clear, although there is not complete agreement, that the first Africans brought to the colonies (1619–1640) were considered to be "servants" who, at the termination of "service," would become free. However, the term of service was often not specified. There is little evidence to show that Africans had written contracts which specified conditions of servitude. On the other hand, white indentured servants had indentures: contracts, that spelled out the responsibilities, etc., of both master and worker.

• As time passed on, especially after about 1950, the term "Negro" as a reference for Americans of African descent has been little used. The reason for this is that early records of slavery referred to Africans as "Negro servants" or simply as "Negroes." This is considered to be a degrading reminder of the enslavement of Africans. "Afro-Americans" or, more recently, "African-Americans" is a more acceptable term, especially since other Americans are referred to in such a manner—for example, Irish-Americans, Polish-Americans, Korean-Americans, and so on.

• It is a matter of record that in a variety of ways thousands of transported Africans resisted enslavement. There are historical accounts of at least fifty slave revolts at sea. In one revolt led by Cinque, son of an African chief, the slaves actually captured the slave ship, *Amistad*. These brave men eventually returned to their African homes.

Some of the transported Africans resisted by starving themselves. Some attacked their kidnappers with their bare hands or with the chains that held them and were killed in the unequal struggles. Many committed suicide. *The American Negro Reference Book* (Prentice-Hall, Englewood Cliffs, NJ), page 5, makes reference to African suicides in the following manner: "One trader remarked that the slaves were so wilful and loth to leave their own country that they often leaped out of canoes, boat and ship, into the sea, and kept under water till they were drowned. They preferred a watery grave or to be devoured by sharks to enslavement in some foreign land."

Once landed and sold into bondage, slaves found other ways to resist. They worked only as hard as was necessary to escape the overseer's whip; some protested by damaging equipment and crops. Along with the thousands of protests by individual slaves, there were numerous group uprisings. Some of the revolts were led by slaves, while others were led by former slaves. One of the most famous of the slave leaders was Gabriel Prosser. In 1800 he led about one thousand slaves in a well-organized attack on Richmond, Virginia. The revolt was not successful. Thirty-five of the slaves, including Prosser, lost their lives as a result of the rebellion.

• Slave unrest caused state legislatures to pass laws that strictly regulated slavery. Slaves were forbidden to talk to free African-Americans, to leave their plantations, to own guns, or to meet in groups. In some places it was even against the law to teach a slave to read or write. They could not marry without their master's consent. The laws protected the property rights of slave-owners; thus, if a slave ran away he or she was accused of "theft of self."

• In 1630 there were only about 60 Africans in the colonies. By 1760, this population had grown to about 326,000, most of whom were slaves. At the beginning of the Civil War (1860), this figure increased to about 4,440,000, of which 3,950,000 were enslaved and 490,000 were free. It is estimated that from 1619 to 1860 some 15,000,000 Africans were taken from their homes in Africa to be sold as slaves in the New World. However, probably half of the transported Africans never completed the voyage. As has been mentioned elsewhere on this page, suicides accounted for many deaths, but diseases contracted on the unbelievably filthy slave ships were the causes of most deaths.

DUTCH AND SWEDISH COLONIES

The text, illustration, and map on these two facing pages offer opportunities for a productive presentation-type lesson on the Dutch and Swedish colonies.

Procedure

1. Make a transparency of the facing page for yourself, and photocopies for your students.

2. Read and/or paraphrase the narrative material on this page. Ask the questions printed in bold type as they appear, and project the transparency when appropriate.

In 1609 the Dutch (Netherlands) hired Henry Hudson, an Englishman, to search for a water route to the Indies. He sailed west to the North American coast. **According to the map what were the first two bays he explored?** (*Chesapeake Bay, Delaware Bay*).

Hudson came to what is now called New York Bay. He thought he had found the long sought passage to the Indies as he sailed up the broad river. But as he sailed northward the river became more and more narrow. Eventually, his passage was completely blocked by rapids and waterfalls. He turned around and sailed back to Europe. **What name was given to the river that Hudson explored?** (*Hudson River*).

However, Dutch traders followed up Hudson's discovery when they learned that there were great possibilities for fur trading in the Hudson River Valley. Within two years after Hudson's discovery, they established trading posts along the river.

The concern of the first Dutch settlers was to make profits from trading. Then, in 1624 a group of about thirty families sailed for New Netherlands, as the Dutch possessions in America were called. They planned to make America their permanent home. One of the Dutch settlements was at Fort Orange. **Fort Orange is located near where the Mohawk River joins the Hudson River. Its location on the map is marked by a dot. Write** *Fort Orange* **next to the dot.**

In 1626, the Dutch settled on Manhattan Island, near the mouth of the Hudson river. This settlement, called New Amsterdam, was extremely successful. In fact, it has grown to be the largest city in the United States—New York City. **Use the scale of miles to determine how many miles a ship would have to sail up the Hudson River from New Amsterdam to Fort Orange.** (*130*)

Swedes Settle along the Delaware

Still another European country, Sweden, became interested in starting a colony in America. In 1636 a Swedish trading company sent fifty settlers to the region around Delaware Bay. They settled at a place called Fort Christina. Then, they set up small trading posts north and south of the main settlement. **What two rivers flow into Delaware Bay that made it helpful for the Swedes and the Indians to trade?** (*Delaware, Schuylkill*)

In their settlements, the Swedes built cabins made of logs. They had built log cabins in their home country, so it seemed natural to build them in the New World. It didn't take the other pioneers very long to see the advantages of the Swede's snug, solid little houses. Thousands of log homes were built in the years that followed. Many famous Americans, including presidents, were born in such cabins. **Write a title for the picture.** (*Suggestion: Building a Log Cabin —Swedish Style*) **How were the trees cut from the forest?** (*by axe, as compared to saw, as indicated by the nature of the cut*) **How were the notches in the logs crafted?** (*by axe, as suggested by the man with an axe, and the nature of the cut*) **What kind of simple machine is being used to lift the logs?** (*inclined plane*) **What is lying close by the workers ready for use in case of attack?** (*gun*) **While the men are working on the house, what would the women be most likely doing?** (*preparing food, bringing water, taking care of children*) **What word or words describes the way the men are working together?** (*cooperation, team work, etc.*) **What is there about the way the cabin is built that would make it easy to defend?** (*The thick walls would stop arrows or bullets.*)

When the Dutch heard about the Swedish settlements, they became angry. They thought that the lands along the Delaware belonged to them. They were especially upset because the Swedes were cutting into their fur trade. Therefore, one day in 1655, seven Dutch warships with more than 600 soldiers appeared on the river in front of Fort Christina. It was useless for the Swedes to resist such a large force. The Dutch took over the Swedish settlements without a fight. The Dutch, however, allowed the Swedes to stay in the homes they had built. Life for the Swedish settlers did not change when the Dutch captured the Delaware region.

DUTCH AND SWEDISH COLONIES

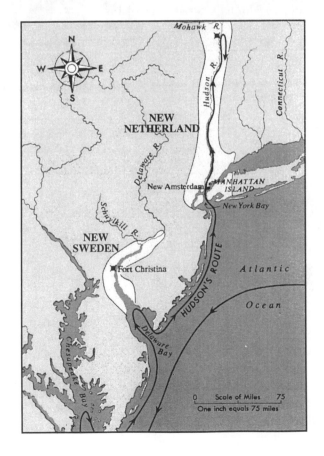

Name: _____ Date: _____

MINORITY EXPLORERS AND BUILDERS

French Huguenots Strengthen the English Colonies

Thousands of Pilgrims, Puritans, Quakers, and Catholics left the British Isles because they were not permitted to worship as they pleased. More than one million French Huguenots, members of a Protestant sect, were not allowed to settle in French colonies. Because of this, France lost many of its finest citizens. The French loss was America's gain. The English colonies were enriched by the Huguenots who settled in them. The Huguenots had special skills as craftsmen, artists, and textile (cloth) workers. Also, they were willing to stand up for their religious and political beliefs. This spirit became a part of thousands of Americans who are descended from them.

Paul Revere was from a Huguenot family. He was a famous silversmith and patriot.

Jews Help Strengthen the English Colonies

Jewish influence in the development of the New World began even before Columbus. Columbus consulted Jewish scholars and referred to Jewish-made maps before starting his first voyage. Five or six of his crew members were Jews by birth. The first Jews to settle in North America landed on Manhattan Island in 1654. When the American Revolution began in 1776 there were about 2500 Jews in the colonies. Jews played an important part in developing colonial trade. Trade helped the colonies grow strong and prosperous. Trade also helped people in widely separated parts of the colonies to understand each other. One of the greatest Jewish merchants was Aaron Lopez of Newport, Rhode Island. At one time, he had thirty ships selling American products all over the world.

Moses Lindo's business and technical skill helped establish indigo as a leading crop in South Carolina. A royal blue dye was made from the indigo plant.

African Explorers in the New World

Almost every Spanish or French explorer included Africans in his exploring party. Thirty men of African descent were with Balboa when he discovered the Pacific. Perhaps the most outstanding African explorer was Estevanico (Little Stephen). He and three companions were the first to explore what is now New Mexico and Arizona. Estevanico's knowledge of Indian languages and customs and his outstanding scouting abilities helped him in his work. Later, he led another exploring party into the regions north of Mexico. Estevanico was killed on this expedition, but his discoveries were useful to Coronado. Africans accompanied the Frenchmen who explored Canada and the Mississippi Valley. France's claims to Louisiana were based, in part, on the fact that French pioneers settled the regions first. Many of those pioneers were African.

Estevanico was especially good as an explorer because of his excellent scouting abilities.

Name: _____ Date: _____

MINORITY EXPLORERS AND BUILDERS

African-American Craftsmen in the Colonies

Southern plantations were like separate communities. As in any community, skilled and unskilled laborers were necessary. African-Americans performed most of the labor in the fields, the homes, and the shops. On a single plantation it was possible to find African-American carpenters, blacksmiths, shoemakers, weavers, knitters, and leather workers. In colonial cities African-Americans worked as butchers, cooks, bakers, bricklayers, pipe makers, silversmiths, and upholsterers. Many individual African-Americans achieved fame for their craftsmanship. One notable example was Benjamin Banneker, who was not only a skilled craftsman, but also a great surveyor, mathematician, astronomer, and publisher of a widely used almanac.

African-American craftsmen helped build Monticello, Thomas Jefferson's beautiful home.

1. With which man mentioned on these two pages is each of the following most closely related?

Indigo _____

Arizona, New Mexico _____

astronomy _____

trading _____

Huguenots _____

exporter of
colonial products _____

2. Draw a circle around the sentence that proves the following statement is true: Jews came to the New World long before Jamestown was settled.

3. Underline the sentence that proves the following statement is true: Huguenots would not have been permitted to settle in French Quebec or in the French lands near the Mississippi River.

4. What are two reasons why Estevanico was a successful explorer?

_____

_____

5. According to the picture, what kind of animal helped Estevanico in his explorations?

_____

6. What were the three *main* kinds of work African-Americans performed on southern plantations?

_____

_____

_____

7. What was made from the indigo plants shown in the picture on the opposite page?

_____

8. In what ways did the Jewish merchants help create a feeling of oneness, or unity, in the colonies?

_____

_____

_____

9. Benjamin Banneker was a very important part of the planning and building of Washington, D. C., as the nation's capital. What two special abilities did he possess that were probably the most useful?

_____

_____

10. How were Africans important to French claims to Louisiana?

_____

_____

Name: _____ Date: _____

WORKING IN A COLONIAL HOME

Each person in a colonial home contributed to the good of the family. Almost everything the family used they had to grow or make. The illustration above shows how a typical family might spend its evenings.

1. Study the picture and complete the listing below.

Family Member	Task
Grandmother	
Young boy	
Mother of the children	
Father of the children	
Girl	
Grandfather	

2. What would be your guess as to what is in the horn hanging from the gun that is over the fireplace? _____

What is in the pot into which the young girl is dipping candles? _____

3. Notice the open space with a door on the left side of the fireplace. What is your guess as to what the space is used for? _____

4. Not including candles, what are two other ways to have light at night (as indicated in the picture)?

_____

5. Think of the changes in living today as compared to colonial times. Complete the paragraph that follows with words from your own knowledge and experience.

Today a furnace that burns _____ , _____ , or _____ keeps us warm. Homes are lighted by _____ , and cloth is woven in _____ . Bread is bought in a _____; shoes are repaired by a _____ .

MAPPING THE THIRTEEN COLONIES

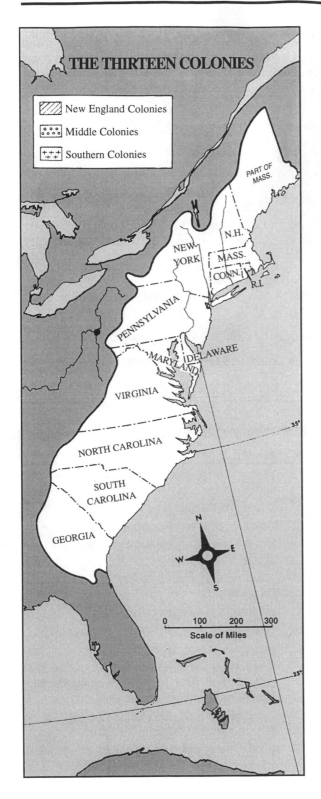

Reading and Completing Maps

1. At the time of the Revolutionary War the Northern Colonies were Connecticut, Rhode Island, Massachusetts, and New Hampshire. Later, Maine was created from Massachusetts, and Vermont was carved out of New Hampshire.

On the map, show the original four colonies by drawing diagonal lines across them as shown in the map key.

2. The Middle Colonies were New York, Pennsylvania, New Jersey, and Delaware. On the map show these colonies by drawing small o's in them as shown in the map key.

3. The Southern Colonies were Maryland, Virginia, North Carolina, South Carolina and Georgia. Show these colonies on the map by drawing small +'s in them as shown in the key.

4. The eastern boundary of the colonies was the Atlantic Ocean. Label the **Atlantic Ocean** on the map.

5. Spanish Florida was to the south of the colonies. Label **Spanish Florida**.

6. France claimed all the land that was west of the colonies. Write **French Claimed Land** on the map in the proper place.

7. The most northeastern lake represented is **Lake Ontario**. Label it on the map.

8. The lake that is southwest of Lake Ontario is **Lake Erie**. Label it on the map.

9. The lake that is north of Lake Erie is **Lake Huron**. Label it on the map.

10. The dark line on the western edge of the thirteen colonies is the "ridge" of the Appalachian Mountains. Carefully label the Appalachian Mountains, and on both sides of the line draw a series of symbols (⋀⋁⋀⋁) to better show the mountain chain.

11. Traveling the Ohio River was the easiest way to reach the land west of the Appalachians; it was a "water highway." The river begins at the junction of the Allegheny River (from the north) and the Monongahela River (from the south). Label the **Ohio River**. Also, the dot at the point where the Ohio River begins is Pittsburgh, which was the starting place for westward-journeying pioneers. Label **Pittsburgh**.

12. Label the **St. Lawrence River** which flows in a northeast direction from Lake Ontario.

COLONIAL EVENTS: 1600 – 1770

Time Lines

It is easy for young students to become "lost" in the sequence of events that are reported in a typical textbook narrative. This is understandable; a multiplicity of events occurred at the same time that the event being explained took place. Time lines can help students to make chronological sense out of all the events. Also, since time lines are essentially single-line bar graphs, they enable students to see proportionate lengths of time between events.

These two facing pages will enable you to make a "grand" time line, which will be completed by students, across a wall of your classroom.

Procedure

1. Hang a taut string across one of the walls of the classroom.

2. Tie ribbons on the string, each 1' apart. If there is a shortage of linear space, the ribbons could be 2' apart. In the first case each space could represent 10 years; in the second case each space may represent 30 years, and so on.

3. Divide students into groups of 2, 3, or 4. Each group will be responsible for hanging and illustrating a certain number of events. For example, assume there are 28 events to be recorded; if there were seven groups, each group would be responsible for 4 events.

4. The facing page illustrates how a part of the time line might be arranged and illustrated.

5. The students should print and illustrate the events at their desks, and then attach them to the string with clothespins or some other clipping device.

Significant Events in American History: 1600 – 1765

Date	Event
1607	Settlement of Jamestown (English)
1608	Settlement of Quebec (French)
1619	House of Burgesses (Virginia)
1619	First Africans imported
1620	Pilgrims land at Plymouth
1624	Settlement of New Netherlands (Dutch)
1630	Settlement of Massachusetts Bay (Puritans)
1634	Settlement of Maryland
1635	Settlement of the Connecticut Valley
1636	Harvard College established
1642	Compulsory school laws passed in Massachusetts
1656	First Quakers reach New England
1659	First Quakers hanged in Boston
1660	English Navigation Acts regulate colonial trade
1670	Settlement of North Carolina
1676	Bacon's Rebellion in Virginia

Date	Event
1682	William Penn establishes the Pennsylvania colony
1688	Quakers speak out against slavery
1692	Salem witch trial (19 persons executed)
1712	Slave uprising in New York (6 suicides, 21 executions)
1731	Start of first public library in Philadelphia (Benjamin Franklin)
1732	Settlement of Georgia colony
1735	Trial of Peter Zenger (freedom of the press)
1754	Beginning of French and Indian War
1763	End of French and Indian War (French lose all of Canada and land between the Appalachian Mountains and Mississippi River)
1763	Proclamation of 1763 (settlement beyond the Appalachian Mountains restricted)
1770	Population of colonies estimated at 2,148,000; slave population at more than 350,000

6-6

COLONIAL EVENTS: 1600 – 1770

1600 — 1620 — 1640 — 1660 — 1680

1607: Settlement of Jamestown

"Work or starve!"

1624: Settlement of New Netherlands

Henry Hudson sails up the Hudson to the falls.

1619: House of Burgesses

Laws made here!

1619: First Africans imported

...and this is the land of the free?

1636: Harvard College established

More than 350 years old and still going strong!

Harvard College Degree

1642: Compulsory school laws in Massachussetts

"...and you go straight to school!"

1659: First Quakers hanged in Boston

"I will not change my beliefs!"

1660: English Navigation Act regulates colonial trade

"Thou shalt not trade with any nation except ENGLAND!"

1682: William Penn founds the colony of Pennsylvania

Penn makes a treaty with the Indians

1670: Settlement of North Carolina

"So many pine trees! We can make money from the pitch and turpentine!"

—continued →

COLONIAL INGENUITY

The inventiveness of early Americans in meeting the needs of everyday living and working was remarkable, if not truly ingenious. This activity will help your students develop an appreciation of the colonists' resourcefulness. It will also provide them with practice in making inferences from observations.

Procedure

1. Make a transparency of the drawings at the bottom of this page.

2. Project each drawing separately, and ask the questions suggested in the right column. Accept any thoughtful answer.

1. **Covered bridge:** What would be reasons for covering a bridge? (*protect the wood; provide shelter in a storm*)

2. **Seed grinder:** *Note*: Do not identify by name at first. What purpose would this device have in food preparation? (*crushes herbs, seeds, kernels, mint for tea*)

3. **Egg beater:** *Note*: Do not identify by name at first. What might this machine be used for? (*egg beater*) Explain how it works. (*twisting motion turns shaft*)

4. **Snake fence:** Why would colonials make a fence in such a way? (*no posts to rot; no nails are necessary; easily repaired*)

5. **Farm harrow:** *Note*: Do not identify by name at first. What would be the purpose of this implement in preparing land for planting? (*levels the ground; breaks up clods*)

6. **Well sweep:** Something is missing from this well sweep that would make it operable. What is it? (*a counter-balancing weight*)

7. **Stockade fence**: Why are the logs pointed? (*harder to climb over, would impale an invader; points shed snow and rain, and this would retard rotting from the top*)

8. **Yokes and pokes:** What is the purpose of the broad yoke and pointed poke? (*yoke prevents cattle from going through fence palings; poke prevents cattle from jumping fences*)

EVERYDAY THINGS USED IN COLONIAL AMERICA

This activity will help students develop understandings of the practical tools colonials used in their everyday existence. It will also help sharpen students' listening, visualizing, and writing skills.

Procedure

1. Make a transparency of Figures 1 and 2.

2. To use Figure 1:

   a. Project the transparency.

   b. Read one of the descriptions from "Descriptions for Figure 1."

   c. Students are to jot down which one of the objects they think is begin described.

   d. Call on a student to suggest an answer.

   e. Discuss the object.

Descriptions for Figure 1

- A light, tough, cone-shaped container made from animal horn; used to keep gunpowder dry. (*powder horn*)
- A round pan with a hinged lid fastened to the end of a long handle; pan is filled with hot coals; used to warm beds. (*warming pan*)
- A scissors-like cutting tool; used to trim the wicks of candles, especially to keep them from smoking excessively. (*candle snuffer*)
- Two grill-like plates fastened to the end of long handles; resembles a large pair of pliers; used for baking a kind of cake. (*waffle iron*)
- A metal rack designed to hold bread upright as it is being toasted by hot coals. (*bread toaster*)
- Metal shaped in such a way that mud, dirt, ice, snow would be scraped off a boot passed over it; generally fastened to a porch or step near a door. (*foot scraper*)

- A hollow, metal tube containing a plunger; ground meat placed in tube is pushed into sausage sack by plunger. (*sausage gun*)
- A kind of hinged hammer fastened to a door; tapping the hammer on the door summoned the inhabitants of the house. (*door knocker*)
- A small metal box in which hot coals were placed; used to keep one's feet warm in churches and other places. (*foot stove*)

3. To use Figure 2:

   a. Project the transparency.

   b. Students are to write their own descriptions. Encourage them to use a style similar to that used in Figure 1 descriptions; that is, first write a description, then follow with a function. *Note*: It would be helpful to tell the purpose of the implement.

   c. Some suggested descriptions follow:

- ***Butter churn*** - A conical shaped, cask-like container made of wood slats; a hole in the top center piece through which a plunger is inserted; up-and-down motion of plunger churns cream into butter.
- ***Bellows*** - Two wooden, fan shaped pieces of wood attached by pleated leather; not unlike an accordion in appearance; air nozzle at one end, two handles at the

BUTTER CHURN

BELLOWS

Figure 1

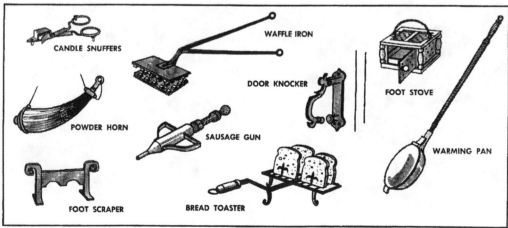

Note: Illustrations on this page not to scale

Figure 2

Name: _____ Date: _____

SYMBOL OF AMERICA: THE KENTUCKY RIFLE

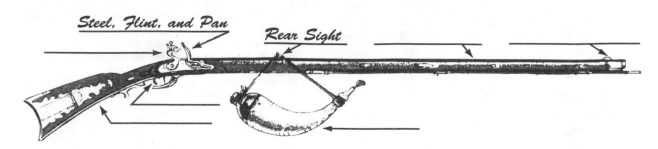

Rifles like the one shown above were first made in Pennsylvania in the early 1700's. They became affectionately known as "Kentucky" rifles after Daniel Boone and other pioneers made them famous.

Before the invention of the Kentucky rifle, the most popular gun in the colonies was the musket. But the musket was not well suited to frontier life. It was too heavy to carry on long journeys. It was inaccurate and it had an effective range of fewer than 100 yards.

The Kentucky rifle was a great improvement on the musket. The musket barrel had a smooth bore, or interior, in which the lead bullets fitted loosely. The rifle barrel had *rifling* or spiral grooves, cut into the bore. The grooves made the bullets spin as they were fired; this increased the accuracy of the gun.

Also, the rifle bullet fitted tightly in the barrel. Therefore the full force of the exploding powder was used to expel the bullet, making it travel much farther and faster than the musket ball.

Other advantages of the rifle were that it used less powder and smaller bullets than the musket. These things were important to pioneers, who took long journeys, and to hunters, who might stay in the woods for months and had to carry all their powder and shot with them.

Of course, the advantages of the Kentucky rifle were also important to soldiers. Early in the Revolutionary War, the British were astounded at the range and accuracy of American guns. The British army had no such weapons as these.

Defeating the British and winning the West for America were difficult jobs. The Kentucky rifle did much to make both jobs easier.

Loading and Firing the Kentucky Rifle

Name: _____ Date: _____

SYMBOL OF AMERICA: THE KENTUCKY RIFLE

1. The story on the opposite page tells you that the musket was not well suited to frontier life. On the lines below, list briefly the disadvantages of the musket as compared with the Kentucky rifle.

a. _____

b. _____

c. _____

2. What was there about the rifle's barrel that helped make the rifle more accurate than the musket?

_____

_____

3. What improvement did the rifle have over the musket to help the rifle bullet travel faster and farther than the musket ball?

_____

_____

_____

_____

4. Which of the two guns used the most powder and lead?

_____

5. What features of the rifle were important to pioneers and hunters?

_____

_____

_____

6. Read the descriptions below of some of the parts of the Kentucky rifle. Then write the name of each part in the proper place on the diagram on the opposite page. Some parts have been labeled for you.

Stock—the wooden part that rests against the shoulder when the gun is aimed

Barrel—the metal tube through which the bullet travels

Sights—aiming devices; one at the rear and one at the front of the barrel

Trigger—the lever that fires the gun

Hammer—springs forward when the trigger is pulled, striking the *flint* against the *steel*. Sparks ignite powder in the *pan*, which in turn fires powder in the barrel.

Horn—container for gunpowder

7. The drawings on the opposite page show how a Kentucky rifle was loaded and fired. Match the descriptions below with the drawings. Write the number of the correct drawing in front of each description.

_____ The ramrod tamps down the bullet.

_____ Grains of powder are poured into the pan of the rifle.

_____ A lead bullet and a greased patch are put into the barrel.

_____ The hammer strikes the flint against the steel, causing sparks.

_____ The pioneer aims the rifle.

_____ A measure of powder is poured into the barrel of the rifle.

FREEDOM OF THE PRESS: THE PETER ZENGER CASE

The following story can be read to your students as an example of how individual Americans have fought and suffered for the freedoms we have and enjoy today, and that are embodied and guaranteed in the first ten amendments to the Constitution. Amendment number three states, in part, *"Congress shall make no law respecting an establishment of religion . . . ; or abridging the freedom of speech or the press. . . . "*

The photocopy on the facing page of Zenger's paper will give your students an opportunity to study from an original source, and to understand Peter Zenger's feelings as expressed by himself.

An important right for which the colonists fought was freedom of the press. One thing this means is that newspapers and books have the right to criticize public officials. In the colonial period, however, the governor of a colony had the power to censor the press. This meant that he could regulate the newspapers of the colony. Often governors punished and put into prison the people who published articles that criticized the government. The governors feared the power of the newspapers. Newspapers might unite the people and encourage them to rebel against the king's government.

In 1733 there was only one newspaper in the entire colony of New York, and it was controlled by the governor. This meant that the people could read only what the governor wanted them to read. This bothered Peter Zenger, the son of an immigrant from Germany. Zenger and a group of his friends decided to publish a newspaper that would print the truth, no matter what the consequences to themselves might be. They called their paper the *New York Weekly Journal*.

As might be guessed, not long after Zenger printed criticisms of the governor, he was arrested and put in jail. His newspapers were burned by the order of the governor. Zenger did not let being in jail stop him. Even while he was there waiting for his trial, he smuggled articles out of jail to be published in his paper.

Most people thought that Zenger would be given a jail sentence because he had criticized the government. But Zenger obtained the help of the most able and most famous lawyer in the colonies—Andrew Hamilton of Philadelphia. Hamilton was eighty years old at the time. But, he agreed to work for Zenger when he learned that many other lawyers in the colonies had refused to help him. This was because of their fear of the governor.

Hamilton's body was weak from old age, but his mind was keen and sharp. In defending Zenger, Hamilton argued that what Zenger had done was not a crime. Hamilton said that the articles Zenger wrote were true. No man should be punished for writing the truth. In a stirring speech to the jury, he said " . . . the question before . . . you, gentlemen of the jury, is not of small nor private concern, it is not the cause of a poor printer, nor of New York alone . . . No! It may . . . affect every freeman that lives under a British government . . . It is the cause of liberty . . . the liberty of speaking and writing truth."

What was the decision of the jury? Let Zenger himself tell it: "The jury withdrew and in a small time returned, and being asked . . . their verdict . . . answered . . . *Not Guilty*. Upon which there were three huzzas [cheers] in the hall which was crowded with people, and the next day I was discharged from my imprisonment."

The Zenger case was important in the history of freedom for several reasons. For one thing, it showed how one determined freeman could stand up against the power of an unjust government and win. It encouraged other newspaper publishers to print the truth as they saw it. When people can read different points of view about an issue, they can make more-informed decisions.

Name: _____ Date: _____

FREEDOM OF THE PRESS: THE PETER ZENGER CASE

T H E
New - York Weekly JOURNAL

Containing the (freſheſt) Advices, Foreign, and Domeſtick.

MUNDAT November 25th, 1734.

To all my Subſcribers and Benefaɛtors who take my weekly Journall.

Gentlemen, Ladies and Others;

Line
(1) A S you laſt week were Diſ-
(2) appointed of my Journall,
(3) I think it Incumbent up-
(4) on me, to publiſh my
(5) Apoligy which is this.
(6) On the Lords Day, the Seventeenth
(7) of this Inſtant, I was Arreſted, taken
(8) and Impriſoned in the common Goal
(9) of this City, by Virtue of a Warrant
(10) from the *Governour*, and the Hono-
(11) rable *Francis Harriſon*, Eſq; and others
(12) in Councill of which (God willing)
(13) yo'l have a Coppy, whereupon I was
(14) put under ſuch Reſtraint that I had
(15) not the Liberty of Pen Ink, or Paper,
(16) or to ſee, or ſpeak with People, till
(17) upon my Complaint to the Honourable
(18) the Chief Juſtice, at my appearing
(19) before him upon my *Habias Corpus* on
(20) the *Wedneſday* following. Who diſ-
(21) countenanced that Proceeding, and
(22) therefore I have had ſince that Time,
(23) the Liberty of Speaking through the
(24) Hole of the Door, to my Wife and
(25) Servants by which I doubt not yo'l
(26) think me ſufficiently Excuſed for not
(27) ſending my laſt weeks *Journall*, and
(28) I hope for the future by the Liberty of
(29) Speaking to my Servants thro' the
(30) Hole of the Door of the Priſon, to
(31) entertain you with my weekly *Journall*
(32) as formerly. *And am your obliged Humble Servant,*
J. Peter Zenger.

Study this photograph of one of Peter Zenger's newspapers. Do not allow the spelling of some of the words or the formation of some of the letters to confuse you. For example, notice how the S is formed in the word *freshest* at the top of the paper. *Note*: The numbers in the left margin are not part of his original paper; they were put there to help you complete this activity.

1. In the first nine lines of the column Zenger explains why his paper wasn't published the previous week. What was his excuse?

_____

2. How does Zenger spell the following words in his column? Headline: Monday? _____
Line 8: Jail? _____ Line 9: City? _____

3. In lines 14–16, Zenger tells his readers there are certain things he was not allowed to do while in jail, including having pen, ink or paper. What else wasn't he allowed to do? _____

4. Complete the following sentence: On lines 17–27 of the article, Zenger explains that he was able to gain the right to speak to his _____ and _____ through a _____ in his prison door.

5. According to lines 31–32, what does Zenger plan to do about future issues of his paper? _____

_____

MULTI-CULTURAL ADDITIONS TO STANDARD ENGLISH

In our teaching of American history we may have the tendency to stress the wars, depressions, and disasters to the neglect of social developments such as progress in education, science, and health. Language development and usage may be another aspect of American history that is neglected. The United States is a very large country containing numerous regions and more than 255 million people. Furthermore, our population is made up, largely, of people who have descended from a myriad of ethnic/language backgrounds. To further increase the "mix," tens of thousands of immigrants enter our country each year.

Although schools teach standard English, the people in each region occasionally use words and expressions that original settlers brought from the mother country and passed on to their children, who passed them on to their children, and so on.

The use of old-world words and phrases adapted and interspersed while speaking English may not be related to one's level of education; a college professor of English, an administrator in a business or industry, or a farmer may all use regional words at one time or another. Most likely this would occur when family and friends get together. It would be unlikely that dialect words would appear in writing unless done so for a specific purpose.

Language deviations, as in the context explained above, are part of the United States' rich multi-cultural heritage. They are to be valued and treasured, and they are as much a part of America as Japanese sushi, Scottish meat pies, Italian veal parmigiani, Polish kielbasa, Mexican tacos, or Indian succotash. Richness of language is a part of American life we can all enjoy and that may help bring smiles to our faces.

"Pennsylvania Dutch" is a good example of regional language and dialect. Many of the early settlers in Pennsylvania were Germans, and the country from which they came was called "Deutschland." Over the years the "Deutsch" part of the name came to be pronounced "Dutch." This twist of language has led many to believe that the Pennsylvania Dutch are from the Netherlands (Holland); of course, this is incorrect.

The accompanying student activity page, on "Pennsylvania Dutch," will provide an interesting language experience for your students. First, you may want to acquaint them with the above information and some of the facts that follow.

- Germans first entered Pennsylvania under William Penn's charter in 1681.

- The main flow of German settlers to Pennsylvania began about 1717. Their numbers increased rapidly and by the time of the American Revolution their numbers made up about 30% of Pennsylvania's population. Also, at about that time there were some 225,000 Germans scattered among all of the other colonies.

- German settlers in Pennsylvania were inclined to make their homes in the southeastern part of the colony—the present-day counties of Lancaster, York, Berks, Lehigh, and Northhampton.

- There were numerous reasons for the pre-Revolution migration of Germans from Germany: religious and political persecution, constant wars that devastated their villages and farms, excessive taxes to pay for the wars. Many Germans were persuaded to come to Pennsylvania as a result of advertisements extolling the colony's attractions.

- General Nicholas Herkimer (1728–1777) who commanded the American troops at the Battle of Oriskany was not one of the Pennsylvania Dutch, but his parents were Germans. Herkimer died as a result of wounds suffered in the battle. Herkimer, New York, is named after him.

Glossary of Pennsylvania Dutch Words

Note: After your students have tried to decipher the sentences on the facing page, review the sentences and provide the proper translation.

bauch: stomach	**goutz**: bark	**shteddle**: village, town
bendle: string	**koos**: kiss	**slipperich**: slippery
bissel: little, little while	**kronk**: sick	**spossich**: funny
crotz: scratch	**loblich**: silly	**unfershtendich**: ridiculous
fahoongart: hungry	**rootsh**: crawl	**weetich**: angry
gabut: tired	**shnell**: quick, quickly	**woonerfitzich**: nosey, snoopy, curious

Name: _____ Date: _____

MULTI-CULTURAL ADDITIONS TO STANDARD ENGLISH: PENNSYLVANIA DUTCH

The sentences below contain words and phrases in italics that are frequently heard in the "Pennsylvania Dutch" region of Pennsylvania and other parts of the country where the earliest settlers were German.

Read each sentence carefully and try to determine what the strange words mean. Write your interpretation of the words on the line at the end of the sentence.

1. "It hurts me in the **bauch**. Maybe I ate too many green apples." _____

2. "I need a little piece of **bendle** to tie this package." _____

3. "Come here for a **bissel**; I want to talk to you." _____

4. "It feels so good when I **crotz** it." _____

5. "He was so **fahoongart**; I thought he'd never stop eating." _____

6. "I'm very **gabut**; I'm going to bed." _____

7. The dog gave a loud **goutz** when he saw the cat. _____

8. His mother gave him a **koos** and told him he was a good boy. _____

9. "I was so **kronk** in the boat. I thought it would never stop rocking." _____

10. "He is so **loblich**; he's never serious." _____

11. "I have never seen a baby **rootsh** so much! She is all over the floor." _____

12. "She completed the puzzle so **shnell**. She must be very smart." _____

13. "The road was so **slipperich** I thought that we would never get to the **shteddle** in time to see the New Year's Day parade." _____ , _____

14. "I never laughed so much in my life; it was so **spossich**!" _____

15. "It was the most **unfershtendich** thing I have ever seen. The man pulled the plant out of the ground to see how it was growing!" _____

16. "He was very **weetich** when he found that someone had stolen his bicycle." _____

17. "You get into so much trouble because you're so **woonerfitzich**. Stop asking so many questions!" __

_____

Name: _____ Date: _____

BEN FRANKLIN: INVENTOR, PATRIOT, STATESMAN

1 Benjamin Franklin was born in Boston in 1706. His parents hoped that he would become a minister, but there was little money for his education. After only two years of school, Ben was kept at home to learn his father's trade—the making of soap and candles.

2 Ben had no interest in soap and candles and continued to educate himself by reading everything he could lay his hands on. At the age of twelve he went to work for his older brother, James, who was a printer. His pay was small, but he used half of it to buy books and the rest for food.

3 A few years later James Franklin began to publish a newspaper. Ben, who loved to write, decided to compose an essay for the paper. He knew, however, that James would not print the essay if he knew it to be the work of his young brother. So in the dark of night, Ben slipped it under the door of the printing shop. He had signed the essay "Silence Dogood." This and several more of Ben's essays were printed in the paper and received many compliments.

4 All his life Ben Franklin was interested in the world around him. He asked himself such questions as, "What is lightning?" At that time no one knew the answer. Ben decided to find out. In 1752 he conducted his famous experiment with a kite. He flew the kite during a thunderstorm. When sparks jumped from a metal key attached to the kite string, Ben had proved that lightning was really electricity. Also, he might easily have lost his life.

POOR RICHARD'S ALMANAC

For years Ben wrote and published this book. It became famous for wise sayings like these:

1. "Well done is better than well said."
2. "The worst wheel of the cart makes the most noise."
3. "The rotten apple spoils his companions."
4. "Don't throw stones at your neighbors if your own windows are glass."
5. "Three may keep a secret if two of them are dead."
6. "He that speaks much, is much mistaken."

---

5 This experiment led to Franklin's invention of the lightning rod. He was one of the first men in the world to experiment with electricity.

6 Ben was too old to fight in the Revolutionary War, but without his help the colonists might not have won. It was Ben Franklin and two other Americans who persuaded France to support the colonies.

7 After the war, at the age of eighty-one, Franklin played an important part in forming the Constitution for the new nation. Time after time, when arguments grew bitter and tempers wore thin, he stepped in to calm the delegates. Perhaps he told a funny story or suggested a compromise on which all could agree. He even gave in on many of his own points to win agreement.

8 Few men in the history of the world have been good at as many different things as Ben Franklin was. As a famous American writer said, "In any age, in any place, Franklin would have been great."

BEN FRANKLIN: INVENTOR, PATRIOT, STATESMAN

Each of the statements below can be related to one of the numbered paragraphs on the opposite page. Write the number of the paragraph on the line before the statement.

_____ Ben was able to use the results of an experiment to invent a useful thing.

_____ Ben was one of the world's great men.

_____ Ben was not stubborn in his beliefs about what should be in the Constitution.

_____ Ben represented the American colonies in France.

_____ Ben's father was not wealthy enough to educate him.

_____ Ben was a member of the Constitutional Convention.

_____ Ben was curious about lightning.

_____ Ben was an important figure in the fight for independence.

_____ Ben did not want to follow his father's trade.

_____ Ben was curious about nature.

_____ Ben educated himself by reading.

_____ Ben went to work for his brother to learn the printing trade.

_____ Ben tricked his brother.

_____ Ben was willing to make sacrifices for his education.

Poor Richard's Almanac

Study the sayings of Poor Richard in the box on the opposite page. On the line before each statement below, write the number of the saying that means the same thing.

_____ Those who associate with bad people may also become bad.

_____ If you want to keep something quiet, tell no one.

_____ A person who talks a lot will often be wrong in what he says.

_____ Actions mean more than words.

_____ The poorest worker is often the worst complainer.

_____ If you are not perfect, do not criticize others.

To go ahead. At the age of seventeen, Ben left his brother's home in Boston. After many adventures he arrived in Philadelphia. The artist who made the drawing below read Ben's own description of his arrival. See if you can put back into words what the artist drew. That is, write a careful description of what you see in the drawing. Use the reverse side of this page for your description.

MAP LOCATIONS IN EASTERN NORTH AMERICA: 1492–1775

This activity will help imprint map locations in the minds of your students and also serve as a review.

Procedure

1. Make a transparency of the map for projection.

2. Have your students number a piece of paper from 1 to 23.

3. Read the descriptions of the places to be located. Students are to jot down A, B, C, D, E, F, G, H, or I as their response to each description.

4. After all items have been read tell the correct responses. Students should correct their own papers.

Note: Most, but not all, of the items included have been mentioned in this book; however, those that are not mentioned are almost certain to be included in basic history texts.

People, Places, and Events

_____ Norsemen try to establish a settlement in Vinland.
_____ Columbus first lands in the New World.
_____ The first African indentured servants are brought to an English colony.
_____ Ponce de Leon looks for the "Fountain of Youth."
_____ Champlain starts the first permanent French settlement in the New World.
_____ John Cabot discovers great fishing banks.
_____ An English settlement on Roanoke Island fails.
_____ Fort Duquesne becomes Fort Pitt after the French are defeated.
_____ General Wolfe captures Quebec.
_____ William Penn establishes a Quaker colony.
_____ John Rolfe brings superior tobacco seeds to an English colony.
_____ Roger Williams establishes a colony.
_____ The first log cabins are built.
_____ The Dutch establish trading posts.
_____ The Peter Zenger "freedom of the press" trial is held.
_____ The French and Indians defeat General Braddock.
_____ Frenchmen interested in farming establish farms.
_____ LaSalle explores a great river.
_____ John Smith tells his followers, "No work—no food."

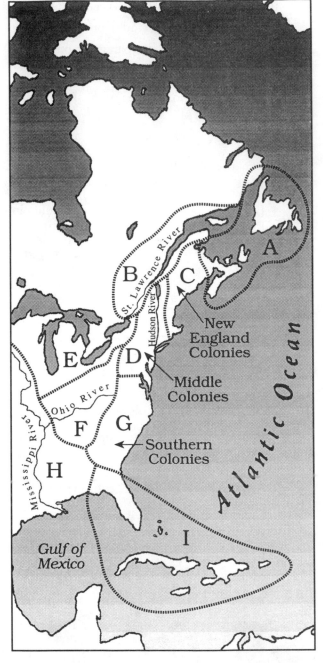

_____ The French fort of Louisbourg is captured by the British.
_____ The first battle of the American Revolution is fought.
_____ New Orleans is founded by the French.
_____ Marquette and Joliet explore the Great Lakes region.

67

SEQUENCES IN EARLY AMERICAN HISTORY

This activity can place your students in a research situation in which the resource material is relatively simple to assemble. A basic history textbook and/or supplementary books such as encyclopedias can be used for most items. Some of the items require exact dates, while others involve some thinking. *Example*: Which came first—log cabins or teepees? The answer is *tepees* because the Indians were here thousands of years before Swedes came to the Delaware River and built their log homes.

Procedure

1. Place your students in research groups of two.

2. Write several of the items below on the chalk board. Allow a reasonable amount of time for the students to research, then discuss, then proceed to another group of items. *Note*: By so doing, the class is kept together and the research is "broken up." No group gets "lost" or far behind.

Items of Research

1. On each line below, two items are listed. Which came first in American history?

____ Henry Hudson	___ John Cabot
____ Sir Francis Drake	___ Henry Hudson
____ Massachusetts Bay Colony	___ Connecticut Colony
____ growing tobacco	___ growing rice
____ House of Burgesses	___ Mayflower Compact
____ Pennsylvania Colony	___ Georgia Colony
____ Benjamin Franklin	___ John Smith
____ Dutch Colony	___ New York
____ Hernando Cortes	___ Christopher Columbus
____ Spanish horses	___ Indian horses
____ Viking settlements in Iceland	___ Viking settlements in Vinland

2. Several events are listed below. Number the events in the order in which they occurred.

____ Pilgrims land at Plymouth.

____ Columbus discovers a New World.

____ King Charles grants Pennsylvania to William Penn.

____ Magellan's men complete the first round-the-world voyage.

____ Indians begin to grow corn.

____ France starts a successful colony at Quebec.

____ Coronado and Estevanico explore the Southwest.

____ The American Revolutionary War begins at Lexington and Concord.

3. Each of the persons named below did things that the world will always remember. Number the persons in the order in which they performed their great deeds.

____ Jacques Cartier

____ Leif Ericsson

____ Christopher Columbus

____ Paul Revere

____ Henry Hudson

4. Which of the events described below occurred first?

____ A battle is taking place in the surf striking the shores of a distant island. In the struggle a great leader is killed.

____ Several soldiers explore an island off the coast of North Carolina. They are searching for clues to help them find out what happened to a group of colonists who have completely disappeared.

Confrontation Between the French and English

FRENCH AND ENGLISH INTERESTS BEGIN TO CLASH

The English settlements were crowded between the Appalachian Mountains and the Atlantic coast. Then, Englishmen became interested in settling west of the mountains, but the French occupation of these lands was an obstacle in the path of the settlers. The French claimed these lands by right of discovery, exploration, and settlement. The English claimed the same land. They believed that the colonies along the Atlantic coast owned the land all the way to the Pacific. It was clear that there would be clashes over the ownership of the interior of the North American continent.

Before 1689 the quarrels between the French and English settlers were not too serious. Both groups of people were busy developing their farms, towns, and industries. They had neither the time nor the desire to go to war against each other.

But after 1689 and for another seventy-four years, there was almost constant trouble between New France and the English colonies. Along with the question of who was going to control the interior, there were other causes for disagreements. For example, during that time England and France were fighting wars in Europe. Naturally, these wars spilled over into the New World.

There were three European wars fought between the English and the French from 1689 to 1748.* After each war land in North America was traded back and forth as though France and England were playing a game. But, of course, it was no game to the thousands of unfortunate French and English settlers. Many of their farms and homes were destroyed. Members of their families were captured, tortured, and killed.

About 1750 the French decided that it was time to let the English know, once and for all, that the land south of lake Erie, known as the Ohio Country, was French. So, the governor of New France sent a party of soldiers into the region. The men buried lead plates in certain important places. The plates stated that the territory belonged to France.

Then, in 1753 the French went a step further. They built several forts in the Ohio region and stationed soldiers in them. Several of the forts were built in what is now Pennsylvania.

Meanwhile, the English were not sitting quietly by. They formed a company, called the Ohio Company, to settle and develop the land occupied by the French.** The company built trading posts and began to trade with the Indians. This cut into the trade the French had previously enjoyed with the Indians.

The Ohio Company complained to the governor of Virginia that the French were trespassing on land that belonged to the company. The governor had already been told by the government in England to oppose all French expansion into the Ohio Country. So, he decided to warn the French that they would have to leave the region. To do the job, he chose twenty-one-year-old George Washington. Washington and a small party of men made their way over very difficult country to the headquarters of the French commander. The commander listened politely to Washington. However, he insisted that the land belonged to France, and that the French had no intention of leaving.***

Extra Information and Suggestions for Teaching

* King William's War (1689–1697); Queen Anne's War (1701–1713); King George's War (1744–1748)

** The Ohio Company received a grant of 200,000 acres in the region south of present-day Pittsburgh.

***Individuals or small groups of students can prepare a written dialogue between Washington and the French commander, or they can role-play the situation.

Discussion question: Washington made his debut as an important person in American history in the incident related above. What qualities and/or special knowledge were needed for Washington to carry out his mission? (knowledge of the forests, ability to lead soldiers, military knowledge, tact and diplomacy, poise, courage)

Name: _____ Date: _____

FRENCH AND ENGLISH INTERESTS BEGIN TO CLASH

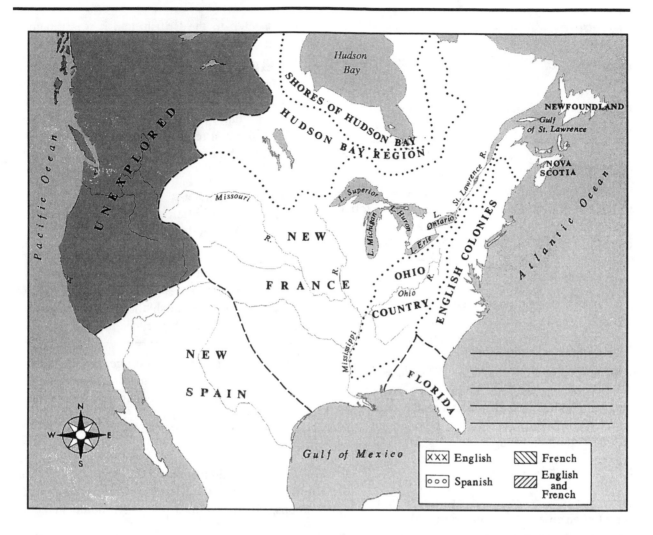

1. By completing the map above, you can gain a better understanding of the position of the French and English in North America about the year 1715.

a. Write the title of the map, "*French, English, and Spanish Claims in North America about 1715*," on the blank lines near the bottom of the map.

b. On the map, draw X's to show the English possessions—English Colonies, Nova Scotia, Shores of Hudson Bay, and Newfoundland.

c. Show the Spanish possessions of Florida and New Spain with small o's.

d. Show the French possessions in New France with \\\\\\\\ lines.

e. The lands labeled Ohio Country and Hudson Bay Regions were claimed by both England and France. Draw //////// lines over all the land claimed by both countries.

f. Draw heavy lines on all the boundaries shown by · · · and - - - for NEW SPAIN and UNEXPLORED.

g. Which country claimed the Great Lakes? _____; the Mississippi River Valley? _____.

HIGHLIGHTS AND MAP OF THE FRENCH AND INDIAN WAR

Procedure

1. Photocopy and distribute the map on the facing page.

2. As you mention the following highlights of the war, have your students label the numbered places on the map.

Highlights

Both the French and English realized that control of the Ohio Valley was dependent upon a fort at the junction of the Monongahela (1) and the Allegheny (2) rivers, which is the beginning of the Ohio River (3). The French got there first and quickly built Fort Duquesne (4).

The British decided to send a large force under General Braddock to capture the fort. Braddock, a proud and stubborn man, refused to take the advice of his colonial officers which was to **not** march a large army through the wilderness, but to use Indian fighting tactics and scatter his forces into smaller groups.* He insisted on having a road built through some 200 miles of forest so that heavy cannon and supplies could be brought with his army. The road was called Braddock's Road (5).

Near Fort Duquesne in July 1755, Braddock's army was attacked by a smaller force of French and their Indian allies. Braddock insisted that his men in their bright red uniforms fight in the open. His soldiers were slaughtered; almost 1,000 were killed or wounded while the French lost about 20 men. Braddock himself was killed. George Washington helped lead the defeated army back to Virginia.**

The next two years brought more victories to the French. They captured Fort Oswego (6), on the southern shore of Lake Ontario (7), and Fort William Henry (8), south of Lake Champlain (9).

A new leader in England, William Pitt, was put in charge of the war. Pitt chose the best military leaders he could find; then, he supported them vigorously. His efforts brought results. In 1758, Fort Duquesne fell to the British, and it was renamed Fort Pitt. Today it is called Pittsburgh.

Next in the war, Louisbourg (10) was captured. In 1759 Quebec (11) surrendered and, finally, Montreal (12). These British victories brought the war to an end. The French gave up all they possessed in the vast region known as Canada and the Ohio Valley. Spain possessed land west of the Mississippi River.

3. Have your students complete the small map showing the distribution of land in North America after the French and Indian War.

Point out that in 1763 the two dominant countries in the continent were England and Spain. However, France re-emerges with the acquisition of Louisiana from the Spanish; then, the United States purchases Louisiana from France in 1803.

---

* An interesting comment on general Braddock: Benjamin Franklin wrote in his *Autobiography* that he warned Braddock, "The only danger I apprehend of obstruction to your march is from ambuscades of Indians."

Braddock replied, "These Indians may, indeed, be a formidable enemy to your raw American militia, but upon the King's regular and disciplined troops, sir, it is impossible they should make an impression."

** Discussion questions: Is "Indian-type" warfare carried on in modern times? (*Yes—underground fighting in World War II with the United States Rangers and British Commandos; guerilla war in Vietnam with the Green Beret*) Why is it difficult to defeat guerillas? (*Their bases of operation constantly change; they are difficult to identify and capable of blending into civilian populations; they conduct warfare in small groups. Consequently, they employ hit-and-run tactics, conduct surprise attacks, and suffer minimal personnel loss when captured or killed.*)

Name: _____ Date: _____

HIGHLIGHTS AND MAP OF THE FRENCH AND INDIAN WAR

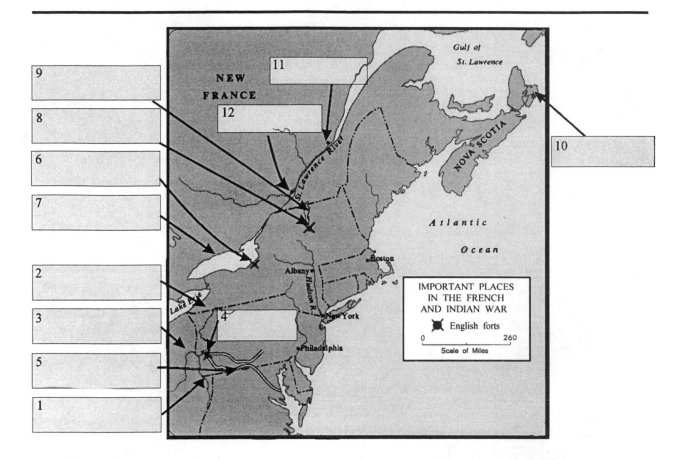

The Map of North America in 1763

At the end of the French and Indian War the map of North America was considerably changed.

1. Complete the 1763 map to better show the changes.

a. Draw diagonal lines (*///////*) in the area labeled "Canada" and "The 13 Colonies." (British)

b. Draw horizontal (≡≡≡) lines in the area labeled "Louisiana" and "New Spain." (Spanish)

c. At the time the map shows, 1763, both Spain and Russia claimed Oregon. Draw crossed (▦) lines in this area.

d. In the area labeled "Russian," draw small crosses (⁺ ⁺ ⁺ ⁺)

Name: _____ Date: _____

HOW THE BRITISH CAPTURED QUEBEC

1. The key to the conquest of New France was Quebec. This city and fort was built on a cliff high above the St. Lawrence River. It was protected by the St. Lawrence, by the steep cliff, and by walls. French troops guarded the area night and day. General Wolfe, the English commander, decided that to capture the fort his soldiers would have to climb the cliff.

2. Wolfe learned from two French deserters that the French expected supply boats to arrive on the night of September 12, 1759. He decided to send British boats to Quebec ahead of the French boats. The French would not realize until too late that the boats they had allowed to land were British.

3. That night British boats sailed along the shore near Quebec. The darkness of the night made it difficult for the French to see the boats clearly. Wolfe was in one of the leading boats. He predicted that he would be killed in the battle for Quebec.

4. As the boats neared the shore, a French guard called out, "Who goes there?"

"France," answered an English soldier who spoke French.

"What regiment?" asked the suspicious Frenchman.

"Of the Queen," quickly responded the English soldier.

"Don't make so much noise. The English will hear you," replied the guard.

5. The boats finally touched the shore. Twenty-four volunteers found and climbed a path up the steep cliff. At the top they surprised a French outpost and captured or killed all but two of the guards. At the sound of the shots and the cheers of success, Wolfe and his men scrambled up the narrow path.

6. In the morning the French commander General Montcalm looked out over the flat plains north and west of the city walls. To his surprise, he saw the companies of Redcoats lined up in battle formation. Montcalm ordered his own troops out to meet the English. In the battle that followed both Wolfe and Montcalm received the wounds that killed them. Quebec and all of New France fell to the British.

1. Each picture on this page is described by one of the paragraphs above. In the circle in each picture, write the number of the paragraph that describes it.

2. Answer the questions that follow on the reverse of this photocopy:

a. How did each of the following help the British to win the battle of Quebec?

- Two French deserters • a dark night
  • a French-speaking soldier

b. Write a caption for each of the pictures which expresses the main idea of the picture. You may use a complete sentence or a phrase.

SECTION 8

England and Its American Colonies Disagree and Separate

BRITAIN'S POLICIES AGGRAVATE AMERICAN COLONIES

The factual segments that follow highlight some of the events that contributed to the build-up of hostility between the "mother country" and its rebellious "off-spring"—the American colonies.

Suggested Procedure

After reading, or otherwise presenting, the fact segments below, have your students try to convey, via cartoons, how the colonials felt about the offensive actions of the British. The cartoon at the bottom of this page may serve as an example.

● ●

Things That Rankled American Colonials

● *The often ill-disguised, condescending, and contemptuous attitude of the British toward the colonials:* Britain's disdain for colonials was very apparent. For example, in the British pre-revolution armies stationed in America, British officers of the same rank as provincial officers were given superior authority and consideration. This practice was a reflection of British contempt for American military knowledge and experience.

● *The often-vetoed laws, actions, and appointments of colonial legislative bodies:* Britain's "right to rule" the colonies was reaffirmed by the British Parliament's passage of the "Declaratory Act" (1766) that stated, in part, that the colonies "were subordinate unto, and dependent upon" the British government in all cases; thus, British laws had precedent over colonial laws. For example, after the Boston Tea Party (1773) the British government passed a series of so-called "Coercive Acts." One of these acts radically altered Massachusetts's self-government by Britain's assuming the right to appoint the members of the upper house of the colony's legislature. Formerly, the members of the upper house were elected by the voters of the colony. Obviously, the upper house would follow the wishes and orders of the governor.

● *The passage of the Proclamation of 1763:* The use and regulation of the former French-controlled lands west of the Appalachian Mountains became a bone of contention between the British and the colonials. To demonstrate their authority, the British enacted the Proclamation of 1763, which barred settlement of the new territories until an indefinite future date. The British hoped that by restricting colonial settlement they could better control the colonies. The colonials, many of whom had settled in the region before the French lost it, were extremely resentful. Also angry were some of the colonies, Virginia and North Carolina for example, that claimed their western boundaries extended all the way to the Mississippi River, if not the Pacific Ocean.

● *The Quebec Act, an exacerbation of the resentment caused by the Proclamation of 1763:* After the French and Indian War, Britain possessed the Ohio Valley and, as has been mentioned, prohibited colonial expansion into the region. The Quebec Act added salt to these wounds because it extended French-populated Quebec's boundaries south to the Ohio River and west to the Mississippi River. Furthermore, what was, in effect, a new colony was to be administered by an appointed governor with no legislative body. "Why," asked many colonists, "are the defeated French being allowed in that region while we, the victors, are not?" And, "Why is there an appointed governor? Does this mean that the British plan to take away the right of self-rule in the eastern colonies?"

● *The Quartering Act (1765), a violation of the principle that "persons' homes are their castles":* The thought of having to provide living space and provisions for British troops was unacceptable to the colonials, especially to those people living in Boston, who would be the most immediate hosts. The colonials held the opinion that such a thing would not be permitted in Britain and shouldn't be permitted in Britain's colonies. Further, the colonials said that the real reason the troops were in Boston was to enforce British rule and to punish the colonies for the Boston Tea party and other acts of resistance.

Note: The 3rd amendment to the Constitution was specifically added to ensure against any attempt to require the population to quarter troops. The amendment states, "No soldier shall, in time of peace, be quartered in any house, without the consent of the owner, nor in time of war, but in a manner prescribed by law."

● *The Writs of Assistance (1751), considered to be a violation of the rights of British citizens:* A Writ of Assistance gave custom officials and others the right to search homes for smuggled goods without specific cause, or simply on suspicion or whim. A knock on the door at any time of the day or night could mean that government officials were demanding entrance. *Note*: The Writs were so annoying to the colonials that the fourth amendment, which unequivocally prohibits "unreasonable searches and seizures," was added to the Constitution.

Name: _____ Date: _____

A PATRIOT SOUNDS AN ALARM IN THE NIGHT

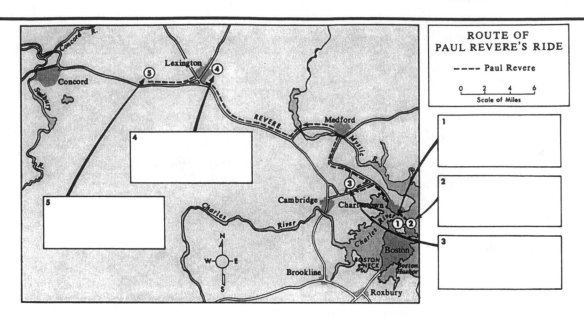

The Story of Paul Revere's Ride

On the night of April 18, 1775, Paul Revere received a message from a friend. The message told him that the British troops were going to march on Lexington and Concord to seize arms that the colonials were storing. Paul's job was to warn the people. **In box 1 on the map write:** *Paul receives a message.*

But, first, Paul warned another of his friends. This friend quickly climbed the tower of the Old North Church in Boston. He hung two lanterns there. This signal told the people of Boston that the British troops were on their way. **In box 2 on the map write:** *Paul's friend sends a signal.*

Meanwhile Paul jumped on his horse and raced for Lexington. He was seen by two British officers who tried to capture him but failed. In escaping Paul had to change his plans and travel by another road. **In box 3 write:** *Paul escapes capture.*

Paul arrived in Lexington about midnight. He warned John Hancock and Sam Adams, two of the most important Patriot leaders, that the British were coming. **In box 4 write:** *Paul warns Hancock and Adams.*

Paul turned toward Concord. Along the way he was captured and his horse was taken away from him. But he managed to talk his captors into letting him go. **In box 5 write:** *Paul is captured, but released.*

Paul walked back to Lexington. The British were just arriving. As they were marching past the house where Hancock and Adams had stayed, Paul slipped out the back door with a trunk. The trunk contained secret papers about the American's plan to fight for their rights.

Another rider, William Dawes, also rode from Boston that night. He started from Boston Neck and rode southwest to Roxbury, then north to Cambridge. From Cambridge he rode to Lexington. He was forced to turn back at the very place Paul was captured. *Show Dawes route by drawing small x's along the road.* It was another patriot, Dr. Samuel Prescott, who actually carried the alarm to Concord.

To go ahead: Imagine yourself to be Paul Revere on his ride through the countryside. As is indicated in box 5 in the map, you are stopped by the British guards. How would you talk yourself out of the situation? Write a few questions that might be asked by the British; then, write Paul's responses. Perhaps, you can read your dialogue to the class.

THE FIRST CONTINENTAL CONGRESS AND PAUL REVERE'S RIDE

1. The following account of the First Continental Congress can be read to your students as a preliminary to understanding Paul Revere's ride.

2. After reading the account orally, read selected verses from Longfellow's poem "Paul Revere's Ride." The verses concern those parts of the story that tell of Revere's experiences prior to reaching Lexington.

First Continental Congress

The Virginia House of Burgesses invited each colony to send representatives to a meeting to be held in September, 1774. The purpose of the meeting, called the First Continental Congress, was to consider ways of uniting to resist British laws. Twelve colonies sent delegates.

The Congress drew up a statement called the Declaration of Rights and Grievances. The Declaration stated the rights of the colonists and explained why Americans were opposing Parliament's laws. The king was asked to repeal the laws. Perhaps the most important accomplishment of the Congress was the plan to stop all trade between Britain and the colonies.

About five months after the Congress, General Gage, the British military commander of Massachusetts, heard that the colonials were storing weapons and supplies at Concord. Gage decided to capture the supplies. He knew that there might be fighting if he tried to carry out the plan. He tried to keep the plan secret—a strong force of about 700 troops was going to march to Concord on the night of April 18, 1775.

The colonials found out about the plan, and that is when Paul Revere and William Dawes entered the picture. They were to gallop before the marching troops to warn the people the British were coming.

Paul Revere's Ride

1 It was one by the village clock,
2 When he galloped into Lexington.
3 He saw the gilded weathercock
4 Swim in the moonlight as he passed.
5 And the meeting-house windows blank and bare,
6 Gaze at him with a spectral glare,
7 As if they already stood aghast
8 At the bloody work they would look upon.

9 It was two by the village clock,
10 When he came to the bridge in Concord town.
11 He heard the bleating of the flock,
12 And the twitter of birds among the trees,
13 And felt the breath of the morning breeze
14 Blowing over the meadows brown.
15 And one was safe and asleep in his bed
16 Who at the bridge would be first to fall,
17 Who that day would be lying dead
18 Pierced by a British musket-ball.

19 You know the rest. In the books you have read,
20 How the British Regulars fired and fled,—
21 How the farmers gave them ball for ball,
22 From behind each fence and farm-yard wall,
23 Chasing the red-coats down the lane,
24 Then crossing the fields to emerge again
25 Under the trees at the turn of the road,
26 And only pausing to fire and load.

27 So through the night rode Paul Revere:
28 And so through the night went his cry of alarm
29 To every Middlesex village and farm,—
30 A cry of defiance and not of fear,
31 A voice in the darkness, a knock at the door,
32 And a word that shall echo for evermore!
33 For, borne on the night—wind of the past,
34 Through all our history, to the last,
35 In the hour of darkness and peril and need,
36 The people will listen and wake to hear
37 The hurrying hoof-beats of the steed,
38 And the midnight message of Paul Revere.

Discussion

1. According to the account on the previous page did Revere actually reach Concord? (*No*)

2. Where in the verses are there examples of:

- **figurative language?**

3 He saw the gilded weathercock
4 *Swim in the moonlight* as he passed.
5 And the meeting-house windows blank and bare,
6 *Gaze at him* with a spectral glare,

- **alliteration?**

5 And the meeting-house windows *blank and bare*,
20 How the British Regulars *fired and fled*,—

- **foreshadowing?**

15 And one was safe and asleep in his bed
16 Who at the bridge would be first to fall,

Name: _____ Date: _____

PAUL REVERE: PATRIOT, SILVERSMITH

Paul Revere was born in Boston in 1735. The docks and wharves of Boston were his playground.

After some schooling, Paul went to work with his father to learn the silversmith's trade.

When he was twenty-one, Paul fought with the British in the French and Indian War.

After the war, Paul was married and went into his father's silver business.

He joined the Sons of Liberty and helped to organize and carry out the Boston Tea Party.

On April 18, 1775, Paul rode to warn the colonists that British troops were coming.

During the Revolution, Paul designed and printed the first issue of Continental paper money.

He also learned how to make gunpowder and directed a powder factory in Massachusetts.

Later Paul expanded his business. He was the first American to make copper plates for ships.

Name: _____ Date: _____

PAUL REVERE: PATRIOT, SILVERSMITH

1. Study each picture on the opposite page and read the text below it. Match each of the nine titles below with one of the pictures. Write the number of the picture on the line before each title.

_____ Colonials under British officers

_____ Pouring tea into the Boston harbor

_____ Boyhood: a time for fun

_____ A master craftsman at work

_____ A warning to the colonists

_____ A new bottom for a great ship

_____ An important business in wartime

_____ Printing money to pay the troops

_____ Learning a trade in his father's shop

2. The pictures themselves and the text tell you much about Paul Revere and the time in which he lived. Write the number of the picture that tells more about each of these facts.

_____ Paul directed a dangerous business during the Revolution.

_____ Fine pieces of silverware were made in small shops in Paul Revere's day.

_____ The port of Boston was a busy place.

_____ After the colonies revolted they printed their own money.

_____ A silversmith's apprentice learns the simple jobs first.

_____ British officers did not think highly of colonial troops.

_____ Paul's work after the war was not entirely concerned with silver.

_____ In Paul Revere's day, the fastest way to send a message was by horseback.

_____ Paul worked with organizations formed to resist the rule of Britain.

3. Picture 3 shows Paul as an officer drilling colonial troops. The British soldiers seem to think that this is a very humorous situation.

Find three things about the appearance of the colonials that the British might have thought were comical.

_____

_____

_____

4. A famous poem about Paul Revere contains these lines:

> "So through the night rode Paul Revere;
> And so through the night went his cry of alarm
> To every Middlesex village and farm,—
> A cry of defiance and not of fear,
> A voice in the darkness, a knock at the door,
> And a word that shall echo for evermore!"

Underline the line of the poem that is illustrated by picture 6.

5. According to the story told below the pictures, how old was Paul when he made his famous ride?

_____

6. Picture 4 shows Paul working on a silver teapot. Why is the pot he is handling resting on a padded surface?

_____

7. What is Paul pointing toward in picture 6?

_____

Notice the person answering his knock. Write a sentence or two that tells what he might have thought upon hearing the news.

_____

_____

_____

_____

DECLARATION OF INDEPENDENCE

These two pages offer additional information about the Declaration of Independence. It is suggested that the actual Declaration be read, in part, to your students.

The discussion question on the opposite page offers an opportunity for students to think and respond.

A Patriotic Victory

Before the British were driven out of Boston by the Continental Army, they had decided to send a force to North Carolina and South Carolina. The British believed that their chances of success there were good because there were many Loyalists in the Carolinas.

The British sent secret agents to meet with the Loyalist leaders in the two colonies. They worked out a plan for seizing control from the Patriots. It called for the Loyalists to march to the coast from the inland highland regions. At the same time, the British navy would attack coastal cities and try to land British soldiers. Then, the British and Loyalists could join forces. Together they could advance into Georgia to the south and Virginia to the north.

It was a good plan, but like many plans it did not work. The Patriots in the two colonies heard about the intentions of the Loyalists and their British friends. They raised an army of their own and met the Loyalists in a brief but important battle in North Carolina in February, 1776.

When the British fleet arrived off the coast, Patriots, not Loyalists, were there to greet them. The Patriots kept the British from landing men and supplies. The Loyalists were badly defeated. Finally, with a new-found respect for the bravery and fighting skill of the Americans, the British sailed for New York. The British would have to make new plans for subduing the colonies.

Congress Makes a Decision

The American victories in the South encouraged all Patriots, especially the members of the Continental Congress. Separation from Great Britain was fast becoming the main thought in the minds of the delegates. Virginia had already declared its independence of Great Britain. Several other colonies had instructed their representatives to work for independence. Few delegates wanted to be the first to bring up the question of independence because of their fear of punishment by the British. Congress was waiting for some brave person to bring the question of independence out into the open.

That brave person was Richard Henry Lee of Virginia. On June 7, 1776, he stood up in Congress and said, "Resolved, that these united colonies are, and of right ought to be, free and independent states . . . all political connection between them and . . . Great Britain is, and ought to be, totally dissolved." Lee's resolution was discussed for almost four weeks. Finally, on July 2, 1776, Congress voted on the question of independence from Great Britain. Twelve of the thirteen colonies represented in Congress voted in favor of separation.

The Declaration of Independence

At the time that Lee offered his resolution to Congress, a committee was chosen to write a statement that would explain the colonists' ideas on independence. The chairman, or head of the committee, was Thomas Jefferson of Virginia. There were four other members of the committee, including Benjamin Franklin of Pennsylvania and John Adams of Massachusetts. However, most of the statement, which is called the Declaration of Independence, was written by Jefferson. The Declaration was approved by Congress on July 4, 1776.

DECLARATION OF INDEPENDENCE

At the time that he wrote the Declaration, Jefferson was only thirty-three years old. He was one of the most brilliant men in the colonies. Almost everything he tried to do he did well. He was an excellent lawyer. His writings were known throughout the colonies.

The second paragraph of the Declaration is perhaps the best known. In it are the famous words "all men are created equal." The paragraph then goes on to say that God has given everybody certain rights, including "life, liberty, and the pursuit of happiness." Men establish governments to protect these rights for everybody—rich or poor, strong or weak. If the government does not protect those rights or if the government does not represent the people, then the government should be changed.

The Declaration states clearly and simply the reasons why the colonists no longer wanted to belong to Great Britain. More than twenty-five wrongs committed against the colonists by the British are listed. Included in the list are such things as:

"For depriving us, in many cases, of the benefits of trial by jury"

"For cutting off our trade with all parts of the world"

"For imposing taxes on us without our consent"

"For quartering large bodies of armed troops among us"

The Declaration makes it clear that the king and his government were asked many times to stop treating Americans unfairly. Finally, in the last part of the Declaration, independence is declared. To make sure that everybody would understand what Americans meant by independence, Jefferson wrote that the colonies now had full power to make war and peace. He also wrote that Congress had the right to make treaties with other countries, to carry on commerce, and to "do all the other acts and things which independent states may of right do."

Insights, Commentaries, Discussion

• Not all of Jefferson's ideas as to what should have been included in the Declaration were acceptable to Congress. One notable deletion was his severe indictment of the British crown for its part in supporting slavery and the slave trade. The passage that was stricken from the final draft follows: He (George III) has waged cruel war against human nature itself, violating its most sacred rights of life and liberty in the persons of a distant people who have never offended him, captivating and carrying them into slavery in another hemisphere, or to incur miserable death in their transportation thither. . . ."

Southern delegates, not without some support of Northerners, rejected the passage. Even in those high-minded, idealistic times, the obvious hypocrisy and contradiction of the existence of slavery and the words of the Declaration, "all men are created equal," were not honestly admitted, and the wrong was not rectified. It remains for the 13th amendment to the Constitution (1865) to declare that, "neither slavery nor involuntary servitude . . . should exist in the United States. . . . "

• *How do you think the Declaration of Independence affected each of the following?* (1) People who wavered between supporting the Patriot or Loyalist factions? (*It forced decisions.*) (2) The patriot armies? (*Enlistments increased and morale improved because purposes were clearly stated.*) (3) Merchants trading with England? (*They were distressed at the impending economic losses from loss of trade.*) (4) Indians? (*It gave them a better chance to resist westward migration.*) (5) France and Spain? (*They were happy to see a crack in the British empire; it would divert British armies and navies from European wars.*) (6) African-Americans? (*Many saw the conflict as a chance to gain freedom. Many enlisted in the British or colonial forces.*) (7) The future? (*It gave a great boost to the desires of others to establish a democratic government—notably the French, who, a few years later, carried out a revolution against the French monarchy.*)

THE BRITISH PLAN TO WIN THE WAR

The information on this page and the two accompanying student activity pages can do much to help students understand the basic strategy of the British to win the war, especially as it pertains to relationships between history and geography.

It seemed to the British that the best way to defeat the American rebels would be to cut off the New England states from the other states. If the lines of communication between the North and the South were cut, it would be easy to attack and win each part separately. The key to the plan was the state of New York. That state acted as a wedge between the North and the South.

General St. Leger was to move southwest along the St. Lawrence River to Lake Ontario. Then he was to travel east along the Mohawk River to Albany on the Hudson River.

General Burgoyne was to move south from the city of Montreal in Canada. Then he was to continue to travel south along Lake Champlain and Lake George.

General Howe was to move north up the Hudson River. All three of the British armies were to unite at Albany. The British would then control a line from Montreal to New York City.

A Great American Victory

Unfortunately for the British, things did not work out as they had planned. For reasons that are not clear, General Howe moved his army south to Philadelphia instead of north. He intended to capture the city. Washington moved his troops to Philadelphia in an effort to stop Howe. At Brandywine, near the city, the two forces met. Washington could not stand up against his more powerful foe and had to retreat. Howe entered Philadelphia in September, 1777. Washington set up winter headquarters at Valley Forge a few miles away.

Howe had won Philadelphia, but in so doing he had not moved north to help Burgoyne and St. Leger. The British forces coming south from Canada had no way of knowing that Howe was not carrying out the plan. As you shall see, this was an important reason why the British failed to separate New England from the other states. Some historians think that Howe's blunder eventually cost the British the war.

While Howe was trying to capture Philadelphia, General St. Leger was running into difficulty on the Mohawk River. Frontier Patriots, including a number of Germans led by General Nicholas Herkimer, stopped St. Leger.* In a fierce battle fought in a thunderstorm, the Patriots defeated the British. Those British troops and their Indian allies that survived the battle retreated into Canada. Of course, they never joined forces with Burgoyne who was moving south along Lake Champlain.

But the worst was yet to come for the British. In October, 1777, General Burgoyne was met by a force of Americans near Saratoga, New York. His army was outnumbered by the Americans, who swarmed into the area from hundreds of miles around. The British soldiers, aided by hired German soldiers called Hessians, fought bravely. But, they were surrounded by Americans who cut off their source of supplies from Canada. With no hope of aid from either St. Leger or Howe, the British had no choice but to surrender. Thus, the British plan failed. The Americans had won the greatest victory in the war.

---

* The Battle of Oriskany started as an almost certain victory for the British who had trapped Herkimer's troops in a steep-sided ravine. However, a thunderstorm halted the fighting because the guns could not fire when the gunpowder was wet. During the lull, Herkimer ordered his men to fight in groups of two. This was important because earlier in the battle his men had been fighting singly from behind trees and rocks. The enemy waited until a colonial soldier had fired his gun and then attacked him with bayonets and tomahawks. With two Americans fighting back-to-back, this was not possible because one man was watching and reloading while the other was firing. *Note*: Herkimer received a leg wound in the battle. Later, the leg was amputated, but Herkimer did not survive.

Name: _____ Date: _____

THE BRITISH PLAN TO WIN THE WAR

The British planned to win the war by separating the New England Colonies from the Middle Colonies and the Southern Colonies. Then, once the colonies were separated, they would fight battles within the sections. In war this strategy is called, "Divide and Conquer."

1. Show the New England Colonies (VT, NH, MA, CT, RI) with light diagonal lines (///////). Draw the lines from the Hudson River, Lake George, and Lake Champlain to the Atlantic Ocean.

2. Show the Middel Colonies (NY, PA, DE, MD) with light horizontal lines (≡≡≡).

3. Show the Southern Colonies (VA) with light crossed lines (▦▦). *Note*: Not all the Southern Colonies are shown on the map. They would include Virginia, North Carolina, South Carolina, and Georgia.

4. Study the map in order to complete the sentences that follow.

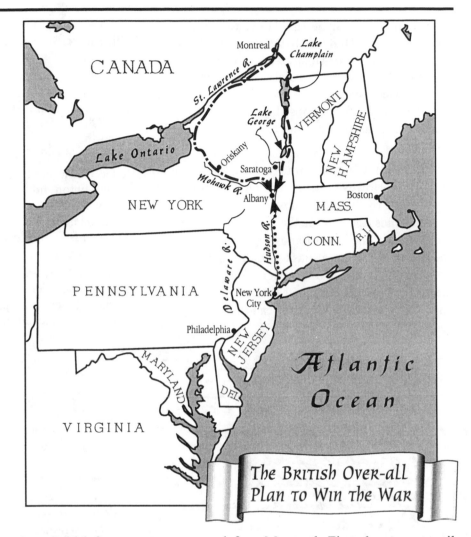

The BRITISH Over-all Plan to Win the War

The ---------- line shows that a British force was to move south from Montreal. First, they were to sail south on Lake _____, then along the shore of Lake _____, and then to the _____ River and to Albany. The -··-··-··- line shows that another force was to proceed to Albany from the west. First, the force would march from Montreal southwest along the _____ River, then along the eastern shore of Lake _____, and then east along the _____ River to Albany. The ······ line shows that another force was to move north from _____ and up the _____ River to Albany.

This was a good plan but it didn't work! The force from the west was defeated at Oriskany (shown on the map). The force from the north was defeated at Saratoga. The force from New York didn't go north up the Hudson; instead, they went south to capture Philadelphia. The result of it all was a great victory for the Patriots.

Name: _____ Date: _____

A SECRET MESSAGE TO GENERAL BURGOYNE

Remember that General Howe was to take his troops up the Hudson River to meet General Burgoyne at or near Albany. Instead he took them to the south to capture Philadelphia by sailing up the Chesapeake Bay and attacking the city from the rear. Those British troops that were left in New York were placed under the command of General Clinton.

General Clinton wrote a letter to General Burgoyne. However, he feared that the letter might be captured by the Americans. Therefore, he wrote a secret message within the letter. But General Burgoyne had no way of knowing how to decipher the message. Then a mask with an opening was delivered by another messenger. When the mask was placed over the original letter, the secret message was revealed. You can read the message below.

1. According to the secret message why did Clinton feel he wouldn't be able to do much to help Burgoyne? _____

_____

2. Underline the words in the message that tell how Clinton felt about Howe moving south instead of north.

3. How did Clinton try to help Burgoyne? The letter below contains a secret message that tells what Clinton did. Find the message and underline the words in it. Start with the words, "General Clinton left" at the end of the first and second lines. The words in the secret message are always at the ends of the lines.

4. Read the entire letter. Then on the other side of this paper answer these two questions: (1) Why did Burgoyne send troops to Bennington, VT? (2) What was the result of the Bennington raid?

GUERRILLA WARFARE IN THE REVOLUTION

Americans learned the art of guerrilla warfare (strike the enemy in surprise attacks and move out) from the Indians. The British approach to combat was to march headlong, with guns and bayonets at-the-ready, into the enemy. The British disdained guerrilla fighting; they thought it was cowardly. However, they paid heavily for their attitude in Braddock's defeat at the beginning of the French and Indian War, in the battle at Lexington and Concord, and throughout the entire Revolutionary War.

Procedure

Orally read the story about Francis Marion. The question in the next column will be helpful in leading discussion.

1. What were some of the advantages Marion and his followers had over the British? (*They were fighting for freedom; they were well acquainted with the terrain and the nature of the land; they were difficult to pursue through the swamps; they had no such place as a permanent headquarters to attack; they were supported by the people of the area; they could blend in with the population of the region.*)

2. What were some of Francis Marion's personal characteristics that helped him to be successful? (*cautious, thoughtful, organized, resourceful, courageous, patient*)

The Swamp Fox and His Men

Some of the most important fighting in the Revolution took place between small groups of British and American soldiers rather than between large armies. The battles were fought on lonely stretches of roads or trails, in dismal swamps, or in thick forests. Sometimes an engagement would last only a few minutes, sometimes an hour or more. Usually it was the Americans who were attackers and the British who were defenders. The British never knew when one of their posts, a detachment of their troops, or their wagon trains carrying supplies would be attacked. The Americans would suddenly appear, fight furiously, and then disappear.

To follow the attackers was hopeless. In the South the Americans used the swamps as hideouts. British troops who were foolish enough to attempt pursuit often became lost. Sometimes they were pulled under by quicksand. Many were killed by snakes and alligators. If they survived all these dangers, they risked capture by the Americans.

The Americans who made up these guerrilla forces are hard to describe because of their great variety. Many were African-Americans who were fighting side-by-side with men of Scottish, Irish,

English, French, and German backgrounds. Sometimes a group might all have the same uniform; but more often, no two members would be dressed alike. The men all had certain characteristics in common. They were bold, brave, hardy, resourceful, and skillful.

The leaders of these fierce Patriots were everything that their men were and more. Several are famous. Perhaps the greatest was Francis Marion, the "Swamp Fox" of South Carolina. He gained the "Swamp" part of his nickname because he attacked the enemy from the deep dark swamps.

Marion gained the "Fox" part of his name because of his cleverness. He was brave, but never foolish. He carefully planned every mission. He would not move his men during the day if he could help it. He preferred the cover of darkness. He seldom used known trails that would make it too easy for the enemy to ambush (surprise) his men. His men were taught to whistle in such a way that they could communicate with each other even at night. No one, not even his most trusted officers, knew Marion's complete plans. "Captured men," he said, "can be made to talk." The men Marion commanded were said to be among the best disciplined in the American armies.

FREEDOM FIGHTERS

The material on these two pages is concerned with minority individuals and groups that fought in the American Revolution. The arrangement of the material makes it suitable as a presentation-type lesson with activity.

Procedure

1. Make a transparency for yourself, and photocopies for your students, of the facing page.

2. As each segment (indicated by the illustrations) is treated, your students may make brief notes on the lines next to each illustration. Then, have them agree on captions for the pictures, and write them on the top lines.

3. Questions that you may ask your students after each segment has been presented follow:

Haym Salomon Gave His Life for Freedom

- What are some of the important facts about Salomon? (*He was a Polish Jew; he was arrested twice as a spy; he raised thousands of dollars for Washington's army; he was only 45 when he died.*)

- How do you know from the story that the drawing shows Salomon after his second capture? (*The first time he was released from prison; the second time he escaped, and that is what the illustration shows.*)

Europeans Aid Washington

- Match the general with the country from which he came: (*Pulaski and Kosciusko from Poland, DeKalb and Von Steuben from Germany, Lafayette from France*)

- How did the availability of friendly foreign ports help American ships during the Revolution? (*Ships could be repaired; supplies could be replenished; the harbors were safe.*)

African-Americans Help Washington

- Why is Crispus Attucks especially remembered? (*He was the first American to be killed in the struggle for freedom.*)

- Why were African-Americans welcomed into the navy? (*Many of them had experience on American fishing and merchant boats.*)

John Paul Jones

- In what way did Jones bring the war directly to the British people? (*His ships raided the British coasts.*)

- What prompted Jones to leave his homeland? (*He thought he might not be fairly treated in a trial related to a sailor he had killed.*)

Suggested Picture Captions

Haym Salomon: A stone wall hides Haym Salomon from the British.

Europeans Aid Washington: A foreign general offers his opinion to Washington.

African-Americans Help Washington: Jack Sisson batters General Prescott's door.

John Paul Jones: Captain Jones has his ship tied to the *Serapis* for a hand-to-hand battle.

Haym Salomon Gave His Life for Freedom

Haym Salomon was born of Jewish parents in Poland in 1740. Early in his life he became a fighter for freedom in his own country. Because of this, he was forced to leave Poland. In 1772 he came to the American colonies. Soon he began working to help the American struggle for independence. In 1776 he was arrested and jailed by the British. He was released from prison, but in 1778 he was arrested once more. He was condemned to die by hanging. Haym managed to escape to Philadelphia. There he put his business talent to work to raise many thousands of dollars for Washington's army. He worked so hard for the American cause that he ruined his health. He died almost penniless at the age of forty-five. He gave his life for freedom as surely as though he had died on the battlefield.

Europeans Aid Washington

Many Europeans hoped that the Americans would win the fight for independence. They helped in many ways. Sometimes Europeans joined Washington's forces and fought as enlisted men or officers. Four of the most important foreign officers were Generals Pulaski and Kosciusko from Poland and Generals DeKalb and Von Steuben from Germany. The most popular foreigner was General Lafayette from France. Sometimes American ships were allowed to enter friendly foreign ports where they could be safe from the enemy. While there, the ships might be repaired or supplies might be taken on board. Some foreign governments loaned or gave money to the Americans so that they could carry on the war. The most important foreign aid came from France. Without French soldiers, sailors, supplies, and money, the Americans might not have won their independence.

African-Americans Help Washington

The first American to die for the cause of freedom was Crispus Attucks, an African-American who was killed in the Boston massacre. Before the Revolution ended, some 5,000 African-Americans had served in the colonial armed forces. They fought from Concord and Lexington to Yorktown. They served as soldiers, laborers, skilled workers, hospital attendants, spies, messengers, and scouts. Many who had experience on American fishing and merchant ships joined the navy. Jack Sisson and others of the Rhode Island First Regiment battered down the door of General Prescott of the British army and then captured him. Peter Salem, who fought at Bunker Hill was praised by his officers as performing "like an experienced officer as well as an excellent soldier."

John Paul Jones—Naval Hero

John Paul Jones was born in Scotland in 1747. At the age of twelve, he became an apprentice seaman. At an early age he was given command of his own ship. Unfortunately, he killed a sailor who attacked him during a mutiny. Jones feared that he could not prove he had fought in self-defense because the mutineers would lie about what had happened. So, he fled to Virginia. When the Revolutionary War broke out, he volunteered for naval duty. Soon, he was made captain and was given command of a small fleet. He was so daring that he even raided the coasts of Great Britain. His most famous battle was with the British warship *Serapis*. The British commander asked Jones if he was ready to surrender. Jones answered, "I have not yet begun to fight." His men boarded the *Serapis* and sank it. Jones's fleet sank or captured more than three hundred British ships.

Name: _____ Date: _____

FREEDOM FIGHTERS

_____

_____

_____

_____

_____

_____

_____

_____

_____

_____

_____

_____

_____

_____

_____

_____

_____

_____

_____

_____

_____

_____

_____

_____

_____

_____

_____

_____

_____

_____

_____

_____

_____

Name: _____ Date: _____

WASHINGTON'S VICTORY AT YORKTOWN ENDS THE WAR

The War Finally Ends

In the spring of 1781, the British general Cornwallis marched north into Virginia. He planned to capture the colony with the help of other British forces that were already there. But his attempts to win control of Virginia were unsuccessful. Finally, Cornwallis and his army moved to Yorktown, a small village on a peninsula that jutted out into Chesapeake Bay. He felt sure that position was a safe one. British ships could help in any land battles he might fight; if a retreat were necessary, British ships could help his troops to escape.

During the time that Cornwallis was trying to win the South, Washington's troops were watching the British at New York City. French troops under the command of General Rochambeau were also watching the British. Washington decided that the time had come to attack New York City. But, just before the planned attack, he received news that a French fleet was sailing for Chesapeake Bay. Immediately, he changed his plans. This was his chance to trap the British. The combined French and American forces marched to Virginia.

At about the same time Washington arrived at Yorktown, the French fleet arrived at the mouth of Chesapeake Bay. They landed about 3,000 more troops. This increased Washington's force to about 17,000. He bombarded Cornwallis's position for about three weeks. Cornwallis could not escape by sea because the French fleet at the entrance of Chesapeake Bay kept the British ships from escaping. Moreover, the French defeated a British fleet that had come from New York to rescue Cornwallis. With all means of retreat cut off, the British position on the peninsula was hopeless.

On October 19, 1781, Cornwallis surrendered. British rule over the colonies she had founded 174 years before came to an end.

Understanding

1. Circle the sentence that tells why Cornwallis positioned his army on the Yorktown peninsula.

2. Underline the sentence that tells why Washington gave up his plans to attack New York.

3. Circle twice the sentence that tells why Cornwallis could not escape from Yorktown by sea.

4. In what way—other than by their warships—did the French help Washington at Yorktown?

_____

_____

5. The picture below shows Washington overlooking the battleground at Yorktown. Respond to the following questions based on what is shown in the picture and what you know from the story.

a. What fleet is in the harbor?

_____

b. What is there to indicate that the British are surrendering?

_____

c. Why is the man at the cannon signaling?

_____

THE AMERICAN REVOLUTION IN THE HEADLINES

This activity can have significant historical subject matter outcomes. Also, it can provide opportunities for "whole language" experiences; i.e., the students will have to isolate main ideas and supporting detail, and also compose short sentences and/or phrases to tell a story.

Procedure

1. Have your students imagine that they are newspaper editors. Their particular job is to write headlines for the news stories that will be published. When composing their headlines they should keep certain things in mind:

- Capture attention with a short title that conveys the main idea of the story.
- Use subtitles that bring out some supporting details and/or highlights of the story.
- Employ gradually decreasing type size as lesser ideas are mentioned.
- Identify (when appropriate) the place of origin of the story and the date.

2. Stories to be headlined may come from your basic history text or from some other source. Here are some suggestions of important events that would have been reported about for the period of time from the Boston Massacre to the surrender of Cornwallis at Yorktown:

- Boston Massacre
- Battle of Lexington and Concord
- Declaration of Independence
- Siege of Boston and the assumption of Commander-in-Chief by George Washington
- Battle of Bunker Hill
- Battle of Trenton
- Wintering at Valley Forge
- Battle of Saratoga
- Benedict Arnold turns traitor
- Surrender of Cornwallis at Yorktown
- John Paul Jones in the *Bonhomme Richard* battles the *Serapis*

3. The student-created headlines would make an interesting bulletin board. After designing and composing the headlines on ordinary paper, they can be carefully printed on larger paper.

4. The headline below is an example of how the surrender of Cornwallis at Yorktown might appear in a newspaper. *Note*: The headline would make an effective example for your students if shown via a transparency.

BRITISH SURRENDER TO WASHINGTON!

BRILLIANT MANEUVER BY FRENCH FLEET BLOCKS ESCAPE OF BRITISH FLEET

**174 YEARS OF BRITISH RULE
COMES TO AN END**

7247 REDCOATS SURRENDER

Yorktown, Virginia, October 19, 1781

THE TREATY OF PARIS—1783

The following account of the peace treaty that officially ended the war between Britain and its American colonies will supplement information in your students' basic text.

The map at the bottom of the page may be enlarged and photocopied for completion. The key at the top of the map suggests symbols that may be used.

• •

The news of the British surrender at Yorktown spread rapidly throughout the colonies. People were overjoyed that, after more than six years of fighting, the end of the war was in sight. However, two years were to pass before an actual peace treaty with Britain was signed. During those years British troops occupied some parts of the country. The fear was always present that war might break out again.

The British had had enough of the war. They were fighting not only their former colonies, but also France. To make matters worse for the British, Spain also had entered the war against Britain in Europe. So, Britain was fighting a war in both Europe and North America.

At the time France came to our aid, the United States had agreed not to make a separate peace treaty with Britain. However, it became clear that France was concerned more about itself and Spain than about America. Also, Spain was trying to persuade the French to keep United States boundaries east of the Appalachian Mountains so that Spain could take over the Mississippi Valley. In short, the peace negotiations were becoming a tangle of intrigue. So, to protect the interests of their own country, American representatives made a treaty of peace without the French.

The United States was well-represented by Benjamin Franklin, John Adams, and John Jay at the peace talks. These men had a variety of talents. Their ability, plus the willingness of the British to be generous to their former colonies, resulted in a peace treaty that was favorable to the United States. The agreement, called the Treaty of Paris, was

signed in September, 1783. The treaty had the following provisions:

1. American independence would be recognized.
2. The boundaries of the United States would be the Mississippi River on the west; Florida on the south; Canada, the Great Lakes, and the St. Lawrence River on the north; and the Atlantic Ocean on the east.
4. Americans could fish off the coasts of Canada.
5. Both the United States and Canada could use the Mississippi River without interference.
6. Congress would recommend to the states that Loyalists be given back any property taken from them during the war.
7. Americans should pay any debts owed to British subjects.
8. Britain would remove all troops from American territory as soon as possible.

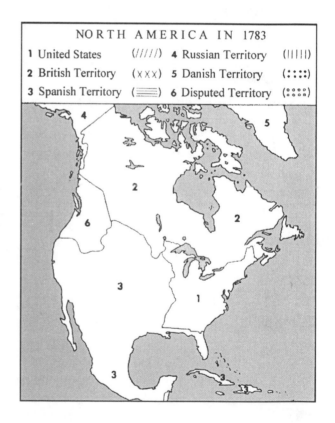

NORTH AMERICA IN 1783			
1 United States	(/////)	**4** Russian Territory	(⦚⦚⦚⦚⦚)
2 British Territory	(xxx)	**5** Danish Territory	(⦂⦂⦂⦂)
3 Spanish Territory	(≡≡≡)	**6** Disputed Territory	(⦂⦂⦂⦂)

Name: _____ Date: _____

CROSSWORD PUZZLE: FROM COLONIES TO INDEPENDENCE

Across

1. The French and Indians traded goods at the Montreal fur _____.
2. Cornwallis surrendered there.
7. Aide to General Washington (initials)
9. Peace treaty city after the Revolution
10. River along which the Dutch set up trading posts
12. He helped design the city of Washington, D. C. (initials)
13. A southern colony (abbr.)
14. The color of their coats made British soldiers easy targets.
16. Quakers were the first settlers in this colony. (abbr.)
18. He wrote the Declaration of Independence. (initials)
19. American officer who accompanied General Braddock on a march through the wilderness
20. City at the mouth of the Mississippi River (abbr.)
22. Second smallest colony (abbr.)
23. A substance dumped into the harbor of Boston
27. They settled New Amsterdam.
29. City where Washington took command of patriot troops
31. Name given to those who fought and supported the war for independence
34. Person for whom Pennsylvania is named
35. New Amsterdam became __ __. (abbr.)
36. They settled on the Delaware River.

Down

1. Foreign country that helped the patriots fight the Revolutionary War
3. A plan for the Northwest Territory: _____ of 1785
4. The crop that helped the Virginia colony to achieve prosperity
5. The patriot who helped Paul Revere spread the news, "The British are coming!" (initials)
6. Event in Boston in which several patriots were killed: Boston _____
8. First permanent French settlement in Canada
11. A patriot victory was won there on Christmas Day, 1776.
15. Religious group that settled Pennsylvania

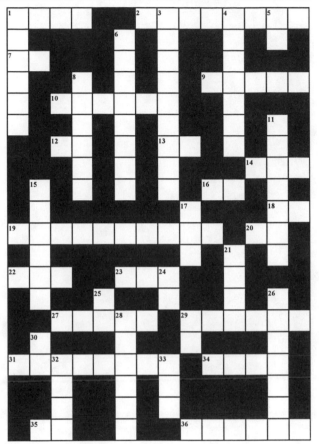

17. The British and Americans (won, lost) the French and Indian War.
21. Traded to the French by the Indians
24. Eastern mountain barrier to westward expansion (abbr.)
25. A part of three northern colonies that later became a state (abbr.)
26. The "Lost Colony"
28. Most American colonists made a _____ between being a patriot or being loyal to the king.
29. Publisher of "Poor Richard's Almanac" (initials)
30. First permanent English colony in North America was located in this colony: _____. (abbr.)
32. A person loyal to the king during the Revolution was called a _____ .
33. Nickname for a leading colonial patriot: _____ Adams

Abbreviations Used

Appalachian Mountains: AM	New Orleans: NO	North Carolina: NC	Vermont: VT
Delaware: DEL	New York: NY	Pennsylvania: PA	Virginia: VA

SECTION 9

People, Issues, and Events After the Revolution

ORGANIZING AND GOVERNING THE NORTHWEST TERRITORY

This page presents background information on the Ordinance of 1785, which was concerned with sectioning the recently gained Northwest Territory, and the Ordinance of 1787, which was concerned with governing the land.

Suggested Procedure

Photocopy the facing page for distribution to your students. Have them take notes and/or answer your questions as you proceed through your presentation.

Background and Questions

It is easy to look back now and criticize the Articles of Confederation and the men who tried to work with them. But, we must remember that those were very difficult times for our country. It was the beginning of our government, and we had much to learn. In spite of the weaknesses of the Articles, Congress accomplished some very fine things. For example, Congress did see the war to a successful conclusion. It did negotiate the very favorable Treaty of Paris. Congress did provide a national government when there was none. In the four years after the end of the war, some laws were passed that proved to be of great benefit.

What were four important accomplishments of the government under the Articles of Confederation? (The war was won; a favorable peace treaty was obtained; a national government was provided; several beneficial laws were passed.)

Probably the most important laws had to do with the surveying and government of the Northwest Territory. (The old Ohio country was part of this territory.) At that time, this was the northwestern part of the United States. So, these laws were called the Northwest Ordinances. Ordinance is another name for law.

Study your map. What were the boundaries of the Northwest territory? (North: Great Lakes and Canada; West: Mississippi River; South: Ohio River; East: Pennsylvania, Virginia) Which one of the Great Lakes did not border the territory? (Ontario)

The first thing that had to be done before orderly settlement of the territory could take place was to find out what was there. The land had to be marked and divided in some way so that settlers would know exactly what land they were buying. Some decision had to be made as to how much the land would cost an acre. The Land Ordinance of 1785, one of the Northwest Ordinances, provided for these things.

First, surveyors went into the region with their instruments. Their orders were to make accurate maps of the region. On the maps they were to show the lakes, streams, springs, and possible locations for mills, mines, salt licks, and anything else of importance. They were to divide the land into townships. Each township was to be divided into sections. The ordinance also provided that one section in each township was to be used for the support of education in the township.

How many sections were in a township? (36) What were the dimensions of a section? (one square mile) How many sections of a township were to be set aside for education? (one)

The land was to be sold in parcels of one or more sections. Of course, if a person bought a section and wanted to sell part of it, he was free to do so. The government would not sell the land for anything less than one dollar an acre.

How much would it have cost to buy four sections of land from the government at the lowest possible price? (4 sections X $640 = $2560)

The Government of the Territory

It was not enough for the Northwest to be surveyed, mapped, and marked off into townships. Other problems had to be solved. How was the territory to be governed? Would the people who settled there be treated as colonists, or would the land and people be organized into states? These problems were settled for the Northwest Territory by the Ordinance of 1787.

One part of the Ordinance stated that slavery would not be allowed anywhere in the Northwest Territory. This was important to the future history of the United States. By including this provision, the government showed an interest in limiting the spread of slavery.

The Ordinance provided that the Northwest Territory would eventually be organized into three, four, or five states. However, before any states were formed, certain steps had to be taken. Congress was to appoint a governor and the officials to govern the entire territory. When the territory reached a population of five thousand or more free men, it could have an assembly. The assembly would then make laws to govern the territory. It could also send a representative to Congress.

Finally, when one part of the territory reached a population of 60,000 free men, it could apply to Congress to be admitted as a state of the United States. If Congress agreed that the territory was ready to join the Union, it would vote *Yes.*

What steps were to be followed before a territory could become a state? (A governor is appointed; when the population has reached 5000 an assembly is elected; when the population has reached 60,000 the territory may apply to Congress for statehood; Congress says yes or no to the request.)

The first state to be made from the Northwest Territory was Ohio in 1803. This was only sixteen years after the Ordinance became law. In the years that followed the states of Indiana, Illinois, Michigan, Wisconsin, and part of Minnesota were carved from the original territory.

Name: _____ Date: _____

ORGANIZING AND GOVERNING THE NORTHWEST TERRITORY

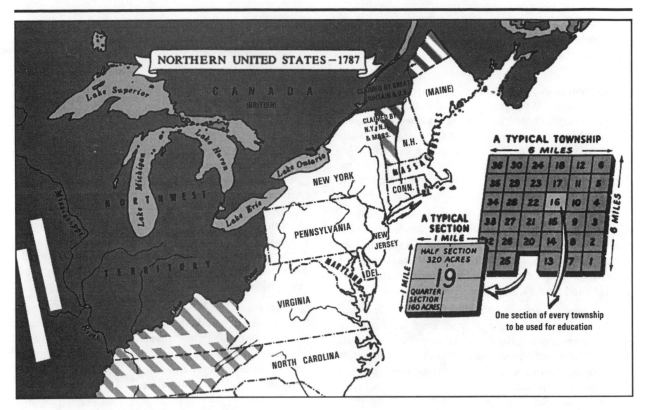

As the title of the map indicates, the map shows the northern part of the United States as it was in 1787.

1. Some of the map has been left unlabeled. You can make it more understandable by following these directions:

a. The land west of the Mississippi River was Spanish territory. Write "Spanish Louisiana" in the area and draw diagonal (////////) lines within it.

b. The land south of the Ohio River to the dashed (-------) border was claimed by Virginia. In small letters write "Virginia(?)" The question mark indicates that the claim was in question.

c. The land south of the land claimed by Virginia, and east of the Mississippi was claimed by North Carolina. Write "North Carolina (?)" in the area.

2. What three states claimed the land between New York and New Hampshire? _____, _____, and _____.
What state was later made from the disputed land?

_____

3. What two countries claimed the land on Maine's northern border?

_____   _____

UNDERSTANDING THE CONSTITUTION

Following are some insights into the Constitution in the form of extra information and some related open-ended questions that can become the basis for discussion.

1. **Information:** It became clear that the Articles of Confederation did not provide for a central government strong enough to hold the 13 states together. Frequently, disputes between states were occurring, some of which could have easily erupted into war. For example, New York taxed farm products from New Jersey. Of course, Jerseymen got even by finding ways to tax New Yorkers.

Discussion Question: What are some kinds of disputes that might arise between two or more states that share a river as a common boundary? Examples: New Jersey and Pennsylvania with the Delaware River; Vermont and Connecticut with the Connecticut River; Georgia and South Carolina with the Savannah River.

Rivers frequently shift their courses. What happens when one state gains or loses land as a result? In recent years there have been discussions between the United States and Mexico over shifts in the course of the Rio Grande. Does one country have the right to dam a river and use the water for irrigation or hydroelectric power if the other country does not want to have this done? How does one state get another state to stop polluting a river?

2. **Discussion Question:** Suppose there were a need to make a constitution today. What present-day Americans would you choose to be members of a constitutional convention such as the one held in 1787? Why? *Should certain professionals—lawyers, educators, physicians—be more heavily represented than others? On what basis should delegates be apportioned—geography, population, ethnic groups, industries?*

3. **Information:** The Constitution was not enthusiastically received by everybody in the states. There were many who opposed its adoption, and there were many criticisms of what it provided and what it did not provide. The most glaring weakness was the absence of provisions to protect the freedom of people. Additionally, Patrick Henry and others expressed the fear that the sovereignty of the states would be destroyed by too strong a central government. To combat anti-constitution propaganda, Alexander Hamilton, James Madison, and John Jay, with the support of many others known as Federalists, published a series of 85 articles in which they explained the constitution. This collection of papers is known as *The Federalist* papers and was quite influential in forming public opinion favorable to the Constitution. Hamilton was the most prolific of the three writers with about 50 articles to his credit.

4. **Information:** The makers of the Constitution did not allow themselves to get bogged down in discussions of the details that would be necessary to administer the country. Instead, they set forth broad yet specific outlines of the government. They realized that detailed administrative instructions would become outmoded as the country grew in size and population. Accordingly, Congress was given power in the so-called elastic clause (Article I, Section 8, final paragraph) to make "all laws which shall be necessary and proper for carrying into execution its stated purposes." Consequently, Congress has been able to do many things not mentioned in the document. For example, it makes laws regulating the use of nuclear power—something which could not have been provided for back in 1787.

5. **Information:** One of the most important features of our Constitution is that both the national government and the states share the responsibility of running the country. This sharing of responsibility, or division of powers, between the states and the national government is known as the "federal system."

To make sure that there are no misunderstandings, a list of Congress's powers was included in the Constitution. There is no list of powers for the states. The states (the people) have the powers that are not specifically allotted to Congress. Section 8 of the Constitution lists the powers granted to Congress.

Discussion Question: What kinds of powers would the states most likely have?

❑ *Provide for education*

❑ *Enact marriage and divorce laws*

❑ *Regulate the sale of alcoholic beverages*

❑ *Issue licenses to practice law, medicine, etc.*

❑ *Issue licenses for specific trades such as plumbing, surveying, etc.*

❑ *Provide for public protection*

❑ *Pass taxes to obtain revenue to properly provide for state expenses*

❑ *Provide for protection of the environment*

❑ *Regulate fish and game*

❑ *Regulate banking*

❑ *Regulate waterways within the state*

❑ *Provide for human welfare*

UNDERSTANDING THE CONSTITUTION

Amendment 1 (Religious Speech, Press, Assembly, Petition)
Congress shall make no law respecting an establishment of religion, or prohibiting the free exercise thereof; or abridging the freedom of speech, or of the press; or the right of the people peaceably to assemble...

Amendment 2 (Soldiers)
No soldier shall, in time of peace, be quartered in any house, without the consent of the owner, nor in time of war, but in a manner to be prescibed by law.

Amendment 4 (Unreasonable searches)
The right of the people to be secure in their persons, houses, papers, and effects, against unreasonable searches and seizures, shall not be violated...

Amendment 6 (Right to a trial)
In all criminal prosecutions, the accused shall enjoy the right to a speedy and public trial, by an impartial jury... wherein the crime shall have been committed...

Amendment 13 (Slavery forbidden)
Neither slavery nor involuntary servitude, except as a punishment for crime... shall exist in the United States...

Amendment 15 (Voting)
The rights of the citizens of the United States to vote shall not be denied or abridged by the United States or by any state on account of race, color, or previous conditions of servitude.

Amendment 19 (Voting)
The rights of the citizens of the United States to vote shall not be denied or abridged by the United States or by any state on account of sex.

Amendment 26 (Voting)
The rights of the citizens of the United States, who are 18 years of age or older, to vote shall not be denied or abridged by the United States or by any state on account of age.

Very few changes have been made in the Constitution over the past 200 years. Most of those changes or additions, called **amendments**, have been concerned with ensuring the rights and freedoms of the people. Parts of some of the most important amendments are listed in the scroll above.

Study the amendments outlined above; then, react to the true or false statements below.

1. A person who is 19 years old is not allowed to vote.   **T   F**

2. A person who commits a crime in New Jersey can't be tried for that crime in another state.   **T   F**

3. The United States can deny women the right to vote if they are divorced.   **T   F**

4. Persons from foreign countries, can be denied the right to vote even if they have become citizens.   **T   F**

5. Newspapers that criticize the government can be shut down by the government.   **T   F**

6. If the United States is not at war but there is a housing shortage at an army camp, home owners can be made to furnish rooms to soldiers.   **T   F**

7. A policeman can stop people walking on a street and search them.   **T   F**

8. Any state can pass a law denying African-American women the right to vote.   **T   F**

9. Prisoners of war can be brought to the United States and be declared slaves and then forced to work, and denied the right to return to their country after the war.   **T   F**

10. A law could be passed by Congress and signed by the president stating that all persons under 18 must attend a church of their choice.   **T   F**

ALEXANDER HAMILTON: PATRIOT, STATESMAN

Procedure

1. Make a transparency of the illustrations.

2. Project the transparency; then, orally read one of the paragraphs.

3. After a paragraph has been read, have your students write the number of the illustration that best applies to the paragraph.

4. After reading the eight paragraphs, ask for volunteers to read their lists of numbers in chronological sequence.

5. Project the transparency once again.

6. Students are to think of two nouns and two verbs that apply to a particular illustration (except #1). Here are some examples for illustration #2:

Nouns	Verbs
barrels, plates	selling, buying
sacks, hat	talking, computing

Alexander Hamilton

_____ In 1776 twenty-one-year-old Hamilton recruited and trained a company of soldiers. He was a brave and skillful officer. In 1776 he became an assistant to General Washington.

_____ Alexander Hamilton was born in the West Indies. When he was only eleven years old, his father left his mother. His mother died two years later. Relatives then cared for him.

_____ While in King's College, Hamilton took up the Patriot cause. Yet, he had the courage and fairness to save the Loyalist president of the college from a Patriot mob.

_____ Alexander was a brilliant boy. When he was seventeen, friends sent him to school in New York.

_____ Hamilton made some enemies. One of them, Aaron Burr, challenged him to a duel with pistols. On July 11, 1804, at Weehawken, New Jersey, the two met. Burr shot and killed Hamilton.

_____ Young Hamilton went to work for a merchant. Although young, he was capable of dealing with experienced lawyers, merchants, and planters.

_____ After the war Hamilton was active in New York politics and law. He is remembered for his fight for the ratification of the Constitution and for his work as Secretary of the Treasury.

_____ While in winter quarters in Morristown, New Jersey, Hamilton fell in love with Betsy Schuyler. They were married in 1780. Seven children were born to them.

THE "WHISKEY REBELLION": A TEST FOR THE NEW GOVERNMENT

The information on this page may add detail to your textbook's treatment of the "Whiskey Rebellion," the first test of the new government's willingness and ability to exercise its powers as provided in the Constitution.

One of the first things the United States government had to do was put the country on a sound financial or money base. Washington chose Alexander Hamilton to organize the Department of the Treasury.

Hamilton felt that it was important for the country to gain the respect and support of people at home and abroad. One way to do this was to pay back the money both the Congress and the states had borrowed during the Revolution. Moreover, Hamilton felt that the national government should take over the debts of the states. He argued that the money had been borrowed for the good of all the states. Therefore, the whole country should be responsible for the debts.

The question then was this: Where was the government going to get the money? Part of the money was raised through *a tariff, or tax on goods imported into the country*. Another source of income was the money received from the sale of public lands in the Northwest Territory. But, it soon became clear that much more money was needed. Hamilton then proposed and Congress approved an excise tax on whiskey produced in the United States. *An excise tax is a tax on things produced within the country*. This tax was hated by farmers in the West and led to the Whiskey Rebellion.

What caused the farmers to revolt? It was difficult for the western farmers to transport their farm products to the markets in the East. There were no roads over which they could drive their wagons. To carry a load of corn in a wagon over the mountains was almost impossible. Therefore, they made their corn, rye, or wheat into whiskey. A keg of whiskey was worth several wagonloads of corn, and it could be carried over the mountains on the back of a horse or mule.

The farmers refused to pay the whiskey tax. But, they did not stop there. They tarred and feathered tax collectors, started riots, and organized a force to attack the government fort at Pittsburgh. President Washington promptly ordered about 15,000 troops led by Hamilton to the scene of the disorders. The mere presence of the troops was enough to end the rebellion. The Treasury Department agents successfully collected the tax from that time on. Also, the government under the Constitution showed that it had the will and the power to enforce the laws.

What provision in the Constitution gave the federal government the right to quell the Whiskey Rebellion? *Article I, Section 8, Paragraph 15, which states that Congress shall have the power "to provide for calling forth the militia to execute the laws of the Union, suppress insurrections, and repel invasions."*

Has the United States' government exercised this power since the Whiskey Rebellion? *Yes, several times, such as in 1962, in Mississippi, to quell riots that occurred when James Meredith, an African-American, enrolled in the University of Mississippi, the first person of his race to do so.*

Some questions to ask in the event that the information on this page is presented in oral or photocopy form follow:

1. What were Hamilton's feelings about paying back money borrowed by the federal government and the money borrowed by the states during the Revolution? *It should be paid to establish the United States' good credit with other countries.*

2. What is a tariff? an excise tax? *A tariff is a tax imposed on goods brought into the country; an excise tax is a tax on goods produced within the country.*

3. Why did states prefer to make whiskey from corn, rather than sell the corn? *Much more money could be made from the whiskey, and whiskey was relatively easy to transport to the East.*

4. Why was it difficult for farmers to transport farm products to the East? *There were no roads over the mountains.*

Name: _____ Date: _____

SEQUOIA: INDIAN SCHOLAR

Sequoia was greatly honored for his work in developing a written language for the Cherokee. Sequoia National Park, the home of the great sequoia (redwood) trees, was named after him.

Sequoia was a Cherokee Indian born in Tennessee about 1770. He never saw a book until he was about thirty years old. When he finally saw books, he realized that they were tools for learning that his people needed. Up to that time, none of the Indian tribes in our country had developed a written language. Sequoia made up his mind to find a way to put the spoken words of the Cherokees on paper.

His own people did not understand what he was trying to do. Once, his wife burned work that had taken Sequoia years to develop. He left his tribe to live alone in the woods so that he could work. This, too, was misunderstood by the other Indians. They thought he was practicing witchcraft and that he would bring great trouble to the tribe. One day a group of Indians burned Sequoia's cabin to the ground. Sequoia's work was once more destroyed. So, he started all over again.

At first, Sequoia set out to make a separate symbol for every Cherokee word. He gave up this method because he realized that a person would have to remember thousands of symbols. This would be too difficult. Even he could not remember all the symbols he had made. Then he came up with the idea of making a symbol for each of the eighty-six sounds in the Cherokee language. Every Cherokee word is made up of one or more of these sounds. After twelve years of work, Sequoia developed an alphabet. He was then able to put every Cherokee word into written form.

The chiefs saw that he had done a wonderful thing. They encouraged their people to learn to read. Cherokees of all ages learned Sequoia's alphabet. Soon newspapers and books were being printed in the Cherokee language.

Sequoia went on to become a great leader of his people. In Washington he ably represented their claims to the lands in Arkansas and Oklahoma to which the Cherokees had been removed from the East. Later he helped other Cherokee tribes move to Oklahoma. It was his hope that all the Cherokees, who had been separated into many groups scattered over many parts of the country, would come together once more into one great tribe. It was while looking for some Cherokees rumored to be in northern Mexico that he died, at about the age of seventy-three. His statue represents Oklahoma in Statuary Hall in the Capitol Building in Washington, D.C.

1. ***Some Facts about Sequoia***

a. His tribe: _____

b. His place of birth: _____

c. His place of death: _____

d. His age at death: _____

e. Two ways his earlier efforts at making an alphabet were destroyed:

    (1) _____

    (2) _____

f. Length of time it took to develop his alphabet:

_____

g. Two ways he is honored today:

    (1) _____

    _____

    (2) _____

    _____

2. Underline the sentence that tells why he did not make a separate symbol for every word in the Cherokee language.

3. Sequoia used some English letters in his Cherokee alphabet. What are some of the letters as shown in the picture?

_____

THOMAS JEFFERSON: STATESMAN, PRESIDENT

(1) Thomas Jefferson was born into a well-to-do Virginia family in April, 1743. (2) His father taught him how to ride, hunt, shoot, and take care of himself in the woods. (3) Tom was taught to respect work and working people. (4) Tom's father was a self-educated man who taught his son to love books and learning.

(5) At the age of seventeen, Thomas entered William and Mary College in Virginia. (6) He studied Greek, Latin, mathematics, and science for up to fifteen hours a day. (7) He was a brilliant student.

(8) In 1767 Tom became a lawyer. (9) Soon he was presenting cases before the court, and he had more cases than he could handle. (10) After he married in 1772, he stopped practicing law. (11) He spent his time managing his estate—Monticello. (12) He also became more involved in politics, where he put his knowledge of law to good use.

(13) Jefferson was a member of the Virginia House of Burgesses at the time when the king was punishing Boston for the Boston Tea Party. (14) He showed great courage by writing a paper that sharply criticized the king. (15) Later, as a member of the Second Continental Congress, he was selected to write the Declaration of Independence.

(16) During the Revolution, Jefferson continued to serve in the Virginia legislature. (17) Among his proudest accomplishments was the law he wrote for complete religious freedom in the state. (18) He also served as Governor of Virginia during the difficult war years of 1779–1781. (19) Once, Jefferson fled from Monticello only a few minutes before the British arrived. (20) Following the war Jefferson served as the United States representative in France.

(21) Washington, our first President, asked Jefferson to be his Secretary of State. (22) Jefferson and Secretary of the Treasury Hamilton often disagreed. (23) The two men were very different in personality, background, and beliefs. (24) Jefferson had great faith in the ability of the people to govern themselves. (25) Hamilton thought that the government should be in the hands of a few. (26) As the country became stronger, Jefferson's ideas won out over Hamilton's.

(27) Jefferson was President from 1801 to 1808. (28) During his first term, the country purchased and explored the Louisiana Territory. (29) The freedoms and rights of the common man were increased. (30) Jefferson was followed in office by his friend James Madison.

(31) Jefferson retired to his Virginia home. (32) There he experimented successfully with scientific farming. (33) He continued to study and write. (34) This great American died on July 4, 1826, fifty years after the adoption of the Declaration of Independence.

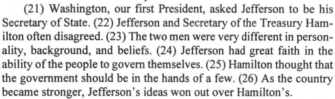

1. A sentence from the story can be used to describe each of the pictures on this page. In the box in the upper right of each picture, write the number of that sentence.

2. Which sentence tells that Jefferson supported religious freedom? _____ spent time in France representing the United States? _____ was the writer of the Declaration of Independence? _____ had a college education? _____ was governor of Virginia? _____

98

SECTION 10

Interest Grows in the Lands Beyond the Mississippi River

THREE AFRICAN-AMERICANS IN THE FAR WEST

York, Traveler with Lewis and Clark

One of the men with Lewis and Clark on their journey up the Missouri River in 1804–1806 was a tall, strong, African-American known as York. York must have been an outstanding member of the exploring party because he is mentioned several times in the *Journals of Lewis and Clark*. York excited great interest among the Indians. Their admiration and respect for him contributed to the success of the expedition.

Jim Beckwourth, Mountain Man

The name Jim Beckwourth can be found in many of the accounts of the explorations of the Rocky Mountains and the regions to the west of them. Beckwourth was a fur trapper and scout. Beckwourth Pass in the Rocky Mountains is named after him. Beckwourth's book, *The Life and Adventures of James P. Beckwourth*, is a valuable source of information about the early West. Beckwourth describes the rough-and-ready life of the mountain men, as they were called, in colorful detail. He lived among the Indians for a time and even became a war chief of the Crow Indians. His description of the Indian way of life has helped us to better understand these early Americans.

George Bush, Settler in Washington

Among the first Americans to see the Pacific Northwest was George Bush, who worked for the Hudson Bay Company. When Bush visited the region in 1820, he realized that this was a place where he could settle and bring up a family in freedom. Twenty-two years later, Bush returned to Puget Sound, Washington, where he started his own settlement. He built a saw and grist (flour) mill. Bush did well. He shared his good fortune with other settlers by helping them to get started. Later, the United States and Great Britain quarreled over the ownership of Oregon. The occupation of the land by Bush and other Americans helped the United States gain permanent possession of Oregon.

1. York first saw the Pacific Northwest in 1805. How many years afterwards did George Bush first visit the region? _____

Note: Write your answers to questions 2–5 on the other side of this photocopy.

2. York is showing his rifle to some Indians who had never seen a rifle before. Write three or four questions that the Indians might ask about the weapon.

3. Write five facts that you can learn about Jim Beckwourth and his work by studying the illustration of him.

4. In what way did George Bush help establish the United States claim to Oregon?

5. What was one special reason why George Bush wanted to bring his family to Oregon?

6. On the lines beneath the pictures write brief captions for each. Use the information in both the picture and the narrative.

THE EXPEDITION OF LEWIS AND CLARK

Perhaps the greatest real estate bargain in history occurred when the United States, under Thomas Jefferson, bought Louisiana from France for approximately $15 million, or three cents an acre. But, what was in the land—commonly called the "Louisiana Purchase"—remained to be discovered. So, in 1803 President Jefferson appointed two men, Meriwether Lewis and William Clark, to lead an expedition from St. Louis on the Mississippi River, up the Missouri River, across the Continental Divide (Rocky Mountains), and down the Columbia River to its mouth on the Pacific coast.

Procedure

The numbered segments of information below all contain details about the expedition. The segments are numbered in sequence from the beginning to the end of the journey. As you relate the sequences, have your students make notes in the boxes on the map on the facing page. Help students trace the arrow from each numbered box to the place in the river where the incident occurred. You may also want to write the information on a projected transparency. After the map has been completed it would be helpful to have students follow the route of travel and orally retell the story. *Note:* When the students write in the boxes, it need not be a word-for-word repetition of what you say.

1 Pittsburgh, August 20, 1803: The explorers load men and supplies on a flat boat for a journey down the Ohio River to St. Louis, on the Mississippi River.

2 St. Louis, May 14, 1804: The expedition, consisting of three boats, 50 men, and six tons of supplies, starts up the Missouri River. It is slow progress; the boats must be poled or rowed every foot of the way.

3 December, 1804: The expedition halts at Fort Mandan (North Dakota) to prepare for the winter of 1804–1805. An Indian woman, Sacajawea, and her French, fur-trader husband, Charbonneau, enter the camp; they will join the expedition as interpreters and guides.

4 Missouri Falls, early June, 1805: There is no way the boats can go over the falls. It takes 30 days to transport the boats and supplies around the falls.

5 The expedition meets the Shoshoni Indians; Sacajawea is reunited with her brother who is a chief. The expedition obtains horses from the Indians for its coming climb across the Continental Divide of the Rocky Mountains.

6 The expedition encounters incredible difficulties in crossing the mountains: snow, sleet, loss of some horses, near starvation, land and snow slides, and hordes of wasps. Finally, the men find streams that flow west. They find the Snake River, build boats, and paddle to the Columbia River, which takes them to its mouth on the Pacific coast.

7 The journey ends, November 15, 1805: The ocean is sighted. Now, preparations must be made for winter. Fort Clatsop is established. During the winter boats are constructed in preparation for the return trip in the spring. On March 23, 1806 the long journey home begins.

8 The round trip—8000 miles, more than 3 years—ends at St. Louis. Much has been accomplished. By right of exploration and discovery, the USA has established a strong claim to the Oregon Country; relations with the Indians of the region have begun; extensive fur trade has begun; significant scientific knowledge of the territory has been gained.

Name: _____ Date: _____

THE EXPEDITION OF LEWIS AND CLARK

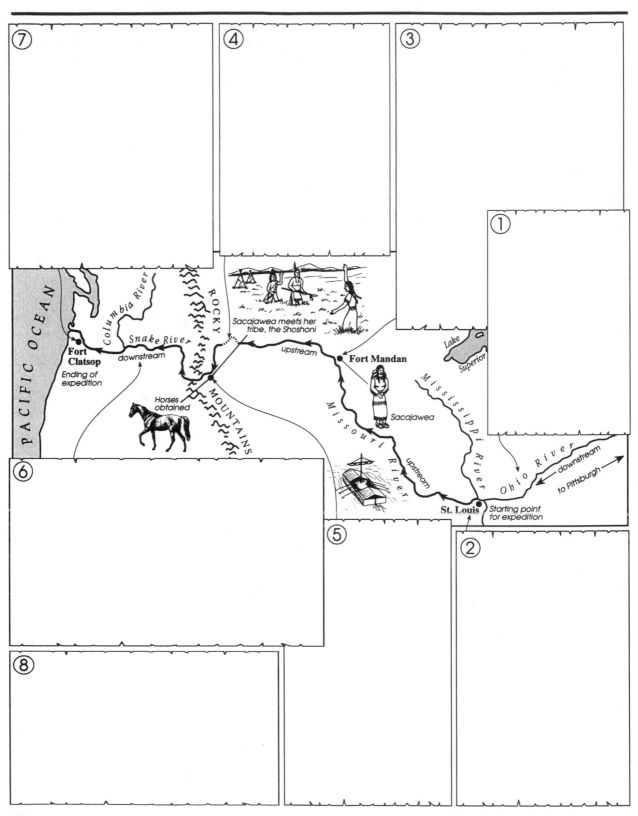

⑦

④

③

①

PACIFIC OCEAN

Columbia River

ROCKY

Snake River

Fort Clatsop
Ending of expedition

downstream

Horses obtained

MOUNTAINS

Sacajawea meets her tribe, the Shoshoni

upstream

Fort Mandan

Sacajawea

Lake Superior

Mississippi River

Missouri River

upstream

Obio River

downstream

to Pittsburgh

St. Louis
Starting point for expedition

⑥

⑤

②

⑧

SACAJAWEA AND THE LEWIS AND CLARK EXPEDITION

1 Sacajawea and her French, fur-trader husband met Lewis and Clark at a Mandan Indian village in what is now North Dakota. Sacajawea was 16 years old at the time. When she was only 12 years old she had been captured by unfriendly Indians who carried her eastward, hundreds of miles from her home. She became the wife of the Frenchman shortly after being captured.

At the time she met Lewis and Clark, she was pregnant, and in February, 1805, she gave birth to a boy, who was given the French name, Jean Baptiste. Later he came to be called Pomp, an Indian name meaning "first-born."

Sacajawea and her husband were hired to become interpreters and guides for the expedition. Interpreting was a most important job; it was through Sacajawea only that the expedition leaders would be able to talk to the Indians they would meet.

In the spring of 1805, the expedition once more started up the Missouri. Sacajawea's baby was strapped in a papoose carried on his mother's back. Sacajawea was looking forward to the possibility that she might be reunited with her people, the Shoshonis.

2 A short distance past the point where the Yellowstone River meets the Missouri River a sudden storm came up. The largest boat filled with water and began to sink. Sacajawea remained calm even though she had her young son to take care of. As belongings of the expedition floated past her, she fished them out of the water. Among the things she rescued were compasses, surveying instruments, books, and clothing. This was typical of Sacajawea—whenever an emergency arose, she met it bravely and resourcefully. Meriwether Lewis wrote of her in his diary that she was as brave as any man on board and that she saved most of the light articles that washed overboard.

3 As the expedition made its way up the Missouri, Sacajawea began to recognize more and more of the land where she had been born. She had a wonderful memory of her early life and surroundings. Time-after-time she would pause, look around, and point the way for the expedition.

Some Indians came walking through the tall grass. Sacajawea recognized them as members of her tribe, the Shoshoni, and shouted for joy. She found friends from her childhood, including another young Indian woman who had been captured with her but who had escaped. She even was reunited with her brother who was a Shoshoni chief.

4 As the explorers moved up the Missouri River, ever westward, Sacajawea was of great help in finding food, medicinal plants, and in interpreting. Very often she took care of the sick men, every one of whom became ill at one time or another during the journey. She continued to carry her young son in a papoose on her back, a load that even the men would have found difficult. She and her husband walked hundreds of miles along the river bank, assisting Lewis, who was taking notes on the land, plants, and animals. Nowhere in the diary that Lewis carefully kept is there a remark saying that Sacajawea complained.

Finally, the expedition reached the Pacific Ocean and Sacajawea saw not only the ocean, but also the carcass of a huge whale that had stranded itself on the shore. It had been stripped of meat and blubber by the Indians.

It was now approaching winter, and preparation had to be made to meet the severe weather. For protection, a small fort called Fort Clatsop was built. The Indians in the region were friendly, but, even so, there were always sentries on duty—it was a real military post. The fort was completed by Christmas and a party was held. Sacajawea, ever generous, gave Captain Lewis twenty weasel tails which she had carried hidden for many weeks.

5 In the spring, the long trip eastward across the continent began. If the expedition had known, they could have sailed home on an American ship that was anchored offshore. The ship would have sailed all the way south around South America and then north to the United States.

When Sacajawea and her husband reached the Mandan Indian villages, they decided to stay there. But later, on the invitation of Lewis, who became governor of Louisiana, they did visit him and live for some time in St. Louis.

For many years no one knew for sure what happened to Sacajawea after the expedition. It seems clear now that she lived to be 100 years old and then died on an Indian reservation in Wyoming.

Sacajawea, who was also known as Bird Woman, is fondly and respectfully remembered by all who knew her or who have written about her. Her name is on dozens of statues, mountains, lakes, monuments, and paintings. Florence Warren Seymour in her book *Bird Girl*, sums up Sacajawea's character when she writes that the Bird Girl's "spirit was indeed that of a bird soaring above hardship and difficulty," and that she is for all Americans, "a symbol of bravery and endurance."

Name: _____ Date: _____

SACAJAWEA AND THE LEWIS AND CLARK EXPEDITION

_____

_____

The following activity is based on the story of Sacajawea on the opposite page and the illustrations on this page.

1. Some facts about Sacajawea:

a. Age when captured _____

b. Age when married _____

c. Native Indian tribe _____

d. Son's name _____

e. Age when she died _____

f. Place she died _____

2. What were Sacajawea's two main duties on the expedition? _____ _____

3. On the lines below picture 1 write a full sentence that explains what is taking place in the picture. *Note*: The event is mentioned in section 1 of the story.

4. On the lines below picture 2 write the sentence from the story that best describes what is taking place in the picture.

5. On the lines below picture 3 write a sentence or two that tells what Sacajawea might have been thinking when she first encountered members of her old tribe.

6. On the lines below picture 4 write the sentence from section 4 that best describes the scene.

7. Make a list of adjectives and/or phrases that describe Sacajawea's character.

_____

_____

_____

8. Sacajawea, as mentioned in section 5 of the story, visited and later lived in St. Louis. The sights she saw must have been very strange to her. How did she react? What did she think? In the list below find one item and write your impression of her thoughts and feelings:

☞ Stores filled with goods

☞ Houses with kitchens, fireplaces, bedrooms

☞ The school—books, desks, pencils, paper—that her son, Pomp, would attend.

Use the other side of this paper for your answer.

_____

_____

_____

_____

SECTION 11

Our First War as an Independent Nation

Important Locations in the
War of 1812

THE WAR OF 1812: SOME HIGHLIGHTS

The following two pages utilize the "interrupted narrative" method of presenting information, a method which requires active response on the part of the learners. The approach is predicated on the theory that because many students will not apply a study method to their reading, a study method should be built into the reading. This approach to studying not only will make the subject more understandable, but also can build significant work-study and reading comprehension skills.

The War of 1812 is an appropriate topic on which to employ the interrupted narrative approach. After your students have attempted the pages on their own, discussion should follow.

The following information may prove to be helpful additions to the information your students will study.

. . . .

Chief Tecumseh of the Shawnee Indians

The Indian leader Tecumseh (1765–1813) realized that the only way his people could halt the westward expansion of the United States was by doing two things:

(1) Gather the various tribes between the Appalachians and the Rockies into one united front and thus gain fighters and resources.

(2) Join with the British against the Americans in the War of 1812. If the British won the war, the Indian reward could be repossession of the Northwest Territory.

Tecumseh did succeed in bringing many of the tribes into his confederation, and they gave considerable help to the British war effort. However, in the Battle of the Thames, near Ontario, in 1813, Tecumseh was killed by American forces. There was no Indian leader of his stature to take his place, so the confederation he had forged died with him.

Naval Battle on Lake Erie

Control of the Great Lakes was an essential objective of both British and American strategy for winning the war. It was in this American campaign that Captain Oliver H. Perry's fleet won a decisive victory in 1813 over the numerically superior British squadron on Lake Erie. One famous quotation that came from the battle was Perry's laconic message to Major General William Henry Harrison, commander of the American western army, who later became president: "Dear Gen'l: We have met the enemy, and they are ours, two ships, two brigs, one schooner and one sloop. Yours with great respect and esteem. O. H. Perry."

Not so well known is the fact that 10 percent, or some 430, of Perry's crews were African-Americans. It is also noteworthy that at the Battle of New Orleans, the most famous battle of the war and considered by many to be one of the greatest of all American victories, General Jackson had some 600 African-American troops to whom he said, "The American nation shall applaud your valor, as your general now praises your ardor."

The Ocean and Coastal War

In 1812 there was no navy in the world that could compare with Britain's in terms of number and quality of war ships and merchant marine. Since the defeat of the Spanish Armada in 1588, Britain truly "ruled the waves." So, pitting the small American navy against the British navy seemed almost certain to result in a disaster for the United States. Nevertheless, the United States, a country less than 25 years old, made the attempt.

The United States had only six first-class warships and some 500 merchant ships that were fitted with cannon and given authorization to attack British commerce. At first, this hastily created navy had spectacular success: The U.S.S. *Constitution* met H.M.S. *Guerriere* and shelled it into surrendering; the U.S.S. *United States* caught up with H.M.S. *Macedonia* off the coast of Africa, rendered the ship helpless with severe shelling, and then sailed it to Connecticut as a prize of war. The armed merchant ships, called privateers, captured more than 1300 of Britain's ships.

However, the British ships kept coming in greater and greater numbers. They blockaded United States' ports so effectively that very few ships could make their way to the open sea; thus, American trade came to a virtual standstill. To add to the chagrin of the United States, British ships raided, burned, and plundered small American coastal towns, almost at will.

The greatest injury to the country's self-esteem occurred when a British fleet sailed up Chesapeake Bay, landed an army on its shores, and sacked Washington. The British then turned their attention to Baltimore at the head of the bay, but there they were stopped; they did not take Baltimore. And it was there that Francis Scott Key, who was being held prisoner on a British warship that was shelling Fort McHenry, wrote the stirring words of the "Star Spangled Banner."

Name: _____ Date: _____

THE WAR OF 1812

It wasn't very long after the American Revolution that England and France were at war again. Both nations began to use force to regulate American trade. They each wanted to stop the United States from trading products to its enemy. Both nations attacked our ships.

1. *What are some of the goods that one country would not want its enemy to import during a war?*

_____

_____

Jefferson thought that he could convince England and France to leave our ships alone by prohibiting the shipment of American goods to their countries or any other country in Europe. _____

_____

_____

To carry out this plan Congress passed the Embargo Act of 1807.

2. *To help explain Jefferson's reasoning write the following sentence in the space set aside in the above paragraph: If our ships were not on the seas, there was no way they could be attacked.*

The embargo was a failure. It hurt the United States far more than it hurt England or France. Business was so poor that tens of thousands of people in the port cities were out of work. People from all over the country, and especially the New England merchants, protested against the embargo. Finally, in 1809 the embargo was discontinued.

3. *What device has the cartoonist used to show what happened to American shipping during the*

Embargo of 1807? _____

_____

Try to think of a short sentence that could be spoken by the American merchant shown in the cartoon. Write your sentence in the empty space. If you can't think of a suitable sentence, write this: The embargo—a way to put the country to sleep.

James Madison, who followed Jefferson as President, also tried to keep the country from going to war over freedom of the seas. At times it seemed that the United States should go to war against both England and France. However, the British were much harder on the Americans than the French were. The British actually fired upon our battleships. They often impressed, or forced, sailors from American ships to work in the British navy. Furthermore, Indians from Canada were still raiding American settlements in the Northwest. The British who controlled Canada received much of the blame for the raids.

Some American congressmen known as War Hawks pressed hard for war. They said that war with great Britain would give the United States a good reason to invade Canada and capture it. In this way Indian raids would be stopped and Canada would provide cheap land for American settlers. Madison asked Congress to decide the question of war with England. In June, 1812, they voted *Yes*. The fighting that took place during the next three years is known as the War of 1812.

4. *Circle the two sentences that tell how the British navy acted against United States ships and men.*

5. *Underline the two sentences that tell why the War Hawks wanted war with Britain.*

THE WAR OF 1812

Fighting the War on Land

Just as the War Hawks desired, an invasion of Canada was planned and carried out. In 1812 American forces attacked British forts at Detroit and Niagara. A third force advanced on Montreal. The Americans were beaten back by British soldiers, the Canadians, and their Indian allies. The Canadians were defending their own country, and they fiercely resisted the advance of the Americans. The Indians saw the war as a way to keep American settlers from moving into Indian territory.

6. *On the map label Detroit at ①, Niagara at ②, and Montreal at ③.*

7. Why did Indians support the Canadians in the war?_____

_____

American forces made a second attempt to invade Canada in 1813. The American forces won some important battles. Toronto, the city where the Canadian government met, was taken but not held. In spite of all the United States' efforts, the end of the year saw Canada still in the hands of the Canadians.

8. *Label Toronto at ④ on the map.*

In 1814 the British invaded the United States. After years of fighting in Europe, they had finally defeated the French. Now they could devote their full energies to the war with the United States. First, they planned to separate New England from the rest of the country, as they had tried to do in the Revolutionary War. But the result was the same—failure. An American fleet on Lake Champlain, commanded by Captain Thomas McDonough, destroyed the British fleet as it tried to sail south on the lake.

9. *Label Lake Champlain at ⑤ on the map.*

The second part of the British plan called for attacks on American cities and villages along the coast. These places could offer little resistance to the British. So, the British were quite successful. Even Washington, the capital of the United States, was captured. President Madison and his wife, Dolley, were forced to flee from the city. The British burned the White House and some other public buildings in revenge for the United States' capture and burning of Toronto, Canada.

10. *Label Washington at ⑥ on the map.*

Circle the sentence that tells why the British burned the White House and other buildings in Washington.

The third part of the British plan was to capture New Orleans. This would help them to control the Mississippi River. The British sent about 7500 well-trained and experienced troops to New Orleans. General Andrew Jackson and about 5000 untrained troops met the British attack. The battle which was fought on January 8, 1815, was a terrible defeat for the British. About two thousand of the British soldiers were killed or wounded. The Americans lost no more than 75 troops. At the time of the battle, neither Jackson nor the British knew that a peace treaty had already been signed between the United States and Great Britain.

Important Locations in the **War of 1812**

Name: _____ Date: _____

WORD SEARCH: PEOPLE AND EVENTS—1775 TO 1860

W	A	S	H	I	N	G	T	O	N	F	U	L	T	O	N	S
G	A	A	S	T	E	A	M	B	O	A	T	X	V	K	N	T
E	T	R	E	N	T	O	N	F	R	A	N	C	E	O	C	L
R	C	A	W	F	R	A	N	K	L	I	N	B	S	L	O	A
I	A	T	Y	I	Z	G	A	G	E	K	C	R	A	A	N	W
E	L	O	O	W	T	R	E	V	E	R	E	A	C	F	S	R
A	I	G	R	H	M	H	D	H	X	F	Y	D	A	A	T	E
L	F	A	K	I	O	A	M	N	F	O	W	D	J	Y	I	N
W	O	B	T	T	R	M	T	E	X	A	S	O	A	E	T	C
O	R	O	O	M	S	I	J	K	X	L	M	C	W	T	U	E
L	N	S	W	A	E	L	N	P	Q	I	R	K	E	T	T	R
F	I	T	N	N	S	T	G	O	L	D	C	T	A	E	I	I
E	A	O	U	V	A	O	B	C	O	N	C	O	R	D	O	V
C	D	N	G	H	I	N	Q	U	E	B	E	C	E	J	N	E
O	R	E	G	O	N	K	M	O	N	T	C	A	L	M	L	R

Word Search

Here is a challenge! Find and draw circles around the thirty words and phrases in the puzzle that are concerned with people, places, events, and things. Fourteen items are in the vertical columns, fourteen more items are in the horizontal columns, and two items are listed diagonally. Following is a list of the words and phrases contained in the puzzle.

WASHINGTON	STEAMBOAT	GAGE	FRANCE	SARATOGA
MONTCALM	REVERE	TEXAS	GOLD	QUEBEC
ERIE	LAFAYETTE	BOSTON	CALIFORNIA	ST. LAWRENCE RIVER
CONSTITUTION	SACAJAWEA	YORKTOWN	WOLFE	JEFFERSON
FULTON	BRADDOCK	WHITMAN	FRANKLIN	WAR WITH MEXICO
OREGON ✔	TRENTON	MORSE	CONCORD	HAMILTON

107

A Singular Person and Event

NARCISSA WHITMAN AND CROSSING THE ROCKIES

Procedure

1. Orally or through photocopies make the story of Narcissa Whitman available to your students.

2. Using information from the story have your students write captions for the illustrations.

3. The outline page can be completed as you orally read the story or from photocopies.

1 Narcissa Prentiss, one of six children, was born in upstate New York. She attended the Female Seminary in Troy, New York. Then she went on to graduate from a higher level school, the Franklin Academy. Upon graduation she became a teacher in a small school, but her real desire was to be a missionary among the Indians. She was told that that kind of work was not acceptable for an unmarried woman.

2 Narcissa met her husband-to-be, Marcus Whitman, a medical doctor, in a casual way, but they soon fell in love. Marcus also wanted to become a missionary in the far west, where he had heard many of the Indians wanted to know more about Christianity. This was very fortunate for Narcissa because it made it possible for her to realize her lifetime goal. As the wife of a missionary, she also could be one. So, the two became engaged and made plans for their future missionary work.

3 Narcissa wanted to be married quickly, but Marcus said that first he wanted to go west to see for himself what conditions were like. Marcus set off on his exploratory trip and came back convinced that it would be possible for a woman to cross the Rocky Mountains in a wagon—something that had never been done before. Narcissa was delighted with this news. Soon they were married and began to make plans for the long and dangerous journey.

4 The overland journey was incredibly difficult, but Narcissa was an equally incredible woman. Perhaps the most difficult part of the journey occurred whenever one of the many rivers had to be crossed. More than once it seemed that all would be lost—animals, wagons, belongings—in the swirling waters. Narcissa and another missionary wife, Eliza Spaulding, gained strength and support from each other.

5 Finally, after six months on the trail, the missionary party reached Fort Vancouver, close to where the Willamette River joins the Columbia River near the Pacific coast. The Hudson Bay Company, a British company, had built the fort and carried on a profitable fur trade with the Indians of the region. The fort was strong and well supplied. Narcissa stayed there for a well-earned rest but, even so, she spent time teaching the young children who stayed at the fort.

6 Marcus went back up the Columbia River to find a site for their mission. He chose a spot where the Snake River joins the Columbia River. The mission, Waiilatpu, is not far from present-day Walla Walla, Washington. The year was 1837, the year Narcissa became twenty-nine years old.

7 The Whitman's mission was in the lands of the Cayuse Indians. The couple worked hard to teach Christianity to the Indians, to take care of their sick, and to teach them to read. Frequently, Narcissa was left alone in their small cabin while her husband was off taking care of the sick. During the first year at Waiilatpu, Narcissa had a baby, Alice Clarrisa, who was a source of great joy to the couple. But then, a most tragic event occurred. One day Alice Clarrisa wandered off, fell into a nearby stream and drowned.

8 Narcissa grieved for her beloved child, but life had to go on. The work of the mission was very demanding. So great was Narcissa's love for the poor and unfortunate that she adopted and took care of eleven children—white children, Indian children, and children of mixed races. Some of the eleven children were from a family—the Sagers—in which both the mother and father had been killed on the trail. Narcissa raised them all as though they were her own.

9 Many of the Cayuse misunderstood the good intentions of the Whitmans. They were resentful of the preaching of the two missionaries, who said they should give up hunting and become farmers. Pioneers were arriving in greater numbers each year and settling on Indian lands. Finally, some of the settlers brought a disease—measles—to the region. Hundreds of the Cayuse, especially children, caught the disease and died. These circumstances led the Cayuse to attack the Whitman mission on November 29, 1847. Narcissa and Marcus were both killed, along with twelve other people at the mission.

10 What was one of the results of the dedication, work and ultimate sacrifice of the Whitmans? The fact that Narcissa and her friend Eliza Spaulding had successfully crossed the mountains encouraged others to try. In the spring of 1843 a great emigration of Americans to the west began. Some 1200 men, women, and children were on the trail. The hundreds of wagons and two thousand animals—horses, oxen, mules, cows—stretched for miles over the plains and through the mountains. The next year saw another great emigration, and the next year, and the next year, and so on.

11 When it came time for the final settlement as to which country—the United States or Great Britain—would possess the Oregon Country, the presence there of thousands of American settlers was the most important factor in the final decision: the present-day states of Washington and Oregon became United States possessions. It was Narcissa and Marcus Whitman, who first made the path that others would follow.

Name: _____ Date: _____

NARCISSA WHITMAN AND CROSSING THE ROCKIES

The four illustrations on this page show events or situations mentioned in the story of Narcissa Whitman. On the lines below each picture, write a caption consisting of at least two sentences that describes what is shown. Use details in the pictures to make your captions full, detailed, and interesting.

Name: _____ Date: _____

NARCISSA WHITMAN AND CROSSING THE ROCKIES

The outline below can be completed with information from the story about Narcissa Whitman. Try to fill all the blanks beneath each major topic. Use phrases or full sentences, but whichever one you choose to use, try to use it consistently throughout the outline.

1. Narcissa's early life

    a. _____

    b. _____

    c. _____

2. Narcissa's ambition made possible

    a. _____

    b. _____

    c. _____

3. Narcissa's marriage delayed

    a. _____

    b. _____

    c. _____

4. The journey west

    a. _____

    b. _____

    c. _____

5. The journey's end

    a. _____

    b. _____

    c. _____

6. The search for a mission site

    a. _____

    b. _____

    c. _____

7. At home in the mission

    a. _____

    b. _____

    c. _____

8. A family of eleven

    a. _____

    b. _____

    c. _____

9. Death at the mission

    a. _____

    b. _____

    c. _____

    d. _____

    e. _____

10. Emigration grows

    a. _____

    b. _____

    c. _____

11. Winning the Oregon Territory

    a. _____

    b. _____

    c. _____

SECTION 13

Growth in Industry, Agriculture, Transportation, and Communication

JOHN FITCH: PIONEER STEAMBOAT INVENTOR

The information on this page will broaden your students' understandings of the transportation revolution brought about through the use of steam power to move boats over water. Prior to the steam engine, people relied on muscle power, animals, wind, and favorable currents to propel their canoes, boats, barges, and ships. In the developing United States, where roads into the interior were rare, steamboats were able to follow the natural highways of rivers.

Suggestions for teaching

Present the information on this page to build background about America's first successful steam-driven vessel, the *John Fitch*. It would be helpful to the development of your students work-study skills if they took brief notes from which they may later study or speak. One example of cryptic notes follows the information.

1. Two distinctive terms are used to identify steam-driven vessels. A *steam ship* is one that sails on open seas such as the Atlantic Ocean. *Steamboats* sail on inland waters such as rivers and lakes. The smaller vessel, the steamboat, was developed first.

2. John Fitch was a New Englander who did not have much formal education, but he had a natural instinct for mechanics. He knew that steam had the power to move gears and wheels. "Why," he asked himself, "can't I use steam to drive a boat forward?" He determined to put his ideas to work; he would build a steamboat.

It occurred to Fitch that the thing to do was to hitch a steam engine to oars; only instead of moving the oars with muscle power, he would use steam power. After many trials and errors he produced such a boat. The result was a strange looking contraption. The boat looked like a great canoe with six oars on each side—except that there were no paddlers.

People hooted and laughed when they saw Fitch's creation. Few people wanted to get too close; they saw smoke billowing out of the smokestack. They were afraid the boat might blow up. But, Fitch had the last laugh. When he pushed the throttle into forward and the oars began to lift and dip, and the *John Fitch*, as the boat was named, began to move across the water, people had second thoughts. Fitch had created America's first successful steamboat.

Fitch went on to improve his invention. Before 1800 he had launched three steamboats on the Delaware River. The boats carried passengers from Burlington, New Jersey, to Philadelphia, Pennsylvania. In the three years his boats operated, they sailed more than 2000 miles up and down the Delaware River.

Fitch redesigned his original boat by getting rid of the oars. He replaced them with a central paddle wheel that was set within the hull. The wheel operated in a manner similar to the way a duck's feet work to paddle through water. Unfortunately, Fitch's boats frequently broke down. Also, many people remained frightened of the boats and preferred to use horse-drawn carriages.

The passenger line Fitch operated began to lose money. The great losses Fitch and his partners suffered forced them to go out of business. Fitch's interest in steamboats remained, but his debts were so great that he had to turn to other ways to make a living. But, Fitch had shown the way, and others who were better financed improved on his ideas. By 1850 steamboats had become a familiar sight on America's rivers.

Example

- Steamboats (inland waters); steam ships (open sea); note spellings

- John Fitch: New Englander

- Fitch's idea: hitch oars to an engine

- Fitch's first steamboat: 6 oars each side

- People's reaction: laughter, fear

- Passenger service: Burlington, NJ, to Philadelphia, PA; sailed more than 2000 mi.

- Original oared boat redesigned to use center-mounted paddle wheel

- Frequent breakdowns and passenger fear led to financial loss and business shutdown

- Fitch, a pioneer, showed the way for others

- By 1850, steamboats common on rivers

The illustration of Fitch's oared steamboat, the *John Fitch*, is shown at the top of the facing page with space allotted for taking brief notes.

Name: _____ Date: _____

JOHN FITCH: PIONEER STEAMBOAT INVENTOR

John Fitch's original oared vessel, the *John Fitch*

Notes:

_____

_____

_____

_____

_____

_____

_____

_____

_____

_____

_____

_____

_____

THE ERIE CANAL: A WATER HIGHWAY TO THE WEST

The facing page will provide an opportunity for your students to better understand one of the first steps in the building of the United States canal system. They will be aided in their understanding of the topic through the use of the "interrupted narrative" approach, applied on other pages throughout this book. You will notice that some of the questions asked require more than the mere noting of facts. These questions require the learner to work with the facts and, they thereby enhance comprehension, skill development, and retention.

The following information and suggestions relative to the topic of canals should prove helpful in your presentation and discussion.

Erie Canal

The Erie Canal stands as a monument to the foresight and perseverance of DeWitt Clinton. As early as 1812 Clinton and another canal enthusiast, Gouverneur Morris, tried to interest the federal government in the canal, but they were turned down. New York State then financed the canal for about $7,000,000. It was a great investment. By 1882 the state had taken in about $121,000,000 in tolls. Today the Erie Canal is part of the New York State Barge Canal System. The new system connects the Hudson River, the old Erie Canal, Lake Champlain, the Finger Lakes, Lake Erie, and Lake Ontario. Thus, about 90 percent of new York State's population lives no more than a thirty minute drive away from some part of the system.

October 26, 1825, was a great day for New York State and the nation. On that day the *Seneca Chief* became the first barge to make a complete trip on the canal from Buffalo to New York City. Thousands of people lined the banks of the canal and cheered, shot off cannons, and blew horns to show their joy and pride.

The original Erie Canal has been enlarged and improved many times over the years and continues to operate as part of the New York State Barge Canal System. Unlike many other early canals that have been discontinued due to the competition of railroads, airplanes, and superhighways over which huge trucks roll, the canal is still part of a vital link to the west.

Other Early United States Canals

In 1829 the Chesapeake and Delaware Canal was completed. This all-water route made it possible to transport people and freight from and to New York, Philadelphia, and Washington, D.C., without venturing into the Atlantic Ocean and sailing around the Del-Mar-Va peninsula. Thus, dangers were lessened as well as costs and travel time.

Neither the Erie Canal nor the Chesapeake and Delaware Canal required locks; that is, barges could travel through the passage without being raised and lowered. However, the Sault Sainte Marie Canals—which connect Lakes Superior and Huron—required locks because the two lakes were at different levels. The locks of this canal were completed in 1855.

Discussion Questions

What kind of problems may be encountered when a state wants to build a transportation facility such as a canal?

1. *Getting authorization from the state legislature*. This may prove troublesome. For example, vested interests such as competing transportation facilities may lobby to oppose the measure.

2. *Financing*. Shall the costs of construction and land acquisition be paid from general taxes? Bond issues? Tolls? Some tax payers will argue that the transportation facility should be paid for by those who use it.

3. *Acquiring the land*. Land speculators should be foiled. Eminent domain (the power of a government to force the sale of land needed for the public good and use) may have to be exercised.

4. *Construction*. Specifications must be printed on which bids from construction companies are made.

5. *Environment*. What will be the effects of the canal on wildlife habitats? Plants? Erosion?

6. *Maintenance*. Shall state employees or private contractors maintain the facility? How is money for maintenance to be raised and allocated?

THE ERIE CANAL: A WATER HIGHWAY TO THE WEST

Transporting people and products in colonial days was dangerous, expensive, and very slow. By 1820, twenty-five of every one hundred Americans lived west of the Appalachians. The few roads and trails over the mountains could not handle the ever-increasing traffic between the east coast and the new settlements. Better means of transportation were needed.

1. In 1820, the population of the United States was about 10,000,000. According to the information above, how many people lived west of the Appalachians? _____

New York State was especially concerned about the problem. It took three weeks to transport products from Buffalo in the western part of the state to New York City in the east. Freight charges were as high as one hundred dollars a ton. *2. What would it have cost a farmer to transport two tons of wheat and one-half ton of corn from Buffalo to New York City?* $ _____

The state decided to build a canal to connect Lake Erie and the Hudson River. Goods could then be carried north from New York city on the Hudson River, and then west on the canal to Lake Erie. *3. According to the map, what other river would be along the route of the canal?* _____ *4. What city is at the eastern end of the Mohawk River?* _____ *5. Once the canal boats reached Buffalo, what lake would provide another waterway to the west?* _____ *6. About how many miles would products travel between New York City and Buffalo?* _____

Work on the canal was begun in 1817 and completed in 1825. The "big ditch," as it was called, was forty feet wide at the top and twenty-eight feet wide at the bottom. The water in the canal was about four feet deep. Even with modern bulldozers and earthmovers, removing so much dirt would be a tremendous task. Imagine the difficulty in those days of wagons, horses, shovels, pick axes, and wheelbarrows!

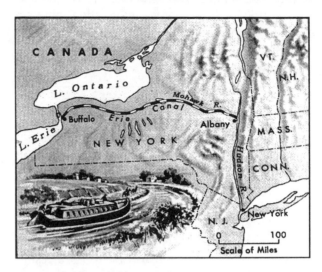

The canal was successful beyond the wildest dreams of the planners and builders. The cost of moving freight from Lake Erie to New York City was reduced to ten dollars per ton. *7. How much would the farmer referred to in question 2 pay to transport the same amount of wheat and corn via the canal?* $_____ *How much was saved?* $_____

The time needed for the trip was cut to eight days. Thousands and thousands of pioneers were encouraged to move west to Ohio, Illinois, Indiana, Michigan, and Wisconsin. The effect on New York City was great. Its population almost doubled from about 100,000 to 200,000 between 1820 and 1830.

The success of the Erie Canal encouraged the construction of other man-made waterways. By 1850 there were more than three thousand miles of canals in the country.

8. How many days were saved in transporting goods from Buffalo to New York City as a result of building the Erie Canal? _____ *9. Notice the canal boat in the map. What power is being used to pull the boat?* _____ *10. Thought question: Why was the height of the canal boats kept quite low?* _____

_____

114

IMPROVEMENTS IN ROADS

Following is some extra information about the development of roads in the United States and some suggestions for teaching, including questions for discussion.

Travelling by Land

Today it is possible to board an airplane in Boston, Massachusetts, and to land in an airport in New York City forty-five minutes later. In 1700 that same trip overland took from eight to ten days. Any person making such a journey had to ride a horse, walk, or take passage on a coastal ship. The trails that served as roads were so bad that wagons or stagecoaches could not use them. As a result, people in those days rarely travelled for pleasure. Emergencies and business were the two main reasons why people suffered the hardships and risked the dangers of travelling.

One brave lady named Mrs. Knight did travel overland from Boston to New York in 1704. She wrote about the difficulties that most colonial travellers faced. Here is how Mrs. Knight described part of her journey.

> ". . . we had near fourteen miles to ride to the next stage [place] where we were to lodge [stay]. I asked him [the guide] of the rest of the road. . . . He told me there was a bad river we were to ride through, which was so very fierce a horse could sometimes hardly stem [cross] it."

Later, Mrs. Knight reached the river. She described her crossing this way:

> ". . . we entered a thicket of trees and shrubs. . . we were on the descent of a hill. . . it was totally dark. . . but I knew by the going of the horse we had entered the water. . . . I rallied my courage. . . gave reins to my nag [horse]. . . in a few minutes got safe to the other side."

As the colonies grew, more and better roads were built. One road ran along the coast from Massachusetts to the Carolinas. By 1776 it was possible to board a stagecoach in New York and to arrive in Philadelphia, ninety miles away, in only two days. This coach ride was unpleasant compared to travelling today by car, train, or airplane. Sometimes, the passengers were thrown from the coach. Or, the coach might have to be floated on logs across streams.

Most colonial roads were simply made of dirt. It was not until after the colonial period had ended that an improved road was built. In 1792 construction was begun on a new kind of road that connected Lancaster, Pennsylvania, with Philadelphia. Two years later the road was ready for use. It was the wonder of its day. The builders of this sixty-six-mile highway used a new method of road building. They put down ten inches of stone, and then laid one inch of gravel or tiny stones on top. The road was slightly higher in the center so the water would run off it. The road could be used in all kinds of weather. Another unusual feature of the road was that the more it was used, the stronger and harder it became. Soon many other roads were built in the same way as the Lancaster road.

Suggestion

1. Photocopy and distribute the students' page which contains graphics related to roads.

2. Refer to *Figure 1*, which shows a stagecoach crossing a river. Ask your students what facts are shown in the picture?

- ◇ raining
- ◇ four horses
- ◇ three windows in coach
- ◇ baggage on top of coach
- ◇ man in front pulling
- ◇ two men in back pushing
- ◇ one man using a pole as a lever
- ◇ three lady passengers seeking shelter under an umbrella and cloth
- ◇ rail fence

Ask your students what inferences we can make about the following:

- ☐ women's feelings at the time?
- ☐ relationships among the three women and among the three men pushing the coach?
- ☐ destination of the passengers?

IMPROVEMENTS IN ROADS

3. The new kind of road described is shown in *Figure 2*. Have your students write the given particulars of the road in the appropriate boxes.

A. Ten inches of large stone on the bottom

B. One inch of gravel or tiny stone on top

C. Higher in the middle for water runoff

D. Cross-section of a McAdam road

A Connecting Link of Stone and Gravel

Up to 1803 the national government left the building of roads to the states and private road-building companies. As a result, few new roads were built. Many people thought that only the national government could take on the expense and responsibility of road building. The people of the Ohio Territory were especially worried about transportation. In 1803, they asked Congress to build a road connecting the East and the West. Congress promised to do so.

Congress kept its promise and voted money for the construction of a road from Cumberland, Maryland to Wheeling, Virginia. Before construction even started, it was decided to extend the road farther west to St. Louis, Missouri, on the Mississippi River. The new highway used the system of road building developed by John McAdam. That is, one inch of gravel was laid over ten inches of large stone. By 1819, the National Road, as it was called, had reached Wheeling. Finally, it reached Vandalia, Illinois, in 1838.

Suggestion

1. Your students may complete the map of National Road, *Figure 3*, by labeling as follows:

❶ Cumberland
❷ Wheeling
❸ Columbus
❹ Indianapolis
❺ Vandalia
❻ St. Louis

2. Show the route of the road by drawing a line connecting all the cities that have been labeled. Also, write **National Road** on the line below the map.

3. Label the states that the National Road went through or touched as follows:

A. Missouri   E. Virginia

B. Illinois   F. Pennsylvania

C. Indiana   G. Maryland (use abbreviation: MD)

D. Ohio

4. Using the Scale of Miles shown in the key, determine the length of the National Road. (*Approximately 560 miles*)

5. Assume that it was possible to travel thirty miles a day in a stage coach on the National Road. How many days would it take to travel from Wheeling to Columbus? (*Approximately 4 days*) From St. Louis to Wheeling? (*Approximately 15 days*) How long would it take a modern car travelling at an average speed of 50 miles per hour to make the trip from St. Louis to Wheeling? (*Approximately 9 hours*)

Discussion Questions

1. How did poor travel and communication conditions affect the unity of the colonies and, later, the states? (*Adversely. The people of the various colonies and states were strangers to each other.*)

2. What factors contributed to the slow development of good communications? (*Great distances, thick forests, wide rivers, hostile Indians, and, in the pre-Constitution days, the lack of a strong central government to initiate and coordinate a road building program*)

3. How do our present excellent communication systems contribute to the unity of the nation? (*People all over the country see the same programs, read the same newspapers, hear the same radio broadcasts, see the same motion pictures, and are easily able to travel to the farthest destination in the country by airplane, car, or train.*)

117

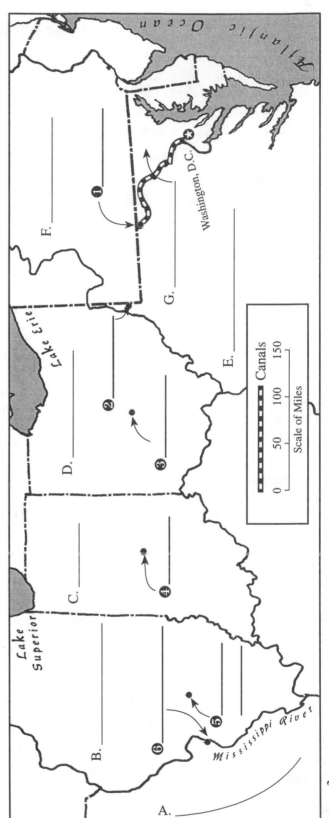

Figure 1: *Rough Traveling in Colonial Times*

Figure 2: **D**

Figure 3:

THE BEGINNING OF RAILROADS IN THE UNITED STATES

Peter Cooper of New York was one of the pioneers of railroading. He had heard that the Baltimore and Ohio Railroad Company was trying to move wagons on tracks by using sails. He thought that nothing would come from that idea. He decided to build a small locomotive and to prove that steam power could be applied to railroads.

After much hard work and many discouragements, Cooper created a small but sturdy steam locomotive called the *Tom Thumb*. To win public support, he decided to give a public demonstration of his invention on the tracks of the Baltimore and Ohio. In August, 1830, twenty-four nervous passengers boarded a coach placed on the rails. Cooper fired up his boiler. Steam hissed from the valves. Sparks and cinders flew out of the smokestack like firecrackers. The coach was pulled along the rails by the *Tom Thumb* at the amazing speed of six miles per hour. The first steam locomotive built in America was a great success.

In the first ten years after Cooper's demonstration, about 2900 miles of railroad track were laid. By 1850 this figure had grown to 9000 miles. By 1860 it was more than 30,000 miles. As railroad mileage increase, the importance of canals and steamboats decreased.

There were several reasons for the success of the railroads. Tracks could be laid along the rivers as easily as canals could be built. In addition, they could be laid in places where there were no rivers or where it was too expensive or impossible to dig a canal. Another important reason for the rapid growth of the railroads was their great speed. In just a few years after the *Tom Thumb*, trains traveled at speeds no canal boat, steamship, or horse-drawn wagon could match.

---

1. Identify each of the following as related to the development of early railroads:

Peter Cooper: _____

Baltimore and Ohio: _____

The *Tom Thumb*: _____

August, 1830: _____

2. What were three reasons why railroads grew so rapidly?

a. _____

b. _____

c. _____

3. The picture shows an amusing incident in the early days of railroading. What words (adjectives) could be used to describe the following?

bull: _____

engineer: _____

farmer: _____

4. On the back of this page, write one-sentence remarks that each of the following might have made: bull, engineer, farmer, passenger.

TRANSPORTATION BY LAND AND WATER

The years from 1830–1860 saw a rapid growth in railroad mileage along the Atlantic coast and the region beyond the Appalachian Mountains and the Mississippi River. With the railroad came growth in population because formerly remote areas were made accessible to settlers. With the influx of settlers, especially west of the Appalachians, came the growth of communities to service their needs.

Procedure for Completing the "Railroad Mileage: 1830–1860" Line Graph

1. Your students can reach a better understanding of the growth of railroads and, simultaneously, have an experience in making and interpreting line graphs by completing the line graph on the facing page.

Railroad Mileage: 1830–1860*		
Year	Mileage	Rounded
1830	23	(not rounded)
1835	1,098	1,100
1840	2,818	2,800
1845	4,633	4,600
1850	9,021	9,000
1855	18,374	18,400
1860	30,626	30,600

* Source: *Historical Statistics of the United States*

2. Discuss the value of "rounding off" statistics so as to simplify plotting information and the fact that, unlike tables which show exact figures, graphs are used to show trends or comparisons at a glance.

3. Help students to understand that if there are a large number of years to be shown on a graph it is useful to list every five or ten years (or some other multiple of 5) on the horizontal axis. The graph on the facing page depicts trends in five-year intervals. (*1830 has been listed already; your students can complete the year listings with five-year intervals.*)

4. The vertical axis should start at 0 and then progress by equivalent intervals to a quantity higher than the greatest quantity that is to be graphed. (*The next logical progression after the 1860 data is 35,000. Have your students complete the vertical axis with intervals of 2500 miles.*)

5. Your students are now ready to position the dots and draw the lines which show growth. (*Have them place a dot indicating rounded mileage for each year represented whenever the horizontal and vertical values intersect; they should then connect the dots with straight lines.*)

6. After the graph is completed ask questions such as the following: What five-year span showed the greatest percent of increase? (*1830–1835*) What prediction would you make about the growth of railroad mileage for the 1860–1865 span of years? (*Data indicates probable continuance of expansion.*)

Transportation by Steam-driven Vessels

It may come as a surprise to some that steam-driven vessels were utilized in significant ways at least three decades before railroads were widely used. One obvious reason for this was that waterborne craft had ready-made "roads": rivers. Imagine the immensity of the task of laying track from Pittsburgh to St. Louis as compared to floating on the Ohio River current to the same destination. Of course, railroads had their advantages. Railroads could be built to almost any place on land; while rivers could only follow their natural paths.

The data that follows is all that is needed to complete the line graph at the bottom of the facing page. Students—on their own—should repeat the procedure followed to complete the railroad mileage graph.

Steamboat/Steam Ship Growth: 1810–1860*	
Year	Number of Vessels
1810	1
1820	22
1830	64
1840	202
1850	526
1860	868

* Source: *Historical Statistics of the United States*

Name: _____ Date: _____

TRANSPORTATION BY LAND AND WATER

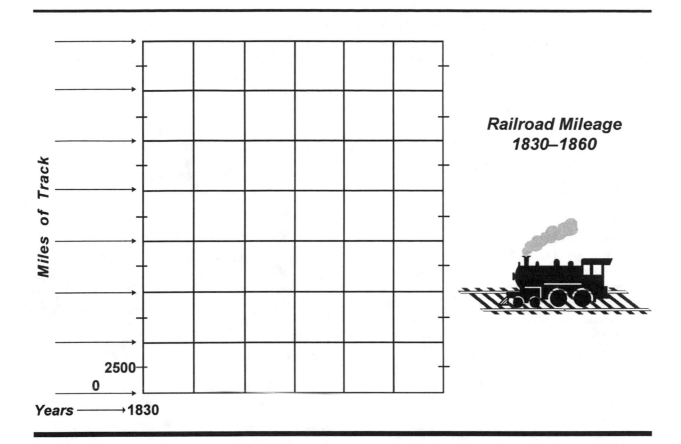

Miles of Track

2500

0

Years ——→ 1830

*Railroad Mileage
1830–1860*

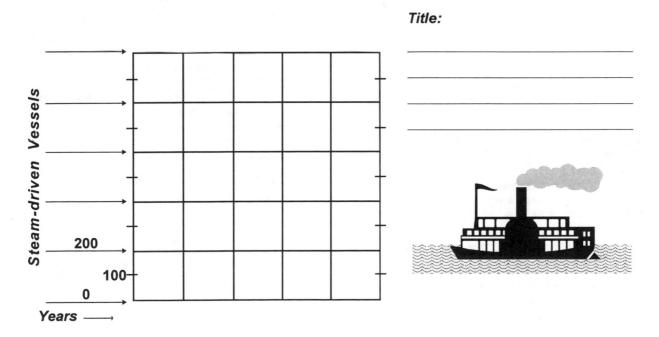

Title: _____

_____

_____

_____

_____

Steam-driven Vessels

200

100

0

Years ——→

120

ROBERT FULTON: INVENTOR

When Fulton was twenty-one years old he sailed ___ to England. While he was there he invented two machines: one that cut marble into slabs, and one that improved canal systems.

After a series of misfortunes the family lost the ___ farm and moved to Lancaster, Pennsylvania. Although the family was poor, young Robert attended school, but spent much time dreaming of future inventions.

Robert Fulton was born in 1765 in a small, stone ___ farmhouse in eastern Pennsylvania. Mrs. Fulton took care of the children, the house, and a beautiful and productive vegetable and flower garden.

Fulton left England and sailed across the English ___ Channel to France. While there he had an idea for a new kind of boat—a submarine. He soon had plans for, and directed the construction of, a vessel that could submerge, move under water, attack an enemy ship, and then surface.

Following the success of the *Clermont*, Fulton ___ continued to design steam-driven vessels. He decided to build a steam warship. In 1815 Fulton died, but others were able to follow his plans so that the *Fulton I*, as the ship was called, was completed.

After his work with submarines, Fulton turned his ___ attention to steam-driven boats. He began his experiments in France; then, he left France and returned to the United States. In 1807 he designed and built the *Clermont*, which ran on the Hudson River. It was a huge success.

1. Each paragraph above tells about one part of Robert Fulton's life. On the line before the beginning of each paragraph write the number of the drawing that is most closely related to the details in the paragraph.

2. In the space before each sentence below write the number of the picture to which the sentence is most closely related.

___ Eventually, underwater boats brought about great changes in naval warfare.

___ The ship sailed up the Hudson River from New York to Albany in 24 hours—a record.

___ In England his interests turned more and more to mechanical things.

___ His father was a farmer who was kept busy working the family's 400 acre farm.

___ Such a ship would be a great help in protecting coastal cities.

___ Even so, Mrs. Fulton scraped up enough money to send Robert to private school.

___ Following his success on the Hudson River, Fulton directed the construction of the *New Orleans* for use on the Mississippi River.

___ Fulton wanted to improve on a submarine first invented in 1776 by David Bushnell.

3. Which picture best fits each caption?

___ Steaming up the Hudson River

___ A "dreamer" at an early age

___ Sighting the shores of England

___ A fighting ship, but a huge target

___ A silent, invisible attacker

___ The Pennsylvania house where Fulton was born

Name: _____ Date: _____

THE CONESTOGA WAGON

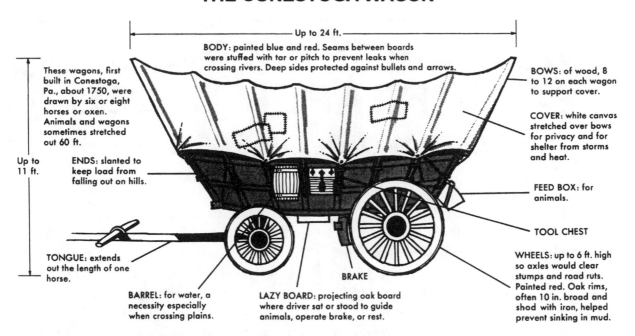

Up to 24 ft.

BODY: painted blue and red. Seams between boards were stuffed with tar or pitch to prevent leaks when crossing rivers. Deep sides protected against bullets and arrows.

These wagons, first built in Conestoga, Pa., about 1750, were drawn by six or eight horses or oxen. Animals and wagons sometimes stretched out 60 ft.

Up to 11 ft.

ENDS: slanted to keep load from falling out on hills.

BOWS: of wood, 8 to 12 on each wagon to support cover.

COVER: white canvas stretched over bows for privacy and for shelter from storms and heat.

FEED BOX: for animals.

TOOL CHEST

TONGUE: extends out the length of one horse.

BARREL: for water, a necessity especially when crossing plains.

LAZY BOARD: projecting oak board where driver sat or stood to guide animals, operate brake, or rest.

BRAKE

WHEELS: up to 6 ft. high so axles would clear stumps and road ruts. Painted red. Oak rims, often 10 in. broad and shod with iron, helped prevent sinking in mud.

For more than 100 years wagons, similar to the Conestoga wagon shown above, were the main means of transportation for pioneer families and moving freight.

Study the drawing and explanations. Then answer these questions.

1. Where were the Conestoga wagons first made? __

_____

2. How long were some of the wagons? _____

_____ How long were they with animals attached? _____

3. What were the purposes of the lazy board? _____

_____

4. What kind of tools were most likely carried in the tool chest? _____

_____

5. What kept the wheels from sinking too deeply into the mud? _____

6. Why were the ends of the wagons so high and slanted? _____

_____

7. What was done to make the wagons usable as boats?

_____

8. What three purposes did the canvas cover serve? _

_____

9. Why were the bottoms of the wagons so high off the ground? _____

_____

10. Certain kinds of sailing boats are called *schooners*. Why do you think the covered wagons were sometimes called prairie schooners? _____

_____

11. To what uses could the canvas cover on the wagon be put at the end of the trip. Try to think of four. _____ _____

_____ _____

12. How could the other parts of the wagon (wood, wheels, spokes, iron rims, the body) be used? _____

_____

_____

_____

CYRUS McCORMICK: AGRICULTURAL INVENTOR

NEW REAPER TRIED
DOES WORK OF SIX MEN
Inventor Plans Improvements

LEXINGTON, VA., July 25, 1832— A new reaping machine that looks like a windmill mounted on a sled, but which may be the answer to a centuries-old farming problem, was exhibited yesterday at the farm of William Taylor of this town. The inventor of the machine, Cyrus H. McCormick of Walnut Grove farm, Rockbridge County, Virginia, was in charge of the demonstration. One hundred or more people were present at the exhibition given for the purpose of promoting interest in the machine.

The truly amazing device cut more wheat in an afternoon than six men swinging scythes, or twenty-four men chopping with sickles.

When asked if this was the first time the reaper had been tried successfully, the young inventor replied, "No, the reaper was first tried last July on my father's farm. Then, a few days later there was a public demonstration in the village of Steele's Tavern, where I cut six acres of oats in an afternoon."

The inventor, who is twenty-two years of age and unmarried, modestly gave much of the credit for the idea for the machine to his father, Robert McCormick, who worked for many years to develop a reaper. "Father's machine," said the young inventor, "was never perfected in the fifteen years he worked on it, but his experience and encouragement helped me to do the job."

After the demonstration the device was moved to the courthouse square in Lexington where many people studied its marvelous mechanical arrangement. One person was heard to say, "No more back-breaking work in the hot sun with a scythe!" Another said, "With the way the country is growing, we'll need this machine to help raise enough wheat to feed the people." Still another was heard to say, "One man will be able to farm much more land than ever before."

Mr. McCormick plans to improve the machine. He isn't satisfied with the way the reaper cuts wet grain, and he has thought of a way to keep the reel from knocking grain to the ground as it moves through the field. He expects to sell reapers for about one hundred dollars each.

Name: _____ Date: _____

CYRUS McCORMICK: AGRICULTURAL INVENTOR

1.   Most news stories provide the answers to five questions for the reader. They are: Who? What? Where? When? and Why?

     After reading the news article on the opposite page, answer the five questions below.

a.   Who is the story about?

_____

b.   What is the story about?

_____

c.   Where did all the events told about in the story take place? (state)

_____

d.   When did the events take place? (years)

_____

e.   Why did the events occur?

_____

_____

2.   About how many people were present at the Lexington demonstration? _____

3.   In what year was the *first successful trial* of the reaper?_____

4.   Where was the *first public* demonstration of the machine held? _____

5.   How large was the field of grain cut by the reaper at the first public demonstration?

_____

6.   How many men using sickles would it have taken to cut the field of wheat Cyrus McCormick cut at Lexington _____

7.   What two improvements did Cyrus plan to make on his machine?

_____

_____

8.   What word is used in the fourth paragraph to describe Cyrus's character?

_____

9.   Which of the results listed below was not mentioned by the spectators as they discussed the machine?

❑ More people would be fed.

❑ One man could farm more land.

❑ The price of wheat would come down.

❑ A farmer would not have to work so hard.

To go ahead. The drawing shows a public demonstration of McCormick's reaper. Write a description of the scene. Tell about the machine itself and the crowd.

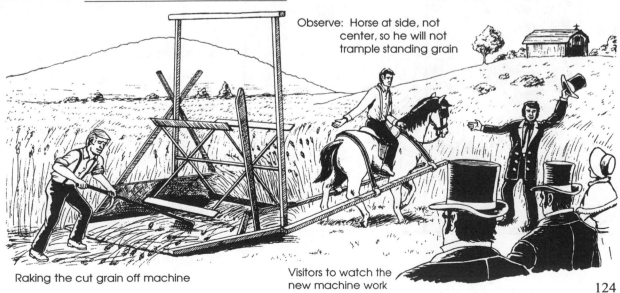

Observe: Horse at side, not center, so he will not trample standing grain

Raking the cut grain off machine

Visitors to watch the new machine work

124

LIFE ON THE PLAINS

Phrases

Each phrase applies to one of the pictures. Write the number of the phrase in the circle in the correct picture.

1   Travelling by wagon   ____

2   Building a house   ____

3   Digging for water   ____

4   Farming with a plow   ____

5   Trying to stop a fire   ____

6   Clouds of grasshoppers   ____

7   Fighting a blizzard   ____

8   Fleeing a tornado   ____

9   Erecting a fence   ____

10 Stuck on the road   ____

Words

Each phrase above is followed by a line. Each of the words below could be inserted before the last word in one of the phrases to make it more meaningful. Write the letter of the correct word on the line after each phrase.

a frightening   **f** sod

b steel   **g** fresh

c muddy   **h** blinding

d grass   **i** barbed-wire

e Conestoga   **j** hungry

To go ahead. Imagine that you became a plains farmer. Write an explanation of the first three things you did upon arriving at your homestead.

TWO AGRICULTURAL IMPROVEMENTS: STEEL PLOWS AND MECHANICAL THRESHERS

Great changes in manufacturing took place in the years around 1800. Changes in farming came about more slowly. A farmer living in ancient Egypt would have had little difficulty using a colonial farmer's tools. The Egyptian used a pointed stick to plow the ground, and so did the Americans. Both the Egyptian and the American cut the grain with a kind of knife called a scythe. After the grain was cut and gathered, both farmers would have to beat the grain with a flail to knock the seeds off the plant. These methods were slow and backbreaking. Label picture 1 above *Using a Scythe*. Label picture 2 *Using a Flail*.

It was almost impossible for one man to farm five acres of land by himself. Yet, each year the world needed more food. Also, more and more people were moving to cities to work in the factories. As a result, there were fewer farm workers to grow crops. It was clear that the world's food needs could not be filled if farmers continued to use their old ways.

One of those who was concerned about improving farming methods was Thomas Jefferson. He reasoned that the moldboard of a plow would turn the soil easily and more thoroughly if it were curved. He had a plow made in this way. The plow was an immediate success. Formerly, farmers had used only the top few inches of soil. Now they were able to dig much deeper furrows and to bring the rich bottom layers of soil to the surface. One result was that soil did not wear out as quickly. The moldboard is part 2 on the plow drawing below. Label the *moldboard* using the line numbered 2. Also label the other parts of the plow as follows: 1. *handles*, 3. *beam*, 4. *share*, 5. *point*, 6. *gauge wheel*. *Note*: The gauge wheel is used to regulate the depth of the cut.

More improvements in plows followed. One of the most important inventions was the steel plow. Formerly, plows were made of wood or cast iron, and soil would stick to them. However, soil did not stick to the steel plow as it did to the old type. Furthermore, the steel plows were able to cut through the thick, tangled grasses of the western plains. The new plows were so popular that they were sold as fast as they were made.

Even after the invention of the reaper, one of the farmers hardest jobs still had to be done by hand. This was the threshing of the grain. The picture at the top of the first column shows how tiring this must have been. A farmer might work three or four days to thresh a bushel of grain. Clever mechanics worked on developing a machine to do the job. Horse-powered threshers (shown below) were soon in use throughout the country. Eventually, steam engines provided the power to thresh grain. *A horse-powered thresher is shown below. Write its title on the blank line.*

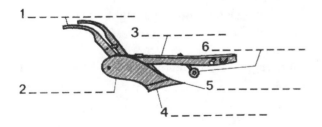

IMPROVEMENTS IN INDUSTRY: MAKING CLOTH

Steam—A New Source of Power

For hundreds of years before the Revolutionary War, ways of making things changed very little. Methods of grinding wheat into flour in colonial America were not much different from methods used in England two hundred years earlier. A housewife in old Boston spun yarn and wove it into cloth in much the same way her great-great-great-grandmother had before her.

1. What three necessities of life are mentioned as not being improved over hundreds of years? ____

_____

2. Think of other ways that life remained relatively unchanged up to 1800. _____

_____

However, the world was changing. It was becoming more crowded with people, especially in the cities. Life was no longer as simple as it once had been. More food, more clothing, more houses, better tools, and better means of transportation were needed. New and better machines for producing things had to be invented. New sources of power to run machines had to be developed.

Since the earliest times power to do work had been supplied by men, animals, water, and wind. However, a stronger source of power, more readily available and more reliable, was steam power. The problem was this: How could this power be controlled so that it could do work?

3. Underline the sentence that suggests the main reason more efficient and faster means of manufacturing were necessary.

Many men had tried to discover how to use steam for power. One of them, an English blacksmith named Thomas Newcomen, invented a steam engine that could pump water out of mines. Unfor-

tunately, the engine was not efficient. It used large quantities of fuel, often broke down, and worked slowly.

James Watt of Scotland was able to make Newcomen's engine efficient. By 1775 he had developed almost all the parts of the steam engine that are now used. He was not satisfied to have his engine used only to pump water. Watt found a way to make the steam engine turn wheels. This was a tremendous development. Now, steam power could be used to drive steamboats, railroad engines, and other machines.

4. Why would it not be true to say that James Watt invented the steam engine? _____

_____

_____

A New Way to Make Cloth

What does the phrase "to spin yarn" mean? It means to take the fibers of such things as wool, cotton, and flax and twist them together. The twisting causes the fibers to form a long, continuous yarn, or thread. When the yarns are woven together, cloth is produced.

During colonial times yarn was made on a spinning wheel. Making yarn on a wheel took much time. Women had to spend hour after hour at their wheels to produce enough yarn to make clothes for their families. Only rich people could afford to buy ready-made clothing. Many inventors tried to find a faster way to make yarn.

In 1764, James Hargreaves of England built the spinning jenny, a machine that really worked. The spinning jenny could spin eight threads at once. Soon, spinning machines were too large to be run by hand power, so water power was then used. Later, steam engines were hitched to the spinning machines.

127

IMPROVEMENTS IN INDUSTRY: MAKING CLOTH

5. *The first power or energy used to spin yarn was human or "muscle" power. What was the next form of power used to spin yarn after Hargreaves invented the spinning jenny?* _____ *What was the third source of power?* _____

Improved methods of spinning then created another problem. Thread was being spun so swiftly that it became necessary to find a faster way of weaving it into cloth. Another Englishman, Edmund Cartwright, produced a power loom, or weaving machine. Then the weavers could keep up with the spinners. Cloth began to be produced cheaply and in large quantities.

6. *How did the improved spinning machines make a problem for the weaving industry?* _____

_____

7. *How was the problem solved?* _____

_____

These great improvements in the textile (cloth) industry had been made in Britain. The British would not allow the Americans to buy the British textile machines or the plans to make them. So strictly did the British guard their secret that textile workers were not allowed to leave the country. British manufacturers were afraid of foreign competition.

However, a young English mechanic, Samuel Slater, carefully studied textile machines. After memorizing the processes used to spin cotton, he secretly left England. After he arrived in the United States, he contacted a wealthy businessman. Together they built a spinning mill in Pawtucket, Rhode Island. By 1790 they were manufacturing cotton yarn in the first cotton spinning mill in America.

Francis C. Lowell, a Boston businessman, visited English textile mills. He found out how to build power looms. He returned to the United States and built the country's first complete textile factory. His factory not only spun cotton into yarn, but also made it into cloth. Formerly, spinning had been done in one factory and weaving in another.

8. *Underline the two sentences that tell what the British did to prevent their spinning and weaving methods from leaving the country.*

9. *In what way was Lowell's factory an improvement over earlier ways of producing cloth?* _____

_____

_____

A Faster Way to Clean Cotton

The invention of the spinning machines and power looms increased the demand for cotton. Enough cotton could be raised, but cleaning the cotton of its seeds took an astonishing amount of time. It took one person about one day to produce one pound of cleaned cotton.

In 1793 Eli Whitney of Massachusetts was visiting Georgia. He saw the great need for a cotton-cleaning machine. He decided to develop such a machine. His cotton gin, as the machine was called, produced more than fifty pounds of cleaned cotton a day.

Many southern farmers stopped raising crops other than cotton because cotton became so profitable. The desire for new cotton-growing lands encouraged western settlement.

10. *What would be one negative (bad or wrong) result of the need to grow more cotton as related to slavery?* _____

_____

_____

REVOLUTION IN COMMUNICATIONS: SAMUEL MORSE

Railroads and roads helped tie together the constantly growing United States, yet faster means of communicating between east and west, north and south, and city and rural areas became necessary. Samuel Morse was probably the most significant contributor to this effort.

Procedure

1. The information that follows will provide background on Morse. After communicating this information to your students, make a transparency or multiple photocopies of the activity at the bottom of the page. The students may decode the message individually or as a group.

2. Your students may wish to compose their own short message. A flashlight may be employed to convey the messages to the class: a short flash for a dot, and a longer flash for a dash. *Note*: The code shown is the International Morse Code which is an adaptation of Morse's original code.

Samuel Morse—Some Facts of His Life

❑ Life span: 1791–1872

❑ Education: Yale University; graduated in 1810

❑ His first successes in life were as an artist in England. He won several prizes for his painting and sculptures. One of his paintings is owned by the New York Public Library; another is hung in New York City Hall.

❑ Quite incidentally he heard that electricity could travel through wire as a current. If this is so, he thought, why couldn't messages be sent through wire? Almost immediately he went to work to make this idea a reality.

❑ After many hardships and disappointments he finally persuaded Congress to appropriate $30,000 to test the apparatus he had devised. A wire was strung between Washington, D.C., and Baltimore, Maryland. With spectators looking on at both ends of the line Morse himself tapped out a message in code, "What has God wrought?" From that moment on there was little doubt that the United States and the world had entered a new era of communication.

A New Way to Write the Alphabet

Samuel Morse created an alphabet of dots and dashes to use on his telegraph. On the telegraph a short click or buzz stood for a dot (·). A longer click or buzz would be a dash (-). Morse kept the code simple so that messages could be sent and received quickly and accurately. Here is the International Morse Code that came into use.

A · -	B - · · ·	C - · - ·	D - · ·
E ·	F · · - ·	G - - ·	H · · · ·
I · ·	J · - - -	K - · -	L · - · ·
M - -	N - ·	O - - -	P · - - ·
Q - - · -	R · - ·	S · · ·	T -
U · · -	V · · · -	W · - -	X - · · -
	Y - · - -	Z - - · ·	

Morse was famous for other things in addition to the telegraph and the code. To learn something else about this great inventor, work out the following message which is written in his code.

JAMES WATT AND ELI WHITNEY: TWO GREAT INVENTORS

The information and graphics on this page will be helpful in teaching the topic, "Improvements in Industry: Making Cloth."

Some Interesting Facts about James Watt

☑ He lived from 1736–1819. At about twenty years of age he became an instrument maker at the University of Glasgow.

☑ Along with being a mechanical inventor, he was a chemist and metallurgist.

☑ He was the first to use steam pipes for heating purposes. As the steam filled the pipes, steam valves let out the hot steam and, thus, warmed a room.

☑ The unit of power, "watt," as in a 60-watt bulb, is named after him.

Some Interesting Facts about Eli Whitney

☒ Whitney had to fight in courts for years to establish himself as the inventor of the cotton gin and the sole owner of the patent for it.

☒ It is highly probable that if the cotton gin had not been invented or if its invention had been delayed that slavery might have died a natural death.

☒ Along with the gin, Whitney was the "father" of mass production methods and the system of manufacturing known as interchangeable parts. Volumes have been written about the sociological effects of these inventions.

☒ Whitney invented a nail-making machine at the age of 13. He taught school for several years to earn enough money to attend Yale College

☒ During the War of 1812, Whitney's manufacturing methods served the country well by producing the guns that were needed. Pratt and Whitney, now known for its production of airplane engines and machine tools, traces its beginnings to Whitney.

Whitney's Cotton Gin

The information and diagram that follows will help your students understand the basic operations of a cotton gin.

Procedure

1. Make a transparency of the diagram, project it, and lead your students through the following steps and explanations.

a. Raw cotton, full of seeds, is fed into the gin.

b. The cotton is pulled into the machine by means of a toothed roller that is turned by a crank.

c. As the cotton is pulled into the gin the seeds fall to a bottom tray; they cannot pass through the grate.

d. A roller with brushes attached sweeps the cotton out of the gin.

e. The cotton is now ready to be spun into yarn.

2. *Notes*:

a. Modern gins are much larger and power operated; nevertheless, the basic principles of Whitney's gin are still used.

b. Numerous uses have been found for the cotton seeds; for example, cotton seed oil is pressed from the seeds and is used as salad dressing, while the seed husks make excellent food for animals.

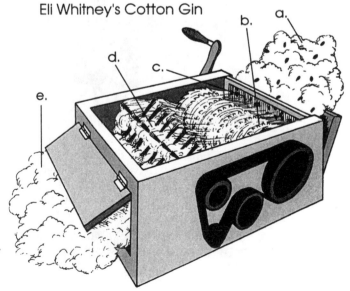

Eli Whitney's Cotton Gin

INVENTIONS: 1780–1870

A proliferation of inventions took place during the years between 1780 and 1870. The following suggested activities will help your students not only appreciate this fact, but also gain skill in classifying information and arranging events in chronological order on a graph (time line).

Procedure

1. *Classifying Information*

a. Write the following headings across the top of a chalkboard: *Industry, Transportation, Communication, Agriculture, Home.*

b. Have your students print the headings across the top of a piece of paper.

c. As you present each invention from the list that follows, ask how it should be classified. Then, write the invention in the proper column on the board with your students following suit.

2. *Completing a Time Line*

a. String a cord along one of the walls of the classroom.

b. Mark off sections of ten years each, starting with 1780.

c. Assign inventions to various children. Each invention is to be recorded on a card, including date and a symbolic sketch as below:

Safety Pin (1846)

Photography (1822)

d. Using clothes pins, hang the cards on the line at appropriate places. If two or more inventions have close dates, strings of different lengths may be hung from the horizontal cord.

Note: It should be realized that not all of the listed inventions were by Americans, although the majority were.

Invention	Date
Photography (C)	1822 *
Ice-Making Machine (H)	1850 *
Telegraph (C)	1840
Gasoline Engine (T)	1860
Typewriter (C)	1867
Bessemer Converter (steel) (I)	1855
Steamboat (T)	1785 *
Steam Locomotive (T)	1804
Corn Picker (A)	1850
McAdam Paving (roads) (T)	1815
Reaper (A)	1834
Pneumatic Tire (air-filled) (T)	1845
Bicycle (T)	1860
Dirigible Airship (T)	1852
Cotton Gin (A)	1793
Safety Match (H)	1844
Hot-air Balloon (T)	1783
Canning Foods (H)	1787 *
Portland Cement (I)	1824
Vulcanized Rubber (tires, rubber boots, etc.) (T)	1839
Lathe (cutting wood, metal) (I)	1800
Sewing Machine (H) (I)	1845
Glider (T)	1853
Safety Pin (H)	1846
Lawn Mower (H)	1831
Elevator (T)	1853

Note: * after a date indicates that the device may not have been invented by one individual at a particular time; rather, the device was perfected over a period of time by several people contributing to the whole. The safety pin, for example, was invented in a matter of hours, but the steamboat was brought to practicality over a period of time by various persons making contributions. For example, many people attribute the invention of the automobile to Henry Ford because his name is so closely associated with the vehicle. In actuality, dozens of inventors contributed to the final invention. Ford had the ability to use the inventions of others along with his own so as to produce a practical automobile.

ASPECTS OF THE INDUSTRIAL REVOLUTION

Following are some bits of information that may be helpful in teaching about the growth of industry in the United States between the years 1800 and 1860.

African-American Inventors

❑ There are few records of inventions by African-Americans before 1860. One reason for this is that inventions by slaves were credited to someone else, most likely their masters or employers, because slaves were not allowed to take out patents on their inventions and because they were not permitted to sign contracts.

❑ Henry Blair of Maryland was the first African-American to be granted a patent. In 1834 he received a patent for a corn harvester that he invented.

❑ The *Negro History Bulletin* for April, 1957, tells the story of Norbert Rillieux, a freedman, who was largely responsible for developing a process and the machinery which could convert sugar cane into sugar crystals more efficiently and more cheaply than had ever before been possible.

❑ The credit for starting New England on its way to becoming the shoemaking capital of the world in the late 1800's and early 1900's belongs to Jan Matzeliger. Matzeliger was not the typical African-American. He was born in South America, but his family migrated to the United States. Although he was young at the time, he was already a fine mechanic having been taught by his father.

Matzeliger's first job was in a shoemaking factory in Lynn, Massachusetts. At that time shoes were made by skilled craftsmen sitting at benches making one shoe at a time, piece-by-piece. He believed there had to be more efficient, less time-consuming, and less expensive ways to make shoes—and he found them.

Whenever he had spare time, which was not frequent, he labored over his shoe machine invention. He had very little money for parts such as iron gears or for tools to work with. Somehow, he managed to find what he needed.

One day after many disappointing attempts, he succeeded in making a model machine that accomplished the most difficult step in shoemaking—fitting the soles of shoes to the upper parts.

His machine was an instant success; it was the beginning of a revolution in the shoemaking process. Here are some of the results of Matzeliger's genius and determination:

● Shoes became far less expensive because the time and the costs of making shoes were greatly reduced.

● New jobs were created because the increase in the demand for shoes brought about an increase in the number of workers needed to make them.

Discussion Questions

What are the advantages of the system of manufacturing—interchangeable parts/assembly line—first developed by Eli Whitney?

1. The costs of manufacturing were decreased. For example, in making guns, machines that made barrels could be set up and used for that purpose only. Workers would become very skillful in working particular machines and could turn out many gun barrels in a short time. The same procedure could be used for making other parts.

2. Formerly, each gun was made by an individual gunsmith. No two guns were exactly alike. The parts could not be interchanged. For example, a trigger from one gun would not fit any other gun.

3. A supply of parts could be kept stored. Damaged or worn out parts could easily be replaced. For example, a soldier fighting in a battle could quickly replace a broken part of his gun, if necessary.

Coal

Few children today have ever seen real coal, much less touched it. But, it was coal—long before oil, hydroelectricity, nuclear power, or solar power—that fueled the industrial world. Steam engines could operate only if coal—wood was an inefficient substitute—furnished heat energy to boil water, generate steam and drive pistons that turned wheels and gears.

An interesting set of statistics follows: In 1820 the United States produced 15,000 tons of coal; in 1850, 7,000,000 tons, and in 1926, the peak year of coal production, 560,000,000 tons. Since that time the country's coal production has steadily decreased, largely because alternate fuels have been developed.

SECTION 14

Acquisitions in the Far West

THE UNION GROWS: TEXAS, CALIFORNIA, AND LANDS BETWEEN

The activity on the facing page will provide your students with an opportunity to find answers to specific questions in various kinds of reference books.

Procedure

1. Secure a variety of history books from the library or make an appointment for your class to use the library. Some of the books available should include standard basic texts, encyclopedias, almanacs, and specialized books on the topics.

2. Place your students in teams of two to find the answers to the questions. The questions do not necessarily have to be answered in the order that follows. Some of the questions are relatively simple to answer; others are more difficult and will require some deeper searching.

3. Give your students an overview on the acquisition of Texas, California, and other areas of the Southwest, but be sparing of details.

4. After you have allowed sufficient time for research—perhaps a period or two—review the findings of the students. Have them make corrections, if necessary. *Note*: Some of the questions would make effective "final test" items.

5. The major territorial acquisitions that "rounded out" the United States are shown below. Photocopies can be made and distributed. The map can be helpful in answering some of the research questions.

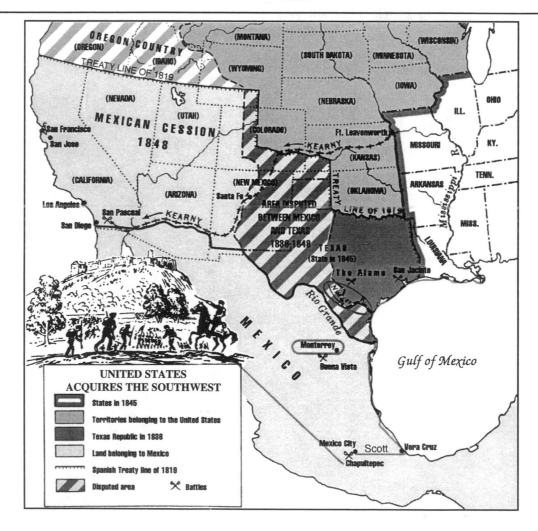

THE UNION GROWS: TEXAS, CALIFORNIA, AND LANDS BETWEEN

The Annexation of Texas

1. In the Texas fight for independence from Mexico, who were two famous men killed in the Battle of the Alamo? _____

2. What was the name of the Mexican general who led the fight against the Texans? _____

_____

3. What name is given to the battle which ended the war in favor of the Texans? _____

4. In what year did Texas become an independent country? _____

5. What name did Texans give to their new country? _____

Sketch a picture
of the flag the
Texans adopted.

6. Who was the first president of the new country?

_____

7. How many years was Texas an independent country before it was annexed? _____

8. What was the date of the annexation of Texas?

_____

9. What is the capital of Texas? _____

10. How many square miles of land does Texas occupy? _____

The War with Mexico

1. After the United States annexed Texas, the exact boundaries of the newly acquired land came into dispute. Mexico said that the _____ River was the southern boundary of Texas, but the United States said that the _____ River was the southern boundary.

2. Two Generals led the American troops in the war. One, _____ who had the nickname _____, landed his troops on Mexico's east coast and then marched over the mountains to capture Mexico City.

General _____, who had the nickname _____ and who later became president of the United States, invaded Mexico from the north. After crossing the Rio Grande River he marched south and captured the important city of _____.

3. What was the name of the peace treaty that settled the war between the United States and Mexico? _____

4. Name the six states that eventually were made from the territory we gained from Mexico.

_____

_____

_____

5. Fighting also took place in California. The American forces were led by Colonel _____. His mission was to cross the deserts of the Southwest and invade California. While he was struggling across the barren land, Americans in California declared their independence from Mexico. They called their new country the _____

_____

At the end of the war California was annexed by the United States. In 1850 California became a state.

6. One more piece of territory was acquired in the Southwest. It became known as the Gadsden Purchase. It was bought from Mexico in _____. The United States paid Mexico $_____ for the land. The land in the Gadsden Purchase completed the southern parts of two states: _____

_____ and _____.

GOLD IN CALIFORNIA

Where the Strike Occurred

One of those who received land from the Mexican government before the Mexican War was John A. Sutter. Sutter at one time had been a captain in the Swiss army, but he became a Mexican citizen in order to qualify for the grant. His dream was to create a great estate in the wilderness of California. He governed his 50,000-acre estate as though it were a separate little country and he was its ruler.

At one time there were more than 18,000 head of horses, cattle, mules, sheep, and oxen grazing on Sutter's land. Men were eager to work for him. His rule was firm but always fair and kind. Many of the Americans who crossed the mountains into California had good reason to be thankful to him. He not only allowed them to rest at his place and repair their equipment, but also helped them to obtain land on which to settle.

All this was to be changed. One day in January, 1848, gold was discovered on Sutter's property. Sutter tried to keep the discovery a secret. He knew that as soon as his workers heard the news, they would desert him to search for gold. His land would be overrun with gold seekers. Mining towns would spring up. Lawless men would be attracted by the gold. The estate he had created and the way of life he loved would be gone forever.

Who Were the Gold Seekers?

It took months for the news of the discovery to reach the eastern United States, but when it did thousands of people caught the "gold fever." They dropped whatever they were doing and made plans to go to California after hearing the magic words, "Gold in California!" The news traveled around the world. Before long, people from many countries including France, Australia, Great Britain, and even China were digging for gold in the rivers and streams of northern California.

It has been estimated that in February, 1849, there were some 54 Chinese in California. By December there were almost 800. One year later, 1850, there were about 4000. The Japanese, apparently, were not attracted by the reports of gold, possibly because the Japanese government discouraged emigration. By a twist of fate (the Mexican War), the gold was discovered just a few days before peace was concluded between the United States and Mexico. Thus, the thousands of Mexicans who came seeking their fortunes were actually entering a region that was formerly theirs. Many African-Americans, both slave and free, worked the diggings. Some of the free African-Americans later migrated to Oregon.

Routes to the Gold Fields

It took a full year from the time that gold was discovered for the first ship from New York loaded with would-be miners to reach San Francisco. Today, a jet plane could easily make the round trip from San Francisco to New York in twelve hours.

One way to get to the gold fields was to sail around the southern tip of South America. A fast ship with favorable winds could make the trip in four to five months. The journey was hazardous and difficult, especially around Cape Horn.

Some of those heading for California travelled by boat and land. They sailed from the eastern coast of the United States to the Isthmus of Panama. Then, they crossed the isthmus by mule or on foot. Hundreds died from malaria before they got to the Pacific coast. Once they reached the Pacific, they took another ship north to San Francisco.

A third way to reach California was to cross the United States on horseback or wagon. Many who were heading to Oregon abandoned their plans when they heard the news of the gold strike, and turned southwest toward California. The trail was studded with skeletons of animals and graves of unfortunate travelers. The worst part of the trip was across the deserts of the Southwest and the daunting heights of the Sierra Nevada mountains.

Name: _____ Date: _____

GOLD IN CALIFORNIA

Gold Seekers' Routes to California

1. Complete the labeling of the map as follows:

A. North Atlantic
B. South Atlantic
C. South Pacific
D. North Pacific
E. New York
F. San Francisco
G. Isthmus of Panama
H. North America
I. South America

2. Read from the map the distance and time (approximate) from New York to San Francisco, and record below.

a. *Transcontinental Route:*

Distance _____

Time _____

b. *Isthmus of Panama Route:*

Distance _____

Time _____

c. *Around South America Route:*

Distance _____

Time _____

3. What was the shortest route in distance? _____

_____

What was the fastest route in time? _____

_____

4. Make your map easier to read by drawing blue "waves" [≋] in all the water areas. Be careful not to interfere with your lettering.

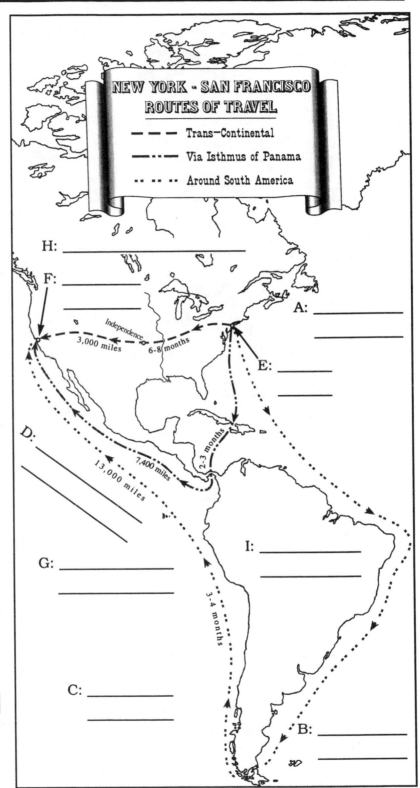

NEW YORK - SAN FRANCISCO ROUTES OF TRAVEL

– – – Trans-Continental
–·–·– Via Isthmus of Panama
·· ·· ·· Around South America

H: _____

F: _____

A: _____

_____

E: _____

Independence
3,000 miles   6-8 months

D. _____

7,400 miles

2-3 months

13,000 miles

I: _____

_____

G: _____

_____

3-4 months

C: _____

_____

B: _____

_____

DIARY OF A FORTY-NINER

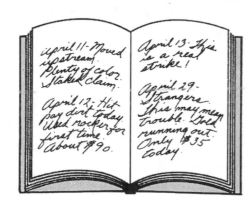

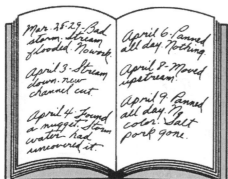

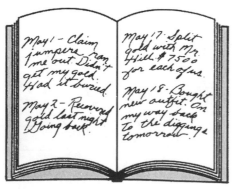

The miner's diary at the left contains several special terms used by the Forty-niners. These terms are listed in the box below. Write the number of each term before its correct definition below the box.

1 grubstake	2 diggings	3 pan	4 color
5 nugget	6 salt pork	7 claim	8 pay dirt
9 rocker	10 strike	11 claim jumper	

_____ An area of unsettled land restricted to the use of the miner who marked it off and "claimed" it

_____ A miner who tries to seize another's claim

_____ A trace of gold in a miner's pan

_____ Gold fields; a place where gold is found

_____ To furnish food and supplies to a miner in return for a share of any gold he might find

_____ A lump of gold; found in various sizes

_____ To separate gold from sand and gravel by washing and shaking the mixture in a pan until the gold particles settle to the bottom

_____ A mixture of sand and gravel containing gold

_____ A simple machine used to separate gold from sand and gravel by rocking the mixture

_____ Pork, heavily salted to prevent spoiling

_____ A large quantity of gold found in one place

Read the diary again and answer the following questions.

1. On what date did the miner first see color? _____

2. When did he find the first nugget? _____

3. When did he know he had a strike? _____

4. How did he fool the claim jumpers? _____

5. What was the total value of the gold he mined? _____

HISTORIC CONVERSATIONS

The couples listed below would certainly have had interesting conversations if time and place had allowed. What might the first named person say to the other in an imaginary conversation? In the space before the question write the number of the sentence from the bottom of the page that best shows a possible conversation between the two. Each of the two persons have something in common with the other.

_____ John Cabot to Leif Ericsson

_____ John Smith to the first Jamestown settlers

_____ Queen Elizabeth to Sir Francis Drake

_____ Thomas Jefferson to Lewis and Clark

_____ Alexander Hamilton to George Washington

_____ Hernando Cortez to his men after landing in Mexico

_____ Christopher Columbus to Ferdinand Magellan

_____ Sacajawea to Narcissa Whitman

_____ A French soldier to his sergeant (Battle of Quebec)

_____ Samuel de Champlain to Jacques Cartier

_____ Peter Stuyvesant to today's mayor of New York City

_____ Henry Hudson to Sieur de La Salle

_____ Cyrus McCormick to Robert Fulton

1. "I have crossed the mountains on foot and by horse, and you have crossed them with a wagon."

2. "You were first; I but followed your path and went a little further."

3. "There is no one to save us but ourselves; we will starve if we do not provide our own food."

4. "You took a great risk by sailing west across the Pacific Ocean to escape the Spaniards, but your resourcefulness saved you."

5. "Your expedition and what you have learned will encourage others to follow."

6. "Sir, I have good news: Our winning the Battle of Saratoga has encouraged the French to aid us."

7. "Had you not taken sides in a war that was not your own, you would have lived to enjoy a hero's welcome in Portugal."

8. "Never have they seen men on horses, or ships with great white sails; they will think we are gods."

9. "Our ships had cabins and other comforts; even so, it was difficult to sail across the stormy North Atlantic. How you did it in your open boats tests my imagination."

10. "Sir, never in my wildest dreams did I ever dream that the city you govern would become one of the world's largest."

11. "Just as the river I explored has been named for me, so should the river you explored be named for you."

12. "I helped the farmers of the country harvest their crops, and you have helped them to bring the fruits of their labors to market."

13. "Sir, I thought I heard stones tumbling down the secret path, and whispered commands."

THE OREGON COUNTRY IS PEACEFULLY DIVIDED

Suggestions for Teaching the Facing Page: The Oregon Country Is Peacefully Divided

1. *Background*

There were two major motivations for American settlement of the Oregon Country. First, eastern missionaries of both the Protestant (Methodist and Presbyterian) and Roman Catholic churches were eager to convert the Indians of the region to Christianity. Second, by 1840 much of the cheap land of the old Northwest Territory had been gobbled up. Where was there to go but the undeveloped Oregon Country where land was cheap and even free, where the soil was fertile, and the climate was excellent? *Note*: In 1843 the 100,000 Americans in Oregon, true to the American tradition of self-government, drew up a constitution to serve them until Oregon became a part of the United States.

Wagon trains to Oregon generally began in Independence, Missouri, on the Mississippi River. Most would-be settlers travelled in the company of others; a lone wagon was highly vulnerable to Indian attacks. Also, if a wagon broke down, an accident occurred, or food ran out there were others in the caravan who were willing and able to help.

Caravans began their 2000 mile journey in the spring—as early as possible. It was crucial to get an early start for two reasons: (1) pasture would be available for the horses and oxen that pulled the wagons, and (2) the Rocky Mountains were all but impassable in winter. At all costs, it was necessary to climb over them before the heavy snows of late autumn and winter.

Once caravans had passed through the 7500 feet-above-sea level South Pass that began the journey across the Rockies, the journey increased in difficulty; at least, the Great Plains had been relatively flat. The country was rough and there were more mountains to conquer. All too frequently animals that pulled the wagons would lie down never to get up again.

Once on the Oregon Trail, settlers could follow it easily. Wagon wheels wore ruts in the earth so deep that some are visible even today. As the distance from Independence increased, so did the fatigue of the animals. One solution to this problem was to lighten the loads that had to be pulled. Countless pieces of furniture, broken wagon wheels and axles, and other precious belongings were discarded and strewn along the trail. Other sad markers of the path were the many mounds of stones with crude crosses that told of those who had died along the way and were buried in a shallow graves.

2. *Discussion*

Place your students in problem-solving situations by having them consider the general question, "What kinds of difficulties would the pioneers have encountered on a wagon trip from the Mississippi River to the Oregon Country?" Following are some specific questions that can be asked to spur their thinking:

A. What kind of food would the pioneers bring to help them through the up-to-six months journey? How could they supplement their supplies? (*Food brought: flour, corn meal, bacon, dried fruits such as apples and peaches, dried vegetables such as beans, salt, tea. Food obtained on the trail: buffalo, occasional deer, and, in desperate situations, a slaughtered domestic animal or one that died on the trail*)

B. How would the wheels and axles of the wagons be greased? (*Tallow from the fat of hogs and cattle*)

C. What fuel could be used for cooking and warmth in regions that were virtually treeless? (*Dried buffalo dung, called "buffalo chips," from the millions of animals that roamed the plains*)

D. Since there were no bridges, how were wagons transported across streams? (*Ropes attached, sides chinked with pitch, then floated across*)

E. What could be done to help sick people? (*Very little: no doctors, primitive medicines; surgical help almost nonexistent in cases such as appendicitis; diseases such as measles, smallpox, and typhus left to run their courses*)

F. How were wagons controlled when going down long hills and mountain sides? (*A partial help: locking wheels with brakes or inserted poles; a negative factor: uncontrollable skids that sometimes overrode draft animals in front*)

G. How were the caravans protected from hostile Indian raids? (*Wagons drawn into a circle as a barricade, children put into wagon beds, men shooting rifles, women loading rifles, water readied to douse fires started by flaming arrows*)

Name: _____ Date: _____

THE OREGON COUNTRY IS PEACEFULLY DIVIDED

Lewis and Clark were not the first Americans to reach the Oregon Country. Captain Robert Gray had sailed his ship, the *Columbia*, from Boston to the Oregon coast in 1792. It was Gray who discovered and named the great Columbia River. Gray 's discoveries and Lewis and Clark's explorations gave the United States a strong claim to the Oregon Country. Moreover, by 1811 Americans were fur trading with the Indians there.

The United States was not the only nation that was interested in Oregon. The British had explored much of the region, established trading posts and forts, and carried on fur trading activities.

A clash between the United States and Great Britain seemed certain. Fortunately, in 1818 before serious trouble started, the two nations reached an agreement. For a ten-year period people from both countries would settle in the region with equal rights.

More and more American settlers began moving to Oregon. Most of them travelled there in covered wagons along the Oregon Trail. Most of the people settled in the fertile valley of the Willamette River of the Oregon Country. There they built their homes, plowed their fields, and raised their families. Before long, they wanted the same rights and privileges they had enjoyed as American citizens in their former homes. They thought that the Oregon Country should become part of the United States.

Fortunately, the United States was able to work out a peaceful settlement with Great Britain. A treaty in 1846 divided the area between the two nations. All the land north of the 49th parallel, plus the island of Vancouver, was to be British. The land south of the line was to be American.

1. Following are several facts mentioned in the narrative. Briefly identify or tell the significance of each.

➔ Ship *Columbia*: _____

_____

➔ Willamette River: _____

_____

➔ 1846: _____

_____

➔ 49th parallel: _____

_____

2. On or from the map:

❑ Draw a circle around the Willamette River.

❑ Draw a heavy line on the 49th parallel.

❑ What three states were made from the Oregon Country?

_____

❑ Note the key to the map. Draw the lines on the map that show Great Britain's part of the 1846 treaty; then, do the same for the United States.

❑ What country claimed the land south of the Oregon Country? _

140

SECTION 15

Fundamental Issues Threaten the Union

HARRIET TUBMAN AND SOJOURNER TRUTH: FREEDOM FIGHTERS

Suggestions

The information on this page may be presented to your students and serve as motivation and preparation for completing the facing student application page.

．．．．．．．．．．．．．．．．．．．．．．．．．．．．．．．．

On July 12, 1914, the citizens of the city of Auburn, New York, dedicated a bronze tablet to an ex-slave. Here is part of the message that was printed on the tablet:

> In memory of Harriet Tubman
> born a slave in Maryland about 1821.
> Died in Auburn, N.Y., March 10th, 1913,
> called the Moses of her people
> during the Civil War. With rare
> courage she led over three hundred
> Negroes up from slavery to freedom,
> and rendered invaluable service
> as nurse and spy.

Also on the tablet was one of Harriet's favorite sayings, "On my underground railroad I never run my train off the track and I never lost a passenger."

What was the Underground Railroad to which Harriet referred? It was not a railroad, and it was not underground. It was a secret organization of brave Americans who had one thing in common: hatred of slavery. Its membership was made up of white Northerners and Southerners and freed or escaped African-Americans. The organization had one main objective: to help slaves gain their liberty.

Here is how the Underground Railroad worked. Suppose that slaves wanted to run away to freedom. They would learn that if they took a certain route north they would eventually reach a free state or Canada. They would also learn that at certain places along the line, or "track," they could expect help. These stopping places were called stations. The friendly people at the stations would give them food, clothing, and shelter. A "conductor," or guide, would help the runaway slaves, or "passengers," to get to the next station.

Travelling or working on the Underground Railroad was extremely dangerous. Most travel took place at night. Often, when fugitives reached a station they would find that they could not stay there. Perhaps law enforcement officers were watching the place. Perhaps the people at the station had been imprisoned. In spite of the danger, however, it is estimated that as many as 75,000 slaves reached freedom on the Underground Railroad.

Harriet Tubman was one of the railroad's conductors. She may have been the most daring agent in the secret organization. After she had gained her own freedom, she returned time after time to slave territory. She led many slaves to freedom, including her own mother and father. Rewards offered for her capture totaled more than $40,000.

Harriet Tubman also played an important role during the Civil War as a scout and spy for the Union forces. Many times she discovered Confederate strongholds and then led Union troops to the locations.

Although she was only five feet tall, Harriet Tubman had great strength and determination. She was willing to risk any danger. Harriet knew how precious freedom was. Yet, she was willing to risk her own freedom to help others gain theirs.

Another great name in the history of the movement to abolish slavery is that of Sojourner Truth, who was born in 1797. There is a wonderful book about Sojourner written by Jacqueline Bernard and entitled *Journey Toward Freedom*. Passages read to your students are sure to capture and hold their interest.

One incident related in the book tells of the time Sojourner was at a camp meeting in an open field where she was scheduled to speak. A gang of rough hoodlums came to the meeting determined to break it up. At first, Sojourner was frightened and hid behind some boxes in a tent. But she felt shame for her fear. So she alone, with no one to support her, left the tent, climbed up on the platform and addressed the mob. She won them over to her side with her hymn singing and earnest preaching. Whenever she stopped they asked her again and again to continue, for she had a beautiful voice.

Finally, Sojourner exhausted to the point of collapse asked the men if they would leave the meeting in peace. As the author of *Journey Toward Freedom* writes, "She closed her eyes wearily. . . She heard a swishing in the grass. It was the feet of her wild young men, sweeping in a solid pack (away) from the field."

Name: _____ Date: _____

HARRIET TUBMAN: LIBERATOR, ARMY SCOUT, AND SPY

To do:

Following are some facts about Harriet Tubman and her work in freeing slaves. With which picture is a particular fact most closely related? Write the number of the fact on the line at the bottom of each picture.

Facts about Harriet Tubman

1. The days were long and hot; her blistered hands became tough.

2. On surprise raids she guided gunboats up rivers.

3. Whole families—men, women, and children—tried to escape from slavery.

4. Along with working in the fields, Harriet performed other chores such as splitting wood.

5. Thorns tore her clothing; vines tripped her as she stumbled through woods.

6. In talks with Quakers she made up her mind to help others escape.

7. Runaways carried their few things in bags and sacks.

8. Army officers trusted and respected her courage and knowledge.

9. She made 19 trips south so as to lead 300 slaves to freedom.

10. Once she arrived in a free state—Pennsylvania—Quakers sheltered her.

11. Harriet had heard that sympathetic people helped slaves escape. She decided to escape alone.

12. Harriet was not well-suited to housework, so she was put to work in the fields.

13. When using roads, runaways had to stay out of sight.

14. Harriet would first scout a river and get to know every twist and turn.

15. Harriet carried a pistol and was ready to use it if she had to.

16. She slept in caves and bushes during the day and followed the North Star at night.

17. She listened carefully to descriptions of the "Underground Railroad."

142

ROLE-PLAYING HISTORICAL EVENTS

Page 25 of this book offers some rationale and information about role playing as a technique for teaching American history. The situations described below can be dramatized so as to encourage student insight about historical events. Before having your students engage in the role-playing, project the pictures via a transparency and read the descriptions orally.

Harriet Tubman Advises a Group of Escapees

The event takes place in a clearing in deep woods. Several African-Americans—men, women, children—are standing and some are sitting on logs. Harriet Tubman is standing in the center of the clearing.

Harriet is explaining procedures and precautions to the people whom she is leading to freedom: how the group will be conducted along the underground railroad, how to guage distance-and-time from station-to-station, how to approach a station and determine whether or not it is safe to enter. She also tells them that if they are captured they will be severely punished. When they reach a free state they will still have to be careful about being apprehended (the Fugitive Slave Law of 1850 provided that captured runaway slaves be returned south).

After she has completed her talk, two or three of the group ask questions. Another person stands and says he wants to return to the plantation; he is frightened. Harriet makes it very clear that turning back is strictly forbidden; that he could be tortured into revealing the locations of stations, etc.

Should We Go to Oregon?

A father (who is a member of the clergy), a mother, two teenagers (a boy about 17, and a girl about 16 years of age), and two younger children are sitting at a table and discussing whether or not they should migrate to Oregon. Various pro and con arguments are advanced. Some of the arguments against the move include the long distance, the possible dangers of sickness and accidents, the necessary loss of their comfortable home. The teenage girl is concerned about leaving her boyfriend; they are planning to get married. The teenage boy wants to study to be a lawyer. The two younger children are concerned about Indians, wild animals, leaving their friends. The mother's family lives near them, and she will miss them.

Some of the arguments for the move include the availability of cheap land, the fertility of the soil, the adventure and excitement of the journey, and the possibility of starting a mission.

The role-players should be encouraged to discuss some of the points that are brought up for example, the young childrens' fear of Indians might be lessened by pointing out there would be several hundred people in the wagon train, all well armed.

Note: As an alternative to the role-playing, have your students each write a paragraph describing one of the scenes above. Then have them assume the identify of one person in the scene and write a paragraph describing that person's reactions to the situation. The completed narratives could then be read to the class.

Name: _____ Date: _____

POPULATION STATISTICS THROUGH 1860

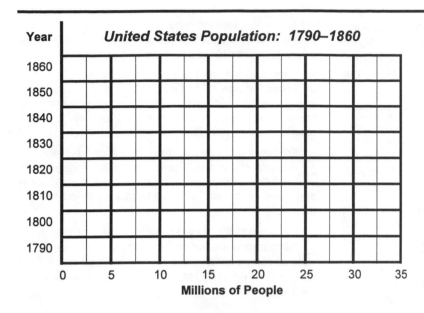

United States Population: 1790–1860

Year | Millions of People (0, 5, 10, 15, 20, 25, 30, 35)

1860, 1850, 1840, 1830, 1820, 1810, 1800, 1790

Population Growth

The population of the United States grew tremendously in the years 1790–1860, as shown in the figures below. Show the same information on the incomplete bar graph on the left.

U. S. Population: 1790-1860*			
1790	4,000,000	1830	13,000,000
1800	5,000,000	1840	17,000,000
1810	7,000,000	1850	23,000,000
1820	10,000,000	1860	31,000,000
* Rounded to nearest million			

Population Centers Change and Move

Improvements in transportation brought great changes in the location of the country's population. Cities that did not exist in 1800 were important by 1850. Cities that were once well known became less important. Also, no longer were all the major cities located along the Atlantic coast.

The graphs at the right will help you understand some of the changes.

1. How many of the ten largest cities in 1800 were near or on the Atlantic coast? _____
How many in 1850? _____

2. What cities on or near the Atlantic coast were listed in 1800 but not in 1850? _____

_____

_____

3. What was the approximate population of New York in 1800? _____
in 1850? _____

4. Approximately how many more people lived in Philadelphia in 1850 than in 1800? _____

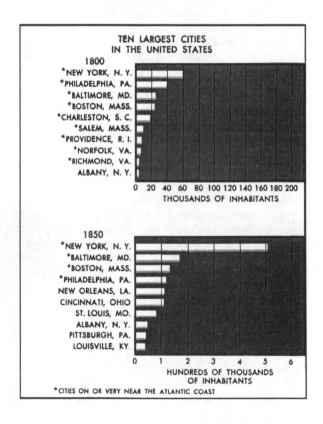

TEN LARGEST CITIES IN THE UNITED STATES

1800
*NEW YORK, N. Y.
*PHILADELPHIA, PA.
*BALTIMORE, MD.
*BOSTON, MASS.
*CHARLESTON, S. C.
*SALEM, MASS.
*PROVIDENCE, R. I.
*NORFOLK, VA.
*RICHMOND, VA.
ALBANY, N. Y.

0 20 40 60 80 100 120 140 160 180 200
THOUSANDS OF INHABITANTS

1850
*NEW YORK, N. Y.
*BALTIMORE, MD.
*BOSTON, MASS.
*PHILADELPHIA, PA.
NEW ORLEANS, LA.
CINCINNATI, OHIO
ST. LOUIS, MO.
ALBANY, N. Y.
PITTSBURGH, PA.
LOUISVILLE, KY.

0 1 2 3 4 5 6
HUNDREDS OF THOUSANDS OF INHABITANTS
*CITIES ON OR VERY NEAR THE ATLANTIC COAST

FREDERICK DOUGLASS: ABOLITIONIST, WRITER

Frederick Douglass was one of the most courageous and effective persons to fight the evils of slavery. The story told in the paragraphs that follow and the illustrations on the next page will help you understand his life.

1. Each of the paragraphs that follows is related to one of the pictures that shows a part of Douglass's life. On the line at the beginning of each paragraph write the number of the picture to which it is most closely related. Use context clues and natural sequences to help you.

When he was about seven years old he was removed ___ from his grandmother's house and plantation to a different plantation. Life there was very hard. He was always cold in winter because clothes and bedding were very scarce; he tried to keep warm by sleeping in a closet. He was frequently beaten for the slightest offense, and he never got enough to eat. (*par. 1*)

Frederick became friends with people who hated ___ slavery and who worked to eliminate it. He spoke out against slavery constantly. Time after time he was beaten by thugs who opposed his beliefs, but he never gave in to them for his own safety. Eventually, friends and supporters collected enough money to buy his freedom from his old master. (*par. 2*)

Frederick decided he must escape or die in the effort. ___ Some friends helped him disguise himself as a sailor; African-American sailors had much more freedom of movement than ordinary slaves. After many close calls he finally made it to a free state—New York. Later, he went to Massachusetts where he took a new name: Frederick Douglass. (*par. 3*)

When Tommy, the young boy Frederick was to look ___ after, was being taught to read, Frederick would watch and listen carefully. Tommy's mother taught Frederick as though he was her own son. However, when Tommy's father found out that a slave was being taught, he got very angry and forbade his wife to continue the teaching. (*par. 4*)

When Frederick was about ten years old he was ___ brought to Baltimore to "take care" of the young son of a wealthy family and to do certain domestic chores. He was relatively well treated in this situation. He experienced comforts of living he had never known before. (*par. 5*)

Frederick spoke out not only for slaves, but also for ___ all people who were treated unequally and denied their rights. This included women who were denied the right to vote, Indians who were being cheated, and people of different nationalities and religions. He became a friend and advisor to President Lincoln.(*par. 6*)

Luck ran out for Frederick. His master died, and ___ Frederick was sold to a new master who was cruel beyond belief. Frederick resisted the master's efforts to break his spirit and was beaten again and again for his rebelliousness. (*par. 7*)

Frederick's interest in reading continued. He found ___ newspapers in trash cans. When he needed help understanding words, it was given by neighborhood children who liked him. He became a very good reader. (*par. 8*)

Frederick Bailey (later Douglass) was born on a plan- ___ tation on the eastern shore of Chesapeake Bay in the state of Maryland. As near as can be known, the year was 1817. In his early years he was lovingly cared for by his grandmother.(*par. 9*)

2. Each of the following sentences is closely related to the main idea of one of the paragraphs above and adds detail to the main idea. On the line before each sentence write the number of the paragraph to which the sentence best belongs. *Paragraph numbers are at the end of each paragraph.*

Then he was "free at last" to come and go and speak ___ as he pleased.

He found discarded newspapers and books to read, ___ but he kept them hidden.

He seldom saw his mother because she was a slave ___ on a distant plantation.

One time after he fought his master and defeated ___ him, his master hired him out to other plantation owners because he didn't want his other slaves to know that Frederick had humbled him.

He said teaching a slave to read would give him ___ "dangerous" ideas about freedom.

To bring his ideas to more people's attention, he ___ published a newspaper called *North Star*, and he also became active in the Underground Railroad.

Tommy's mother made Frederick feel cared for and ___ respected.

He was always hungry—so hungry that he ___ scrambled for the crumbs that fell from the table.

With a new name it would be harder for slave hunters ___ to trace him.

145

FREDERICK DOUGLASS: ABOLITIONIST, WRITER

Events in the Life of Frederick Douglass—Fighter for Freedom

The picture story on this page shows some important events in the life of Frederick Douglass. The pictures are numbered in the order in which the events occurred, that is, chronologically.

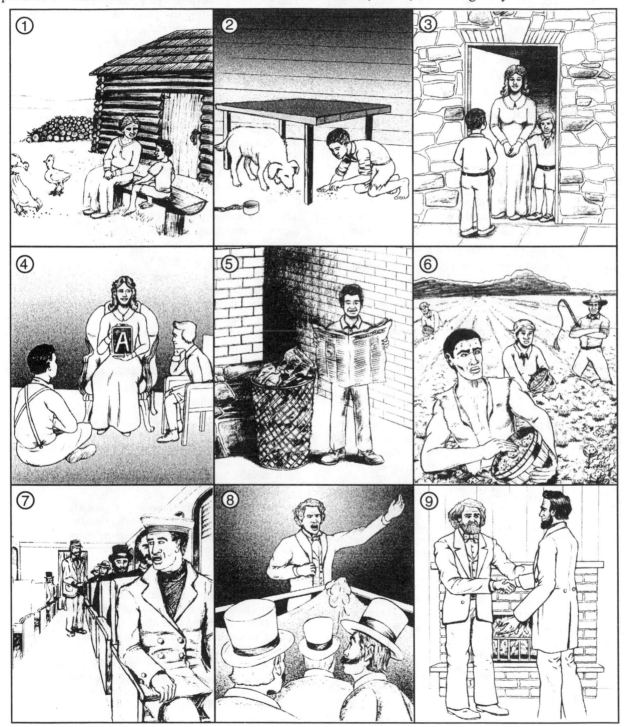

UNCLE TOM'S CABIN: A NOVEL ABOUT THE EVILS OF SLAVERY

The novel *Uncle Tom's Cabin,* by Harriet Beecher Stowe, is a long one, some 500 pages in the Library of America edition. It is, no doubt, too long and difficult for the average student to read. Nevertheless, the story should be known. It tells the story of slavery in graphic, yet eloquent, words. It is so moving a story that in its first year, 1852, it sold some 300,000 copies, a phenomenal amount in those days. There is no question that the book had a profound influence in turning public opinion against slavery.

Suggestions for Teaching

1. Orally read the chronological synopsis of *Uncle Tom's Cabin* that follows. Elaborate and discuss sequences as they are met. A copy of the book would be useful, especially to read selected passages.

2. Photocopy the accompanying student application page. Instruct your students to write a short essay about one of the illustrations. Here are some suggestions:

❑ Crossing the Ohio River from Kentucky into Ohio: Describe the scene, including a paragraph each on the river, the pursuers, and Eliza with her child.

❑ The fight at the stone fort: One paragraph each on a dialogue between the runaways and the slave catchers, the fighting itself, and what might have happened after the fight.

Synopsis of *Uncle Tom's Cabin*

Note: As the story opens, Tom (Uncle), Eliza Harris, and her little boy, Harry, are the slaves of a kind master.

1. Master had fallen into debt and he was going to sell Tom, Eliza, and Harry to settle his debts. Eliza overheard that she and little Harry would be sold to different masters. She knew that if that happened, she probably would never see Harry again.

2. Eliza decided that she and Harry would run away. Eliza, carrying Harry, stopped at Uncle Tom's cabin and warned him that he was to be sold. Tom told Eliza that he would not run away. Eliza said that she would try to make it on her own even though she knew it was winter, the dangers were great, and she would be severely punished if she were captured.

3. Eliza ran for the Ohio River; once across she and little Harry would be safe. The river was choked with ice floes. But, Eliza was desperate. Holding Harry tight in her arms she jumped from floe to floe and made it to the Ohio shore. The men who were chasing her with dogs couldn't believe that what she had done was possible.

4. A kind man pulled Eliza and her child up the river bank. The man told her that people who lived in a nearby farm would help her. She made her way to the farm where she was warmly welcomed and given food. They told her they would

help her escape to Canada by means of the Underground Railroad.

5. While Eliza and Harry were hidden and protected, Uncle Tom was being transported on a boat to the South where he was to be sold at a slave auction. On the boat was a charming young white girl, Eva, who made friends with Tom. One day Eva fell overboard. Tom dived into the water and rescued her. In gratitude, Eva's father bought Tom from the slave trader. Tom then became Eva's guardian and servant in her father's beautiful New Orleans home.

6. Eliza's husband, George, had lived on a different plantation than his wife. He, too, was determined to find freedom or die trying. His hope was that he would be reunited with Eliza and little Harry in Canada. After a number of dangerous adventures when he was almost captured, he found shelter in one of the very stations where Eliza and Harry were hidden. They were overjoyed to be together.

7. The Quakers who were sheltering Eliza, George, and little Harry learned that slave catchers had found out where the fugitives were hiding. The small family, two other slaves who were also runaways, and a brave Quaker man quickly boarded a carriage pulled by fast horses.

8. The runaways were armed and determined to fight rather than surrender. Because their pursuers were gaining on them, they stopped their carriage and scrambled up a hill to a natural rock fort and confronted their pursuers. In the fight that followed, the leader of the slave catchers was wounded. His cowardly followers fled and left him to die. The runaways took pity on him, loaded him in their carriage and continued on to the last station. They were sheltered there while arrangements were made to take them across Lake Erie in a steamboat to Canada and freedom.

9. Meanwhile, Tom's new master was kind to him. Little Eva loved Tom, helped him to learn to read and write better, and spent many hours reading and discussing the Bible with him. But, Eva became very sick with a childhood disease. Each day she became weaker until, finally, she died in her father's arms.

10. After Eva died, her father had a great change of heart about slavery; he saw it for the evil thing that it was. He resolved to free Tom and his other slaves. Before he could do that he was stabbed to death while trying to stop a brawl between two men.

11. From that time on Tom's life became increasingly difficult. He was put up for sale at a slave auction, and he was bought by a cruel, savage, and coarse man, Simon Legree. He whipped Tom time-and-time again. One day he ordered Tom to whip another slave, but Tom would not do that; he would rather die than follow such an order. Because Tom refused, he was whipped until he was senseless and bleeding slowly to death. Tom lingered on for a short while, but his injuries were so great that he died. Tom's last thoughts were that he would be free at last, but free in Heaven.

147

UNCLE TOM'S CABIN: SCENES FROM THE NOVEL

Name: _____   Date: _____

THE FUGITIVE SLAVE ACT OF 1850

Prior to 1860 the two great regions of the country, "the North" and "the South," were finding it increasingly difficult to agree on several matters. One of the causes of constant trouble was the issue of slavery. In an effort to resolve some of the differences between the regions, the Compromise of 1850 was passed. As you may know, in a compromise each side "gives in" a little in order to solve a problem.

One of the parts of the Compromise was the Fugitive Slave Act of 1850. This act was an attempt to calm Southerners who were suffering financial loss because many of their slaves were escaping to the North with help from people who lived there.

Here are some of the provisions of the Fugitive Slave Act:

1. Runaway slaves were to be returned to the state or territory from which they had escaped.

2. All citizens were to aid in carrying out the law; for example, citizens had to assist in the capture of slaves.

3. Anyone who in any way aided a slave to escape would be fined $1000 and imprisoned for six months for each slave helped. Of course, this meant that anyone who was a part of the Underground Railroad would be severely punished.

Attempts to enforce the law were strongly resisted by those who hated slavery. They especially disliked "slave hunters"—who collected rewards for captured slaves—and officers of the law whose responsibility it was to apprehend slaves. Many runaway slaves were, themselves, prepared to fight to the death rather than return to the South.

To do:

1. Suppose you were an ordinary citizen who was called upon to help capture a runaway slave under the provisions of the Fugitive Slave Act. Circle the sentence that tells what you would be expected to do.

An officer attempts to arrest a runaway

2. Suppose you were a member of the Underground Railroad. As such you helped nine slaves to escape. What would be your punishment, if caught?

_____

3. Write a sentence that might tell what each numbered person in the picture was thinking at the time of the event.

① Officer with badge and stick: _____

_____

② Man holding warrant that gives legal permission to arrest the runaway: _____

_____

③ Man standing in front of the runaway: _____

_____

④ Boy with hoop and stick: _____

_____

⑤ The runaway: _____

_____

149

JOHN BROWN'S RAID ON A UNITED STATES ARSENAL

The following account of John Brown's raid would be of interest to your students. It may be orally read by the instructor or, perhaps, by a student. At the end of the reading questions could be raised: Was John a hero or was he a criminal? Was he justified in taking the law into his own hands? Did the raid do any good? What might have been some positive results of a successful slave rebellion? Some negatives? How might Martin Luther King, an advocate of nonviolence, have reacted to the event?

An Attempt to Start a Slave Rebellion

For most abolitionists, the Dred Scott decision did not settle the slavery issue. Some became even more determined to find ways to get rid of slavery. They immediately went to work to elect men who would represent their point of view in Congress. Or, they contacted those who were already in positions of power and let them know how they felt about the slavery issue. Some of the abolitionists were willing to go beyond these accepted ways of bringing about changes.

A very determined abolitionist, John Brown, took the law into his own hands. He had been deeply involved in the trouble in Kansas and had not hesitated to kill those who opposed his way of thinking. His plan was to start a rebellion among the slaves against their masters. He thought once the revolt was started, it would spread throughout the South.

Brown planned to make the rugged mountains of western Virginia the headquarters for his operations. From there he would ride forth from time to time, attack isolated plantations, and free the slaves. He would arm the slaves and they would become part of his growing army. Eventually, he hoped to have a force that nothing, not even the United States Army, could successfully oppose.

First, Brown needed guns and ammunition. He decided to capture the United States arsenal at Harper's Ferry, Virginia. On the night of October 16, 1859, he and his followers, five of whom were African-Americans, attacked the lightly guarded supply depot where the supplies and weapons he wanted were stored. The arsenal was easily taken. Then, Brown's men moved to some nearby plantations. They freed about thirty slaves, who were brought back to the arsenal.

The alarm went out and United States troops arrived at the scene the next day. Ten of Brown's men were killed. Brown and some of his followers were captured. Brown and six of his men were brought to trial for treason. They were all found guilty and were hanged.

When he was condemned to death, Brown said the following to the court: "This court acknowledges, as I suppose, the validity of the law of God. I see a book here which I suppose to be the Bible, or at least the New Testament. That teaches me that all things whatsoever I would that men should do to me, I should do even so to them. It teaches me, further, to remember them that are in bonds, as bound with them. I endeavored to act up to that instruction. . . . I believe that to have interfered as I have done as I have always freely admitted I have done in behalf of His despised poor, was not wrong but right."

Brown's raid, his capture, trial, and death received great publicity. Many Americans expressed shock and disapproval of his attempt to start a slave rebellion. Other people, both Northerners and Southerners, took advantage of the sensational affair and stirred up more feeling. John Brown and his raid increased the tension that already existed between the North and the South. Americans wondered when the final split would come. As things turned out, they did not have long to wait.

THE ELECTION OF 1860

This page presents concise information on the Election of 1860. The facing page offers a student activity that will help students understand the country's geographical division following the formation of the Confederacy. Also, a work-study skill is suggested: transferring information from one source (a map) to another source (a table).

Who were the Presidential candidates in the election of 1860? What were the platforms, or programs, of the parties that backed them?

The *Northern Democrats* were led by Stephen A. Douglas, who had sponsored the Kansas-Nebraska Act. He and his party believed that the people of each territory, not Congress, should decide whether or not their territory would tolerate slavery.

The *Southern Democrats* were led by John C. Breckinridge of Kentucky. The position of this party was that slavery should be allowed to expand to all states and territories. Furthermore, the party insisted that it was the duty of the national government to protect the institution of slavery, wherever it existed.

The *Constitutional Union* party took a middle-of-the-road approach to the slavery question. This party believed that problems regarding slavery should be solved by compromise and negotiation. This party's candidate was John Bell of Tennessee, a Southerner. In its attempt to appeal to both the North and South, this party chose a New Englander to run for the office of Vice-President.

The *Northern Republican* stand on the slavery question was that there should be no extension of slavery into any new territory. It should be noted, however, that their platform did not demand the abolition of slavery in the states where it already existed.

As can be seen, the Republicans and the Southern Democrats were far apart in their views on slavery. The Constitutional Union party and the Northern Democrats were somewhere between those two extremes.

The Republican candidate was Abraham Lincoln of Illinois. Lincoln had gained a reputation as a great debater when he and Douglas discussed the slavery question before large audiences in Illinois.* These Lincoln-Douglas debates were widely reported in the country's newspapers. They won Lincoln many friends and supporters in the North. They also made him extremely unpopular in the South. The fact that Lincoln and his party favored a high protective tariff made him even more unpopular in the Southern states.

Before the election of 1860, many Southern leaders had declared that the South should leave the Union if Lincoln were elected. They said that the Republican party was a completely Northern party. So, if Lincoln gained the Presidency, the South would have little influence in the national government. Southerners believed that they would be forced to give up slavery. They also feared that many laws harmful to the South would be passed.

The election was held. Neither the Northern or Southern Democrats nor the weak Constitutional Unionists had much of a chance against the Republicans. Lincoln and his party won. Would the South carry out its threat to leave the Union? One after another, seven states in the South announced their secession from the Union. Together they formed a new country which they called the Confederate States of America. Before long, four more states joined the Confederacy.

---

* The *American Negro Reference Book* points out that one of the reasons for New England's relatively small slave population was that New Englanders were shrewd enough to realize that slaves were a potential threat to their safety. There is no doubt that they were justified in their fears. In all the states slaves were restless. Time after time slaves rebelled against their enslavement. Covert rebellion manifested itself in passive resistance, sabotage, escapes, and, in some cases, suicide. Scores of organized rebellions in which slaves used force in an attempt to gain freedom are recorded. This accounts for the harsh slave codes enacted in many states. For petty offenses such as associating with free ex-slaves, slaves could be severely whipped. The white population knew that the desire for freedom is contagious and that slaves might do something violent to gain liberty after contact with freedmen.

Name: _____ Date: _____

THE UNION IS DIVIDED

Confederate and Union States in 1861

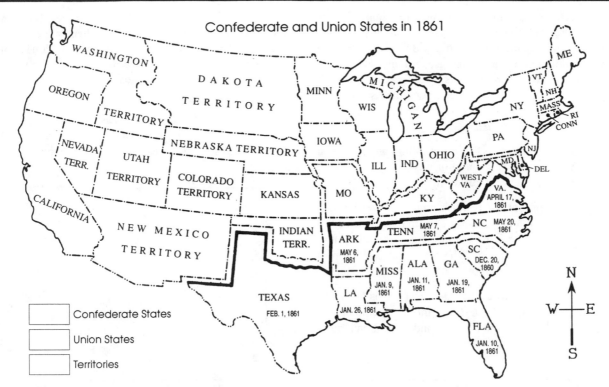

Confederate States

Union States

Territories

Complete the map of the Confederate and Union states in 1861 by carefully following the directions below.

1. The Confederacy included eleven states. They were Texas, Louisiana (LA), Mississippi (MS), Alabama (AL), Georgia (GA), South Carolina (SC), Florida (FL), Arkansas (AK), Tennessee (TN), Virginia (VA), and North Carolina (NC). On the map draw vertical (| | | | |) lines in these states.

2. All the other states shown on the map remained in the Union. Put a check (✓) in all the Union states.

3. Five of the states that stayed in the Union were slaveholding states. They were Missouri (MO), Kentucky (KY), West Virginia (WV), Maryland (MD), and Delaware (DE). Put an X in each of these states.

4. All the remaining areas on the map were territories. Draw small circles (○○○) in the territories.

5. Complete the map by filling in the blank boxes in the key with the symbols you have used in making the map.

6. What was the total number of Confederate states? _____ Union states? _____

7. Which two Union states were farthest west?

_____

8. Which Confederate state was farthest west?

_____

9. The information on the map can be shown in a table. Here is how to do it:

a. Make column headings on a sheet of paper, as follows:

State	Free	Slave*	Date of Secession
Virginia			
Tennessee			
etc.			

* Remember, some Union states were slaveholding states.

b. First, list all the Confederate states; then list all of the Union states.

c. Finally, write in the dates of secession where applicable, and put checks in the proper columns.

AMERICAN HISTORY TO 1860 TRIVIA CHALLENGE

1. This activity will provide an opportunity for the students to work together on a research challenge. It will put them in a position to use many different sources of information: library card catalogs; computer-based catalogs; and many different books including almanacs, encyclopedias, textbooks, and compendiums such as the *Encyclopedia of American History* and the *Concise Dictionary of American History*.

The questions that follow are not in any particular order. Your researchers could just as well start with the last question as the first question.

If it is appropriate, rewards could be given to those teams that complete the questions first, second, and so on. Scoring can be quite simple; e.g., set a time limit such as two class periods. The team that has the most correct responses within the time limit is the winner

2. A second way to utilize the questions is to photocopy the two pages of questions and the "game board" (below). Enlarge the game board and paste it on a piece of cardboard.

Cut out the questions along the dotted lines and paste them on pieces of cardboard. Then, write the answer to each question on the back of its card. You should make enough sets of game boards and cards for two to four students to play at each board.

Finally, provide a spinner with four sides (see drawing) and a set of tokens such as different coins, and place the cards on the game board. The students should take turns answering questions and advancing around the game board.

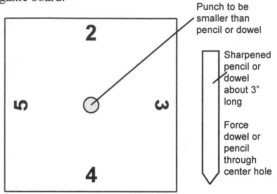

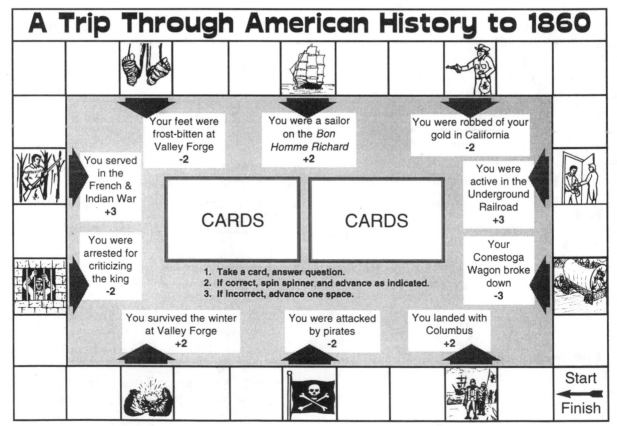

15-12

AMERICAN HISTORY TO 1860 TRIVIA CHALLENGE

1. Title of Frederick Douglass's autobiography

2. State where the Ohio River begins

3. Name of Henry Hudson's ship that sailed up the Hudson River

4. Name of Benjamin Franklin's almanac

5. Number of voyages of discovery made by Columbus

6. Frenchman who first sailed into the Gulf of St. Lawrence and the St. Lawrence River

7. Name of Frederick Douglass's newspaper

8. The real name of Johnny Appleseed

9. Names of the three ships that first brought colonists to Jamestown

10. Number of the constitutional amendment that guarantees freedom of religion

11. Governor of Virginia at the time of Bacon's Rebellion

12. The year Baltimore, Maryland, was established

13. The two symbols on California's first flag

14. Date of the Battle of Bennington in the American Revolution (year)

15. Number of the constitutional amendment that prohibits unreasonable home searches

16. Name of John Paul Jones's ship that fought the *Serapis*

17. Day, month, and year of the "Boston Massacre"

18. Owner of tea chests dumped into the water at the "Boston Tea Party"

19. Year of the Battle of Buena Vista in the War with Mexico

20. Nickname of British general, John Burgoyne

21. Four men from the Massachusetts Bay Colony who signed the Declaration of Independence

22. Day, month, and year Washington crossed the Delaware River to attack the British in Trenton

23. Commander who said, "Don't give up the ship." (War of 1812)

24. Name of Francis Drake's ship when he sailed into San Francisco Bay

25. Nickname of Revolutionary general, Anthony Wayne

26. Builder of the famous clipper ship, *Flying Cloud*

27. Patrick ___?___, who said, "Give me liberty or give me death."

28. Occupation of John Marshall, discoverer of gold in California

29. Fishing banks off coast of Newfoundland: ___?___ Banks

30. Captured Fort Ticonderoga in American Revolution: Green ___?___ Boys

31. U.S. President during the War with Mexico

32. American patriot hanged as a spy by the British (1776)

33. Year Harvard College, United States oldest, was founded

34. First names of Marquette and Joliet, French explorers of the Mississippi River

35. Name of mission established by Reverend and Mrs. Spaulding and Mrs. Spaulding in Oregon

36. How La Salle, French explorer, met his death

37. River on which George Washington's home is located

38. First names of Lewis and Clark, explorers of the Louisiana Territory

39. Inscription on the Liberty Bell: "Proclaim ___?___ throughout all the ___?___ ___?___ "

40. Another name for British loyalists during the American Revolution

15-12

AMERICAN HISTORY TO 1860 TRIVIA CHALLENGE

41. First name of Benjamin Franklin's son who was royal governor of New Jersey

42. Commander of American troops at the Battle of New Orleans (War of 1812)

43. The first regularly published newspaper in the colonies

44. Name of first English child born in America (Clue: Roanoke Island)

45. Nickname of General Andrew Jackson, later President of the United States

46. First year the United States government issued stamps for letters

47. Number of different men who served as president before Abraham Lincoln

48. James Madison, our third president, a graduate of __?__ College

49. Official name of the organization unofficially called "Quakers"

50. One of two nicknames of Abraham Lincoln

51. Texas battle cry in the fight for independence: "Remember the __?__"

52. First permanent Spanish settlement in Florida

53. Place where the "shot heard 'round the world" was fired

54. Indian tribe forced to follow the route that came to be called "Trail of Tears"

55. Execution year of first person executed for "witchcraft" in Massachusetts

56. The woman who fought bravely in the Battle of Monmouth in New Jersey

57. Person who killed Alexander Hamilton in a duel

58. California river where John Marshall found gold in California in 1843

59. Two states where camels were imported to be used for transportation

60. Europeans who established Fort Christina on the Delaware River

61. City in New Jersey where the Colt Six-Shooter was first manufactured

62. British explorer who gave the Columbia River its name

63. Revolutionary patriot who wrote "Common Sense" and "The Crisis"

64. Full name of the president whose father was the second president

65. State that was known as the "Dark and Bloody Ground"

66. Indian name for corn

67. Year the United States Marine Corps was established

68. Person who wrote the "Star Spangled Banner"

69. Writer of "My Country 'Tis of Thee"

70. City in Maryland where the United States Naval Academy was established in 1845

71. Meaning of "E Pluribus Unum" on the Great Seal of the United States

72. Aztec ruler at the time of the Spanish invasion of Mexico by Cortes

73. The year that work on the Washington Monument was begun

74. First Chief Justice of the Supreme Court of the United States

75. Name of Thomas Jefferson's home in Virginia

76. The first steamboat run started by Fulton was between Philadelphia and __?__

77. Indian tribe of which Sacajawea was a member

78. Town (and area) in New Jersey where Washington's troops spent two harsh winters

79. President at the time the White House was burned during the War of 1812

80. The last of the original 13 colonies to be established

155

S E C T I O N   1 6

The Civil War

Abraham Lincoln

ABRAHAM LINCOLN: FROM LOG CABIN TO THE WHITE HOUSE

The story of Lincoln can be utilized in various ways. Here are some suggestions.

1. Orally read the story for the simple purpose of having your students understand something of the humble origins of his life and his steady march to the presidency. Follow with discussion.

2. Arrange some role-playing situations, for example:

✎ A dialog during which Abe's father, Abe's sister, and Abe are discussing how they will cope with the death of Mrs. Lincoln.

✎ A discussion between Abe and his river boat partner as they arrive in New Orleans. Abe's impressions about the city and the slaves should be included.

✎ Abe is in court as a lawyer for Duff Armstrong, the son of Jack Armstrong. A witness is testifying that he saw Duff commit a crime on a moonlit night. Abe is cross-examining him and brings out the fact that the moon was so low it would not have been possible for the moon to have been a helpful light.

3. Photocopy the story and distribute. Then, divide the class into small groups of three or four. Each group is to tell the story of Lincoln in a "filmstrip" they create. *Note*: See the page immediately after the story for a full description of how to make a filmstrip and a "TV Box."

Abraham Lincoln was born in a one room Kentucky cabin; the year was 1809. His parents were poor farmers; they could neither read nor write, but this was quite common in those times. His mother never had the opportunity to know that her son became president of the United States. She died when he was only nine years old. Abe helped make the coffin in which his mother was buried.

Abe and his older sister, Sarah, were motherless for a year. Sarah, who was only eleven years old, took her mother's place—cleaning, sewing, cooking, and even helping her father on the farm. After a while, Abe's father met a young widow from Kentucky, who had three children, and married her. This meant that the merged family lived in the small cabin. Even in such crowded conditions Abe's stepmother was cheerful and kind. She made a warm and loving home for Abe and the other children.

Abe helped his father on the farm; there was never a shortage of work. Whenever his father could spare him, he worked for other farmers for twenty-five cents a day. He became locally famous for his skill with an axe. First, he would chop down trees, then split them into rails or firewood. This hard outdoor work helped him to become very strong. There were few young men in the area who could pin him in a wrestling match.

There was no way that a frontier farm boy could attend school regularly. Abe once said that taken all together he spent less than a year attending school. How did he become educated? He educated himself. He couldn't buy books; there wasn't enough money. So, he borrowed books, always taking care to treat them carefully and return them to their owners in good condition. Over and over again he read stories such as *Robinson Crusoe*, books of poetry, Shakespeare's plays, biographies, and, whenever possible, newspapers.

One of the most eventful happenings in his life occurred when he was eighteen years old. He was hired to help take a flatboat loaded with farm products down the Ohio River, then into the Mississippi River, and then to New Orleans at the mouth of the river. Abe was amazed at the size of the city, its buildings, hard-surfaced streets, and great ships moored to docks or floating at anchor. The sight of slaves being bought and sold, sometimes chained, was something he never forgot. He recognized the evils of slavery. One day, in the distant future, he was to be in the position to bring slavery to its end.

Abe's family moved to Illinois. He helped his father build a cabin and start a farm. When Abe reached the age of twenty-two and had completed all of his responsibilities to his family, he was free to be on his own and make his own life. Eventually,

ABRAHAM LINCOLN: FROM LOG CABIN TO THE WHITE HOUSE

he and a partner started a store in New Salem, Illinois.

An exciting incident occurred soon after Abe moved to New Salem. The leader of a local gang of young men, Jack Armstrong, heard of Abe's skill in running, splitting logs, and wrestling. Jack challenged Abe to a wrestling match. Abe accepted the challenge.

On the day of the match a large crowd was on hand to watch the two grapplers. The two, evenly matched, struggled, each trying to throw the other. Finally, Abe wrestled Jack to the ground and pinned his shoulders. Immediately, Jack's friends jumped Abe. Abe broke free, put his back to a wall and said he'd take them all on—one-by-one. Jack, who was a fair person, came to Abe's aid and told his friends to stop. Eventually, Abe and Jack became the best of friends. Also important, Abe had won the respect of all who were there.

There wasn't enough business to keep the New Salem store going, so it failed. The failure left Abe and his partner in debt. Then, his partner died. Now Abe had to pay the debt all by himself. Abe went to work again—splitting rails and doing all kinds of odd jobs. He learned how to survey land, and even became postmaster of New Salem at the grand pay of fifty dollars a year. It took Abe fifteen years, but he paid back every cent of the money that was owed.

There were some other good results of the work Abe was doing. He made many friends and became known as an intelligent and honest person. He was always ready to help people; for example, he wrote many letters for people who could not do it themselves. He became so well known and liked that he was urged to become a candidate for the state legislature. He lost the election, but on his second try he won. In order to be properly dressed for his new responsibilities he once more went into debt; he bought himself a new suit— the first he ever owned. Abe went on to win a seat in the next three elections.

Abe had always wanted to be a lawyer, so he decided that he would study for the law examination on his own. In those days it was not necessary to attend college to become a lawyer. For three years he studied at every opportunity. When he thought he was ready, he took the test and passed it. A good friend then asked him to be a partner in his law firm. Abe gladly accepted the offer.

Abe was a clever lawyer. He was able to detect flaws in the testimony of witnesses and use them to his client's advantage. In a famous murder trail he was defending the son of Jack Armstrong, his one-time wrestling opponent and old friend. A witness testified that he had seen the murder committed with the moon directly overhead. Abe checked the weather records for the night in question. What did he discover? The moon was very low in the sky—almost set—at the time of the crime. It was clear that the witness was lying. Abe won the case.

Abe served a two-year term in Congress; then, he returned to New Salem to take care of his growing law practice. His interest in politics was renewed when a law, the Kansas-Nebraska Act (1854), was passed. The law provided that the population of a territory, such as Kansas or Nebraska, could decide by vote if the state was to be a "free" state or a "slave" state. Abe was very disturbed about this because he believed it would increase slavery in the country. He wanted slavery to die out. He spoke out against the spread of slavery at every opportunity. Many people agreed with him when he said, "As I would not be a slave, I would not be a master."

Lincoln's views on slavery and his growing popularity led the Republican Party to choose him as their candidate in the Election of 1860. After a strenuous campaign in which he debated his strongest opponent, Stephen Douglas, Lincoln won the election easily. Southerners were extremely disturbed with the results of the election. Even before Lincoln took office, South Carolina seceded from the Union. A few months later, in April, 1861, the Civil War began when South Carolina attacked and won Fort Sumter in Charleston harbor.

PORTRAYING LINCOLN'S LIFE ON A "TV FILMSTRIP"

Lincoln's life lends itself to filmstrip sequences and episodes. Creating such a TV filmstrip in the classroom is very worthwhile because the experience develops reading, organizing, subject matter, whole language, and cooperative learning skills.

Here are some suggestions for implementing the activity:

1. Distribute photocopies of "Abraham Lincoln: From Log Cabin to the White House."

2. Suggest some elements of his life that could be shown on frames. Some examples are his

- cabin birthplace
- trip to New Orleans
- splitting logs
- work as store manager

3. Organize students into groups of 3–4.

4. Explain how a TV filmstrip is developed.
   a. A topic/title is selected.
   b. The topic is divided into subtopics that would make 7–12 frames.
   c. Each frame shows a particular aspect of a topic. Frames can be maps, pictures, diagrams, cartoons, graphs or written material. Frames should have titles and/or captions.
   d. After all frames are created—usually on 8" x 11" paper—they are carefully taped together.
   e. The assembled strip of frames is attached to rollers.

5. Have the students present the TV strip to the class or some other audience such as another class or parents.

6. An interesting additional project is to have the groups write and tape record accompanying scripts, much as is done with commercial sound filmstrips.

7. Suggestions for making the TV box follow:
   a. Select a strong cardboard box—14" x 14" x 8" is a good size.
   b. Tuck the flaps of the box into the box. This gives the box strength and rigidity.
   c. Cut an opening in the box about 7 1/2" x 10 1/2".
   d. Insert dowels into pre-slit holes. Keep the slits smaller than the dowel diameters to prevent the dowels from "wobbling" when turned. Dowels can be purchased from a hardware store, lumber yard, or crafts store. Be sure they are at least 1/2" in diameter.
   e. Decorate the box with contact paper, wallpaper, or coloring.

TV BOX

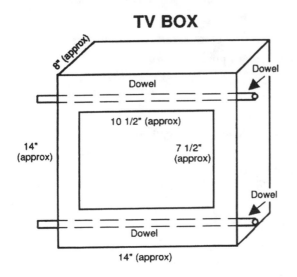

TV FILMSTRIP

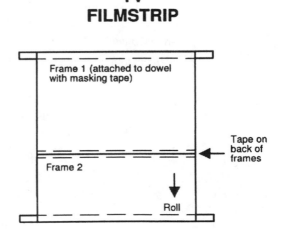

TWO GREAT SECTIONS FIGHT A CIVIL WAR

At first, the United States government did very little to stop the Southern states from seceding. The North wanted to avoid bloodshed. Northerners kept hoping the Confederate states would give up their ideas of secession and come back to the Union.

Jefferson Davis, the president of the Confederacy, did not think that the North would sit quietly forever and watch the Union break up. He decided to act quickly. He ordered the seizure of all United States government property in the Confederate states. This property included such things as forts, army camps, post offices, and arsenals. There was little opposition to this act.

However, the United States troops at Fort Sumter in the harbor of Charleston, South Carolina, resisted. The Confederates had demanded the surrender of the fort several times. Each time the commanding officer, Major Robert Anderson, refused. Promptly at dawn on April 12, 1861, Confederate guns began firing on the fort. Sumter's guns answered back. Anderson and his men held on for thirty-four hours, but his position was hopeless. Anderson surrendered the fort.

The bombardment of Fort Sumter made it clear that the South not only had left the Union, but also would fight to stay separate. On the other hand, by resisting the attack on Fort Sumter, the North had shown that it would fight to keep the South in the Union.

Which of the following is the most important thing to remember about Fort Sumter?

_____ The loss of the fort meant that Charleston harbor would be open to Confederate ships.

_____ It was the final event that brought about the Civil War.

President Lincoln had sworn to "preserve, protect, and defend the Constitution of the United States," and when the South took Fort Sumter, he knew that it was his duty to bring the seceded states back into the Union, using force if necessary. He issued a call for 75,000 soldiers. Thousands of men quickly volunteered for what they thought would be a short war.

President Davis also issued a call for soldiers. His request also brought an enthusiastic response.

Placed at the head of the Confederate troops in Virginia was General Robert E. Lee of Virginia. General Lee was such a capable officer that he had been offered command of the Union forces. He had refused the appointment because he did not wish to fight against the people of his own state.

By July 21, 1861, a Union army of some 30,000 faced an equal number of Confederates in northern Virginia. The Union objective was to capture Richmond, the capital of the Confederacy. For a while it appeared as though the Union attack would be successful. However, more Confederate troops arrived. Before the day was over, the Union troops were fleeing back to Washington. The first great encounter of the war, the Battle of Bull Run, was a Confederate victory.

Understanding

1. Draw a circle around the listing of the kinds of United States property seized by the Confederates at the beginning of the war.

2. Circle the sentence that tells that the Confederates did not want to take Fort Sumter by force.

3. Underline the words that tell why Lincoln had to take steps to keep the Southern states from leaving.

4. Underline twice the sentence that tells why General Lee would not accept command of the Union armies.

5. What was there about Richmond, Virginia, that made it an important Union objective? _____

_____

_____

6. A *civil war* is one that is fought within a country between groups or sections of the country. Why has it been said that a civil war is the worst of all kinds of wars? _____

_____

_____

_____

TWO GREAT SECTIONS FIGHT A CIVIL WAR

Plans for Winning the War

After Bull Run the North realized that it would not be easy to defeat the South. What to do?

First, it was important to the North to keep the South from trading with other parts of the world. This was because the South did not have many factories that produced guns, ammunition, clothing, medicine, or the numerous other things an army needs. The Confederacy hoped to get necessary war supplies from foreign countries in exchange for its cotton. To prevent this, Northern warships would try to block all ships entering or leaving Southern ports.

Second, Northern plans called for an invasion of the South. Northern generals thought that by gaining control of the Mississippi River they could separate the western Confederate states from the eastern states.

Another part of the North's invasion plans was to divide the Confederacy east of the Mississippi River. The idea was to separate the northern Confederate states from those farther south.

The invasion also called for the capture of Richmond and the coastal regions east of the Appalachian Mountains. If the North could force the Confederate capital to surrender, the South might become discouraged. Furthermore, the coastal cities were the most important centers of population, transportation, and business in the South.

The Confederacy's plans for winning the war were mainly defensive. That is, their main tasks were to break the blockade and to stop the invading Northern armies. They thought that European nations, especially Britain, would help them break the blockade in order to get Southern cotton. Southerners also felt sure that they could hold back the Union armies.

Understanding

1. Complete the map below as follows:

a. To show the Northern blockade, draw a chain (⊖⊂⊃⊂⊃⊂) along the coasts from Texas to Maryland. Label the chain **Northern Blockade** in two or three places along the chain.

b. To show the North's invasion plans, draw a heavy line along the Mississippi River from New Orleans to Missouri. In the box with the arrow pointing to the Mississippi River, write **Control the Mississippi; divide the confederacy east and west**.

c. Draw a heavy line from Memphis to Atlanta to Savannah. In the box with the arrow pointing to the line, write **Divide the Confederacy north and south**.

d. In the box with the arrow pointing to Richmond, write **Capture Richmond and coastal regions**.

2. What were the Confederate states west of the Mississippi River? _____

_____

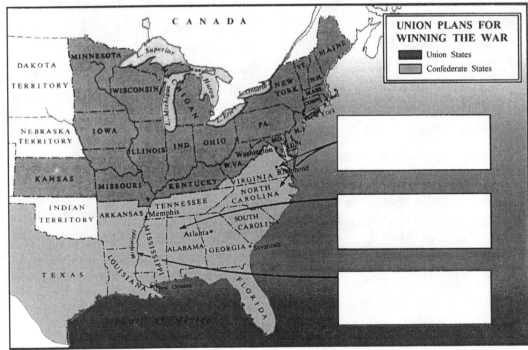

A GREAT NAVAL BATTLE

_____ It has been said that the Civil War, or the "War Between the States" as some call it, was the first "modern" war because many new ways of fighting were introduced. Although most of the changes were in methods of land fighting, one of the most important changes came about in naval warfare. For the first time, two ironclad ships, the *Monitor* and the *Merrimack*, engaged in a battle at sea.

_____ At the beginning of the war, the North declared a *blockade* of the South. This meant that no ships were to enter or leave southern ports. Any ships—foreign or southern—that tried to "run the blockade" were to be stopped. The South had few factories. To obtain the manufactured goods needed to carry on the war, it had to carry on trade with other nations. Some ships got through the blockade, but before long the South was being seriously hurt.

_____ To help break the blockade, Southerners conceived the idea of remodeling a wooden steamship, the *Merrimack*, and covering its sides with iron plates. Enemy cannon balls would simply bounce off the slanting iron sides. They also equipped their iron boat with ten guns and a cast-iron ram. The ram was used in charges on enemy ships. It could make great holes in a ship's hull.

_____ The captain of a northern wooden warship who had the misfortune to attack the *Merrimack* wrote "at least fifty solid shots struck her (the *Merrimack*) on her slanting sides, without producing any apparent effect." No ordinary ship could stand against the iron monster.

_____ But spies had told the Union naval authorities about the *Merrimack* long before it was launched. So the North also built an iron-plated ship. The Union ship, the *Monitor*, was said to resemble a "cheese-box on a raft." It had a revolving turret, or iron tower, and two very powerful guns.

_____ The two ships met on the morning of March 9, 1862. The previous day the *Merrimack* had sunk one ship, forced another to surrender, and was planning to sink a third Union ship, the *Minnesota*, the next morning. Imagine the *Merrimack's* surprise when dawn broke and revealed another iron ship standing ready to protect the *Minnesota*!

_____ The two ships fought for hours, but neither could sink the other. They seemed to be perfectly matched. Each of them withstood scores of direct hits by cannon balls. Finally, the *Merrimack*, withdrew. It never again came out to fight.

_____ One thing was a clear result of the battle. Wooden warships were things of the past. Naval warfare would never be the same again.

A GREAT NAVAL BATTLE

1. From the ten sentences below, choose the eight that best summarize the paragraphs in the story on the opposite page. Write the letter of each of the eight sentences on the line before the paragraph it describes.

a Wooden warships prove to be helpless against the *Merrimack*.

b Wooden warships will no longer be useful in fighting at sea.

c The trade of the South is seriously slowed down by the blockade by northern ships.

d The South breaks a blockade of its ports.

e A battle rages between two equally matched opponents.

f The Civil War marks the beginning of new warfare techniques.

g The *Merrimack* becomes the model for many other southern ships.

h The North hears about Confederate plans and takes action to counteract them.

i The *Merrimack* successfully attacks two ships.

j A ship is designed that might break a blockade.

2. The drawing on the opposite page shows an artist's impression of the battle between the *Monitor* and the *Merrimack*. From the descriptions given in the story, you should be able to label all three ships shown in the picture.

Label the drawing by writing *ME* for *Merrimack*, *MO* for *Monitor*, and *MI* for *Minnesota* beside the proper ship.

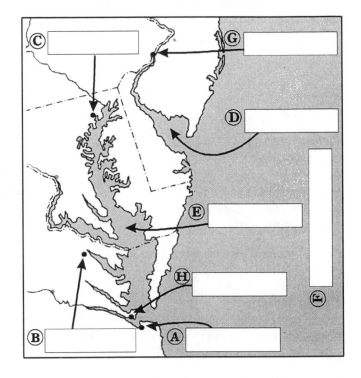

3. Label the following places on the map above:

Ⓐ Norfolk   Ⓔ Chesapeake Bay

Ⓑ Washington   Ⓕ Atlantic Ocean

Ⓒ Baltimore   Ⓖ Philadelphia

Ⓓ Delaware Bay Ⓗ Hampton

4. The map includes the area where the battle between the *Monitor* and the *Merrimack* took place. To mark the position exactly, put an X in the water area between Hampton and Norfolk. This water area is called Hampton Roads.

AFRICAN-AMERICANS FIGHT FOR FREEDOM

Some facts related to African-American participation in the Civil War are listed below. Your task is to select facts from the list and write a short article that could accompany the picture at the top of the next column. Imagine that the picture and your article will be published in a prominent newspaper.

Some tips in writing your article:

✍ Your paragraphs should be brief with sentences that are short—newspaper style.

✍ You should have an opening paragraph that is related to the picture.

✍ You may want to combine several related facts in one paragraph.

✍ After you have composed your article on another piece of paper, edit it and copy it in the space below the picture.

Note: The abbreviation A-A in the listing stands for African-American.

Listing of facts

➡ Approximately 185,000 A-A's served in the Union Armies.

➡ A-A's had their own regiments; most of their officers were white.

➡ There were 166 all-A-A regiments in the Union army.

➡ Two-thirds of the A-A soldiers were from the South; they had escaped to the North.

➡ At first, A-A troops received one-half the pay of white troops. This was changed in 1864 when Congress authorized full pay and "bounties," bonuses paid for enlisting in the army or navy.

➡ 20,000 A-A's served in the Union navy. They made up twenty-five percent of Navy sailors.

➡ About 38,000 A-A soldiers were killed in the Civil War.

➡ Twenty-two A-A's were awarded the Congressional Medal of Honor, the USA's highest award for bravery.

➡ Some of the names of the A-A regiments were Kansas Colored Volunteers, Fifty-fourth Massachusetts Volunteers (two of Frederick Douglass's sons were in this regiment), Fourteenth Regiment of Rhode Island Heavy Artillery.

➡ An A-A regiment was one of the first to enter Richmond, the Confederate capital, when General Grant captured the city. When Lincoln toured Richmond he was escorted by A-A cavalry.

➡ A-A regiments participated in some 500 Civil War engagements.

➡ It was after the Emancipation Proclamation (1863) that Lincoln authorized the use of A-A troops.

➡ About 90 A-A soldiers became commissioned officers. ("Commissioned officers" includes such ranks as lieutenant, captain, etc.) The highest ranking A-A officer was Martin R. Delany, a Major of Infantry.

➡ By the end of the war, A-A regiments made up about 10 percent of the Union army.

_____

_____

_____

_____

_____

_____

_____

_____

_____

_____

_____

_____

_____

_____

_____

_____

Name: _____ Date: _____

LAND BATTLES OF THE CIVIL WAR

Certain places are numbered in the story that follows. Write the number of each place in the correct circle on the map.

The North began to carry out its plans for winning the war. In 1862 General Ulysses S. Grant began a campaign to gain control of the Mississippi. He moved on Fort Henry (1) and Fort Donelson (2). These two forts guarded the northern approaches to the Mississippi River. After capturing them, he moved southward and took the important river ports of Memphis (3) and Vicksburg (4). Meanwhile, a combined army-navy force under the command of Admiral Farragut captured New Orleans (5) and then advanced northward to join with General Grant. This split the Confederacy into an eastern and a western section.

The war in the East was going badly for the Union. The Union armies were stopped in their efforts to capture Richmond (6). Then, General Robert E. Lee put the Union armies on the defensive by invading the North. However, his advance was halted at Gettysburg (7), Pennsylvania, in July, 1863.

President Lincoln gave Grant command of all the Union armies. Then, Grant took personal charge of the Union's forces in the East. He led a drive to Richmond and captured it.

While Grant was engaged in the battle for Richmond, General William T. Sherman of the Union army was marching southeastward from Chattanooga (8), through Atlanta (9) and to the Atlantic coast. Sherman's march was a military success. His army left a path of destruction fifty or more miles wide and hundreds of miles long. Sherman's idea was that the South would stop fighting only if it could no longer make war. After reaching Savannah (10), he turned north to join with Grant.

After Grant took Richmond, Lee withdrew his forces and headed for the mountains of western Virginia with Grant in pursuit. Lee realized that it was no longer possible to win the war. There was no point in shedding more blood for a hopeless cause. On April 9, 1865, Lee surrendered to Grant at Appomattox Court House (11), Virginia. This was almost four years after the fall of Fort Sumter.

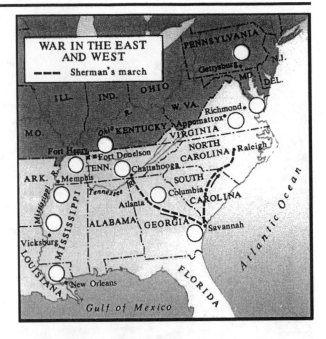

Understanding

1. Circle the sentence that tells why Fort Henry and Fort Donelson were important.

2. According to the map in what state is Memphis?

_____

Vicksburg? _____

3. Underline the sentence that tells the effect of Admiral Farragut and General Grant capturing the Mississippi River.

4. What did General Lee of the Confederacy do to put the North on the defensive? _____

_____

5. Underline twice the sentence that tells why General Sherman destroyed such a large area of land in the Confederate states.

6. How did General Lee show his concern for lives and property by not continuing the war after General Grant captured Richmond? _____

_____

_____

THREE FAMOUS AMERICANS IN THE CIVIL WAR

The battle between the *Monitor* and the *Merrimack* changed naval warfare forever.

John Ericsson, Inventor from Sweden

When John Ericsson (1803–1889) of Sweden was only ten years old, he built a model sawmill that was perfect in every detail. Before he was fifteen years old, he had mastered the skills and knowledge needed to hold a job as a draftsman, surveyor, and engineer. As Ericsson grew older, he became interested in steam-driven ships. This interest led him to the United States in 1839, and he began to build ships for the United States navy. Ericsson was happy and successful in the United States. In 1848 he became an American citizen.

When the Civil War broke out, Ericsson supported the Union. He hated slavery. He was happy to use his talents to help fight against it. It was fortunate that Ericsson was on the side of the Union. This is why:

The Confederates covered an old warship, the *Merrimack*, with iron plates. They armed it heavily with guns and sent it out to attack Union ships. On its first day out, March 8, 1862, the *Merrimack* met and easily sank two Union ships. It was clear that wooden ships could not endure against the ironclad ship. With their new weapon, the Confederates hoped to break the Union's blockade of the Confederate coast.

On March 9 the *Merrimack* sailed out again. Its crew was looking forward to another day of victories. Instead of meeting helpless wooden ships, though, the *Merrimack* met a Union ship, the *Monitor*, which was also an ironclad. For about four hours the ships bounced shells off each other's hulls, but little damage was done. Finally, both ships returned to their bases. The *Merrimack* never sailed again. It was destroyed by the Confederates themselves to keep the Union from capturing it.

Where does Ericsson come into the story? It was he who suggested to the United States government that an ironclad could and should be built. This was only three months before the famous *Monitor-Merrimack* battle. It was he who designed the *Monitor* and who took charge of building it. If this Swedish-born American had not made his contribution, the story of the Civil War would have been very different.

John Ericsson

1. How old was Ericsson when he came to the United States? _____

2. Underline the sentence that tells why Ericsson helped the North rather than the South.

3. Circle the sentence that tells what the Confederates hoped to accomplish with their ironclad ship.

4. Underline the sentence that tells why the Confederates destroyed the *Merrimack*.

5. Some people called the *Merrimack* a "cheese-box on a raft." In the picture circle the ship that fits that description.

6. The last sentence in the story of Ericsson suggests that without his boat the story of the Civil War might have been very different.

In what way would the war have been different? Write your answer on the reverse side of this page.

Carl Schurz

1. Why did Schurz leave his homeland? _____

_____

_____

_____

Name: _____ Date: _____

THREE FAMOUS AMERICANS IN THE CIVIL WAR

Carl Schurz, General and Statesman

Carl Schurz (1829–1906) was born in Germany. He came to the United States in 1852. At the age of thirty-four, he became a Major General during the Civil War. In 1869 Schurz was elected United States Senator from Missouri. As a senator and later as Secretary of the Interior, he performed outstanding services. He fought vigorously to have the American Indians treated fairly. Then, as a newspaper writer, book author, and speaker, he helped others understand and love his adopted country. Carl Schurz wrote on every imaginable subject—from a two-volume biography of Henry Clay to the political, social, and economic events of his times. He was a reformer and crusader. He exposed and publicized corruption in government. He courageously opposed the political bosses of the times. One person speaking of Schurz said, "You knew where to find him always, and that was in the right place."

Schurz was forced to leave Germany when a revolution that he took part in failed.

Robert Smalls, Captain and Congressman

As dawn broke on May 13, 1862, Confederate guards at Fort Sumter were surprised to see one of their ships, the *Planter*, steaming past the fort. However when the *Planter* flashed the proper signals, it was allowed to pass. The guards had no way of knowing that on board the ship were African-American slaves who had captured the *Planter* and who were sailing it to freedom. Robert Smalls, the leader, was able to pilot the ship and give the proper signals because he had been a member of the *Planter's* crew.

Smalls's daring act was given wide publicity. He became a member of the Union navy and was made pilot of the *Planter*. Once, while his ship was being shelled by the Confederates, the captain of the *Planter* deserted his post. Smalls led the ship to safety. As a reward, Smalls was made captain of the ship.

After the war Smalls served in Congress for ten years. He worked tirelessly to have laws passed which helped African-Americans gain their civil rights. One law he supported as a member of the South Carolina legislature established free public schools for both African-Americans and white children in South Carolina.

Smalls smuggled his wife and two children aboard the *Planter* and took them to freedom with him.

2. How does the picture help you to know that Schurz left Germany secretly? _____

_____

3. Schurz held all the positions listed below. Check only the ones mentioned in the story.

____ Lawyer	____ Minister to Spain
____ Army officer	____ Senator
____ Newspaper owner	____ Newspaper writer
____ Secretary of the Interior	

Robert Smalls

1. According to the caption how did Smalls's family get to the *Planter*? _____

_____

2. Circle the sentence that tells why Smalls was able to sail the *Planter* past Fort Sumter.

3. How was Smalls rewarded for saving the *Planter*?

_____

4. Underline the sentence that tells why Smalls is remembered by educators.

Name: _____ Date: _____

CLARA BARTON: SCHOOL TEACHER, CIVIL WAR NURSE

December 25, 1821, was an especially happy Christmas for the Barton family in Oxford, Massachusetts. Their new baby, Clarissa Harlowe Barton, was born. Clara, as she came to be called, was much younger than her sisters and brothers; she learned much from them. David taught her to ride wild colts at a very early age. Before Clara was three years old Dorothy and Sally taught her to read. Stephen taught her arithmetic.

At the age of fifteen, Clara applied for a teaching position in a one-room school and was given the job. Now that she had the job, could she keep it? Forty pupils were to be in her school, and four of the boys, all of them as old as Clara and much bigger, were known troublemakers. But, before two weeks were over, Clara proved to the boys that she could run faster and bat a ball farther than any of them. She won their respect.

Clara's reputation as a teacher grew. Eventually she moved to New Jersey, where free public schools were rare. Clara insisted that the children of poor people had a right to an education, and offered to serve three months without pay if the town would make the school free to all.

Clara's real life's work, however, began when the North and South were locked in war. Wounded men were dying by the thousands through lack of care. Clara determined that she would become a nurse at the front. No woman had ever been a battlefield nurse before, but Clara finally got the job.

Clara spent years at the front. Bullets, rain, cold, mud, and disease meant nothing to her as long as there was a wound to be dressed or a dying soldier to be comforted. She earned the title "Angel of the Battlefield" from the grateful soldiers.

After the war, Clara continued to help people. She traced thousands of men missing in the war. She went to Europe and helped victims of other wars. Finally, she helped to organize the American Red Cross and became its first president.

Read the questions below and underline the ones that are answered in the story.

1. How old was Clara when she died?

2. How many children did the Barton's have?

3. What did David teach Clara?

4. What did she learn from her mother?

5. Was Clara successful in her first job?

6. What did Clara do during the war?

7. How long did she teach school?

8. Where in New Jersey did she teach?

9. Where and when was she born?

10. What did Clara pioneer in New Jersey?

11. What did Clara do after the war?

12. What was her last big job?

THE DEATH OF ABRAHAM LINCOLN

On March 4, 1865, Abraham Lincoln was sworn in for a second term as President of the United States. At the time he expressed the hope that the nation would soon be reunited. He made it clear that he did not want to punish the Confederate states for breaking away.

Then on April 14, 1865, just five days after Lee surrendered, the President was shot as he sat watching a play. The next day he died. The country was shocked and saddened by his death. One man who loved Lincoln was Walt Whitman, one of America's finest poets. He wrote the poem that follows soon after the death of Lincoln.

O CAPTAIN! MY CAPTAIN!

1. O Captain! my Captain! our fearful trip is done,
2. The ship has weather'd every rack, the prize we sought is won,
3. The port is near, the bells I hear, the people all exulting,
4. While follow eyes the steady keel, the vessel grim and daring;
5.   But O heart! heart! heart!
6.   O the bleeding drops of red,
7.   Where on the deck my Captain lies,
8.   Fallen cold and dead.

9. O Captain! my Captain! rise up and hear the bells;
10. Rise up—for you the flag is flung—for you the bugle trills,
11. For you bouquets and ribbon'd wreaths—for you the shores a-crowding,
12. For you they call, the swaying mass, their eager faces turning;
13.   Here Captain! dear father!
14.   The arm beneath your head!
15.   It is some dream that on the deck,
16.   You've fallen cold and dead.

17. My Captain does not answer, his lips are pale and still,
18. My father does not feel my arm, he has no pulse nor will,
19. The ship is anchor'd safe and sound, its voyage closed and done,
20. From fearful trip the victor ship comes in with object won;
21.   Exult O shores, and ring O bells!
22.   But I with mournful tread,
23.   Walk the deck my Captain lies,
24.   Fallen cold and dead.

Understanding

1. To what do each of the following words in the poem refer?

line 1: *Captain* _____

line 1: *trip* _____

line 2: *ship* _____

line 2: *prize* _____

line 3: *the port is near* _____

line 19: *the ship is anchor'd safe and sound* _____

_____

line 20: *object won* _____

2. Circle the two lines in the poem that suggest that the poet does not want to believe that Lincoln is dead.

THE CENSUS: COUNTING THE PEOPLE IN THE COUNTRY

The Constitution provides that "Representatives and direct taxes shall be apportioned among the several states which may be included within this Union, according to their respective numbers." It is obvious that this part of the Constitution could not be carried out unless an accurate count, or census, of the population was conducted. The Constitution provided for the actual census as follows: "The actual enumeration shall be made within three years after the first meeting of the Congress of the United States, and within every subsequent term of ten years, in such manner as they shall by law direct." *Note*: The United States was the first nation to provide by law for periodic census. Also, the census is now used for many other purposes in addition to mere enumeration of the population for determining representation.

Suggestions for Teaching

1. One reason for the following activity is to demonstrate that statistical information may be more clearly presented in tables and graphs than in narrative form.

2. Provide your students with a photocopy of the blank table at the bottom of the page.

3. Orally read the narrative below. After each relevant paragraph is read, have your students complete the blank spaces in the table. *Note*: It may be helpful to complete the table with your students via a transparency or the chalkboard. Also, some subtraction will be necessary.

Counting the People

When George Washington became President, no one knew for sure how many people lived in the United States. So, in 1790 a census was taken.

It was not easy to take the first census. The men hired to do the counting had to be brave. They had to know how to survive in the wilderness. Much of the country was wild and undeveloped, so travelling was done on foot, except for the times when horses or canoes could be used. Many of the places the census takers visited were not shown on maps. In the country west of the Appalachian Mountains, Indians were a danger.

In spite of all the hardships, the job was done in nine months. When all the figures were added up, it was found that the population of the country was about 4,000,000 people. Only 200,000 of these people lived in towns and cities. The remaining 3,800,000 lived in farm areas.

The Constitution provides for a census to be taken every ten years. A study of the population figures over the years tells much about the growth of the United States.

The census of 1830 revealed that we had about 13,000,000 people. Some 12,000,000 of these people were living in farm areas.

Between 1830 and 1860 our population more than doubled. In 1860 there were 31,000,000 Americans. About 25,000,000 of these people lived on farms. As you can see, a greater proportion of Americans were living in cities and towns in 1860 than were in 1830.

Other interesting facts have been uncovered by the census takers. In 1860, there were about 4,500,000 African-Americans living in the nation. These figures had grown from 757,000 in 1790, and 2,300,000 in 1830. The 1990 census showed there are about 30,500,000 African-Americans in the country. This means that about eleven of every one hundred Americans are African-American.

Population Growth of the United States: 1790–1860

Year of Census	Population of the Country	Population Living in Farm Areas	Population Living in Towns and Cities	African-American Population
1790				
1830				
1860				

SECTION 17

Developing the Great Plains

Engraving by H. B. Hall's Sons

Name: _____ Date: _____

SOLDIERS OF THE PLAINS

From the end of the Civil War until 1898, most of the activity of the United States Army took place in the West. It was the Army's job to keep peace and order in the region. There were many problems. First, the area to be policed was vast in size; one-half of Europe could easily fit into it. Second, much of the land in this region was desert and mountains. Third, the Indians in the West fought desperately to preserve and protect their way of life. Fourth, the cattlemen, sheepmen, and farmers there fought bitterly against each other. Fifth, there were "bad men" who recognized no law but their own. They preyed on Indian, cattleman, farmer, town dweller, and soldier with equal disregard.

After the Civil War the national army was greatly reduced; rarely were there more than 25,000 soldiers in it at any one time. Most of those soldiers were stationed in the West. But, what the western army lacked in numbers, was more than made up in quality. Many of the soldiers were veterans of the Civil War and had served in the Confederate and Union armies. One writer, S. E. Whitman, in his book *The Troopers* describes western soldiers as being tough, competent, and "battle seasoned." Whitman went on to compare the soldiers with polar bears in their ability to withstand bitter winters.

About 20 percent of the troopers serving in the West were African-Americans. Many of them were ex-slaves who had proved their capabilities in the Union armies in the Civil War. Since jobs were scarce after the war, millions of ex-slaves could not find work, but there were opportunities in the army. Troops were needed to fight in the so-called "Indian Wars." Many more African-Americans than were actually needed applied for appointment. The thought of having a steady income, food, clothing, shelter and, most of all, the dignity and respect that came with being a soldier was very attractive.

The Army was not desegregated at that time, so four African-American regiments were formed: the 9th and 10th Cavalry, and the 24th and 15th Infantry. These regiments had splendid records. General Merritt, who commanded some of these troops, said of them that they were "brave in battle. . . and most efficient in the care of their horses, arms, and equipment." That General Merritt and many others who praised the troops were correct in their opinions is shown by the fact that nine of the African-American troops who participated in the Indian Wars were awarded the Congressional Medal of Honor—the nation's highest award for bravery.

1. Circle the two sentences that describe the area within which the army operated.

2. Underline the sentence that tells why the Army and the Indians often fought.

3. Why might veterans of the Civil War be especially good soldiers in the western Army? _____

_____

4. Underline the sentence that tells why African-Americans wanted to enlist in the Army.

5. What proof is offered in the story that supports the widespread opinion that African-American troops per-

formed courageously?_____

_____

Note: Answer questions 6 and 7 on the reverse side of this paper.

6. In the opening paragraph one sentence reads, "cattlemen . . . and farmers . . . fought bitterly against each other." Write your opinion as to why these two groups were enemies. Think of roaming cattle and farmers' crops.

7. Study the picture that shows soldiers enduring a plains blizzard. Explan why the soldier in front has dismounted from his horse.

PLAINS SETTLERS, INDIANS, AND BUFFALO

Procedure:

1. Photocopy the next four pages and distribute.

2. Direct your students to read the narrative until they find a reference to a question that is on page 173. They are to answer the question, then read on until they meet another question to be answered, and so on through the entire narrative.

The West Needed More Farmers

The population of the West in 1870 was light and scattered in spite of the activity of the cattlemen, sheepmen, and miners. Settlements, mining developments, and cattle ranches occupied only a small part of the total land area. The few cowtowns located on the railroad lines were not large. In the West the cows and sheep far outnumbered the people.

In the early days the Interior Plains or "Plains" were almost completely covered with grass. Trees could be found along the banks of streams and rivers and in some mountain areas, but it was possible to go hundreds of miles and not see a tree. *Question 1, p. 173.*

Water is scarce in the western part of the Plains. Denver, in the extreme western part of the region, averages about 14.8 inches of precipitation a year, while St. Louis in the east averages 35.4 inches. Western rivers are shallow compared to eastern rivers. There are very few lakes in the Plains except in the northeastern part. *Question 2, p. 173.*

Because there were few trees, Plains settlers could not get lumber for houses, barns, or furniture. There was little wood for fires. The settlers had no material, not even rocks or stones, that they could use for fences. *Question 3, p. 173.*

If the Plains between the Mississippi River and Rocky Mountains were to be developed fully, they needed more people. They needed people who could settle permanently on the land and improve it. What the region really needed was farmers. *

Farmers do more than simply increase the population by moving to a place with their families. Farmers attract other people to the area in which they settle. Farmers need workers who can provide services such as transportation and communication. They need businesses which will supply them with farm machinery, seeds, lumber, clothing, and hundreds of other things. They also need teachers, ministers, doctors, and lawyers. *Question 4, p. 173.*

The Homestead Act of 1862 made it possible for a settler to get one hundred and sixty acres of land free. However, many Americans interested in farming hesitated to take advantage of this offer. Unfriendly Indians in the West were the most important reason for their hesitation.

The Indians had good reason to be unfriendly. They had been pushed from one place to another for three hundred years. Settlers starting with the Spaniards had squeezed the Indians out of their original homes. Indian lands were sometimes taken without payment. Treaties and agreements with the Indians were broken many times. *Question 5, p. 173.*

PLAINS SETTLERS, INDIANS, AND BUFFALO

The Indians had not given up their lands meekly. They fought bravely against great odds. Thousands of their people had been killed. They often retreated, but at the first opportunity they took up the fight again.

The Plains Indians saw the Civil War as a chance to fight for their land. Their leaders took advantage of the fact that the Union armies were fighting against the Confederate armies. They attacked wagons, trains, and stagecoaches to discourage people who were travelling to or through the Plains. They attacked army forts and settlements. They tore down telegraph lines and ripped up the railroads. Some gave help to the Confederacy. These Indians thought that they would have a better chance of keeping their hunting grounds if the Confederacy won. *Question 6, p. 173.*

After the Civil War, the Indians became even more desperate. Their main source of food and clothing was the buffalo. But these great animals were being killed by the hundreds of thousands. To provide meat for the construction crews, the builders of the transcontinental railroad hired hunters to kill the buffalo. One famous hunter, "Buffalo Bill" Cody, is said to have killed four thousand of the animals himself.

After the railroads were completed, buffalo were killed for sport. People riding on the trains would pass the time away by shooting buffalo from the windows. Buffalo robes became popular in the East. Professional hunters went to the Plains and killed thousands more. *Question 7, p. 173.*

The great buffalo herd of the Plains was almost destroyed. In the early 1860's there were about 15,000,000 buffalo on the Plains. By 1890 hardly a buffalo could be found in all the West. The end of the buffalo meant the end of Indian resistance. The Indians were forced to go into reservations. If they had not, they would have starved to death. *Question 8, p. 173.*

One of the few areas left to the Indians by the United States government was the western part of the Plains. Even this region was not completely theirs. Many Indians were forced to live in certain areas, called reservations. Some Indians, however, refused to accept the reservations and continued to live outside of them.

In recent years, the United States government has tried very hard to treat the Indians fairly. In 1946 an Indian Claims Commission was set up. This Commission hears claims by American Indian groups against the United States. The Commission has often decided that a particular group of Indians was unfairly treated. In many cases the Indians have been given money awards. In one recent year the Commission awarded the Indians more than $43,000,000.

There are about one hundred Indian reservations in the United States today. No Indian is forced to live on a reservation now, although many Indians prefer to do so to help preserve their cultural heritage. Indians are citizens of the United States and may come and go as they please. Of course, they may vote and hold public office.

Americans today are proud of the pioneers who faced the danger and terror of Indian attacks. We also admire the Indians who fought so bravely. Americans regret the harsh and often unfair treatment of the Indians. *Question 9, p. 173; then, answer the questions at the bottom of the second column, page 174.*

PLAINS SETTLERS, INDIANS, AND BUFFALO

1. a.   On the map on page 174 draw light diagonal lines in the section labeled Interior Plains.

  b.   What three groups of mountains are within the Plains? _____

_____

  c.   What great river flows almost entirely within the Plains and then joins the Mississippi River? _____

_____

  d.   What mountains form the western border of the Plains? _____

  e.   As the diagram next to the map shows, the land of the Plains gradually rises from east to west. How many feet higher in elevation is Denver than St. Louis? _____ feet

2.   What are three reasons why there is a shortage of available water in the Plains:

_____

_____

_____

3.   In what ways did the shortage of lumber affect the Plains settlers?

_____

_____

4.   In paragraph 6 it is stated that farmers need "services such as transportation and communication." What would be one communication service? _____

_____

transportation service? _____

5.   If you had been an Indian, how would you respond to a settler who asked, "Why are you being unfriendly to us?" _____

_____

6.   Why did the Indians tend to help the Confederacy during the Civil War? _____

_____

_____

_____
_____
_____
_____

7. a.   List as many facts as you can find in the picture. Be brief, as in the example:

✍	Herd dividing	✍	
✍		✍	
✍		✍	
✍		✍	
✍		✍	

  b.   Write a two- or three-sentence caption in the space below the picture. On the reverse side of this page express your feelings about the scene.

8.   Why did the destruction of the buffalo herds force the Indians into reservations? _____

_____

9.   What is the United States government doing to try to compensate Indians for past wrongs done to them?

_____

_____

Name: _____ Date: _____

PLAINS SETTLERS, INDIANS, AND BUFFALO

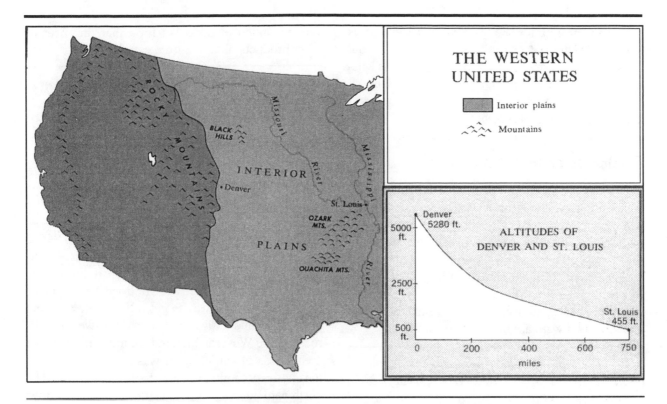

THE WESTERN
UNITED STATES

▨ Interior plains

〰 Mountains

ALTITUDES OF
DENVER AND ST. LOUIS

Pioneer Family from Norway

windmill for pumping water from underground sources

leaky sod roof

rain barrel

A TYPICAL INTERIOR PLAINS HOME

Understanding the Picture

1. From what country did the settlers in the picutre come? _____

2. In what two ways does the family obtain water?

_____

_____

3. According to the information in the picture, what is one of the disadvantages of a sod roof? _____

_____

4. What is being used to prop up the front of the house?

_____

5. How might the dog be useful? _____

_____

_____

6. What does the man on the left have that shows he is ready for attacks? _____

_____

174

CATTLEMEN AND FARMERS IN THE EARLY WEST

The information below presents some facts and insights that can prove helpful in teaching about cattlemen and farmers in the West beyond the Mississippi River. Each paragraph is followed by an "open-ended" question that may stimulate your students' thinking and discussion.

Raising Cattle in the West

The oldest industry in what is now the southwestern part of the United States is cattle raising. The Spaniards were responsible for the industry's beginning. There were neither cattle nor horses in the New World before the coming of the Spaniards. The Spaniards brought cattle and horses with them to present-day Southwest United States. Some of the animals escaped from the herds. Only the fastest and strongest were able to survive.

> *Do you think the Spaniards' cattle and horses eventually found their way beyond the Appalachian Mountains to the east coast? (Probably not. The great distance, the deserts, the Mississippi River, and the mountains would have been great obstacles to overcome.) If not, how did cattle and horses come to the East? (The English and French settlers brought them, along with poultry, hogs, etc.)*

The cattle roamed free for about three hundred years. From time to time the Spaniards, and later the Mexicans, rounded some of them up. The beef obtained from these cattle was very tough. The hides, however, made excellent leather, and that is what the Spaniards wanted. But, in those regions there was not much of a market for either the meat or other products obtained from cattle.

> *Why wasn't there much demand for meat and other cattle products in those regions? (The population was too thin and scattered. To transport the cattle or the products obtained from them to Spanish communities on the west coast or in Mexico would have been difficult because of the distance, deserts, and mountains.)*

As you will remember, the United States added California, Arizona, New Mexico and Texas in the 1840's. Then in the 1860's the first transcontinental, and other east-west railroads, were built. At last there was a way to get cattle to the growing population and cities in the East. However, railroads in the West ran hundreds of miles north of the great herds of cattle. So, it was necessary to drive the cattle over dusty trails to the railroads. The northward journey of the cattle and the cowboys was called the "long drive."

> *What were some of the problems that cowboys would have to be overcome on the long drive? (Finding enough pasture and water for the animals, Indian raids, keeping the herd together, stampedes caused by such things as lightning, and animals such as wolves and mountain lions were only a few of the problems met and, in some way, overcome.)*

The East's demand for Western beef increased each year. In 1866 about 250,000 cattle made the

CATTLEMEN AND FARMERS IN THE EARLY WEST

long drive. By 1871 the number had increased to over 600,000. The cattle sales brought great profits to Western cattlemen. They also gave the railroads a good income. This encouraged the building of more railroad lines. It also encouraged men to start cattle ranches on the plains to the north of the railroads.

> *The cattle had to be transported live on the railroads. Why would this be so? (There were no refrigerated cars to preserve meat.)*

Trouble over Western Lands

The earliest cattlemen grazed their cattle on government land. They did not have to pay rent for the use of the land. Sheepmen also wanted to use these lands. They moved their sheep into the cattle country, especially into the more mountainous parts. Cattlemen were angry about this. Sheep ate the grass so close to the ground that cattle could not graze on the land. Also, the cattlemen believed that they had more of a right to the grazing land because they had been there first. Bitter battles were fought between cattlemen and sheepmen.

> *It is mentioned in the paragraph that sheep ate the grass close to the ground. How would this gradually bring about the erosion of soil? (When grass is cropped close to the roots, the "cover" for soil is removed. When rains come there is little protection; the force of the raindrops and running water washes away the top soil.)*

Farmers obtained western land through the Farmstead Act of 1862. By the terms of this Act, any American could claim 160 acres of land free. Tens of thousands of acres of land were distributed this way. The farmers fenced their land and this greatly disturbed the cattlemen. Fences were necessary to prevent cattle from ruining crops, but fences made the long drives more difficult. Sometimes cattlemen cut the fences so their cattle could obtain food and water. Then, the farmers would try to get even. In the end the farmers won. Cattlemen were forced to buy large amounts of land and fence it.

> *What were some of the reasons why farmers won the question as to whether or not land should be fenced? (There were more farmers than cattlemen, and farmers had the support of the businesses that serviced and supplied them. This meant that they had more influence in obtaining legislation favorable to them. Also, previous to the Homestead Act the land was "public." Now that the farmers **owned** much of the land, the law was on their side.)*

By 1890 long drives were a thing of the past. New railroad lines had been built out in every direction from the main east-west lines. In this way the problem of getting cattle to market was solved. By 1890 the land of the West was being used by farmers, cattlemen, and sheepmen. Of course, the state and federal governments still held millions of acres in reserve.

Name: _____ Date: _____

THE AMERICAN COWBOYS DURING 1865–1890

Without cowboys the cattle industry in the West during the years 1865–1890 would have been impossible. Who were the cowboys? Where did they come from? From whom did they learn their skills?

The last question can be answered first by stating the simple fact that long before the United States acquired the Southwest, Mexicans were herding the wild cattle found there—the "longhorns." These animals were so called because their horn spread was nothing less than spectacular, as much as six feet from horn-tip-to-horn-tip. The Mexicans' methods of roping, branding, and herding; the kind of saddles they found most useful; and the kind of clothing and equipment necessary to do the work—all of these things were passed on to the earliest American cowboys, who then improved on them and passed their knowledge on to others.

The answers to the other two questions are not simple. As one writer put it: "The cowboys were a mixed bag." What he meant by "mixed bag" was that cowboys were of many different nationalities—mostly American—but also many were Mexican ("vaqueros,"or cowboys), Irishmen, Germans, Englishmen, and others. Many cowboys were ex-soldiers from the Confederate and Union armies, some were adventure-seeking young men not more than seventeen years old. A fair number of cowboys were older men who were tired of the drudgery of farming or mining or, perhaps, wanted to remove themselves from the crowded cities in the East. And, there were still others who were running away from places where they may have had some difficulty with the law. No matter what their background, there was one thing for certain: all cowboys had to "pull their own weight" and work cooperatively with others as a team, or else leave!

The West was especially attractive to recently freed African-Americans. They wanted the independence that came with the wide-open spaces of the West, where persons were judged not by the color of their skin, but by their work, their courage, and their endurance. Estimates vary, but it is quite certain that more cowboys were African-American than any other ethnic group.

Understanding

1. If a statement below is true according to the story and illustration, circle the T at the end of the statement.

a. Mexicans were the first to herd cattle in the Southwest. **T**

b. Most longhorns' horn spreads spanned more than six feet. **T**

c. Cowboys worked as individuals rather than as members of a team when herding cattle. **T**

d. One of the things that attracted African-Americans to become cowboys was the opportunity to be independent. **T**

e. All of the cowboys in the illustration have ropes. **T**

f. The cattle in the illustration are not the longhorn breed. **T**

2. All the statements that follow are true. Underline all of those that are *not* mentioned in the story.

a. Indians were among the early cowboys working for the Spaniards.

b. Longhorned cattle were gradually replaced by other breeds of cattle.

c. Men from Ireland were part of the "mixed bag" of cowboys.

d. More ex-Confederate soldiers became cowboys than ex-Union soldiers.

3. From what you see in the picture, what do you think is happening? Explain your reasons.

_____

_____

_____

_____

Name: _____ Date: _____

COWBOYS: CLOTHES AND EQUIPMENT

The clothing and equipment used by cowboys has a long history—a history that goes back to the Mexican vaqueroes of the early 1800's. American cowboys saw the good sense of the Mexicans and adopted many of their ideas, which are still in use today. You can become more familiar with their dress and equipment, including cowboy horses, by completing the following exercise.

1. Label the diagram, as follows:

A: Wide-brimmed hat
B: Bandanna
C: Flap pockets
D: Gloves with cuffs
E: Leather chaps
F: High boots with pointed toes, high insteps
G: Saddle horn
H: Rolled slicker (cape)

2. Beneath each item listing in the diagram is a blank space. Try to think of one more use of the item and write it on the blank line.

3. Color the illustration in any way that you think is appropriate.

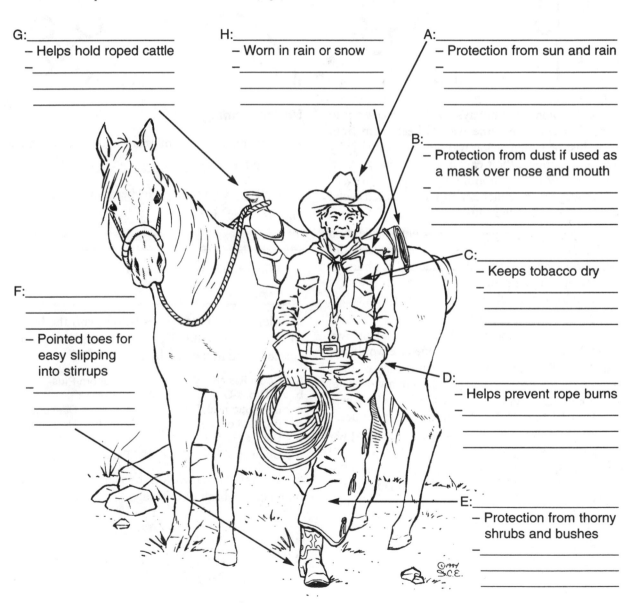

G:_____
– Helps hold roped cattle
–_____
_____
_____

H:_____
– Worn in rain or snow
–_____
_____

A:_____
– Protection from sun and rain
_____
_____

B:_____
– Protection from dust if used as a mask over nose and mouth
–_____
_____
_____

F:_____
– Pointed toes for easy slipping into stirrups
–_____
_____
_____

C:_____
– Keeps tobacco dry
–_____
_____
_____

D:_____
– Helps prevent rope burns
–_____
_____
_____

E:_____
– Protection from thorny shrubs and bushes
–_____
_____

IDENTIFYING CATTLE

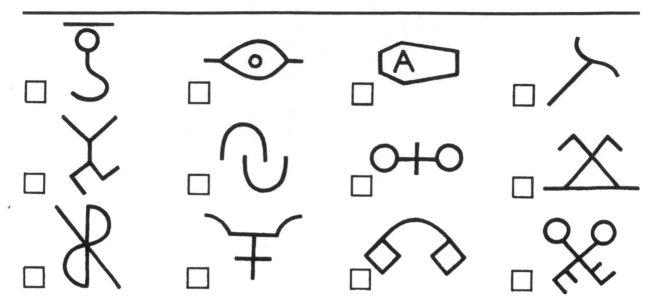

Cattlemen have always found it necessary to mark their cattle in some way to keep them from being lost or stolen. One way to mark cattle is by cutting or clipping their ears in a particular manner. Another way is by tattooing a number on the animal. Today, many ranchers clip a numbered metal band to the ears of the cattle.

However, most past and present ranchers do not use these methods. They do as the Spaniards did long before there was a United States. They burn an identifying mark on the hide of the cattle with a branding iron. The scar left by the hot iron is called a brand.

In the past, as today, each rancher had his own brand. It was understood that no one else would use that brand. Ranchers today deposit a copy of their brand with the government of their county or state. When a brand is registered, the rancher tells where he intends to place the brand on the cattle's hides.

Brands are known by names such as the H bar O (H–O). A brand should be simple. However, it should be designed so that it is difficult to alter. For example, if a brand consisted only of an O, a cattle stealer could easily change the brand by putting a cross in the circle.

Understanding

1. How many ways of marking cattle are mentioned in the story? _____

2. How does a modern rancher make sure that no one else uses his brand? _____

_____

3. Why shouldn't brands be too simple? _____

_____

4. Match the brand names below with the brands shown at the top of this page. Write the letter of the correct name in the box by each brand.

a. Coffin Ranch
b. O-Cross-O
c. Bar Button Hook
d. Buzzard on the Rail
e. Double R
f. Drunken T

g. Longhorn Plus
h. Walking Y
i. Swinging Diamonds
j. Tumbling Horseshoes
k. Walking Keys
l. Pig's Eye

5. Design and name your own brand. Draw your brand on the back of this page.

Name: _____ Date:_____

THE HEROIC RETREAT OF THE NEZ PERCE INDIANS

In 1876 American settlers in the Pacific Northwest claimed land on which the Nez Perce Indians were living. Naturally, the Indians resisted these claims. They had lived in the region long before there was a United States, and they felt that they had first right to the land. Discussions were held in an effort to settle the dispute peacefully. However, the Nez Perce could not accept the only solution that was acceptable to the United States government—removal to a reservation in Idaho. Fighting broke out between the Indians and the settlers. When United States troops stepped in to protect the settlers, the Nez Perce realized that they could not successfully oppose the United States Army. So, about 750 Indians decided to escape into Canada where they thought they could be free.

The great leader of the Nez Perce retreat was Chief Joseph. Over some 1700 miles and for 75 days he led his band toward Canada through thick forests, over blistering plains, rugged mountains, and roaring rivers. The United States Army Cavalry followed in hot pursuit. With less than 200 warriors, Chief Joseph faced a total of more than 2000 troopers. Four major battles and numerous small ones were fought. Even though Chief Joseph's people had to carry wounded warriors, old men and women, helpless children, food, and baggage, he gradually pulled ahead of the troops. Finally believing they were safe from capture, the Nez Perce stopped to rest in the Bear Paw Mountains only thirty miles from the Canadian border. This was a mistake. Colonel Nelson Miles learned of the location of the Nez Perce. He and his men marched 150 miles and surprised the Indians. Even then the Nez Perce chief, who now had fewer than 87 warriors, did not give in easily. Finally, however, after five days of fighting bravely against great odds, the Nez Perce surrendered. The date was October 4, 1877. Chief Joseph and his people were scattered to reservations in all parts of the West.

These are the words of Chief Joseph spoken at the time he surrendered: "I am tired of fighting. Our chiefs are killed. . . . The little children are freezing to death. My people, some of them, have run away to the hills, and have no blankets, no food. . . . I want to have time to look for my children, and see how many of them I can find. . . . My heart is sick and sad. From where the sun now stands I will fight no more forever."

---

1. Why did the Nez Perce Indians resist the claims of American settlers to the Northwest? _____

_____

2. Circle the sentence that tells what the Nez Perce had to do if they wanted their dispute with the United States government peacefully settled.

3. Why did the Nez Perce decide to go to Canada?

_____

4. Supply the facts for each of the parts of the Nez Perce retreat listed below:

• Leader of the Nez Perce:_____

• Distance the Nez Perce travelled in their retreat:

_____

• Number of days the Nez Perce were pursued:

_____

• Number of warriors the Nez Perce had at the beginning of their retreat: _____

• Number of warriors at the last battle: _____

• Number of United States troopers at the beginning of the pursuit: _____

5. What mistake did the Nez Perce make that cost them their freedom? _____

6. Circle the words of Chief Joseph that tell you that not all of the Nez Perce surrendered.

THE FIRST TRANSCONTINENTAL RAILROAD

In 1862 President Lincoln signed laws that made it possible for a railroad to be built from the Missouri River to California. These laws and others passed later provided for cooperation between private railroad companies and the federal government. This was necessary because no private company had enough money to do the job alone.

The United States government and the railroads reached an agreement as to how the expenses of building the railroads would be met, as follows:

➡ For each mile of track laid in a state, a railroad would receive 10 square miles of land along the track.

➡ For each mile of track laid in territory a railroad would receive 20 square miles of land along the track.

➡ The government would loan a railroad company up to $48,000 for each mile of track laid.

➡ The railroads agreed to carry government troops, property, and mail at reduced rates.

1. Here is a problem that will help you understand the financial (money) arrangement between the railroad companies and the government.

How much land could a railroad be given for laying thirty miles of track in a *territory*?
_____ square miles

How much land would be given to a railroad for laying fifty miles of track in a *state*?
_____ square miles

Railroads could sell the land they were granted. The money received helped the railroad meet expenses of labor, materials, and equipment. The amount of money railroads received for the land they sold varied.

FIRST TRANSCONTINENTAL RAILROAD

Name: _____ Date: _____

THE FIRST TRANSCONTINENTAL RAILROAD

2. **Suppose a railroad sold off one square mile (640 acres) of land at $3.00 per acre.**

How much would they have received? $_____

Ten square miles at $3.00 per acre? $_____

Building the Transcontinental Railroad

3. **Complete the blanks in the following paragraph by using information found on the map on the opposite page.**

Two companies, the _____ and the _____, were formed to build the new railroad. The Union Pacific was to start in _____, Nebraska. The Central Pacific was to start in _____, California. The Union Pacific followed the _____ River for several hundred miles and then continued west to _____ Point, Utah. The Central Pacific headed in a northeasterly direction across California and the entire state of _____.

4. **What lake is directly south of where the two railroads were joined?** _____

5. **Through how many states and territories did the completed railroad pass?** _____

Many of the supplies for the Central Pacific had to be shipped from the east coast around South America. On the other hand, the Union Pacific had to haul wood for crossties from the East to the Plains. There were no suitable trees on the grassy plains.

The Central Pacific put down 689 miles of track, and the Union Pacific put down 1086 miles. The Union Pacific could lay track faster because much of its route crossed open plains. The Central Pacific had rugged mountains to cross. In one stretch of sixty miles, fifteen tunnels were dug by the construction workers of the Central Pacific.

6. **What was the length of the completed railroad from Omaha, Nebraska, to Sacramento, California?** _____ miles

The men who built the railroads deserve great credit. They were tough, strong workers. They had to be. The weak could not have endured the long, hot summers and the bitter winters. Many of the workers on the eastern end were recent immigrants from Ireland. Along with them worked many African-Americans, some of whom were working for wages as free men for the first time in their lives.

At first, it was difficult to find workers for the western end of the line. Finally, arrangements were made for some ten thousand Chinese workers to come to America. After the construction was completed, many of the Chinese workers decided to make the United States, and especially the state of California, their permanent home.

7. **People from Europe worked on the eastern railroad, the Union Pacific; whereas, people from China (Asia) worked on the western railroad, the Central Pacific.**

Try to think of a geographical reason why this was so. _____

_____

_____

_____

On May 10, 1869, at Promontory Point, Utah, the transcontinental railroad was finally completed. Governor Stanford of California drove the last spike—a gold one—into the last tie. Then, the engine from the east and the engine from the west were slowly driven until their front "cowcatchers" met. The news was telegraphed all over the country. Americans were proud that day. One of the greatest engineering feats of all time had been accomplished by a country fewer than 100 years old.

SECTION 18

A Singular Person

GEORGE WASHINGTON CARVER: AGRICULTURAL GENIUS

The organization of the facing page and the information on it lends itself to a listening, note-taking, studying experience for your students. A suggested procedure follows:

1. On a piece of paper have your students rule two four-inch columns the length of the paper. Title the columns "Cues."

2. Then, as in a lecture, slowly read or tell the information on the facing page in the order in which it is presented. You may want to elaborate on the basic information. For example, the first paragraph can be supplemented by pointing out Missouri on a wall map. Also, Carver's full name would make for an interesting comment.

3. While you are speaking, students are to take notes in the "Cues" column. As you come to a new topic (indicated by the paragraphs) indicate so to the students; they can make a horizontal line across the cue column. In this way students will have the entire "lecture" broken into major topics. Possible cues for several paragraphs are shown below. Sometimes, a whole phrase might be written as a note, but rarely an entire sentence.

4. Have your students review the lesson by referring to their cue notes. They should attempt to recall and recite the main ideas and details of the reading, triggered by the psychological phenomenon of association.

5. Have your students periodically review the material by attempting to recite from the cue columns, thus strengthening both retention and understanding.

Note: It is essential that instructors go through the entire process with the students several times on different subject matter until the students gain enough skill and confidence to proceed on their own. Students will need help in isolating cues from the bulk of material.

This study method is effective because during the entire procedure students are mentally and physically active. They are responding at maximum level. Their concentration is helped because they have short, numerous, achievable goals. When the information-giving-information-receiving experience is over, students have something tangible to which they may refer and which will help them recall. Therefore, they may prepare for tests more efficiently and effectively.

The cue method of taking notes and studying is especially helpful to those students who are not proficient writers and spellers. They do not get behind and frustrated from writing long sentences or constructing formal outlines. Instructors should write all strange or unusual words, including geography place names, on the chalk board as aids to the note-takers.

Note: An alternate way to apply the "cue" method of studying is to first demonstrate it, then photocopy the facing page, and then have students make cue notes from the printed page.

Cues	*Cues*
P. 1	**P. 4**
• 1864, Missouri, birth	• South: cotton dependent
• Mother/son kidnaped	• Crops fail, prices down = trouble
• Boy returned, mother not	• Cotton: wears out soil
• Boy: George Washington Carver	
	P.5
P. 2	• Carver: rotate crops
• GWC wanted education	• Rotate: change crops yearly
• Kind people help	
• Grad.: Iowa State College, 1894	**P. 6**
	• Small market for peanuts, sweet potatoes
P. 3	• GWC invents new uses for peanuts, sweet potatoes, soy beans, etc.
• Tuskegee Institute, Alabama	
• GWC: agriculture dept. (head)	

GEORGE WASHINGTON CARVER: AGRICULTURAL GENIUS

One night in 1864, a slave mother and her young son were kidnaped from their cabin on a plantation in Missouri. The boy was returned to his master, but the mother was never heard from again. That small boy grew to be one of the greatest agricultural inventors of all time. His name was George Washington Carver.

Young Carver struggled to educate himself. He had a hunger for knowledge that kept driving him on. Through his own efforts and the help of some very kind people, Carver was able to graduate from Iowa State College in 1894.

Carver took a position as the head of the agriculture department of Tuskegee Institute, Alabama. Tuskegee was a small, struggling, African-American college that had a great president, Booker T. Washington. Together the two men made Tuskegee famous throughout the world.

At the time Carver went to Tuskegee the South was too dependent upon the income from one crop—cotton. If a crop failed or if cotton prices went down, the South suffered. Also, planting cotton in the same soil year after year wore out the soil. This made it increasingly difficult for many Southerners to make a living from farming.

Carver believed that the South had to learn to rotate its crops. To rotate crops means to change the kind of crop grown on a particular field from year to year. This helps keep the soil from wearing out.

But Carver also knew that southern farmers would have difficulty selling many of the crops that they could grow. The market for such products as peanuts and sweet potatoes was small. About 1900 Carver went to work to find new uses for old products. He invented hundreds of uses for peanuts: soap, medicine, peanut butter, dye, paper, ink, cosmetics, oil, and many other useful things. He found more than 100 uses for sweet potatoes. Soybeans, which had not had much of a market, became much in demand after Carver found ways to convert them to different kinds of flour and oil.

Manufacturers quickly realized they could make profits from these products. Southern farmers were encouraged to plant these crops rather than just cotton. Southern agriculture underwent great changes. No longer was the South a "one crop" region. The South became more prosperous. Foreign countries also used Carver's ideas for their own betterment.

Carver never became a rich man; in fact, he never patented his inventions. He did not think that it was right for him to make money from his inventions that were gifts from God. However, he was honored all over the world for his achievements. Many fine offers came to him, but he stayed at Tuskegee teaching young students and finding new ways to make life better. It is probably true to say that few people in history have had as much positive effect on making the world a better place to live than this former slave child, George Washington Carver.

SECTION 19

The United States Expands Continentally and Internationally

THE SPANISH-AMERICAN WAR: BACKGROUND

1. United States Involvement with Cuba

As early as 1808, Jefferson thought the United States should own Cuba. When it appeared that Great Britain and France were interested in taking over Cuba, he had his cabinet issue statements that made it clear that the United States would oppose any such action.

Almost every presidential administration up to the Spanish-American War was involved in attempts to buy or annex Cuba. In 1852 President Fillmore would not agree to a proposal by Great Britain and France that Spain's domination of the island be guaranteed. In 1854 the famous Ostend Manifest, which was supposed to be a secret understanding within the United States government but which became publicly known, urged that the United States buy or seize Cuba as a means of ridding Cuba of Spanish oppression.

In 1895 a rebellion started that involved the United States and resulted in the ousting of Spain from Cuba. Prior to our declaration of war with Spain, various locations on the southern coast of the United States were used as bases for attacks by Cuban insurrectionists and American sympathizers against the Spanish colonial government. United States authorities conscientiously tried to halt these activities, but widespread popular support plus the thousands of miles of coastline made it possible for many attacks to be launched.

2. Discussion Question

Who or what blew up the *Maine*? The question remains unanswered, but can provide an opportunity for imaginative thinking. What are some possible answers to the question? (1) *The Spanish government?* Not likely. Spain was working desperately to keep the United States out of its war with the Cuban rebels. (2) *Unauthorized Spanish loyalists?* A good possibility. Hatred and bitterness toward the United States might have motivated irresponsible elements to plan and execute an act of revenge. (3) *The Cuban rebels?* A strong possibility. They would have had the most to gain by such an action because it could have brought the United States into a war with Spain. (4) *American sympathizers of the Cuban revolt?* Not likely. It would be an act of treason against their own country. (5) *A foreign government?* A good possibility. A foreign government might have had something to gain by provoking a war between the United States and Spain. (6) *Accidental external explosion?* A strong possibility. A floating mine could have broken loose from its moorings and discharged itself against the *Maine*. (7) *Accidental internal explosion?* A strong possibility. The *Maine* carried huge amounts of gunpowder. A fire could have broken out below deck and ignited the powder.

3. Sidelights of the Spanish-American War

Battle deaths, 385 (as compared to 53,000 in World War I, and 291,000 in WWII); noncombatant deaths, mostly from diseases such as yellow fever, 2,061; selective service was not used during the Spanish-American War although it later operated during World War I, World War II, the Korean War, and the Vietnam War; four African-Americans units saw action in Cuba (including the famous battle at San Juan Hill with Theodore Roosevelt) and against guerillas in the Philippines; during the Battle of Manila Bay, George Dewey with six ships destroyed ten Spanish ships with no loss of American ships or lives; the American warship *Oregon* steamed some 15,000 miles from the Pacific around Cape Horn to join Sampson's fleet at Santiago de Cuba, thus dramatizing the need for a canal through the Isthmus of Panama for future national defense.

3. Classification of Facts About Puerto Rico

Following is a suggested research project in which students will utilize multiple books.

a. Make photocopies of page 188, "Facts About Puerto Rico ."

b. Have your students read the facts and classify them in the manner described on the student page.

c. After the completion of the activity, have individuals or groups of students select one or two of the categories in the table and find additional facts. The facts may be gleaned from a variety of sources which are readily available.

d. The facts should be stated in clear, brief language and should not contain elements of opinion, but may contain qualifications such as "approximately" or "probably."

e. After researching and compiling additional facts, students may read their lists to the class.

Note: One of the advantages of this activity is that it departs from the traditional narrative report that some students find tiresome to make and/or listen to. Also, students of limited ability may achieve greater success and a feeling of satisfaction in making this kind of report. Finally, it will put students in the position of using a variety of printed material, and will help develop the skill of reading to find specific information.

THE SPANISH-AMERICAN WAR: FIGHTING ON LAND AND SEA

Fighting the War

The first important battle of the Spanish-American War took place in the Philippine Islands, thousands of miles from Cuba. Spain owned the Philippines, and an important part of the Spanish fleet was stationed there.

Commodore George Dewey was in command of the United States fleet that was based near the Philippines. He received a cable from Washington ordering him to use his seven warships to capture or destroy the Spanish fleet in the Philippines. Dewey immediately sailed for Manila Bay, where he found the Spanish fleet. Before the day was over, every Spanish ship had been destroyed. Dewey's ships then guarded the bay and waited for further orders and help before entering the city of Manila.

1.   What nation owned the Philippine Islands at the start of the war? _____

2.   What was the result of the battle in Manila Bay? _____

_____

3.   The map at the right below shows the Philippine Islands and the route taken by Dewey's ships. **On what island of the Philippines is Manila?** _____

4.   What sea did the Americans cross to get to Manila? _____

5.   About how many miles did the fleet sail?
____550   ____700   ____900   ____1100

Meanwhile, another Spanish fleet of seven ships was sailing for Cuba. On May 19, 1898, the fleet steamed into Santiago harbor on Cuba's southern coast. An American fleet commanded by William T. Sampson learned that the Spanish ships were there. Sampson promptly moved his ships and blocked the harbor.

On July 3 the Spanish fleet slipped out of the harbor in a desperate attempt to escape. The Americans discovered what was happening and chased the Spaniards along the Cuban coast. One by one each Spanish ship was overtaken and sunk. The American fleet suffered very little damage.

6.   According to the maps at the left below, in which direction did the Spanish fleet sail in its attempt to escape from the Santiago harbor?

_____

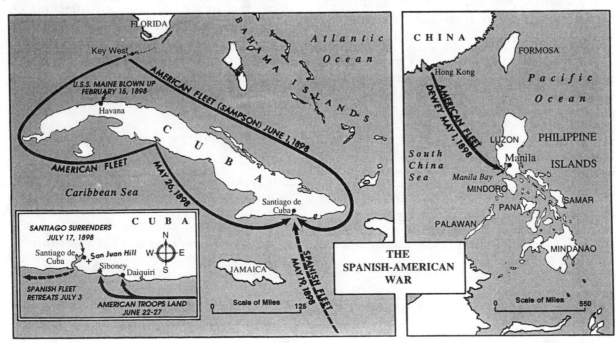

THE SPANISH-AMERICAN WAR: FIGHTING ON LAND AND SEA

While Sampson's ships were blocking the harbor of Santiago, about 16,000 American troops landed nearby to help capture the city. The troops moved toward the high land that overlooked Santiago. Sharp fighting took place. On San Juan Hill an army unit known as the "Rough Riders" won fame for its bravery. When the Spanish fleet was destroyed, these troops then took possession of Santiago.

7. According to the maps on the opposite page when did Santiago surrender? _____

Shortly after the fall of Santiago, the Spanish government asked for peace. It was agreed that all fighting was to stop on August 12, 1898, but this news was delayed in reaching the United States forces in the Philippines. So, on August 13, Dewey and the troops that had been sent to help him marched into Manila. They met very little resistance. The city surrendered the next day.

Representatives of the United States and Spain agreed to a peace treaty in December, 1898. By the terms of the treaty Spain gave up all rights to Cuba. Also, Puerto Rico, the Philippine Islands, and the island of Guam in the Pacific were given to the United States. The United States gave Spain $20,000,000 as payment for the Philippines and Puerto Rico.

The signing of the peace treaty marked the end of the four-hundred-year-old Spanish empire in the New World and the beginning of an overseas empire for the United States.

8. Circle the sentence which helps you to know that the capture of Manila did not require as much fighting as the capture of Santiago.

9. In what way was Puerto Rico treated differently from Cuba in the peace treaty? _____

_____

_____

_____

Helping Cuba

Although the United States could have easily taken Cuba at the end of the Spanish-American War, we did not do so. In fact, we helped the Cubans establish their own government.

There was no real government in Cuba when the war ended. So, for more than two years General Leonard Wood of the United States was Cuba's military governor. He and the United States troops preserved law and order while the Cubans were organizing their own government. During this time representatives of the Cuban people met to write a constitution.

Before the constitution was adopted, the United States asked that certain things be included in it. The United States wanted to make sure that the new government of Cuba would be stable. Therefore, our main request was that the United States have the right to come to the aid of Cuba if its independence was in danger or if law and order needed to be preserved. The requests that the United States made were known as the Platt Amendment.

The Cubans agreed to the Platt Amendment even though they did not like the idea of possible interference by the United States. After the Cuban Constitution was adopted, elections were held. Then, on May 20, 1902, the governing of Cuba by a United States citizen came to an end.

1. Why did the United States have to supply a government for Cuba after the War? _____

_____

_____

2. Circle the sentences which tell why the United States wanted the Platt Amendment.

3. How did the United States show that it had no intention of adding Cuba to its territory? __

_____

_____

Name: _____ Date: _____

FACTS ABOUT PUERTO RICO

To do:

1. Each fact about Puerto Rico listed below can be placed in a specific category of information. The categories are:

➤ History (H)
➤ Education (E)
➤ Geography and Climate (GC)
➤ Government and Politics (GP)
➤ Industry and Trade (IT)
➤ Population (P)

2. After reading the list, decide which category each fact best fits. Write the letter(s) that represent the category on the line before each listing. The first item has been done to help you get started.

H ___ The United States gained possession of Puerto Rico from Spain as a result of the Spanish-American War.

___ Because it is not a state, Puerto Rico does not have representatives in Congress who are allowed to vote.

___ Puerto Ricans make three times more money from manufacturing than from agriculture.

___ Puerto Rico's most important exports are manufactured goods such as chemicals, machinery, clothing, and pharmaceuticals (medicine products).

___ About 30,000 Arawak Indians lived on the island of Puerto Rico at the time it was discovered.

___ Puerto Ricans may vote in United States presidential elections if they live in a state.

___ The University of Puerto Rico has an enrollment of more than 25,000 students.

___ In the early fall, Puerto Rico is often hit by hurricanes.

___ Beginning in 1511 Africans were brought to the island to work as slaves for the Spaniards.

___ Toward the end of the 16th century, the British tried to take Puerto Rico from the Spaniards; however, their efforts failed.

___ New York City has a greater Puerto Rican population than any city in Puerto Rico itself.

___ In 1952 Puerto Rico became a self-governing commonwealth.

___ In 1625 the Dutch tried to take Puerto Rico, but, like the British before them, they also failed.

___ Puerto Rico is about one half the size of New Jersey.

___ Columbus discovered Puerto Rico in 1493 on his second voyage of discovery.

___ In 1873 the Spanish government abolished slavery in Puerto Rico.

___ When the United States took over Puerto Rico, only about 20% of its 900,000 people could read or write; in 1992 about 90% of the population could do so.

___ Puerto Rico has high central mountains with many small rivers flowing from them.

___ Spanish is spoken in Puerto Rican schools; however, starting in first grade English is also taught.

___ Puerto Ricans do not pay income taxes to the United States government even though they are United States citizens.

___ San Juan, Puerto Rico's capital, has a population of about 450,000.

___ About 85% of the things Puerto Rico buys from other countries are bought from the United States.

___ In 1994 Puerto Rico had a population of about 4,000,000.

___ As a result of a mild climate, Puerto Rico's main crops are sugar, bananas, coffee, tobacco, pineapples, and oranges.

___ In 1990 more than 155,000 Puerto Ricans were attending colleges and universities.

___ The United States buys about 90% of all Puerto Rican exports.

___ Puerto Rico is about 100 miles from east to west, and about 35 miles from north to south.

___ About 18% of Puerto Rican workers are in manufacturing, and about 3% work in agriculture.

___ About 20% of Puerto Rico's land is covered by forests.

___ In November 1993, Puerto Ricans voted to decide the future of their government. The election was close: 48.4% for Puerto Rico to remain a commonwealth, 46.2% to become a state, 4.4% to become independent.

Name: _____ Date: _____

THE EARLY HAWAIIANS

People called Polynesians had lived in the Hawaiian Islands for at least one thousand years before Captain Cook landed there. The Polynesians had come to Hawaii from islands to the south. These people also settled many other islands in the Pacific Ocean. So, there is a vast region in the Pacific which has been given the name Polynesia.

The Polynesians were great sailors. They travelled in canoes made from hollowed logs. Some of their canoes were about one hundred feet long and could carry forty or fifty people. Sometimes sails made from fibers of the coconut palm trees were fitted to the canoes. Some canoes had two or three poles extending from their sides to which a log was attached. This kind of canoe was called an outrigger. Outrigger canoes were hard to tip over.

When the Polynesians were going on long voyages, they placed a raised deck between two canoes. A shelter on the deck protected the women and children during storms. Supplies were stored in the shelter. Animals such as dogs, pigs, and chickens rode on the deck. Water was carried in hollow bamboo logs. Fires were built over beds of sand on the deck. Birds and fish caught on the voyage were cooked over the fires. The Polynesians could stay at sea for weeks without suffering any major discomforts.

Understanding

1. On the map below, draw a circle around the Hawaiian Islands.

2. Are the Hawaiian Islands north or south of the equator? _____

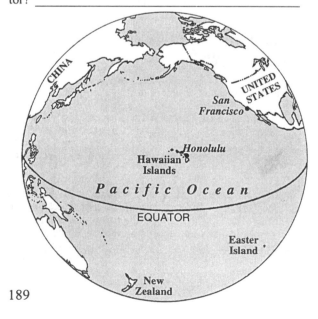

3. Connect the Hawaiian Islands, New Zealand, and Easter Island with straight lines. Label the area within the triangle *Polynesia*. Why is this area called Polynesia? _____

_____

4. Draw a line from Honolulu in the Hawaiian Islands to San Francisco. To show the distance write *2,000 miles* on the line.

5. What name is given to the kind of canoe shown in the picture below? _____

6. How do you know from the story that the Polynesians probably ate pork and eggs on their voyages? ___

_____

7. How did the Polynesians store water? _____

_____

8. How did the Polynesians add to their supply of food on their voyage? _____

_____

_____

Challenge Question: The Polynesians did not have navigation instruments. Yet, they seldom got lost at sea. What is there in the picture that is a clue as to how they navigated? Write your answer on the back of this page.

Name: _____ Date: _____

THE UNITED STATES ACQUIRES ALASKA

Fill in the blank spaces in the paragraphs below with the information from the map.

The map shows that there are only _____ miles of water between Alaska and Russia. The body of water between these two land masses is called the _____. The Russians took profitable harvests of seal and sea otter furs from Alaskan coastal waters and islands in the years prior to 1860.

In 1784 the Russians established a fur-trading settlement on _____ Island. Then they began trapping on the mainland of Alaska. By 1860 the Russians had killed most of the furbearing animals. Then, Russian interest in Alaska began to decline.

In 1867 the Russians suddenly offered to sell Alaska to the United States. Secretary of State William Seward was very interested in the offer. However, some people objected to the purchase. They said that Alaska was worthless. They called Alaska "Seward's Icebox" and the "Polar Bear Garden." Other people said that the government had no right to buy outside territory. By "outside" they meant that Alaska was not adjacent to the United States.

Seward went on a campaign to tell the people and Congress about the value of the territory. He explained that Alaska was a great bargain at only two cents an acre for a total $7,200,000. Alaska was even more of a bargain than Louisiana which had cost about three cents an acre.

Seward told about Alaska's great resources of fish, lumber, and minerals. Then he offered an argument for buying Alaska that was hard to dismiss. "Suppose we did not buy Alaska," he asked, "would you want some other nation to have it?" Finally, Seward pointed out that since it had been legal by the laws of the country to buy Louisiana, it must also be legal to buy Alaska.

The arguments of Seward finally won out. In April, 1867, the United States Senate agreed to the purchase. The purchase of Alaska also included the Aleutian Islands. The United States thus added about 600,000 square miles of land to its territory.

Understanding

1. On the map below circle the *Aleutian Islands*.

2. The body of water just north of the Aleutian Islands is the Bering Sea. Label the *Bering Sea*.

3. Why did the Russians lose interest in Alaska?

_____

Answer the following two questions on the reverse side of this page.

4. Briefly list three arguments Seward offered as reasons for buying Alaska.

5. How might a person in charge of the defense of the United States have answered Seward's question: Would you want some other nation to have Alaska? Explain.

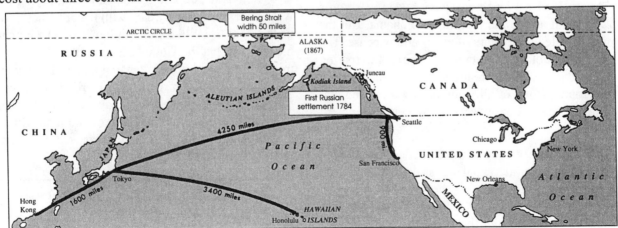

BUILDING THE PANAMA CANAL

The narrative and graphics on this page and the following two should prove helpful in teaching a lesson on the acquisition and building of the Panama Canal. The fourth page—a student response page—tells about George Goethals, the builder of the canal. Significant attention has been given to Goethals's values and character and may, by example, have a positive effect on your students' values.

It is suggested that you make a transparency of the map, picture, and diagram on the third page of this lesson. Then, as you present the lesson you may refer your students to the appropriate graphics.

Notice that each narrative paragraph is numbered. The numerals before the questions on the facing page relate to the numbered paragraphs.

1 Ever since Balboa crossed the Isthmus of Panama in 1513, nations have wanted to build a canal there to connect the Atlantic and Pacific oceans. Such a canal would have saved thousands of miles of sea travel for the Forty-niners and others who followed them. To reach the west coast of the United States by sea from the east coast, people had to sail around South America. By 1900 the need for a canal was even greater. The United States had acquired Alaska, Hawaii, Guam, and Puerto Rico. It also had interests in Cuba and the Philippines.

2 A canal across Central America would also be a help to the defense of the United States. For example, if the country were attacked on its Pacific Ocean side, the ships in the Atlantic could come to their defense more quickly. Also, a canal would make trade with other countries faster. The time needed to sail from New York to China, for example, would be cut in half.

3 In 1881 a French company began work on a canal across the Isthmus of Panama. But the project failed after years of effort and expense. The rugged mountains, the tangled jungle, the roaring rivers, and the heat were too much for the French to overcome. Worst of all were yellow fever and malaria, dreaded diseases carried by certain kinds of mosquitoes.

4 In the early 1900's, the United States decided to try to build a canal across the Isthmus. Such a canal could not be built, however, without the permission of Colombia. This was because the canal was to go through the Panama section of that country. Unfortunately, we could not come to an agreement with Colombia. The dispute centered around what price was to be paid for the land where the canal would be built.

5 Theodore Roosevelt, who was President at that time, was disappointed and angry. He was anxious for the construction of the canal to begin. He thought the Colombians were being unreasonable. The Colombians thought the United States was unreasonable.

6 Even more disturbed were the Panamanians. They believed that the canal would make their region richer. So, they rose in rebellion against Colombia. The Panamanians received encouragement and aid from the United States. On November 3, 1904, Panama declared itself to be a free and independent nation.

7 The United States gave immediate recognition and support to the new country. Two weeks later we made a treaty with Panama that gave us the right to build a canal in Panama. The agreement stated that the United States could have a ten-mile strip of land across Panama as a right-of-way for the canal. In return we paid Panama $10,000,000. We were also to pay Panama a rent of $250,000 each year for the use of the land. Since that time, however, we have increased this rent many times over.*

*   In 1978 the United States Senate voted a treaty that turns over the Panama Canal to Panama on December 31, 1999.

191

BUILDING THE PANAMA CANAL

8 Colombia bitterly protested her loss. The United States argued that the Panamanians had a right to independence if they so desired. Nevertheless, it is easy to understand why Colombia was unhappy. In 1921 the United States voted to pay Colombia $25,000,000.

9 Work on the Panama Canal began in 1904. One of the first tasks was to eliminate yellow fever and malaria. The man who directed the work against those diseases was Colonel William C. Gorgas. Gorgas knew that to eliminate these diseases it was necessary to destroy the breeding places of the mosquitoes.

10 Gorgas had his men drain the swamps where the mosquitoes bred. They sprayed with oil all other places where mosquitoes might lay their eggs. Once, Gorgas angered the canal engineers by spraying cement even before it had dried. However, by such actions Gorgas rid the area of yellow fever and malaria.

11 Meanwhile work on the canal continued. Several chief engineers worked on the job. The man who finally completed the task was George W. Goethals, an army engineer. An idea of the size of the undertaking can be gained by knowing one simple fact: at one time there were 30,000 men working on the job. Deep cuts had to be made through mountains. This required the removal of millions of tons of earth. The courses of rivers were changed, dams and locks were built, and lakes were created.

Finally, in August 1914, some ten years after its start, the canal was completed. The Atlantic and Pacific were joined.

Questions related to the narrative

1. Refer to the map. How many miles shorter from New York to San Francisco is the canal route than the around-South America route? (*8,000 miles*) Assuming an ocean-going ship could sail 400 miles in a day, how many days could be saved by using the canal route? (*20 days*)

2. Why would the canal route have made the products of China less expensive in the United States? (*Transportation costs reduced*)

3. Suppose someone said, "I can't believe mosquitoes could interfere with the building of the Panama Canal." How would you respond? (*Little mosquitoes carry big diseases: malaria and yellow fever*)

4. Refer to the map. How can the geographical location of Panama in relation to Colombia be described? (*A narrow strip of land jutting northwestward out of northern Colombia*)

5. What seemed to be lacking on the part of the Colombians and Americans with regard to the Panama Canal negotiations? (*Patience, willingness to compromise*)

6. What is your opinion relative to the United States helping the Panamanians rebel? (*An "open" question; accept diverse points of view*)

7. Why was the payment of ten million dollars to the new country of Panama especially helpful to them at the beginning of their independence? (*Costs of setting up a new government*)

8. Suppose we hadn't built a canal across Panama. What might have been an alternate route? (*Refer to a map. A route across Nicaragua was a distinct possibility, and was actually considered. The route across the country would have been longer; on the other hand, Lake Nicaragua would have been incorporated into the canal route.*)

9. Why was it important to eliminate the breeding places of disease-carrying mosquitoes as compared to spraying for existing mosquitoes? (*Spraying would have to be done year-round in tropical Panama, and some mosquitoes would still survive. Also, if not eliminated entirely, the mosquitoes would probably have developed immunities over several generations.*)

BUILDING THE PANAMA CANAL

10. What was Gorgas's reasons for spraying cement? (*Cement is wet when first poured; mosquitoes could breed in the dampness.*)

11. What is taking place in the picture? (*The men and machines are cutting through the mountains—the Gaillard Cut. Level after level of land and rock are removed until the "floor" is reached.*)

How does a lock work? (*Refer to the diagram. The Panama Canal is not a sea-level canal; ships must be raised and lowered over the hills. A lock is* a huge tank. After a ship enters the first lock, the gates behind it are closed. Water is pumped into the lock. As the water level rises, so does the ship. The gates to the next lock are opened, and the ship moves forward. The gates behind the ship are locked, as before. Water is pumped in, as before. The reverse procedure is used to lower the ships. **Note**: Your students can follow ship A as it enters the Miraflores Lock on the Pacific side of the Canal, travels east, and exits onto the Atlantic side of the Canal.)

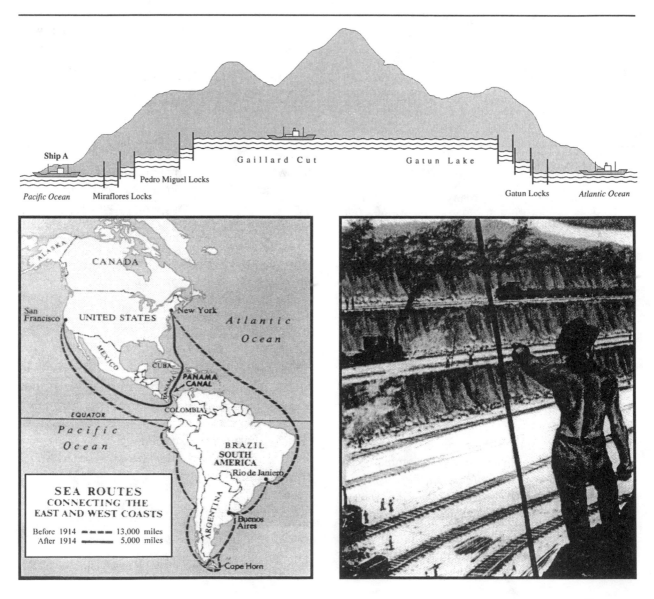

Name: _____ Date: _____

GEORGE WASHINGTON GOETHALS: CANAL BUILDER

Goethals served in Puerto Rico during the Spanish-American War. In World War I he served as a Major-General.

George Washington Goethals's parents had been in the United States ten years when he was born. Before coming to this country in 1848, the Goethals had lived in Holland.

Goethals directed the building of the Panama Canal. This has been called the world's greatest engineering job. The question is sometimes asked, "Why was Goethals able to succeed where so many others had failed?" There is no simple answer to this question, but here are some of the reasons:

Knowledge and experience: It is said that Goethals could do any of the jobs his men were called upon to do. He studied hard. He also actually worked on construction jobs. So when Goethals planned new projects, he was able to combine his book learning with his practical experiences.

Honesty: The men felt that they could trust Goethals. He never broke a promise. He was firm and fair. He never took a penny that did not belong to him even though he was in charge of spending millions of dollars.

Determination: Once during the canal's construction, a great landslide filled in a cut in the mountain that his men had been excavating for years. Many of the engineers were discouraged and thought the canal project should be abandoned. The engineer in charge asked Goethals, "What are we going to do now?" Goethals answered, "Dig it out again."

Loyalty: Once Goethals refused an offer of a million dollars to work for a private company. When asked about it he said, "I owe it to the public to stay here until the canal is finished."

Resourcefulness: During the Spanish-American War, Goethals was in charge of landing troops and equipment on a rough beach in Puerto Rico. But there were no docks and no lumber with which to build them. However, Goethals found a way. He took some barges, filled them with sand, then sank them. The sunken barges served well as a safe landing place.

1. What language was probably spoken from time-to-time in the boyhood home of Goethals?

_____ Spanish   _____ Dutch   _____ Swedish

2. When was Goethals born?

_____ 1838   _____ 1848   _____ 1858   _____ 1868

3. Which of these qualities did Goethals have?

_____ timidity   _____ faithfulness

_____ imagination   _____ greediness

_____ stubbornness   _____ ignorance

4. What were the "docks" in the picture before they became docks? _____

5. In what branch of the army would you guess that Goethals was an officer: Signal Corps, Corps of Engineers, or Infantry? _____

6. Explain briefly why Goethals refused an offer for a better-paying job in private business. _____

_____

7. What fact is told in the caption of the picture that is not mentioned in the story? _____

_____

8. Complete this sentence: Goethals learned from books, but also he learned from _____ .

9. From what you can see in the picture, suggest why the freighter isn't moored to the docks. _____

_____

10. What steps are necessary to transfer the supplies from the freighter to the docks? _____

_____

MATTHEW HENSON: POLAR EXPLORER

On April 4, 1909, six men stood at the North Pole. They were half dead from exhaustion. As they watched an American flag wave in the freezing wind, they gave three cheers and shook hands all around. One of the men was Robert E. Peary, the leader of the group. Four of the men were Eskimo. The sixth man was Matthew A. Henson, an African-American. These men were the first to reach the North Pole.

The association between Peary and Henson had begun nearly twenty-two years before. Peary, a naval officer, had asked Henson to accompany him on an expedition to Central America. The purpose of the expedition was to map possible canal routes. Henson was to be Peary's personal servant. However, soon after starting work, one of the men in the surveying crew quit his job after nearly drowning in quicksand. Peary asked Henson if he was willing to take the man's place. Henson eagerly agreed.

Henson was a fast learner. Before long he could work the surveying transit and other instruments with accuracy and skill. He was strong and could keep going long after other men would stop. He was cheerful, and the other men liked and respected him. Peary noted all of these things. He realized that Matt Henson was a man who could help him carry out his dream of being the first to reach the North Pole.

Peary and Henson went on several polar expeditions together. They had many adventures in which they faced death. Once, Peary's feet were so frozen that the tips of eight toes fell off. This did not stop him from continuing his search for the North Pole. Peary was as stubborn as he was courageous. Another time Henson saved Peary's life by shooting a musk-ox that was attacking Peary. Peary once said of Henson, "I can't get along without him."

Dozens of individuals and organizations have honored Henson for the part he played in Peary's polar explorations. In 1945 Congress awarded him a silver medal and cited him for "outstanding service to the government of the United States." Then, in 1961 a plaque in his memory was placed in the State House in Annapolis, Maryland. On it were the words that many felt should have been said years before. They are, "Matthew Alexander Henson, Co-discoverer of the North Pole."

---

1.   What year will mark the ninetieth anniversary of the first successful expedition to the North Pole?

_____

2.   Number in order of actual occurrence the following events mentioned in the story.

_____   Henson takes the place of one of Peary's surveyors.

_____   Peary realizes that Henson can be of great help on his polar explorations.

_____   Henson is honored by the State of Maryland.

_____   Henson accompanies Peary to Central America as his personal servant.

3.   Circle the word or words that describe why Henson was able to make his co-workers feel better under difficult conditions.

4.   Underline the sentence that tells

☞ Peary's dream.

☞ something about Peary's character.

☞ how the extreme polar cold injured Peary.

5.   What other people were also co-discoverers of the North Pole? _____

6.   On the back of this page write a paragraph that describes the scene shown in the picture. Try to use descriptive adjectives and verbs.

THREE IMPORTANT U. S. POSSESSIONS: SAMOA, GUAM, VIRGIN ISLANDS

American Samoa

In the 1870's the United States became interested in the Samoan Islands, which are about 2500 miles southwest of Hawaii. In 1878 a chief of one of the islands agreed to allow the United States to have a naval station at the harbor of Pago Pago. In return, the United States agreed to help the islanders if they had difficulty with other nations.

In the 1890's it became clear that Germany and Great Britain wanted to take over the islands. The United States discussed the future of the islands with these nations several times over the years. Finally, in 1899, the Samoan Islands were divided between the United States and Germany. Today, our part of the islands is known as American Samoa.

Facts About the Samoan Islands:

Location: South Pacific, about 2500 miles southwest of Hawaii

Land Area: 77 square miles, six main islands

Population: Approximately 47,000 in 1990

Capital: Pago Pago (pronounced "Pango Pango")

Administration: Residents are United States "nationals," not citizens; they are represented by one nonvoting delegate to the House of Representatives.

American Guam

The first European to arrive in the Mariana Islands, of which Guam is but one island, was Magellan (1521). Spain colonized the islands and held them to the end of the Spanish-American War, when they were ceded to the United States. Guam was important to us because it gave us a possession in the far Pacific that would serve as a naval base on the sea route to the Philippines.

In 1941, Japan seized Guam. However, in 1944 American armed forces recaptured the island. Guam was used extensively in the last months of World War II as a supply/staging station for the final assaults on Japan.

Facts About Guam:

Location: The southernmost of the Marianas, about 3500 miles west of Hawaii

Land Area: 209 square miles, the largest island in the Marianas

Population: Approximately 130,000 in 1990

Capital: Agana

Administration: A self-governing, unincorporated territory of the United States; residents are American citizens, but do not vote in presidential elections.

Miscellaneous: Significant United States bases are located there, including Anderson Air Force Base, and naval installations.

American Virgin Islands

The Virgin Islands were discovered by Columbus in 1493. At the time the islands were inhabited by Carib Indians. As a result of diseases introduced by the Spaniards, and deaths brought about by the Spanish subjugation of the islanders, the original inhabitants were all dead or departed by 1600. With the natives gone, the Spaniards introduced Africans into the islands and enslaved them to work on sugar plantations.

Through a series of complicated events (European wars, treaties, etc.), Denmark acquired the easternmost of the islands in the 18th century. The Danes held the islands for almost 250 years. Then in 1917 the Danes agreed to transfer ownership of their islands to the United States for $25,000,000. We were interested in the islands for two main reasons: (1) there was good reason to think that Germany wanted them and (2) the islands would give us a strategic naval base in the Caribbean Sea, made especially important since the opening of the Panama Canal in 1914. Ten years after gaining possession, the United States granted citizenship to the Virgin Island inhabitants.

Facts About the Virgin Islands:

Location: A part of the West Indies in northeastern Caribbean Sea; about 50 miles east of Puerto Rico and 1700 miles south-southeast of Miami

Number of Islands: Three main inhabited islands (St. Croix, St. Thomas, St. John) and about 50 smaller islands

Land Area: 132 square miles

Population: Approximately 102,000 in 1990

Capital: Charlotte Amalie (St. Thomas)

Administration: U. S. Department of the Interior; a delegate is elected to the United States Congress who may vote in committee, but not in the House; Virgin Islanders are citizens, but they are not allowed to vote in presidential elections.

Miscellaneous: Main industry is tourism; hilly land not conducive to extensive agriculture; the British Virgin Islands are to the north and east.

SECTION 20

The United States Expands Its Population

IMMIGRATION: SUGGESTIONS FOR TEACHING

Throughout American history, immigration has been, perhaps, the most significant and dominating factor in shaping the United States. All Americans living today, including the first immigrants—the Indians—have their origination in some place other than North America. And, even today, immigration is modifying the nature of the nation.

These two pages will offer suggestions for teaching about immigration, including commentary, a poem, a helpful book, and activities.

Statue of Liberty

After 1886, for many millions of foreigners, the best-known symbol of the United States was the Statue of Liberty. As emigrants neared their long journey's end at the entrance of New York's harbor, they looked for the magnificent woman with the torch of liberty in her right hand and the tablet bearing the date of the Declaration of Independence in her left hand. The sight was one that would not soon be forgotten. It was among the first visual and emotional contacts emigrants made with what was to become their adopted country.

"The New Colossus," a poem by Emma Lazarus, is inscribed on a tablet in the statue's base. A reading of the poem followed by a discussion of its meaning could be a productive experience for the class. One of the most interesting facets of the poem is the contrasts made between the Old World and the New World.

The New Colossus

Not like the brazen giant of Greek fame,
With conquering limbs astride from land to land;
Here at our sea-washed, sunset gates shall stand
A mighty woman with a torch, whose flame
Is the imprisoned lightning, and her name
Mother of Exiles. From her beacon-hand
Glows world-wide welcome; her mild eyes command
The air-bridged harbor that twin cities frame.
"Keep ancient lands, your storied pomp!" cries she
With silent lips. "Give me your tired, your poor,
Your huddled masses yearning to breathe free,
The wretched refuse of your teeming shore.
Send these, the homeless, tempest-tost to me,
I lift my lamp beside the golden door!"

Immigrant interviews

Arrange to tape-record interviews with one or more immigrants known to students in the class. Relatives of the students would be especially appropriate to interview. If a tape recorder is not available, the interviewer can take careful notes. In either case, questions should be prepared beforehand. Most of the questions should be of such a nature that they require a response beyond a mere "yes" or "no." Some sample questions follow:

1. *What was there about your home country that made you want to come to the United States?*
2. *Why did you choose the United States rather than some other country?*
3. *How did you get here?*
4. *Please describe your route and tell some of the problems you faced on the journey itself.*
5. *What were your reactions when you finally reached the United States?*
6. *What was your first job, and what were some of the problems you had adjusting to the United States?*
7. *How did you prepare to become a citizen?*
8. *Now that you have gone through the entire immigration process, what advice would you give to someone who was interested in emigrating to the United States?*
9. *Some people have said that naturalized citizens often become better citizens than those who are born in the country. How would you react to that?*

Note: It would be helpful to have a mock interview or two in the classroom before your students conduct the real interviews.

Book suggestion

Mary Antin, who came to the United States as a child immigrant from Russia, wrote *The Promised Land*, a book that tells in simple, yet eloquent language, what it meant to her and her family to have the privilege of living in America. Some of the experiences she relates are full of humor; others are very sad. A selection from *The Promised Land* can be found in number 208 of Commager and Nevins, *The Heritage of America*.

Commentary on African-Americans as Immigrants

Almost every immigrant group—Germans, Poles, Italians, Chinese, etc.—has faced consider-

IMMIGRATION: SUGGESTIONS FOR TEACHING

able discrimination in the United States at one time or other. But these groups have largely overcome prejudices against them and have climbed up the political, economic, and social ladders. Yet, the progress of one great immigrant group, African-Americans, has been considerably more frustrated. Why has this been so? (*African-Americans have not had the same opportunities—educational, economic, and political—extended to them as have been extended to other groups. Other minority groups may have been denied opportunities temporarily, but African-Americans have been denied opportunities consistently for almost four hundred years by individuals, private organizations, and, even worse, by local, state, and national governments. Even today, for example, in some sections of our country, African-Americans are kept from voting by economic and physical intimidation. Because of the color of their skins, African-Americans are easily singled out as targets for discrimination. Also, the intentional and unintentional stereotyping of African-Americans in such things as history books, plays, movies, TV shows, songs, and jokes has often built unfavorable images in the minds of many white Americans, thus making it easier for them to rationalize their denial of opportunity to African-Americans.*)

The Oath of Allegiance

The final step for aliens who are applying for United States citizenship is to take an oath of allegiance in court before a federal judge. When the solemn swearing-in ceremony is over, the new citizens are congratulated, and each is given a certificate of citizenship. Each can then proudly say, "I am an American."

The full Oath of Allegiance follows:

I hereby declare, on oath, that I absolutely and entirely renounce and abjure all allegiance and fidelity to any foreign prince, potentate, state or sovereignty, to whom or which I have heretofore been a subject or citizen; that I will support and defend the Constitution and laws of the United States of America against all enemies, foreign and domestic; that I will bear arms on behalf of the United States when required by the law; that I will perform noncombatant service in the armed forces of the United States when required by the law; that I will perform work of national importance under civilian direction when required by the law; and that I take this obligation freely without any mental reservation or purpose of evasion; so help me God.

Note: Natural-born citizens of the United States are not required to take an oath of allegiance. Some have argued that they should. What are your students' opinions?

E Pluribus Unum

It is reasonable to assume that each country of the world (some 170 at latest count) is represented in the United States by immigrants. To emphasize this tremendous diversity, have each student volunteer to "adopt" one of the countries. The country could be one with which the student's family is connected.

Each country should be represented by a flag made by the adopting student. The flags may be put on display with a suitable caption, for example, "E Pluribus Unum," (Out of Many—One). *Note*: *The World Almanac and Book of Facts* and various young persons' encyclopedias contain pictures of the world's flags.

"E Pluribus Unum"

Book

Leonard Patrick O'Connor Wibberley has written an informative and entertaining book titled *The Coming of the Green*. The "Green" in the title refers to the Irish. The book tells why the Irish came to America, how they prepared for their journey, what the journey itself was like, and what the Irish did once they got to the United States. Some of the things mentioned in the book show how indomitable the Irish, and all immigrants, were in pursuing their search for a better life. Mr. Wibberley tells the reader that Irish Catholics had been forbidden to go to school in the old country, and "were almost a hundred per cent illiterate," and that when the immigrants arrived in America they pushed wheelbarrows on which they loaded their possessions and children. The immigrants were glad to be paid six dollars a month as they worked on the canal-, railroad-, and road-building jobs.

IMMIGRATION FACTS: 1820–1992

In 1790 the population of the country was about 4,000,000. By 1990 the population had grown to about 250,000,000. People coming here from foreign countries accounted for much of the growth. After they arrived most immigrants married and had children of their own, and their children had children, and so on. The population just grew and grew.

Bar Graph

The bar graph on the opposite page will help you understand that during 200 years of immigration there were great increases and great declines in the immigration rates. Complete the blanks in the paragraph with numbers and years from the bar graph.

1. From 1831 to 1850 _____ immigrants entered the United States. Between 1851 and 1870, the number who entered more than doubled to _____. In the forty-year period from 1871 to 1910 a total of _____ immigrants landed on our shores. From 1911 to 1930 there were _____ immigrants. The greatest drop in the number of entering people occurred from _____, with only _____ immigrants entering. The figures began to climb again in the twenty-year period from 1951 to 1970. The period from 1971 to 1990 saw the second highest number of immigrants: _____.

2. In the bar graph, find the answers to the following questions:

a. How many more people entered the United States in the 1911–1930 period than in the 1931–1950 period? _____

b. During the two twenty-year periods between 1891 and 1930 many countries in the world suffered hard times. Families could not find enough work to properly feed, clothe, house, and educate themselves. How many people took advantage of the opportunity to find a better place to live by entering the United States in those years? _____

c. According to the bar graph what is the total number of people who have entered the United States between 1831 and 1990? _____

Circle Graph (opposite page)

1. Write the title for the graph on the blank lines next to it: Immigrants from Around the World, 1820–1990.

2. To distinguish parts of the graph, use colors for the segments.

3. On the back of this page, summarize the main idea or "message" of the graph and include supporting detail.

Completing a Bar Graph

From what four countries of Europe have the most people emigrated to the United States? The following figures tell you: Germany, 7,500,000; Italy, 5,400,000; United Kingdom, 5,200,000; Ireland, 4,700,000.

Use these figures to complete the bar graph below. Some help has been given to get you started.

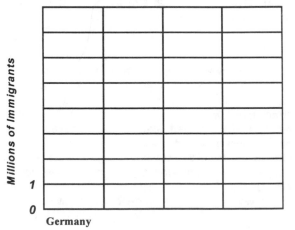

European Countries Sending the Most Immigrants to the U.S.A.: 1820–1992

Name: _____ Date: _____

IMMIGRATION FACTS: 1820-1992

*Immigrants Entering the United States: 1831–1990**

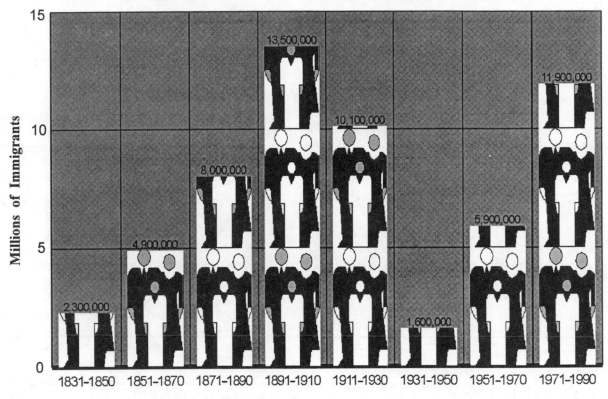

Years

*Figures rounded to the nearest 100,000

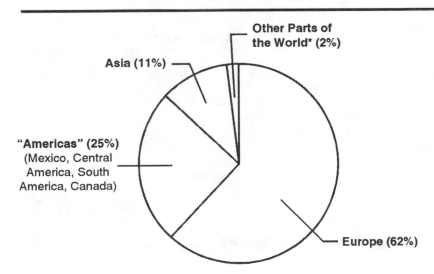

Asia (11%)

Other Parts of the World* (2%)

"Americas" (25%)
(Mexico, Central America, South America, Canada)

Europe (62%)

Title: _____

_____

_____

_____

* Other Parts of the World: Australia, New Zealand, Oceania, Africa, etc.

Note: Data for both graphs from *Statistical Abstract of the United States, 1992.*

Name: _____ Date: _____

EMIGRATION: THE VOYAGE TO A NEW HOME

It took courage and determination to be an emigrant. Many problems had to be solved and many dangers faced. For emigrants from Europe and Asia, one of the most fearsome things was the crossing of the ocean.

_____

_____

_____

Average emigrants of the 1800's and the early 1900's did not occupy pleasant, clean ship's cabins. They did not pass the days by playing shuffleboard or lounging in deck chairs. They did not spend the evening hours dancing to the music of an orchestra. _____

_____

_____

Emigrants did not eat three well-cooked meals a day in an attractive dining room; they cooked their own meals. They brought all the food they thought they would need for the voyage. Of course, without refrigeration food often spoiled. If the emigrants' food gave out before the end of the voyage, they faced starvation. __

_____

_____

_____

Emigrants lived and slept in the steerage, a dark space deep within the ship. They shared this space, which might have been originally designed for cargo, with hundreds of other people. Such crowded conditions were unhealthy and sickness was common. _____

_____

_____

_____

However, emigrants were usually sturdy and strong. They had great patience and were not easily discouraged. The very fact that they were willing to risk their lives and endure hardships indicates that they were not ordinary people. They kept their spirits up by singing, talking, and planning for the future. _____

_____

_____

_____

Finally, after many days and weeks at sea, the ships reached the shores of the emigrants new homes. Soon, they would be landing. A new life was about to begin. _____

_____

_____

Understanding

1. A paragraph is made up of a main topic and supporting details. With that in mind, decide in which of the paragraphs above each of the following sentences should be placed. Write the sentences in the space provided.

Sentences

✍ Then, other emigrants would offer food they could spare to those who had nothing.

✍ The friends they had made on the long voyage would go their separate ways.

✍ Some emigrants had never seen an ocean.

✍ The days passed very slowly.

✍ Sometimes, adult emigrants taught children the geography, history, and language of the United States.

✍ The long nights were not quiet; babies cried, sick people coughed and tossed restlessly on their sleeping pallets.

2. The illustration shows a boatload of emigrants entering New York harbor. The Statue of Liberty is in the background. Imagine yourself an author who is going to write a paragraph based on what is seen in the picture. You might start your paragraph like this: *As the ship passed the Statue of Liberty . . .*

Note: Write your paragraph on the reverse of this page.

Name: _____ Date:_____

AMERICANS: OUT OF MANY—ONE

Two Americans From Varied Backgrounds

Mary McGuire (Irish)
Anthony Lazzaro (Italian)
— James Lazzaro
— Nicholas Lazzaro
— Angela Lazzaro
— Michael Lazzaro

Maria Zorro (Mexican)
Robert LaCrosse (French)
— Linda LaCrosse

— Wanda Lazzaro
— Peter Lazzaro

Elsi Rothacker (Swiss)
Chiang Chung (Chinese)
— Helena Chung
— Judith Chung
— Tanya Blackhawk
— Christopher Blackhawk

Anna Rostovich (Russian)
John Blackhawk (American Indian)
— Simon Blackhawk
— Katherine Blackhawk

The Great Seal of the United States carries this motto: **E Pluribus Unum**. This is a Latin phrase that means: Out of Many—One. After you study the genealogical (descendant) diagram of two imaginary children and answer the questions about it, you will better understand one of the interpretations of the motto.

1. From how many different nationalities are Wanda Lazzaro and Peter Lazzaro descended? __

2. From how many different nationalities was Nicholas Lazzaro descended?_____
Simon Blackhawk?_____

3. Who was Tanya Blackhawk's mother? _____
_____

4. Who were Michael Lazzaro's two grandfathers?
_____
_____

5. Who were Tanya Blackhawk's two grandmothers? _____
_____

6. What are the names of Tanya Blackhawk's two aunts? _____
_____

To do: On the reverse side of this page make your own imaginary genealogical chart. Use the chart above as a model. Here are the rules.

a. Think of the names for four men and four women from eight different countries. Try to think of names that represent a country, for example: Peggy O'Brien (Ireland); Karl Mannheim (Germany), and so on.

b. You can "marry" any two people you want.

c. Diagram the descendants of the first four married couples to the last two children.

RESEARCHING SUBTOPICS OF MAJOR THEMES: MULTI-CULTURALISM

Perhaps the most neglected aspect of teaching the language arts is the oral presentation of the results of research. The following activity will not only provide an opportunity for students to effectively express themselves, but also increase their ability to find information on a particular topic and organize it for presentation.

Because we are a nation of many different racial, ethnic, and cultural backgrounds, it would be advantageous to devote a period or two to multi-culturalism as it pertains to American history and contemporaneous times.

To do:

1. Explain the significance of the expression: "*E pluribus unum*" or "Out of many—one."

2. Each student is to choose a topic for presentation, research it, and make an outline, which will also serve as a guide for oral presentation.

3. Prepare or otherwise obtain at least one instructional aid (map, diagram, tape, picture, realia, etc.) to accompany the presentation. Utilize appropriate music, poems, dances, etc.

4. Time the presentation so that it is no less than four nor more than six minutes.

5. Presentations are not to be read, although certain parts of a presentation may be read. The prepared outline should be used as a guide.

6. Keep in mind that topics should not be broad in scope. For example, not about all the special foods prepared by an ethnic group, but one particular food—its ingredients, how cooked, how eaten, and so on.

7. The following is a list of suggestions that may be utilized or serve as examples of the nature and scope of topics:

➢ Bagpipes of Scotland
➢ Polish polkas
➢ Aspects of a language
➢ Particular foods of a nation or group
➢ A poem or two, for example, poems of Bobby Burns of Scotland

➢ Swiss yodeling
➢ A Spanish dance, Highland Fling, Irish Jig, etc.
➢ Mexican Mariachi bands
➢ Japanese origami; Haiku
➢ Jewish holidays; e.g. Rosh Hashana
➢ Brazilian Mardi Gras
➢ Explanations of the flag of a particular nation
➢ Christmas as celebrated in a particular country
➢ Explanation of a physical or political map of a particular country
➢ Games played in a particular country
➢ Pictures, overhead transparencies, post cards for a particular country
➢ Explanations of stamps from a particular country
➢ Tape recordings of a country's music; for example, West Indies music

This same approach can be utilized in other areas of the curriculum, for example, early American history.

➢ Ships of the early explorers
➢ Colonial homes, tools, clothing, etc.
➢ Revolutionary soldiers (uniforms, weapons, etc.)
➢ Indian customs, homes, weapons, etc.
➢ Aspects of the Civil War
➢ Life on the Great Plains
➢ Gold seekers
➢ Early mechanical transportation (steam boats, trains, automobiles, air ships, etc.)
➢ Elements of World Wars I and II
➢ The effects of geography on American history; for example, the effect of the Appalachian Mountains on western movement, the St. Lawrence Seaway, early canals and their routes, the Mississippi River and the western movement
➢ Traditional children's games
➢ Early mechanical toys
➢ Square dances; early songs
➢ Particular types of architecture, for example, Victorian
➢ Providing artificial light: candles, lamps
➢ Spinning and weaving cloth in early America
➢ Realia and artifacts from America's past

Beginnings– Automobiles and Airplanes

Charles Duryea

Frank Duryea

Henry Ford

AUTOMOBILES: A BRIEF HISTORY AND DISCUSSION

Clever inventors had tried for years to make a vehicle that would move over roads without an animal pushing or pulling it. They were trying to develop a self-moving vehicle, or automobile. As early as 1796, a French army officer had built a steam-powered vehicle that pulled cannon over land. In 1829 Englishmen were startled to see a "steam-carriage" moving over the roads at an average speed of fifteen miles per hour.

In the United States many men had experimented with steam automobiles. The most famous of these men were the Stanley brothers. Their Stanley Steamers were bought and successfully driven by many people from about 1896 to 1925. These steamers were so powerful that few dared run them as fast as they could go. And few people really felt secure with a boiler full of live steam riding with them over the road.

The steamers had a rival in electric cars. There were certain advantages to the electric cars. They ran very quietly. They did not need fuel. But they had major faults, too. They lacked power for steep hills, snow, and sand.

In 1893 the first successful gasoline-powered automobile was driven in Springfield, Massachusetts. The car had been built by Charles and Frank Duryea. By 1900 a number of other American inventors had also built cars run by gasoline. These cars became so popular that manufacturers eventually stopped making electrics and steamers.

Henry Ford was one of the men who experimented with gasoline-powered automobiles. He completed his first model in 1896. Then, he decided to enter the automobile manufacturing business.

At that time automobile companies built one car completely before they started to work on the next car. Ford found that manufacturing one car in this way took many hours of work. This made the cars too expensive for most people. Ford was bothered by this. He wanted to produce a good car at a price the average family could afford.

Ford realized that he could never manufacture cars cheaply by using the old methods. He began to use the system of interchangeable parts first developed by Eli Whitney. In this system each worker becomes expert at performing one particular job.

The same parts on all of Ford's cars were identical. Each axle was like every other axle. Each door handle was like every other door handle. Any steering wheel could be interchanged with any other steering wheel.

Then Ford borrowed another idea known as "assembly line" production. Here is how this system worked:

The frame of a car was placed on a moving belt. The moving belt took the frame from worker to worker. Each worker did one thing to the frame. Meantime, the body of the car also was being assembled, or put together, on another moving belt. Finally, the frame of the car, with all its parts attached, was joined to the completed body of the car. This took place at the ends of the lines.

The interchangeable-parts system and the assembly line cut down the time needed to make the parts of a car and to assemble them. Because fewer man-hours of work were needed, a finished car cost less. In fact, the prices of Ford's new cars were cut by more than half.

Discussion

"Automobiles have been an important factor in American life in the past and exert an even stronger influence today." Elements to consider:

Employment: Manufacturing, selling, transporting, road construction, toll collectors, insurance agents, car hops at drive-ins, advertising agencies, oil fields and refineries, and many others.

Natural resources: Significant portions of our natural resources are used in the automobile industry, including iron, copper, oil, rubber, plastics from coal, etc.

Social: The automobile has caused considerable changes in the organization and relationships of families; crime is facilitated in that the automobile is frequently used as an accessory; automobile mobility has contributed to the growth of suburbs, family movement from region to region, and the growth in mobile homes; tourism has become one of the nation's top industries; spectator sports have been helped; local, state and national governments have derived revenue from sales taxes, gasoline taxes, parking meters; air pollution.

THE WRIGHT BROTHERS FLY AN AIRPLANE AT KITTY HAWK

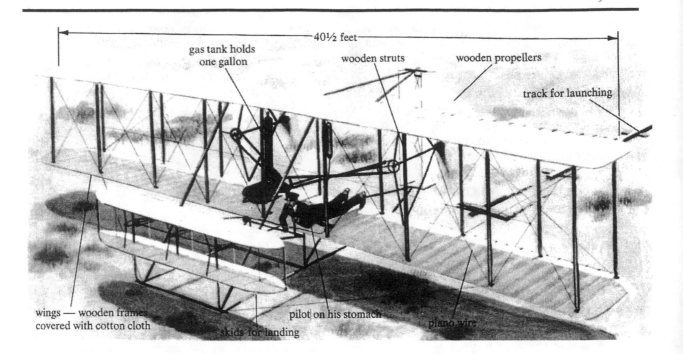

wings — wooden frames covered with cotton cloth
gas tank holds one gallon
wooden struts
wooden propellers
track for launching
40½ feet
pilot on his stomach
skids for landing
piano wire

The Wright brothers' first airplane weighed about 600 pounds and cost about $1,000. The original model is now on display at the Smithsonian Institute in Washington, D.C.

To make a successful motor-driven airplane it was necessary for the Wright brothers to experiment, observe, and research. They studied birds and how they flew. They made kites of different shapes and sizes to determine which kind gave the best performance. They made model gliders which they tried out in a wind tunnel.

Finally, the brothers put together all that they had learned and built their airplane. They decided to try it out at Kitty Hawk, North Carolina, where the winds and weather conditions were favorable. Under its own power the airplane flew for twelve seconds and traveled 120 feet. Before the day was over, December 17, 1903, their plane had made three more successful flights.

To do

Study the diagram and its caption (above) and the narrative on this page. Then complete the table in the next column.

Facts about the Wright Brothers' First Airplane			
Weight		Cost	
Wing span		Place first flown	
Number of propellers		Date of first flight	
Type of motor		Length of first flight	
Gas tank capacity		Duration of first flight	
Type of landing gear		Pilot's position during flight	
Where displayed			

205

Name: _____ Date: _____

FIRST SOLO ATLANTIC FLIGHT

LINDBERGH DOES IT! TO PARIS IN 33½ HOURS

FLIES 1000 MILES IN SLEET AND SNOW
GIGANTIC CROWD MOBS FLIER
LINDY RESCUED BY TWO FRENCH AIRMEN

FELL ASLEEP SEVERAL TIMES
ASKS FISHING BOAT: "WHICH WAY TO IRELAND?"
FUEL ALMOST GONE ON LANDING

PARIS, May 21, 1927—A crowd of 100,000 cheering French welcomed the weary flier at Le Bourget Field. Some people broke through the police lines in an attempt to pull Lindy from his plane, or to get souvenirs.

A GREAT EVENT IN AVIATION HISTORY

After the experiments of Wilbur and Orville Wright, aviation developed rapidly. Perhaps the industry received its greatest boost when Charles A. Lindbergh flew across the Atlantic Ocean alone in a single-engine airplane. The entire world was awakened to the possibilities of air travel between continents.

Above is an example of how the news was reported. Read the news, and study the map and picture. Then check the statements below *true* or *false*.

T	F	Statement
		He almost ran out of gas.
		He flew over northern England.
		He flew about 3600 miles.
		His plane had four engines.

T	F	Statement
		He flew north of the 60° N line of latitude.
		The flight took place more than sixty years ago.
		He flew from west to east.
		He had clear weather all the way.
		He had difficulty keeping awake.
		He was in the air about one and a half days.
		He saw no ships at sea.
		He was rescued from crowds.
		Paris is farther north than New York.

SECTION 22

World War I Through the Great Depression

Name: _____ Date: _____

EUROPEAN NATIONS CHOOSE SIDES IN WORLD WAR I

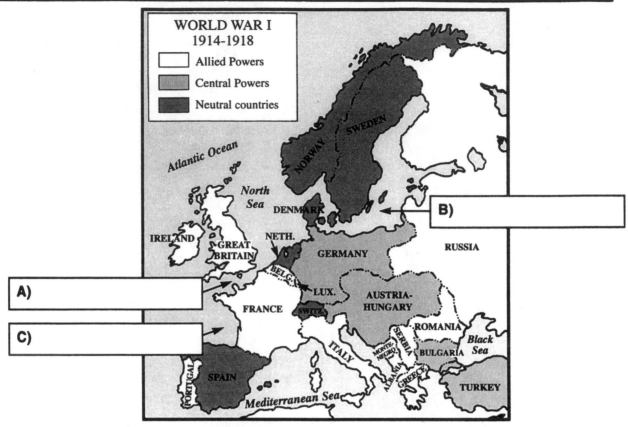

The map shows the lineup of the three groups of European nations at the beginning of World War I.

1. According to the map what nations made up the Allied Powers?

_____   _____

_____   _____

_____   _____

_____   _____

_____   _____

_____   _____

_____

2. What nations made up the Central Powers?

_____   _____

_____   _____

3. What nations were neutral?

_____   _____

_____   _____

4. What three Allied Power nations bordered on the Central Power nation of Bulgaria?

_____   _____

_____

5. What four Allied Power nations did not border on any of the Central Power nations?

_____   _____

_____   _____

6. Add to the map, as follows:
   A. *English Channel*
   B. *Baltic Sea*
   C. *Bay of Biscay*

THE SINKING OF THE *LUSITANIA*

Suggestions for Teaching

1. Read the two paragraphs in this column to your students. Then, after a short discussion, read the report on the sinking of the *Lusitania* or photocopy and distribute.

2. From the information presented in the report have your students imagine they are headline writers for a newspaper. On a separate piece of paper, have them prepare a headline for a feature story about the disaster. The story should have a main headline followed by three or four subheadings, the size of the print gradually diminishing.

3. An example headline is printed at the bottom of the page.

President Woodrow Wilson had some definite opinions about the war in Europe. In the beginning he clearly stated that the United States would be neutral. But, as the war in Europe intensified, both the Central Powers and the Allies took and sometimes destroyed American property. Their navies interfered with our shipping to prevent American food and supplies from reaching their enemies.

The Central Powers, especially Germany, did more to anger Americans than the Allies. They torpedoed neutral merchant ships and passenger ships. Without warning, torpedoes were launched from submarines. The people on the attacked ships had little chance to get into lifeboats. These and other actions turned most Americans against Germany and its partners.

The Sinking of the *Lusitania*

On May 7, 1915, the *Lusitania*, owned by Britain's Cunard Line, was sunk off the coast of Ireland by torpedoes launched from the German submarine, U-2. No warning was given to the *Lusitania,* which was carrying 1959 passengers and crew. There were 197 Americans on the ship; 128 of them died from the explosions or from drowning. In all, 1198 people were killed.

Two torpedoes struck the forward part of the ship. Unfortunately, the point of impact of the torpedoes was only 150 feet from a storage compartment that held small arms ammunition and which also exploded. The ship sank in less than 18 minutes after being struck. Considering the speed at which the *Lusitania* sank, it is remarkable that anyone survived.

One survivor standing by the ship's rail said that he actually saw the U-2 which was about 100 yards away. He watched in amazement as one of the torpedoes sped toward the ship and exploded on impact. Many other passengers who were in their cabins were caught completely by surprise when the torpedoes hit.

The American government strongly protested the unprovoked and cowardly attack on an unarmed ship. President Wilson resisted the urging of many Americans to declare war. However, he did notify the German government that if such an act occurred again it would "be regarded by the government of the United States . . . as deliberately unfriendly." The German government, however, would not apologize for the attack.

THE *LUSITANIA* SUNK BY A SUBMARINE

DEAD: 1198, INCLUDING 128 AMERICANS

TWO TORPEDOES STRIKE AS HORRIFIED PASSENGERS WATCH

Strong American Protest
Many Urge War

NEW YORK, MAY 7, 1915

WORLD WAR I: AMERICANS FIGHT ON LAND AND SEA

Discussion

What are some of the sacrifices and negative aspects of war? (1) Human: Men, women and children lose their lives, and many people, both civilian and military, are seriously wounded. The loss of lives and permanent wounds have serious repercussions in the disruption of families. (2) Freedom: During war censorship is often imposed. Movements in travel and choice of work may be restricted. (3) Material: Consumer products such as gasoline, food, and heating oil become scarce because of war demands. (4) Careers: Young people may be forced to leave school, and businesses may have to be abandoned. (5) Destruction: Transportation facilities, homes, schools, churches, dams, bridges may be devastated. (6) Natural resources: The excessive demands of war bring about a more rapid depletion of forest, mineral, and other natural resources. (7) Social: Undesirable changes in the family and social structure may occur. For example, the soldier father and working mother may have less time for their children. (9) Economic: Preparing for and fighting war is costly. The aftermath of war, which, among other things, involves care and rehabilitation of veterans, is costly and continues for years after the war is over. The rebuilding of destroyed government and civilian property requires huge sums of money.

The Convoy System

After we entered the war, the United States had to transport its troops, equipment, and supplies overseas by ship. Some of the troopships carried as many as 5000 men. One ship, the *Leviathan* (giant), actually carried over 11,000 men on one trip. Suppose a troopship such as the *Leviathan* or even a smaller ship were sunk. There would be little possibility of saving most of the soldiers and sailors.

The American navy with the help of the British navy worked out a solution to the problem. Neither troopships nor merchant ships were allowed to cross the ocean alone. Instead, a number of ships sailed together. The ships were protected on all sides by warships. This means of protecting ships used during the war is known as the "convoy system."

As a result of the convoy system, only one European bound troopship was sunk by submarines. Thus, a steady stream of men and supplies poured into Europe to help the Allies.

American Land-Troops Engage the Enemy

In 1917 a successful revolution took place in Russia. The new Russian leaders, who were Communists, made a separate peace with Germany. Russia became known as the Union of Soviet Socialist Republics, or the Soviet Union. Now, thousands of Central Power troops, mostly Germans, were free to attack France.

In the spring of 1918, the German armies started a great drive to capture Paris, France. The weary Allied armies were in great need of help. It was at this time that the American troops saw their first important action. Wherever the Germans seemed strongest, American soldiers were sent to fight. Also, the presence of the Americans gave new spirit to the soldiers of France and Britain. The fresh American troops made the difference between victory and defeat for the Allies. The German drive was halted by August, 1918.

General John J. Pershing was commander of the American Expeditionary Force, or A.E.F. He was not satisfied with using American troops only to strengthen the weakened armies of France and Great Britain. He believed we would be of greater service if we fought as an American army. The other Allied commanders came to agree with Pershing. So it was decided that the Americans would fight as a separate army in cooperation with the other Allied armies.

A powerful Allied drive to end the war was planned for the fall of 1918. The drive was a great success. Steadily, the Germans were driven off the land that they had won in the first three years of the war. One after another, Germany's partners gave up. Germany realized that she would not win the war. On November 11, 1918, Germany also admitted defeat and asked that the fighting be stopped.

Name: _____ Date: _____

WORLD WAR I CHANGES THE MAP OF EUROPE

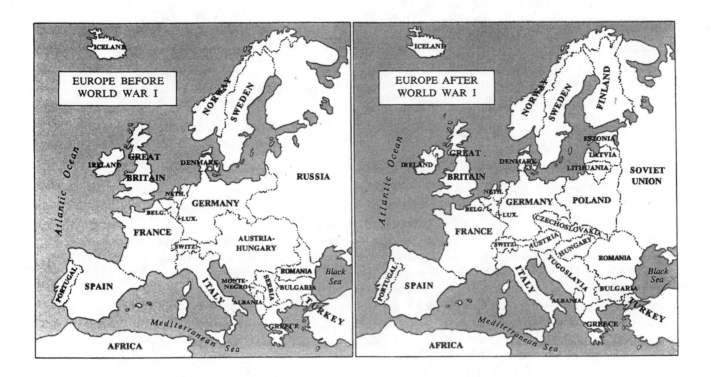

The end of World War I brought many changes to the map of Europe, especially to those countries that were part of the Central Powers. Russia—which was once part of the Allies, but which left the group to make a separate peace with Germany—was also significantly changed. The two maps above show the "before and after" of Europe.

1. According to the maps what countries came into existence after World War I?

_____   _____

_____   _____

_____   _____

_____   _____

_____

2. What five countries were formed from land that was once Russian land?

_____   _____

_____   _____

_____

3. Which country lost the greatest amount of land after World War I? _____

4. What was the former Russia called after World War I? _____

_____

5. Which of the following two countries gained land after World War I?

_____ Romania   _____ Bulgaria

RELIEF TO EUROPE: LED BY HERBERT HOOVER

There is substantial evidence that shows the United States is forceful in war, and equally magnanimous in victory. In fact, the Great Seal of the United States embodies these characteristics in that the eagle holds thirteen arrows in its left talon symbolizing readiness for war, and thirteen leaves on an olive branch in its right talon symbolizing equal readiness for peace. Never was the generosity of our country more manifest than after World War I, except, perhaps, in our humanitarian efforts after World War II.

The following article can be read orally to the class for the purpose of helping students appreciate our efforts on behalf of others, as exemplified by Herbert Hoover and America's charitable organizations.

Herbert Hoover was born in West Branch, Iowa, in 1874. Early in life he decided he wanted to be an engineer. He followed through on his dream and graduated from Stanford University, California, as a mining engineer. He worked on engineering projects all over the world: Australia, China, Russia, South America, Africa, and other places.

Hoover was a Quaker and, as such, believed it was his duty and responsibility to help people wherever and whenever help was needed. During World War I he was appointed United States Food Administrator. It was his job to make sure that food was available for the United States, for members of our armed forces, and for our allies in Europe. "Food will win the war," was the slogan of the time, and there were very few who disputed the truth of this slogan. War-ravaged Europe certainly could not produce enough food for its population; it was up to the United States to do the job.

His work as head of the Commission of Relief in Belgium deserves to be described. Belgium had been crushed by the German invading armies. Within one month of the invasion, Hoover had the first relief ship unloading in Belgium. Then, ship after ship arrived loaded with food for starving Belgians. The diplomatic red tape Hoover had to cut through was staggering. Thousands, perhaps tens of thousands, of lives were saved because of Hoover's organizational genius. One of Hoover's aides in the Belgium relief effort described him as "very direct, positive, able, speaks little, but everything he says counts."

But Hoover was more than a clever organizer. He was a great humanitarian. It was his great concern for people, especially children, that drove him to apply his skills far beyond what might be considered his "duty."

After the war, Hoover went to Europe as Director of the American Relief Administration, which had the job of keeping millions of Europeans, friends and former foes alike, alive while they made the transition from war to peace. Hoover and his aides supervised the distribution of some 27 million tons of food, clothing, seeds, and other supplies to half the countries on the European mainland—from Finland in the north to Armenia in the south. Later, in gratitude, more than four million men, women, and children signed their names to letters and scrolls thanking Hoover for his help.

Hoover's administration worked closely with private organizations such as the American Red Cross and the American Friends Service Committee. In all, perhaps 200 million people were helped—almost twice the population of the United States itself in 1920. In Russia alone, for example, more than eight million children were protected from disease by medical shots. Many of these children would have died if it had not been for this medical help. Also, for more than two years we helped feed eleven million Russians every day.

After the war Europe was so poor that it did not have the money to recover. Therefore, our government loaned billions of dollars to various European countries between 1918 and 1923. The money was used for building roads, factories, farms, and other facilities.

Because of America's help and its own great efforts, Europe was able to regain much of its former strength. The scars of the war—blackened fields, blasted homes, twisted rails, destroyed bridges, people wandering aimlessly from place to place—were no longer visible. Nonetheless, beneath the surface the old feelings of hate, fear, jealously, and revenge were still alive in the defeated powers.

THE 1920'S: YEARS OF GROWTH

After World War I, the United States grew rapidly. Well-established industries, such as the construction industry, steadily increased in size. Other industries that had been very small before the war, such as the aviation industry, grew to be giants.

Some industries, such as the ice-making industry, died out. They were replaced by entirely new industries, such as the refrigeration and air-conditioning industries, which developed after the war.

Statistics of the 1920's			
	1920	**1924**	**1928**
Population (millions)	106.5	114.1	120.5
Families with radios (millions)	very few	1.3	8
Daily newspaper circulation (millions)	27.8	33	38
Automobiles, trucks, and busses (millions)	9.2	17.6	24.7
Tractors on farms (thousands)	246	496	782
Hard-surfaced roads (thousands of miles)	369	472	626
Horses (millions)	19.8	17.4	14.8
Oil pipelines (thousands of miles)	55.3*	68.2	81.7
Airplanes produced	328	377	4346
Telephones in use (millions)	13.3	16	19.3
Movies, average weekly attendance (millions)	40**	46	65

*1921   **1922*

1. How much increase was there in each of the following items during the years from 1920 to 1928:

population: _____ million

newspaper circulation: _____ million

telephones: _____ million

automobiles, trucks, busses: _____ million

tractors on farms: _____ thousand

airplanes produced: _____

2. How much of a decrease was there in the number of horses from 1920 to 1928?

_____ millions

Why do you think the number of horses decreased? _____

_____

_____

3. Why would the number of miles of oil pipelines increase along with the number of motor vehicles?

_____

_____

4. Growth in one industry usually brings about growth in closely related industries. Think of one industry that probably grew because of the growth in newspaper circulation.

_____

5. *Challenge question:* Think of one effect the growth of newspapers would have on the lumbering industry, and one effect it would have on the forests of the country.

a. Lumbering: _____

_____

b. Forests: _____

_____

FRANKLIN ROOSEVELT FIGHTS THE DEPRESSION

Millions Unemployed

Following is a set of revealing statistics on unemployment in the United States from 1929 (the beginning of the Great Depression) to 1944 (the height of World War II). The figures are from *Historical Statistics of the United States*.

The information can be utilized in several ways. For example, facts can be read; trends perceived; conclusions drawn; and picture, line or bar graphs can be constructed.

Year	Number of Unemployed	% of Labor Force
1929	1,555,000	3.20
1930	4,340,000	8.75
1931	8,020,000	15.90
1932	12,060,000	23.60
1933	12,830,000	24.90
1934	11,340,000	21.70
1935	10,610,000	20.10
1936	9,030,000	16.90
1937	7,700,000	14.30
1938	10,390,000	19.00
1939	9,480,000	17.20
1940	8,120,000	14.60
1941	5,560,000	9.90
1942	2,260,000	4.70
1943	1,070,000	1.90
1944	670,000	1.20

Closing the Banks

Franklin D. Roosevelt was sworn in as President on March 4, 1933. The country did not have long to wait before he went into action. On March 6, 1933, he ordered all the banks in the nation to close for a few days. This was necessary because people thought that the banks were not safe. So, they were withdrawing large sums of money from the banks.

In those depression days even banks that were in excellent financial condition could collapse as a result of heavy withdrawals of money. This is because the money in a bank's vault never equals the amount of money customers have deposited. The reason for the difference is that banks loan out money that has been deposited. Banks cannot call back the money they have loaned out quickly enough to pay for large numbers of withdrawals.

Discussion

What kinds of problems would be brought about by closing banks for an extended period of time, say five days? (*Both minor and major problems would result. For example, workers would have difficulty cashing paychecks. Stores and other places of business would have difficulty making change. Businesses might accumulate large sums of money in cash boxes and safes and, thus, be tempting targets for robberies. Renters would not have access to their safe-deposit boxes. Sales would inevitably drop, and business would decline. Depositors would not be able to withdraw money for emergencies. On the international level, trade would be affected adversely. Tourists would not be able to withdraw money for expenses, and traveler's checks would not be taken out or cashed. All in all, the country would undergo an extensive slowdown.*)

The Civilian Conservation Corps (CCC)

During the Great Depression, millions of young men were out of jobs. How could these young men who couldn't find jobs be helped to earn money at useful tasks? The government's answer was to organize the Civilian Conservation Corps (CCC) to provide jobs for men between the ages of 17 and 28. The men might be sent to work in camps thousands of miles from their homes. They planted trees, built roads, bridges, and dams. They cut down trees to make camping grounds, and they dug irrigation ditches. They built up their bodies, learned new skills, and gained confidence in themselves.

Discussion

Is there any need for CCC-type programs today? (*Many have argued that the CCC should be reactivated. They claim that even today there are thousands of youths who are unemployed and who could benefit from the health and educational aspects of CCC-type programs. They say the nation as a whole would benefit because the need for a national program of conservation is greater than ever before.*

*Some have argued against CCC-type programs on the grounds that such programs promote socialism, encourage the growth of bureaucracy, develop semi-military forces that could be exploited, are a form of forced labor, and infringe on personal freedoms. **Note:** It would be interesting to poll the class to see how many would be interested in such a program. Also, do the girls think there should be a separate CCC for girls? Or, should the CCC be co-ed?*)

Name: _____ Date: _____

FROM THE CIVIL WAR TO THE GREAT DEPRESSION: CROSSWORD PUZZLE

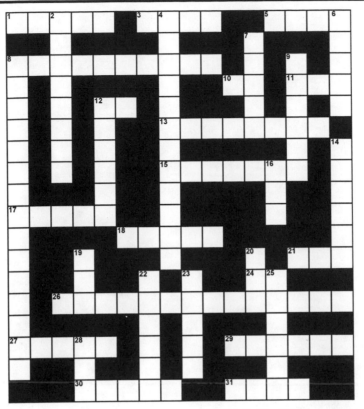

Across:

1. Americans felt _____ about the sinking of the *Lusitania*.
3. Island liberated by Americans in the Spanish American War
5. Where the Civil War began: _____ Sumter
8. Island gained by the U.S. after the Spanish American War
10. Pacific Islands occupied by the U.S. after the Spanish American War (*Abbreviation*)
11. Mail delivery service to country homes begun in 1896 (*Abbreviation*)
12. One of the Central Powers in World War I (*Abbreviation*)
13. Commander of American troops in Europe in World War I: General _____
15. People from Asia who helped build the Central Pacific Railroad
17. Eastern beginning point of the Union Pacific Railroad (*City*)
18. American battleship sunk in the harbor of Havana, Cuba
21. President who followed Herbert Hoover (*Abbreviation*)
24. Some people call it the War between the States; others call it the _____. (*Abbreviation*)
26. Name of the western portion of the transcontinental railroad
27. During the Civil War, Clara Barton was a _____.

29. Chief of the Nez Perce Indians
30. Man who shot Lincoln
31. A fast way of delivering mail: the _____ Express.

Down:

2. Builder of the Panama Canal
4. Name of the eastern end of the transcontinental railroad
6. Nickname for President Theodore Roosevelt
7. Immigrants from Europe who worked on the eastern end of the transcontinental railroad
8. Place where the eastern and western links of the transcontinental railroad were joined
9. One of the Allied Powers in World War I
12. Purchased from Russia in 1867
14. After World War I he saved thousands of Europeans from starvation.
16. Many prairie settlers lived in ___ homes.
19. Confederate military leader
20. Organized by the federal government to provide work for young men during the Great Depression (*Abbreviation*)
22. The brothers who built a successful flying machine
23. Island in New York harbor where many emigrants entered the country
25. President during World War I
28. Submarine (*Abbreviation*)

SECTION 23

American Sports Heroes

SPORTS: SOME HISTORICAL STATISTICS

In some history texts there is much more emphasis on historical elements such as discoveries, wars, and presidents than on social elements such as music, fashions, and architecture. But, the latter elements are also history. This page and several others will offer your students excursions into sports history.

Following are some sporting facts that have "made history." Each set of facts lends itself to interesting bar, picture, or line graphs. Present the facts on an overhead transparency or chalkboard. After discussion, teams of two students may take a set of data and design a graph to show the statistics. Encourage innovation; for example, a bar graph of home runs may show baseball bats for the bars.

Leading Home Run Hitters, 1927–1993				
Year	Player	Club	League	#HR
1961	Roger Maris	New York	American	61
1927	Babe Ruth	New York	American	60
1932	Jimmie Foxx	Philadelphia	American	58
1938	Hank Greenberg	Detroit	American	58
1930	Hack Wilson	Chicago	National	56
1949	Ralph Kiner	Pittsburgh	National	54
1965	Willie Mays	San Francisco	National	52
1977	George Foster	Cincinnati	National	52
1947	John Mize	New York	National	51
1990	Cecil Fielder	Detroit	National	51

Baseball Pitchers with 300 or More Major League Wins	
Pitcher	Number of Wins
Cy Young	511
Walter Johnson	416
Christy Mathewson	373
Grover Alexander	373
Warren Spahn	363
Pud Galvin	361
Kid Nichols	360
Tim Keefe	344
Steve Carlton	329
Eddie Plank	327
John Clarkson	326
Don Sutton	324
Nolan Ryan	324
Phil Niekro	318
Gaylord Perry	314
Tom Seaver	311
Mickey Welch	311
Old Hoss Radbourn	308
Lefty Grove	300
Early Wynn	300

Source: The World Almanac and Book of Facts, 1994

Leading Lifetime Rushers (Football)			
Player	Years	Total Yards	Average
Walter Payton	13	16,726	4.4
Eric Dickerson	10	13,168	4.4
Tony Dorsett	12	12,739	4.3
Jim Brown	9	12,312	5.2
Franco Harris	13	12,120	4.1

Note: The above set of statistics presents an opportunity for your students to practice "rounding," as in arithmetic. Rounding makes it easier to graph quantities and read data. The average yards gained in rushing does not lend itself to rounding because the spread of the figures is too close; no useful purpose would be served by rounding. However, "Total Yards" lends itself to rounding. Rounding to the nearest 100 would be most useful in designing a graph for the data in the table above. For example, Walter Payton's record could be rounded to 16,700.

National Football League Stadium Capacities

The number of people who attend football games is impressive. For young people, especially, some familiar comparable element involving numbers makes statistics more comprehensible. The Los Angeles Memorial Coliseum, for example, has a capacity of 92,480 people. That figure is greater than the combined population of three cities: the capitals of Maine (Augusta: 21,325), Maryland (Annapolis: 33,195), and Missouri (Jefferson City: 35,577). All the people of the capital of New Jersey, Trenton (92,124), could be seated in the Los Angeles Memorial Coliseum.

Stadium	Location	Capacity
Los Angeles Memorial Coliseum	Los Angeles, California	92,488
Pontiac Silverdome	Pontiac, Michigan	80,500
Rich Stadium	Buffalo, New York	80,290
Cleveland Stadium	Cleveland, Ohio	80,098

215

Name: _____ Date: _____

JIM THORPE: ALL-AROUND ATHLETE

T	N	A	S	S	O	C	I	A	T	E	D
V	E	F	J	B	R	O	W	N	G	E	O
J	W	O	A	I	S	T	A	R	I	T	L
A	A	O	K	L	A	H	O	M	A	E	Y
V	T	T	S	O	C	O	S	X	N	D	M
E	H	B	F	A	T	H	L	E	T	E	P
L	O	A	D	S	N	I	R	I	S	H	I
I	H	L	X	N	S	W	E	D	E	N	C
N	A	L	R	F	E	D	I	S	C	U	S
T	C	A	R	L	I	S	L	E	F	O	X
U	K	E	I	S	E	N	H	O	W	E	R
E	D	E	C	A	T	H	L	O	N	Q	

1. Read the story about Jim Thorpe. Notice the underlined words. Find these words in the word search and circle them. There is one abbreviation.

2. The illustrations show Jim Thorpe in some of the events mentioned in the story. Write a three- or four-word caption for pictures 1–3 on the bottom of this page. In square 4 write a headline that expresses the main idea of item 5 in the story.

1. Jim was born in 1888 on an Indian reservation in Oklahoma. He was about 60 percent Sac and Fox Indian, and 40 percent Irish. His Indian name was Wa-Tho-Hack which means "Bright Path."

2. As a young man he was a student in the Carlisle Indian School, Pennsylvania. While at Carlisle he starred in all sports, but especially football. In a game against Brown University, he once kicked the football 83 yards. Carlisle played the West Point (Army) football team and beat them. One of the Army players, Dwight Eisenhower, became President of the United States.

3. Jim took part in the 1912 Olympics held in Stockholm, Sweden. He competed in the decathlon (10 events) and the pentathlon (5 events). Some of the events included in these two categories are throwing the javelin, hurling the discus, and running in races such as the 1500 meter. He won both the decathlon and the pentathlon. At the end of the games, the King of Sweden gave Jim two gold medals and said, "Sir, you are the greatest athlete in the world." Jim, who was very modest, replied, "Thanks, King."

4. After the Olympics Jim played professional football and baseball. One of the baseball teams he played for was the New York Giants. In football, Jim helped form the American Professional Football Association, which later became the National Football League (NFL).

5. In January 1950, the Associated Press asked sports writers to name the greatest athlete of the first half of the 20th Century (1900–1950). Jim Thorpe was the overwhelming choice. Many people go beyond that—they say that he was the greatest athlete who ever lived because he did not star in just one sport, he starred in every sport in which he took part.

BABE DIDRIKSON: SPORTS SUPERSTAR

Mildred "Babe" Didrikson, who added Zaharias to her name when she married, has been called one of the greatest athletes—man or woman—of all time. The amazing thing about Babe, and one of the reasons she deserves such recognition, was the variety of sports in which she starred. The story that follows helps bring understanding as to how and why she earned such lavish praise.

Procedure

1. Photocopy the opposite page and distribute.

2. Orally read or otherwise present the story. As the story is presented urge students to write *brief* notes on the lines provided below each illustration.

3. At the end of all the sequences, have some students read their notes to the class and/or have someone tell the story using his/her notes as prompts.

Note: If possible, obtain *"Whatta–Gal": The Babe Didrikson Story* by W. O. Johnson and N. P. Williamson, or *Babe Didrikson, Athlete of the Century*, by R. R. Knudson. Both books tell exciting and moving details about Babe Didrikson's life.

1. Babe was born in Port Arthur, Texas, in 1911. Her parents had emigrated to America from Sweden.

As a youngster, whenever and wherever it was possible, she ran. Unconsciously, because she had no idea she would become a track champion, she would hurdle the hedges in her neighborhood when she was headed someplace. She was highly competitive. She ran not only to beat others, but also to beat herself. She even raced things. For example, if she were sent to the store she would race the old-fashioned trolley car from stop to stop as people in the trolley cheered her on.

2. It is probably true that in the schools she attended she could have played on any team—football, soccer, baseball, etc.—and easily held her own with any boy athlete. In playground games she was among the first chosen to play on a team. She was such a great hitter of home runs that teammates and spectators began to call her "Babe" after Babe Ruth, the great New York Yankee baseball player.

3. Babe was an outstanding basketball player in high school. One night a scout for an insurance company saw her play. He immediately tried to recruit her for his company's team. The company gained publicity by sponsoring athletic teams. He offered her a job as a secretary on the condition that she would play basketball on the company team. That way she would remain an amateur. She accepted the offer; she would be able to help her family with the money she was paid, and she would still be involved in sports. Babe not only became the fastest typist in the office, but also led the team to second place in the National AAU basketball tournament.

4. Babe loved basketball, but there were other sports that interested her. She turned to track and made up her mind that she would work to represent the United States in the 1932 Olympic Games to be held in Los Angeles. She would compete in both track and field events.

Babe practiced every day for hours at a time to get ready for the Olympic trials. Finally, the competition that decided who would represent the United States in the Olympics was held. Alone, as a one-person team representing her company, she went to the AAU Nationals. The results? She won the team championship with six first places. Babe scored 30 points against the second-place, 22-member team that earned only 22 points. Nothing equal to her performance had been done before, and it hasn't been equaled since. From the Nationals she went on to the Olympics, where she set world records in the 80 meter hurdles and the javelin throw and, of course, earned two gold medals.

5. Babe's next challenge was golf. She went about learning the sport in her usual way; that is, she gave maximum effort and concentration to learning golfing skills. Her hands blistered and bled from gripping golf clubs as she completed her daily goal of driving more than a thousand golf balls with distance and accuracy. The results were predictable. In the 1940's she won seventeen consecutive major women's golf tournaments. She travelled abroad and became the first American woman to win the British Women's Amateur Golfing Championship.

Babe was stricken with cancer when she was only 39 years old. She had major surgery in an attempt to eliminate the disease. After the operation, in spite of the fact she was considerably weakened, she competed in the National Women's Open and won the title. The Associated Press named her the outstanding woman athlete of the first half of the 20th century.

But there was one thing Babe couldn't defeat. Cancer returned. Her weakened body gave up and she died at the premature age of 45.

217

Name: _____

Date: _____

BABE DIDRIKSON: SPORTS SUPERSTAR

JESSE OWENS: OLYMPIC CHAMPION

1. Each paragraph below tells about a major part of Jesse Owens's life. In the box before each paragraph write the number of the drawing that is most closely related to the main idea or details of the paragraph.

☐ *Jesse Owens, one of seven children, was born in 1913 in Oakville, Alabama. His folks were "sharecroppers" on a forty-acre farm.* ___ ___

___ ___

☐ When Jesse was seven years old the family moved to Cleveland, Ohio, where they hoped things would be better. When Jesse was in junior high school the athletic coach, Charles Riley, invited Jesse to try out for the track team. Jesse was thrilled, but he told Mr. Riley that he couldn't practice after school because he had to earn money to help his family. Mr Riley understood that it was necessary for Jesse to work. *He told Jesse he would coach him everyday for forty-five minutes before school .* ___

☐ Jesse went on to senior high school. He became one of the greatest high school runners in the country. *He was so outstanding that dozens of schools mailed him scholarship offers.* ___ But, Jesse wanted to go to Ohio State University (OSU). However, OSU did not offer scholarships. Mr. Riley came to his rescue. *He talked the OSU officials into giving Jesse three part-time jobs.* ___

☐ The Ohio State coach, Larry Snyder, taught Jesse many things about running and broad jumping. For example, he suggested that Jesse do shadow-boxing to improve his footwork. Jesse won race after race. *People began to call him "the world's fastest human being."* ___ ___

☐ After Ohio State, Jesse's next challenge was the Olympic games to be held in Berlin, Germany. Hitler, the German dictator, had no use for African-Americans. *He said that the Germans (Aryans) were the superior people of the world. Jesse proved that Hitler was wrong. Before the Olympics were over, Jesse had won four gold medals.* ___ ___

2. Notice that certain sentences in the paragraphs are italicized and are followed by a blank line or lines. On the lines write the letter of the sentence or sentences (below) that most naturally follow the italicized sentences.

A. Charles Riley, who had many years as a coach, knew instinctively that Jesse had it in him to become a world champion.

B. Jesse's real name was James Cleveland Owens. Everyone called him J.C., which later came to be "Jesse."

C. While Hitler watched with hate in his heart, Jesse broke the world record in the broad jump with a leap of 26'5".

D. Often, there was little to eat and no money to buy food or clothing.

E. He could have had free tuition, free books, free room and board and, in some places, spending money.

F. As a child Jesse was sickly, but, even so, he worked in the cotton fields to help his family.

G. The family was very poor and could hardly make a living from the farm.

H. Another name given to Jesse while he was at OSU was "the Bullet."

I. Jesse wasn't willing to believe the ideas and words of Hitler.

J. The jobs were waiting on tables, working in the library, and operating an elevator.

K. At Ohio State, Jesse broke the world record in the 100-yard dash, the broad jump, the 220-yard dash, and the 220-yard hurdles *all in the same day.*

3. Beneath each picture below, write an appropriate caption. Write the caption as a title or as a descriptive sentence.

Note: The drawings are *not* in the sequence that they occurred in Jesse's life.

ALTHEA GIBSON: WORLD CHAMPION TENNIS PLAYER

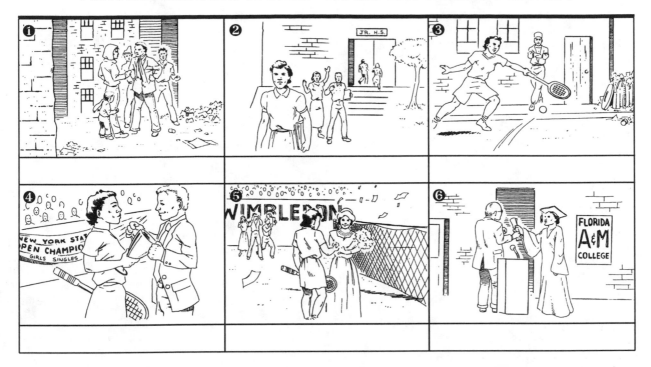

1. Following are some facts about Althea Gibson, champion tennis player. With which paragraph is each picture most closely related? Write the number of each picture before the appropriate paragraph.

___ Althea attended junior high school, but she lacked interest in book learning. She often played "hookey," despite her friends telling her she shouldn't. Eventually, she dropped out of high school.

___ Althea learned to play paddle tennis on the streets of Harlem, a section of New York City. A street recreation leader who was watching her play realized that Althea had the potential to be a fine tennis player. He bought her a racket and taught her the game.

___ Althea was born in North Carolina in 1927. Shortly after her birth her parents moved the family to New York City. She learned to stand up for herself, and she sometimes protected others who couldn't defend themselves.

___ There was no stopping Althea in the tennis world. She won tournament after tournament. At the peak of her career she won the trophy at Wimbledon, England, and the United States National Championship.

___ Later in her life she realized the importance of a good education and earned a degree at Florida A&M College.

___ Within a year after starting lessons, Althea became so good that she won the girls' singles in the New York State Open Championships.

2. On the lines beneath each picture write a brief caption.

3. Select a picture. Then, on the back of this page write what you think Althea might have been thinking or saying in the situation shown in the picture. Here is an example for picture 5: When I was in Harlem, I never dreamed that the Queen of England would be congratulating me for winning a championship in her country.

SECTION 24

World War II

STATIONS: ACTIVITIES RELATED TO WORLD WAR II

1. *What is the "stations" approach to teaching history?*

Definition: A method of teaching designed to develop knowledge and skills in a particular curricular area by having learners engage in a variety of related activities and utilize a variety of materials and equipment under the direction and supervision of the instructor.

2. *What are the physical arrangements in a station setup?*

A variety of activities are set up at "stations" positioned around the classroom. All, or most, of the necessary materials, equipment, books, directions, etc. are at the station. There may be a table where materials of a general nature such as crayons, scissors, glue, etc. are available for general use. *Note*: the facing page shows a stations arrangement related to World War II.

3. *How are records kept of the learners' work?*

Each learner is listed on a chart that also lists the various stations. As the learners complete an activity they initial the chart. Learners also keep personal folders of all the response sheets they have completed. Instructors can tell at a glance how individuals and the class as a whole are progressing. Also, maintaining folders develops organizational skills and a sense of responsibility in learners.

4. *What does the instructor do while learners are working at the stations?*

- Gives special help to slow learners
- Administers materials
- Encourages, praises, prods, suggests
- Evaluates learners

5. *How is the stations approach helpful to learners?*

☞ The learners' interests, needs, and capacities are better realized.

☞ The learners' natural tendencies to move about, talk, and interact are channeled into productive tasks.

☞ The learners are more responsible for their own learning and behavior.

☞ Learners are actively responding both mentally and physically.

6. *How can the stations approach be integrated into the weekly schedule?*

	Mon	Tues	Wed	Thurs	Fri
1st week	RL	RL	S	S	RL
2nd week	S	RL	RL	S	RL

RL: Regular lesson (textbook, lecture, etc.)
S: Stations

7. *What are some elements to keep in mind when utilizing the stations approach?*

☞ Stations supplement the basic subject matter; they are not the basic course.

☞ In some stations it is helpful for students to work in groups of two, but rarely more than two.

☞ Each station should have a tangible result, for example, a completed response sheet, a completed model, map, etc.

☞ At the conclusion of the stations activities, all the stations should be discussed, conclusions drawn, misunderstandings corrected, supplemental instruction given, and so on.

☞ Each station should have a sheet of paper on which the following appear:
- Number and title of the station
- Purpose or objective of the station stated in simple language
- Directions for completing the station

Example

Station 1: Stations Folder

Objectives:
1. To make a folder to hold pages
2. To design a symbol for the cover

Directions:
1. Fold construction paper in half (Figure 1).
2. Make pockets by folding the paper up 2" from the bottom. Staple corners (Figure 2).
3. Design a cover that relates to our unit.

(Figure 1)   *(Figure 2)*

STATIONS: ACTIVITIES RELATED TO WORLD WAR II

❑ "Team Teaching" lends itself well to the stations approach. Each teacher is responsible for a certain number of stations. Interclass movement is provided for.

❑ In some station arrangements each learner should complete every station. In other arrangements it may not be necessary for each learner to complete every station because the stations may range in difficulty.

❑ To save time, space, materials, money, and to take care of large groups, two or more setups of the same station can be provided.

❑ The greater the number of stations, the greater the opportunity to provide for individual differences. Stations may range from "easy" to "difficult."

❑ The number, variety, and difficulty of stations may be such that they may be completed in one session or several sessions.

❑ All of the children are actively responding all of the time.

❑ A large variety of skill outcomes are provided for, as well as a wide range of subject matter outcomes.

❑ Stations provide a fine opportunity for cooperative learning.

❑ Stations can become the basis for an exhibit which parents and other classes may attend. The children explain the stations; they become "teachers."

❑ After the students have experienced stations provided by the teacher, they can become responsible for devising stations. This is the ultimate in teaching; i.e., the children are helped to become independent learners and developers.

❑ The first station should direct learners to make folders to hold all papers. The cover of the folder should have a symbol representative of the theme.

TYPICAL STATIONS SET-UP ON WORLD WAR II

Station 2
Map of Europe.
Students complete
response sheet.

Station 3
Filmstrip of soldiers
being trained.
Response sheet.

Station 4
Map of Pacific.
Students complete
response sheet.

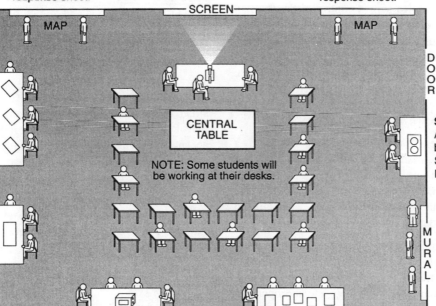

Station 1
Folders. Students
make folders to hold
various photocopies.
Design cover.

Station 9
Chart showing a
diagram of a sub-
marine. Students
complete their own
unlabeled diagrams.

Station 5
Audio tape recording of
bombing of Pearl Harbor.
Students listen.
Response sheet.

Station 6
Mural showing D-Day
invasion of Normandy.
Students complete
with ships, planes, etc.
Pre-sketched back-
ground.

Station 8
"TV" filmstrip on a variety of
World War II topics. Each
student makes one "frame."
Books, newspaper articles,
magazines available.
Frames connected to make
a long roll.

Station 7
Multi-research. Students
find answers to questions.
Variety of books: almanacs,
encyclopedias, books on
World War II, etc.

Note: Central table will
have response sheets
to be completed; e.g.
textbook readings

Note: The stations
set-up shown may
take learners 3-4
periods to complete.

DICTATORS TAKE OVER RUSSIA, ITALY, AND GERMANY

A Dictator for Russia

As you will recall, Russia fought on the side of the Allies in World War I. The ruler, or tsar, of Russia was Nicholas Romanov. Nicholas was a very poor leader. Battles had been lost and millions of Russians had been needlessly killed and wounded through ignorance and neglect. Russian soldiers were terribly discouraged.

The discontent of the people at home was equal to that of the soldiers on the battlefields. Most of the people were very poor, whether they worked on farms or in the cities. They hated the often dishonest and cruel officials of the tsar. During the war, millions of Russians were hungry. Many riots took place in the cities. Government officials were attacked, and stores were looted. Soldiers and civilians wanted a change in the government.

1. Circle the sentence which tells some results of Nicholas's poor leadership during World War I.

2. What two words are used to describe some of the tsar's officials? _____

It was during the days of unrest in early 1917 that a group of revolutionaries seized control of the Russian government. Nicholas was forced to give up his rule. The revolutionaries faced tremendous problems. Also, they had no experience in government. The Communists, who were well organized, took advantage of these problems and seized control of the government. Tsar Nicholas and his family were killed. After the revolution Russia became known as the Soviet Union.

As one of their first acts, the Communists, led by a man named Lenin, made peace with the Germans. The Communists were anxious to have peace for two reasons. They believed that it was hopeless to continue the war. Also, without war, they would be better able to strengthen their control over the Soviet Union.

The Communists took over all means of production, transportation, and communication in the country. Eventually, they took over the ownership of all land. Small and large landowners had to give their property to the government.

The first leader of the Communists, Lenin, died in 1924. The man who eventually took his place, Joseph Stalin, was extremely cruel. People who opposed him were either killed or sent to prison labor camps. Russians who had hated the tsar realized that they had exchanged one kind of dictator for another.

3. How did the Communists make sure that Nicholas would not lead a movement to regain control of Russia? _____

4. Underline the sentence in the fourth paragraph that the following sentence would most naturally follow: The terms of the peace required Russia to give up much of its land.

5. Circle the sentence in the fifth paragraph that expresses the same idea as the following sentence: Factories, railroads, newspapers, and radio stations were placed under government control.

The Soviet Communists wanted to establish their form of government in other countries. It was their plan that these new Communist governments would be loyal to and controlled by the Soviet Communist party. By these means the Soviet Union could conquer the world with little loss of blood and money of its own.

A Dictator for Italy

People in Italy were very dissatisfied after World War I. Many people could not find jobs. Many were hungry. Communists in Italy took advantage of this situation and tried to make things worse. Their idea was that if things got bad enough, the Italians would then accept Communism as a way to obtain a better life. The Communists staged strikes and riots. Law and order seemed to have broken down in Italy.

The violent activities and excitement and the big promises of the Communists were attractive to many Italians. But even more Italians became fearful of the Communists.

Benito Mussolini used the people's fear of Communism for his own purpose. After World War I, he organized a group called Fascists. Like the Communists the objective of this group was to take over and change the government of Italy. The Fascists wanted to replace government by representatives of the people with rule by a dictator.

DICTATORS TAKE OVER RUSSIA, ITALY, AND GERMANY

Mussolini used his Fascist followers to combat the Communists. He met force with force and ended the Communist threat. In the minds of many Italians Mussolini was a hero.

Then, in October 1922, Mussolini demanded that the government of Italy be handed over to him. At first the government, which was headed by a king, refused. But when Mussolini's Fascist forces started to march on Rome, the Italian capital, the government gave in. Thus, Mussolini became dictator of Italy.

1. **Underline the sentence that tells why the Communists tried to upset life in Italy.**

2. **How did Mussolini become a hero to many Italians?** _____

3. **What act of Mussolini forced the Italian government to give in to his demands?** _____

_____

A Dictator for Germany

All of the European countries suffered hardships during the Great Depression, but one of the hardest hit was Germany.

In the early 1930's millions of Germans were desperate. They wanted to do something to change conditions, but they did not know what to do. It remained only for some leader to come along and show them the way. A leader did come along, but, as you shall see, he showed the Germans the wrong way.

The man who took advantage of the discontentment in Germany was Adolf Hitler. Hitler told the Germans they were a "master race" that should rule "inferior" people. Many Germans believed him.

Hitler also told the Germans that Germany was poor because it was not large enough. He said that Germany had to win back the land and resources it had lost. He claimed that Germany was surrounded by enemies and that it was only a matter of time before Germany would be attacked.

Hitler had a great personal hatred for Jews. He unfairly blamed the Jews for Germany's troubles. He told his followers that it would be necessary to get rid of the Jews in Germany.

Hitler's political organization, called the Nazi party, gradually grew in power. In January 1933, the Nazis had Hitler appointed chancellor, the most powerful man in the German government.

1. **What were four things that Hitler told Germans in order to gain their support.**

a. _____

b. _____

c. _____

d. _____

Now that he was chancellor, Hitler arranged to have an election that would put Nazis in control of the German legislature. Here is how his Nazis won the election:

*   He ordered all newspapers that were opposed to him to be shut down.
*   He would not allow opposition political parties to have meetings.
*   He denied the use of radio to people who were against him.
*   People who spoke against him were jailed, beaten, or killed.

Hitler's Nazis easily won the election. At the first meeting of the new legislature the Nazis voted to give Hitler all the powers he needed to become dictator. Hitler was free to rule the country as he pleased.

2. **What are three things that Hitler did to limit the ability of those who opposed him to communicate?**

a. _____

b. _____

c, _____

3. **What did Hitler do to those people who spoke against him?** _____

_____

_____

STALIN, MUSSOLINI, AND HITLER: SOME INSIGHTS

Dictators

■ **Stalin**'s real name was Joseph Dzhugashvili. It was Lenin who suggested the name Stalin, or "man of steel." Stalin was the son of a shoemaker in the southern Russian province of Georgia. He entered a seminary to become a priest, but he was expelled due to his actions against the government and lack of real interest in the Church. He was arrested and sent to Siberia several times for his revolutionary activities, but he always managed to escape. Eventually, however, he succeeded in becoming dictator of the Soviet Union.

Stalin was so cruel in this role that the Soviets themselves repudiated and admitted the terrors and terrible crimes of his 29-year regime (1924–1953) after his death. Millions of people had died directly or indirectly as a result of his actions. His pictures and statues were removed from public places, and cities that had been named in honor of him, such as Stalingrad, were renamed.

■ **Mussolini** was the first of the modern Fascist dictators. The term "Fascist" comes from the Italian *fascismo* which was the name of the Roman symbol of authority, a bundle of birch or elm rods from which an axe head protruded.

Some characteristics of Fascism and what Mussolini stood for follow:

☑ Extreme nationalism and the belief that the people and the nation have a special mission to rule others

☑ Exaltation of a supreme leader

☑ The belief that the individual must be subordinated to the state

☑ Indoctrination and regimentation of the nation's youth

☑ Repression of all other political parties

☑ Denial of free speech, press, and assembly

☑ Racism and the belief that the nation's people are superior to others.

☑ Imperialistic and aggressive foreign policy

☑ Oppression of minority groups on racial, ethnic, and religious grounds

☑ Elaborate system of spying and secret police

☑ State control of educational, recreational, and athletic organizations

☑ Close control or outright suppression of labor unions

Mussolini was born in a small Italian village in 1893. As a student he was rebellious and frequently expelled from school. Despite his school record, and his belligerent and egotistical nature, he managed to earn a degree and teach elementary school for about three years. When WWI broke out, he joined the Italian army, rose to the rank of corporal, and served until he was wounded in 1917.

Through his writings as a newspaper editor and columnist he vented his ire against the socialist government, and played on the discontent of many Italians who thought they had not been rewarded sufficiently for their support of the Allies in WWI. He gathered other dissidents around him and founded the Fascist party in 1919. As leader, he eventually forced King Emanuel II to abandon his throne, and he became dictator of Italy in 1922. He consolidated his power, and then, to show his "greatness," he invaded and conquered weak Ethiopia. The fact that the Ethiopians fought his armored divisions with spears, bows and arrows, sticks and stones did not prevent him from proclaiming his greatness as a military commander.

Italy joined with Germany as an "equal" Axis power, but, in reality, Italy was an underling. In WWII, military disaster after military disaster finally led to Mussolini's overthrow by his own followers. He fled toward Switzerland, but his own secret police captured him. He was returned to Italy, tried, convicted, sentenced to death, shot, and then hung by his heels in a public place for all to see.

■ **Hitler**, it can be said with all objectivity, was a failure as a boy and young man. He was unable to demonstrate conviction or industry of any sort: he never completed high school, and he barely survived by doing odd jobs. His negative attitude was formed early in life. He blamed his lack of success on everyone but himself. He had a hatred, totally unfounded, of Jews whom he blamed for his lack of success. But Jews were not his only hatred. He had no use for democracy or democratic procedures, and he particularly hated anyone who disagreed with him. He would become hysterically enraged at any opposition to his opinions.

Hitler was an Austrian by birth and a German by choice. In 1914 he moved to Munich, Germany. When WWI broke out in 1914, he joined the German army. In the army, Hitler "found" himself and developed qualities of leadership.

After the war Germany was in chaos. People were poor, hungry, jobless, and disillusioned. Hitler capitalized on German discontent and, with others, formed a new political party, the members of which were called Nazis. The charismatic Hitler led the party to eventual domination of Germany.

Hitler's rise to power was marked by ruthless persecution of all who opposed him. His particular targets were the Jews of Germany and of other countries his armies conquered. He picked on the weak and the helpless and in the process had millions of Jewish children and adults murdered by his storm troopers.

How he conducted the war is another story, but in the end he lost. Finally, he killed himself as the Russians and Americans were storming the last bastion of his empire—Berlin.

DWIGHT D. EISENHOWER: WORLD WAR II GENERAL, PRESIDENT

Telegram: "Report immediately to headquarters, Washington, D.C."

The events listed in this column tell in chronological order some of the highlights of the life of former general and president, Dwight D. Eisenhower.

Your task is to match the events with the symbols drawn at random around the page. Write the number and date of the event on the line in the box.

1 *October 14, 1890:* Dwight David Eisenhower is born in Denison, Texas. He is the third child of seven of which one died very young. The family moves to Abilene, Texas. The house he lives in is small, but it is a happy home.

2 *Spring, 1909:* Dwight "Ike" Eisenhower graduates from Abilene (Texas) High School. Ike is known for his mathematical ability.

3 *June 14, 1911:* Ike enters the United States Military Academy at West Point. Four years later he graduates as a 2nd lieutenant. At West Point he continues his excellence in mathematics. He is an outstanding football player until he injures his knee.

4 *March, 1918:* World War I is being fought. Ike trains soldiers in tank warfare at Camp Holt, Pennsylvania. Although he wants to experience combat in Europe, he is too valuable as a training officer to be reassigned.

5 *January, 1933:* Ike is assigned to assist General Douglas MacArthur, and, among other things, he accompanies MacArthur to the Philippine Islands. Both men are destined to become supreme commanders during World War II—MacArthur in the Pacific, Eisenhower in Europe.

6 *December 7, 1941:* Japanese warplanes attack Pearl Harbor, and this leads to America's entrance into World War II. Ike is called to war headquarters in Washington, DC, to help plan the war.

7 *June, 1942:* Ike is made Supreme Commander of American troops in Europe. He directs the invasion of North Africa and Italy. Then, in January 1944, he is made Supreme Commander of the Allied Expeditionary Force in Western Europe. As Commander he directs the final attack on Hitler's forces, including Operation Overlord (Normandy Beach, D-Day, June 6, 1944).

8 *June 7, 1948:* World War II is over. Ike retires from the army and is appointed President of Columbia University in New York, one of America's greatest schools.

9 *Summer, 1952:* Ike is chosen by the Republican Party to run for President. He wins the election. He runs for re-election in 1956 and wins a second term.

10 *March 28, 1969:* At the age of 79, Ike dies. He is returned to his old hometown of Abilene and is buried there.

A $(3 \times 6^2) = ?$

THE D-DAY LANDING ON NORMANDY

Operation Overlord was the beginning of the end of World War II in Europe. The illustration and suggestions for teaching will help your students gain insights and additional understanding of the initial action on the Normandy Beaches on D-Day, June 6, 1944. Concomitantly, they will gain skill in reading and interpreting pictures.

Procedure

Photocopy and distribute the illustration of troops landing on Normandy or make a transparency for projection. How might newspaper correspondents describe the invasion scene? What are some of the details they might want to include in their stories?

After discussing the points that follow you may want to give an assignment: Write a story as it might appear in a newspaper or from the point-of-view of a soldier who is a part of the invasion.

❑ **The beach:** low and sandy; surf not especially rough; some natural protection from observation and gunfire provided by the shelf of land some 100 yards from the waterline; flat beach that lends itself to landing men, equipment and supplies; scrubby vegetation.

❑ **The men:** advancing in lines; most carrying rifles; one man carrying an antitank bazooka; most carrying packs; some running for the shelter of the shelf; some conferring and/or using a field telephone in the shelter of the shelf; medics administering to a wounded soldier.

❑ **Miscellaneous:** two planes overhead; soldier beckoning for help.

Name: _____ Date: _____

JAPANESE-AMERICANS DURING WORLD WAR II

(1) After the Japanese attack on Pearl Harbor, many Americans became suspicious of all people who had a Japanese background. (2) Beginning in the spring of 1942, Japanese-American citizens were taken from their homes and placed in prison camps. (3) They were forced to move so swiftly that often their property was lost, stolen, or sold for a fraction of its real value. (4) More than 100,000 men, women, and children were put behind barbed wire fences. (5) The reason given for relocating these people was military necessity. (6) But it should be noted that no Japanese-American was ever found to be a spy or saboteur.

(7) Many Americans protested the imprisonment of their fellow citizens. (8) Eventually, some of the restrictions on the prisoners were lessened. (9) Some were allowed to work in shipyards, factories, and government offices. (10) But many thousands remained in camps until 1945, when the last one was closed.

(11) At first, Japanese-Americans, called Nisei, were not allowed to volunteer for the armed forces. (12) When they were given that privilege in 1943, they offered their services by the thousands as soldiers, spies, and translators. (13) They were willing to fight for their country even though they had been badly treated by it. (14) As members of the armed forces, the Nisei established records that have seldom, if ever, been equaled. (15) The all-Nisei 442nd Combat Team earned more medals and citations for bravery that any other unit in World War II.

(16) Bradford Smith, in his book called *Americans from Japan,* tells how useful the Nisei were as soldiers, spies, and translators. (17) For example, Smith tells of the bravery of one Japanese-American, Terry Doi. (18) Terry Doi was one of the first soldiers to land on Iwo Jima. (19) He took a flashlight with him as he went into cave after cave. (20) He tried to persuade the enemy to surrender. (21) He saved many American lives this way at the risk of his own.

1. On the line before each sentence below write the number of the sentence in the story that it would most naturally follow.

These Americans believed that Japanese-Americans ___ would help defeat the United States.

These Americans believed that Japanese-Americans ___ would be as loyal to the United States as any other Americans would be.

Some were dismissed from their jobs without explanations, and others were threatened with bodily harm.

He was able to talk to the Japanese in their own ___ language.

2. Underline the sentence which proves that the Japanese at home were loyal to America.

3. Circle the sentence that tells how excellent the Japanese-Americans were as soldiers.

4. Circle the two sentences that describe what is taking place in the picture.

5. What are three kinds of jobs that Japanese-Americans performed in the armed forces?

a. _____

b. _____

c. _____

6. On the reverse of this page write an imaginary conversation between Terry Doi and the Japanese soldiers in the cave. To help you get started, consider what might be the first words Terry would speak? How might the soldiers respond?

Name: _____ Date: _____

ALBERT EINSTEIN: WINNING THE RACE TO DEVELOP THE ATOM BOMB

In 1939 a small group of American scientists became aware that the Nazis were well on their way toward developing an atom bomb. These men brought the matter to the attention of President Franklin D. Roosevelt. Roosevelt saw the danger. He immediately issued orders that put us in a race against Germany to develop the bomb first. As you know, we did win the race, but it was close. When the war with Germany ended, Germany was just a few months away from completing work on its own bomb.

The man who actually wrote the letter warning President Roosevelt of Germany's atom bomb activities was Albert Einstein, a German-born Jew. One of the men who persuaded Einstein to write the letter was Enrico Fermi. Fermi was a world-famous Italian scientist. He had left Italy because he could not bear to live under the dictatorship of Mussolini. Fermi played an important part in America's development of the atom bomb.

Einstein had left Germany in 1933 to visit the United States and England. While he was away, Hitler took power in Germany. Einstein learned from friends that everything he owned had been taken and destroyed. Einstein never returned to Germany. To do so would have been to risk imprisonment and possibly his life because Hitler was determined to destroy the Jews. Einstein was invited to settle in many places. He chose to live in New Jersey, where he took a position at Princeton University. In 1940 Einstein became a citizen of the United States.

Why was Einstein so famous? In 1905 he had announced the mathematical formula that was the first step toward the development of atomic energy. In the years that followed he made other important scientific discoveries. Other scientists were able to take his discoveries and, by combining them with their own, make the atom bomb.

Thus, the persecution of the Jews by Hitler and the dictatorship of Mussolini over the Italians drove two of the most gifted men in the history of science to our country. Einstein and Fermi not only helped us win World War II, but also helped us gain the knowledge necessary to use atomic energy for peaceful purposes.

Nazi storm troopers took possession of Einstein's home and belongings.

---

1. Circle the sentence which tells how near Germany came to winning the race to produce an atom bomb.

2. Underline the sentence which tells what part Enrico Fermi played in warning President Franklin D. Roosevelt about Germany's atom bomb activities.

3. Circle twice the sentence which tells why Einstein could not return to Germany.

4. Underline twice the sentence which tells why 1905 was an important date in the history of the development of the atom bomb.

5. Put a △ before the sentence which says about the same thing as the caption to the picture on this page.

6. Some facts about Albert Einstein:

• Year he left Germany _____

• Year he became a U.S. citizen _____

• Where Einstein settled _____

• First contribution to the development of the atom bomb _____

_____

7. How did Hitler's hatred of Jews help lead to his defeat? (Answer on reverse of this page.)

WINNING THE WAR IN THE PACIFIC

In the six months after the bombing of Pearl Harbor, the Japanese gained control of more than ten million square miles of sea and land in the Pacific and in Asia. They captured many possessions of the United States, Great Britain, and the Netherlands, and several independent countries.

1. Study the map; then, put a check before each of the following places that were part of Japanese-controlled territory.

___ Burma	___ Australia
___ Thailand	___ New Guinea
___ India	___ Outer Mongolia
___ Malaya	___ Sumatra
___ Manchuria	___ Java
___ Borneo	___ Korea
___ French Indochina	

American soldiers, sailors, and airmen played heroic roles in slowing down the advance of the Japanese. For example, on December 10, 1941, the Japanese first landed in the Philippine Islands. American and Philippines troops were greatly outnumbered and had little naval or air support. Yet, they fought so bravely that it took the Japanese until May 6 to force a surrender.

2. The Philippine Islands are labeled and shown on the map. Connect the dots that circle the islands.

3. Approximately how many months did it take the Japanese to conquer the Philippine Islands?

After the surrender, American and Filipino troops were forced to march to the Japanese prisoner-of-war camps. More than 20,000 men died on this long march, which became known as the "Bataan Death March." This march made the Allies more determined to defeat the Japanese and their Axis partners.

4. The Japanese tried but failed to capture Midway Island. If they had captured Midway, they might also have been able to capture the Hawaiian Islands. Draw squares around *Midway Island* and the *Hawaiian Islands*.

Gradually, under the leadership of General Douglas MacArthur, the United States was able to move from a defensive to an offensive position. We began to attack instead of waiting to be attacked. A plan for defeating the Japanese was developed. First, Japanese outposts in the Pacific and Asia were to be recaptured. Then Japan itself was to be invaded.

On August 7, 1942, American troops landed on Guadalcanal in the Solomon Islands.

5. On the map circle this group of islands.

6. Circle the two sentences that describe the plan for defeating Japan.

All the American fighting men, equipment, and supplies were transported to Guadalcanal by ship. It is almost impossible to imagine the conditions the soldiers faced. The thick jungle was infested with scorpions, leeches, rats, spiders, and snakes. Great ants bit the soldiers, who were afraid to call out or move because this would reveal their position to the Japanese.

The Japanese fought the advancing Americans from hiding places in caves, foxholes, and trees. Rarely did the Japanese surrender. They fought to the death. This resulted in tremendous losses of human life on both sides.

In February 1943, the Japanese were finally cleared out of Guadalcanal. In the meantime, Americans were invading other Japanese-held islands. In almost every case, Guadalcanal-type fighting was necessary before the islands were won. Many other islands were recaptured by United States forces, including Iwo Jima, which brought us closer and closer to Japan.

7. On the map find Iwo Jima and circle it.

The United States did not try to take every Japanese island in the Pacific. Instead, we used a system of "leap-frogging." Some islands were passed by, while others were invaded. Slowly but surely the American forces closed in on Japan. By the end of February 1945, the Philippine Islands had

WINNING THE WAR IN THE PACIFIC

been liberated. By the end of August, 1945, Okinawa was captured. Okinawa was only about 350 miles from Japan. Other American and Allied troops pushed the Japanese out of Southeast Asia and China.

8. On the map circle Okinawa, which is south of Japan.

9.   Underline the sentence that explains the "leapfrogging" approach to winning the war.

The next step was to invade Japan itself. It was estimated by United States military experts that an invasion of Japan would cost one million American lives and several million Japanese lives. Therefore, an appeal was made to the Japanese to surrender. They refused. Then, President Harry S. Truman decided to try to end the war quickly by dropping an atom bomb on Japan. The atom bomb had never

before been used in war. It was hoped that its use would convince the Japanese that they had to surrender or be destroyed.

An atom bomb was dropped on the city of Hiroshima on August 6, 1945. Over 70,000 Japanese were instantly killed and four square miles of the city were flattened. Still the Japanese would not surrender. Three days later an atom bomb was dropped on the city of Nagasaki. Again, more than 70,000 people were instantly killed. On August 14, 1945, the Japanese surrendered to the Allies.

10. Circle the sentence that tells that the invasion of Japan would have cost more lives than dropping the atom bombs on Hiroshima and Nagasaki.

11. On the map draw circles around Hiroshima and Nagasaki.

WORLD WAR II IN THE PACIFIC

Japanese-controlled territory at its greatest extent

Name: _____ Date: _____

JACK KENNEDY AND PT-109

It is August 1943, and the United States is fighting a war against Japan. Your name is Jack Kennedy. You are a lieutenant in the United States Navy. You are in command of PT-109 ("Torpedo Patrol" boat) in the South Pacific near the Solomon Islands. Your mission is to "seek and destroy" Japanese ships.

You are on patrol at 2 a.m.; it is a very dark night. Suddenly, the bow of a Japanese destroyer looms over your boat. Before you can launch a torpedo or maneuver out of the way, the destroyer crashes your boat amidship, breaking it in half. The eleven sailors on board—two others had been killed instantly in the collision—abandon the boat, but the surrounding water is on fire from spilled gasoline. The crew swims back to the wreck and clings to its sides during the long night. The Japanese destroyer's search lights sweep the water but do not spot them. The wrecked PT boat is slowly sinking.

Dawn breaks. Several islands are close by, but the sailors fear they are occupied by the enemy. What to do? You decide to have your crew swim to the most remote island; it has the least chance of being occupied by Japanese. One of your crew is seriously burned; he can not make the swim on his own. You take the belt of the man's life jacket between your teeth. You tow the man for four hours through shark-infested waters. Your men struggle on; you offer constant encouragement and serve as an inspiring example. Finally, the breaking surf throws you all on to the shores of the island which has the strange name "Plum Pudding Island."

There is neither food nor water on the island except some unripe coconuts. The men are exhausted; they are bleeding from wounds; they are in desperate need of medicine and bandages. It rains and the men try to catch the falling drops on their tongues, but it is not enough to quench their thirst. You know that to stay on the island means death. Once more you encourage your men to swim to another island. Once more you tow the wounded sailor—this time for three hours. Again, disappointment—there is no water or food on the island. The men are now terribly weak. They have had no food or water for going on three days.

You are the leader. The men depend on you. You cannot give up. While the men are resting, you and another brave and strong member of your crew decide to swim to yet another island. There you find a one-man canoe, a tin of rain water, and a crate that contains crackers and candy. You paddle the canoe and its precious cargo back to where your men are waiting; your companion will swim back the next day. On your return it astonishes you to find your men talking—using pidgin-English and signs—to two native islanders. The natives are part of an American/Australian spy network. They take off in their canoe to report what they have found. They paddle to an island occupied by the Japanese, but on which an Australian spy lives in secret. He radioes to an American ship that the crew of PT-109 has been found. The next day an American PT boat picks up you and your crew.

The news of the dramatic rescue is broadcast to the United States. The manner in which you and your men conducted yourselves is on the front page of newspapers, and your name as leader is spoken again and again in radio broadcasts. You become well known. The publicity is your first step toward becoming President of the United States on January 20, 1961, some twenty years after the incident.

1. On the other side of this page, write a main headline and several sub-headlines that tell the story of PT-109 and its crew. Remember that following the headlines you should tell the place and date where the story was first reported.

2. Write a brief newscast about the event as it could be read over the air waves by a radio news reporter. Remember the four w's (what, when, where, why) of a broadcast.

3. Copy a sentence from the story that explains what is shown in the illustration.

HIROSHIMA: A SHORT STORY

The story that follows, "Hiroshima," is an adaptation of an original story that appeared in *On Becoming a Teacher: Tales of Tears and Laughter* by the author of this book. The adaptation is printed here for several reasons.

☞ It renders the dropping of the atom bomb more than a depersonalized event of World War II.

☞ It highlights the predicament of Japanese-Americans during World War II.

☞ It can help your students realize that there is more than one way of thinking about an issue or event.

☞ It offers a deviation from lesson-to-lesson concentration on a basic textbook.

☞ It suggests other methods of teaching, for example "interviewing" and "guest speakers."

☞ It offers insight and technique in organizing role-playing as an instructional procedure.

☞ It suggests other role-playing situations that could be used in teaching about the atom bomb.

Suggested Procedure

Read the story orally. Follow with some discussion questions:

♦ How do you know that Mitzi is probably going to be a good teacher? What special traits does she possess?

♦ Why were the Japanese, but not the Germans, placed in internment camps?

♦ Should Elliot have told Mitzi how to teach the class?

♦ What might have been some of the things discussed by President Truman and Bess Truman?

♦ Can we think of some other situations relative to the atom bomb issue that could be role-played?

HIROSHIMA

All of the children in Mrs. Blaine's class had been born after 1963. Two or three of the older fathers of the children had served in the United States armed forces in World War II, and several had served in the Korean War. So Mrs. Blaine thought that the unit of study, "America Since 1940," would be especially meaningful to the children. Parents and grandparents would no doubt have personal memories of the many exciting events of the period. The children could conduct interviews, and possibly some of the parents could be invited to the class to tell what they knew from firsthand experience about such events as the bombing of Pearl Harbor and the assassination of President Kennedy.

Because she was one of Professor Elliot's senior cooperating teachers, Mrs. Blaine had only one student teacher assigned to her. The girl was Mitzi Yamaguchi, an American-born girl of Japanese descent. Mitzi's parents, now American citizens, had been born in Japan and had emigrated to the United States in the late 1930's. The lesson Mrs. Blaine had assigned Mitzi to teach was "Japan and the United States in World War II." The teacher's thought was the Mitzi would have a special relationship to the event because the atom bomb had been first released on Hiroshima, Japan.

Mitzi made an appointment to talk to Elliot about the lesson.

As Elliot sat in his college office waiting for Mitzi, he thought about her. He wondered what, specifically, she wanted to see him about with regard to her lesson. She had already shown that she was going to be an exceptional teacher. The lessons she had planned and taught, one in arithmetic, one in reading, and one in music, were all excellent. She had everything—imagination, resourcefulness, organization, and a feeling for detail.

But beyond these things, she had charisma. The kids doted on her. When she taught there were no problems of control and discipline.

When children entered the room in the mornings before school started, they naturally migrated toward Mitzi. She always had something of interest to tell, something that they could see and touch. One time she brought a collection of miniature birds that her grandfather had carved out of scrap wood. Another time she showed some of her own handwork, a wire sculpture of a skier slaloming on the slopes of Mount Fujiyama. It was obvious that she had a great respect for the country of her ancestors.

Most of the kids were curious about Mitzi. Some had never seen a Japanese girl at close range. There were things they wanted to know about her, and being kids they weren't afraid of expressing what was on their minds. Elliot remembered one girl saying to Mitzi in the spirit and tone of frank admiration, "I wish I had dark eyes and black hair like you."

Mitzi smiled and replied, "Well, thank you. I know lots of Japanese girls who would like to have your blue eyes, and blond hair. How about trading?" Then the girl and Mitzi laughed together in perfect rapport, as though they were sharing a joke.

Among the lessons Mitzi had taught was an outstanding music lesson. She brought in a guitar that she told the children she had bought at a flea market for three dollars. When she bought it, it had no strings, and four of the tuning pegs were missing. There was no way to get replacement pegs because the guitar was not a standard make. So her father carved the pegs from wood. Then he refinished the instrument, and Mitzi bought new strings. The guitar was so beautiful and had such a nice sound that any professional would have been proud to play it.

Mitzi formulated her lesson around a folk music theme. She discussed various kinds of folk music and played and sang well-chosen songs as illustrations. But the best part of the lesson was reserved for the end when she played some "fun" songs for the children and sang with them. One of the songs went like this:

> Oh, I bought a wooden whistle,
> But it "wooden" whistle no matter how
> I tried.
> It was a fine wooden whistle but it
> wooden whistle,
> So I sat right down and cried.
> Then I bought a steel whistle and
> it "steel wooden" whistle
> No matter what I would do.
> It was a shiny steel whistle but it
> steel wooden whistle,
> So I sat right down and went
> "boo-hoo-hoo."
> Then I bought a tin whistle,
> Just a plain tin whistle; it
> only cost a dime.
> Just an ordinary whistle, just
> a simple tin whistle,
> An' now I "tin" whistle all the time!

Elliot's office door was open, so when Mitzi appeared he told her to come in. Once more he was struck by her charm and quiet dignity. He could never pinpoint what it was that made her so striking, but it may have had more to do with her personality than her looks. There was a basic simplicity about her, a complete absence of guile or affectation, and an honest and open face that was captivating.

After a minute or so of banter, Elliot asked her what was on her mind—what was it she wanted to see him about. She said, "It's about the World War II lesson, Japan and the United States. I don't know what to do about it."

"Do you mean that you don't understand the subject matter, or that you don't know what methods to use? If it's methods, I would suggest. . ."

Mitzi interrupted Elliot and explained, "No, it's nothing like that. What bothers me is that I have deep feelings about the entire war and especially the bomb. I don't think I could handle it without pushing my feelings on to the kids."

"There will be lots of things you'll have to teach that you are not particularly comfortable with, Mitzi," Elliot re-

plied. "The thing to do is be as objective as possible. Stick to the facts as closely as you can."

"Yes, I know that, Professor Elliot. But this is something beyond the ordinary. Something that happened to my family because of the war and the bomb," she said.

"Well, tell me about it. What makes this topic so special?" Elliot urged.

"It begins with my father and mother," she said. "At the time Pearl Harbor was bombed in 1941, they were living in California. I guess there were bad feelings against the Japanese at the time. Lots of people thought that anybody who had Japanese blood was a potential traitor. There were all kinds of rumors going around: that Japanese submarines had landed spies on California beaches; that saboteurs aided by Japanese-Americans would blow up power plants, railroad tracks, and airfields as preparation for an invasion; that Japanese were secretly training to take over the cities. All kinds of things.

"One time my mother was on a bus—my folks were living just outside of Los Angeles at the time—and a lady demanded that she give up her seat. Well my mother wouldn't do it. The lady called her a bad name, and said that all Japanese should be put in prison."

Mitzi continued, "The government decided that all Japanese were to be evacuated from the west coast. My mother and father were given twenty-four hours notice to pack up their things and be ready to go. They didn't have time to sell any of the things they owned—furniture, their car, the washing machine. After they were evacuated, people just walked into their rented house and took what they wanted. The police didn't seem to care about what was happening.

"My parents made the trip on a bus to what was called an 'assembly center.' The only things they could take with them were some clothes. There wasn't enough room for things like family picture albums, pets, and collections. My father lost a collection of butterflies that it had taken him ten years to put together.

"They were assigned quarters in a tarpaper barracks. It had one big room, and a smaller room with four or five open toilets and several sinks. Four or five families lived there. Barbed wire fences surrounded the place. Spot lights flashed all around the camp at night. Guards with dogs patrolled the place. My mother told me that it was a nightmare. They were treated like criminals. They loved the United States. They couldn't understand why they were being treated so harshly. The United States was at war with Germany. Why weren't Germans interned?"

Elliot interrupted Mitzi at this point and said, "Mitzi, I understand why you would feel bad about your folks' experiences. But you're not teaching about the Japanese internment, you're teaching about the war between the United States and Japan."

"Yes, but all of these things have affected my feelings about the war, and there is more to my story. You see, my mother's parents—that is, my grandmother and grandfather—were still living in Japan during the war," Mitzi continued. Then she hesitated. I had a premonition of what the next part of her story would be, but I just told her to go on.

"Professor Elliot, when the atom bomb was dropped, my grandparents were living in Hiroshima. My grandmother must have been instantly cremated in the heat. Her body was never found. My grandfather lived because he was outside the city at the time the bomb was dropped. He worked on the railroad, but he was so badly scarred by the bomb that little children ran from him when they saw him. He's dead now. We're not sure what he died from, but we think it was radiation."

Mitzi stopped talking for a moment. Then she said, "Do you see why it's going to be hard for me to teach that lesson?"

Elliot didn't know what to say. Tell her that she didn't have to teach the lesson? That couldn't be the answer. What he had said earlier was still true. There would be many topics she would be called upon to teach that would be personally difficult, but nonetheless necessary to teach. If she could resolve this issue, then the next issue would be that much easier to face. Or, so he told himself.

Elliot said to her, "Mitzi, only you can work out this problem. There is no way you can or should be excused from teaching this lesson. Not that you have asked to be excused," he quickly added. "It's an event that happened in American history, an important event. It won't go away. The kids should know about it. You're a teacher. Teach it."

Elliot continued, "My suggestion is that you sit down and think through the subject matter. But even more important to the success of the lesson and your own peace of mind is *how* you teach it. Try to think of a method that treats the subject fairly. There is more than one side to every event. Maybe that can be brought out in some way."

Mitzi sat silently for a minute. Then Elliot saw her face begin to light up just the tiniest bit. A smile began to curl around the edges of her mouth. Elliot detected a glint in her eyes that indicated that she had formulated the beginning of an idea. But she simply said, "Two sides to every event. H'mmm." She hesitated, then said, "Professor Elliot, you've been a great help."

"I have?" Elliot replied. He felt better for, frankly, he had the impression that in some way he had failed Mitzi.

"Yes, sir," she said, "I'll do my best."

The day arrived on which Mitzi was to teach her lesson. Elliot had made up his mind to observe her teach. He

was concerned for Mitzi and more than a little curious as to how she was going to handle the situation. Her plan of attack soon became apparent.

She had the children read the account of the events from their basic history textbooks. As is the case with most textbooks, the authors told the bare essentials of the events chronologically from the bombing of Pearl Harbor to the dropping of the bomb on Hiroshima. The textbook version was quite objective, and failed completely to convey anything of the drama of the story.

After the reading Mitzi said, "Now that we understand the facts of the event we should think about the people who were involved. How might they have felt? We can make inferences about their feelings. You all know what inferences are from Mrs. Blaine's lessons. It's making deductions from the facts."

Mitzi continued, "But, we have to remember that an inference is nothing but a guess. After inferences are made there should be further investigation to determine whether the inferences are true or false.

"I'm going to suggest a new way to make inferences," Mitzi explained. "We will do some role-playing. That is, we'll try to put ourselves in the positions of the people who were living at the time of the bombing of Hiroshima. Some of us can be Americans, some can be Japanese, and some can be from other countries."

The children reacted enthusiastically to Mitzi's suggestion.

Mitzi had a prepared list of topics for the children to role-play. They were as follows:

☐ With his wife, Bess, President Truman is discussing the possibility of dropping the atom bomb. They are going over the pro's and con's.

☐ The pilot of the bomber that carried the bomb is discussing the mission with his copilot as they are winging toward Japan.

☐ The Japanese prime minister is discussing with three members of his cabinet the possibility that an atom bomb might be dropped somewhere in Japan. What should be done?

☐ A family of four Japanese—father, mother, daughter, and son—are seeking protection in a bomb shelter from the attack.

☐ Three American soldiers who have been taking special training for the expected invasion of Japan are discussing what it will mean to invade the islands.

☐ Ten years after the war, a group of college students in a youth hostel in Switzerland are discussing the war, including the atom bomb affair.

Mitzi thoroughly explained each situation, but she was careful not to give her opinions. The interest of the children was high. Mitzi's research of the topics had helped her assimilate many interesting bits of information about the war and the personalities involved. While she was explaining the role-playing situations, she was able to relate information to the children that they might never otherwise have known.

Each role-playing group was assigned a part of the room in which to work out the details of their presentations. The children went to work with a will. There was an industrious buzzing in the room. Occasionally, an excited child's voice would ring out; for the most part the behavior of the children was fine. Elliot made a note on his observation sheet to remember to compliment Mitzi for the thoroughness of her preparation of the children for their tasks.

In about ten minutes the groups were ready for their presentations. Initially, the children were nervous in taking their parts, sometimes giggling and stuttering. Soon, however, one of the advantages of role-playing began to manifest itself; that is, the players settled into their roles and lived them. They forgot the audience and themselves. The audience, too, became lost in the drama.

Many of the aspects of the bombing of Hiroshima were developed. Elliot began to appreciate how clever and resourceful Mitzi was in using this technique. Elements of the event were brought out by the players that Mitzi could not have mentioned without the risk of being thought biased.

The children were fair. They really tried to see the event from both the Japanese and American points of view. For example, one of the girls in the "Japanese Prime Minister's Group" expressed the idea that the Japanese secret service should use all its resources to steal the plans for an atom bomb.

Elliot often brought a small tape recorder to the lessons he observed. It was beneficial to student teachers to play back recordings of lessons they taught. In this way they could analyze their speech, the quality and quantity of their questions and comments, and the oral responses of the children.

Elliot switched on the recorder as soon at Mitzi began her lesson. Here is a transcription of the "college students" group, who were discussing the affair from the vantage point of ten years passage of time.

Japanese Student: Here we are good friends walking across Europe, and just ten years ago our countries were fighting against each other.

German Student: Yes, when the war was being fought, I was only ten years old, but I remember many things about it.

American Student: Me, too. My father was in the army. He fought on Iwo Jima, Guadalcanal, and all those places.

Israeli Student: I don't remember anything much about the war, but I have read a lot about it. I read all about the atom bomb. (Then to the Japanese student): Do you hate the Americans for dropping the bomb?

Japanese Student: At first I did. I wanted to kill every American I saw. But, as I grew older I didn't hate them anymore.

American Student: Why was that?

Japanese Student: Well, I read that the Germans were working to make an atom bomb, and that some of our own Japanese scientists were helping them. I think that if we had developed the bomb first, we would have used it on the Americans.

Israeli Student: Yes, but why did they have to drop it on a city?

Japanese Student: Because all during the war cities were being bombed—not with atom bombs but with other kinds of bombs like block-busters and fire bombs. So, it didn't seem so different to use an atom bomb on a city.

German Student: That's right. We bombed London almost every night. Thousands of people were killed in London from bombs. One night Allied bombers bombed Dresden, one of our most beautiful German cities, and many people were killed.

Israeli Student: Maybe it was better to end the war quickly with the atom bomb. I don't know.

Later, when Elliot talked to Mitzi, he asked her if she thought she had met the objectives of her lesson.

"Yes," she said, "I wanted the children to learn some of the basic facts about the first atom bomb dropping, and I wanted them to do some thinking about the facts. I wanted them to relate to the events of the times as closely as possible. I think that the role-playing showed that they had made good progress in all of these areas."

"But, you know, Professor Elliot," she continued, "I think that I learned more than the kids did."

"How's that, Mitzi?"

"Well, I've got to admit that I was prejudiced against the Americans' atom bomb dropping before I taught the lesson. But I do see now, thanks to the kids, that from the American point-of-view there were some very compelling reasons for the decision. It couldn't have been easy."

Then, as she left my office, she turned her head and said, "Professor Elliot, thanks for not letting me cop out of the lesson. It wouldn't have been professional."

Elliot didn't say anything. He just nodded his head. But he thought to himself that with enough teachers like Mitzi it might just be possible that the world could become a better place to live.

SECTION 25

Post-WWII People and Events

THE UNITED NATIONS

1. This page contains facts about the United Nations that you may pass on to your students.

2. When completed, the diagram on the facing page will show the six major parts of the UN and the principal functions of those parts.

United Nations Facts

☑ Purpose of the UN: To foster world peace and to better the conditions of humans throughout the world.

☑ Number of member nations as of 1994: 188. Switzerland, following its traditional role as neutral is not a UN member; however, the UN Secretariat does have its European office in Geneva.

☑ The headquarters for the UN is in New York City. John D. Rockefeller, Jr., contributed more than $8 million for land acquisition; New York City invested some $26 million to adapt the site; the Ford Foundation gave $6.2 million for the Dag Hammarskjöld Library.

☑ The UN has five official languages: English, French, Russian, Chinese, and Spanish. If a member of the UN speaks in any of the five official languages, the words are immediately translated into the other four languages. Listeners may hear the translation almost simultaneously via special earphones.

☑ In front of UN headquarters, the flags of all member nations are flown.

☑ The UN has its own post office and issues its own stamps.

☑ To pay the operating expenses of the UN, members are assessed in accordance with their wealth. For 1992–1993 the total budget was $2.36 billion. The United States contributes more money to the UN than any other nation—in 1992, $300 million, while many of the smaller countries paid about $100 thousand.

☑ Following is an account of how the United Nations came into being:

In August 1941, President Franklin D. Roosevelt and Prime Minister Winston Churchill of the United Kingdom met on a battleship in the Atlantic Ocean. At the end of the meeting a number of statements known as the Atlantic Charter were issued. The Atlantic Charter gave the hopes and plans of the United States and Great Britain for a fair and just peace after the war. The Charter spoke of the "right of all peoples to choose the form of government under which they will live." Another statement was concerned with the right of all people to "live out their lives in freedom from fear and want."

The Atlantic Charter briefly mentioned a "permanent system of general security." By this Roosevelt and Churchill meant an international organization that might prevent World War III.

At a meeting held in Moscow in October 1943, it was decided to form a new international organization "open to membership of all . . . states large and small." Another meeting, called the Dumbarton Oaks Conference, was held in Washington, D.C., in 1944. Here the structure of the new organization, to be called the United Nations, was discussed. Many points of general agreement were reached although no final decisions were made.

Finally, a conference took place in San Francisco in April 1945. At this conference the charter, or constitution, for the United Nations was written.

About fifty nations were represented at the San Francisco Conference. In about nine weeks the United Nations Charter was written. It was submitted to the governments of all the participating nations for approval. The United States Senate, which has the power under our constitution to accept or reject treaties, voted 98–2 in favor of the Charter. By October 24, 1945, enough nations had voted in favor of the Charter for the United Nations to begin official operations.

Name: _____ Date: _____

THE UNITED NATIONS

The United Nations works to improve living conditions around the world. It takes action against nations that are endangering world peace. To accomplish these goals there are several major parts of the United Nations. Each one of which has specific functions, but each part works in cooperation with the other parts.

To do

1. Notice that each blank box in the diagram has a heading.

2. Find the matching heading below. Then, in the diagram box carefully print the information that follows the word **Function**.

GENERAL ASSEMBLY—Every member nation has one delegate and one vote. . . . **Function**: Discuss world problems and suggest actions to be taken.

SECURITY COUNCIL—15 members, 5 of which are permanent, the other 10 chosen for 2-year terms. . . . **Function**: Keep world peace—even by using force, if necessary.

ECONOMIC AND SOCIAL COUNCIL—54 members elected for 3-year terms by the General Assembly. . . . **Function**: Solve problems of hunger, health, housing, and education.

TRUSTEESHIP COUNCIL—**Function**: Protect and guide places in the world not yet independent.

INTERNATIONAL COURT OF JUSTICE—**Function**: Listen to disputes between nations (example: boundary disputes) and then suggest solutions that are fair to both sides.

SECRETARIAT—**Function**: Manage the business of the UN; notify the Security Council of matters that may lead to war.

MAJOR PARTS OF THE UNITED NATIONS

GENERAL ASSEMBLY
Function: _____
_____
_____

SECURITY COUNCIL	**SECRETARIAT**	**ECONOMIC AND SOCIAL COUNCIL**	**INTERNATIONAL COURT OF JUSTICE**	**TRUSTEESHIP COUNCIL**
Function:	Function:	Function:	Function:	Function:

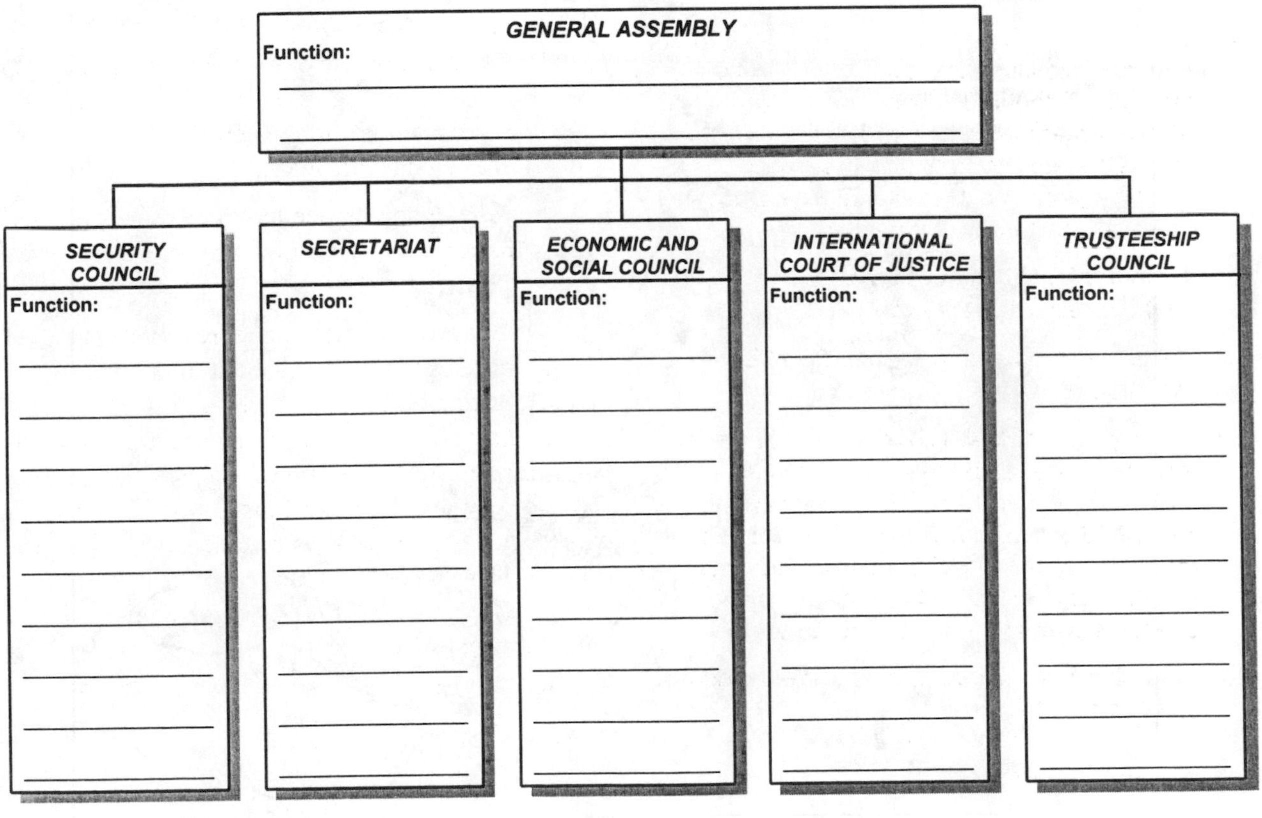

THE IRON CURTAIN AND NATO

The allied victory in WWII made it possible for the Soviet Union to impose Communism on eastern European countries, and by 1948 they had succeeded; almost all of eastern Europe was Communist controlled. These countries included East Germany, Poland, Romania, Bulgaria, Hungary, Yugoslavia, Albania, Czechoslovakia, Latvia, Lithuania, and Estonia.

1.   On the map draw (//////) lines in all the countries mentioned above.

The nations controlled by the Soviet Union were said to be "behind the Iron Curtain." There was very little communication between the Iron Curtain nations and the nations of western Europe.

2. Show the border between the Iron Curtain countries and the western European countries by drawing a heavy line connecting the X's that start on the border between West Germany and East Germany.

In 1945 relations between the United States and the Soviet Union began to deteriorate. A long period—some forty-five years—known as the Cold War began. During this period the United States and the Soviet Union were close to war several times.

In April 1949, the United States entered into an agreement with Canada and several European countries. The North Atlantic Treaty, as the agreement was called, provided that an armed attack against any treaty nation would be considered an attack against all of the nations.

The treaty called for a military force, the North Atlantic Treaty Organization (NATO), to be made up of soldiers and sailors from the fifteen member nations. NATO had the overall purpose of preventing the forceful spread of Communism in Europe.

*3. The following listed countries were part of NATO. On the map write N (for NATO) in the countries: Iceland, Belgium, Turkey, Italy, Denmark, France, Greece, Norway, Portugal, West Germany, Luxembourg, Great Britain, Ireland, Netherlands. **Note**: Spain and Finland were not part of NATO, nor were they Communist nations.*

AFRICAN-AMERICANS AND OTHERS FIGHT DISCRIMINATION

A Time of Little Progress

Many African-Americans hoped that after World War I they would find equality in their own country. There were good reasons for such hope. More than 370,000 African-Americans were serving in the armed forces. Some 300,000 had moved from the South to the North and West to work in defense industries. They expected that their excellent war and work records would influence other Americans to give them their rights. And, finally, early in the war President Wilson had said that the war was being fought "to make the world safe for democracy." Did this not mean that he intended to make democracy work at home?

1. What were some of the things that would have to be done to "make democracy work at home?" _____

_____

_____

_____

African-American hopes were not realized. During and after World War I feelings against them seemed to grow worse. The Ku Klux Klan was revived, and other anti-African-American organizations were started. Newspapers often carried stories about attacks against African-Americans. Thousands of innocent people were left homeless as a result of riots which they did not start. Many African-Americans suffered from harsh discrimination.

In spite of the risks, African-Americans continued to work for their own advancement. The NAACP* was active in suing in the courts for equal rights. The NAACP also worked to have laws passed that were beneficial to African-Americans. Another group, The National Urban League, concentrated on helping African-Americans receive equal standing in the workplace.

2. In what two ways did the NAACP work to advance African-Americans? _____

_____

_____

3. In what way did the National Urban League work to advance African-Americans? _____

_____

_____

Important Gains

During World War II, about one million African-American men and women served in the armed forces. About half of these Americans served overseas. Many more opportunities were open to them in World War II than had been in any other war. One step forward, for example, was the promotion of Benjamin Davis, Sr., to the rank of Brigadier General. Davis was the first African-American in our armed forces to achieve this rank.

During the first years of the war the armed forces were segregated. African-American units lived separately, were trained separately, and served separately. This policy wasted time and money, and it used manpower inefficiently.

Military and government leaders decided to experiment with integrated troops. Some small units of African-American troops were attached to larger units of white troops. Results were encouraging. The men worked harmoniously together and effectively carried out their duties and responsibilities. The war ended before full integration of the armed forces was achieved. But a start had been made.

On July 26, 1948, President Harry S. Truman took a giant step forward in moving African-Americans closer to the goal of equality. He signed Executive Order 9981. This order stated, "there shall be equality of treatment and opportunity for all persons in the Armed Services without regard to race, color, religion, or national origin." Excellent progress in carrying out this order was made; today, the armed forces are totally integrated.

4. Why is Benjamin Davis, Sr., an important figure? _____

_____

_____

* National Association for the Advancement of Colored People

AFRICAN-AMERICANS AND OTHERS FIGHT DISCRIMINATION

5. Why is executive order 9981 important? __

_____

_____

_____

    The next great victory of the civil rights fight came in education. In 1954 the Supreme Court, in the case known as *Brown versus Board of Education*, ruled that it was unconstitutional to have separate schools for African-Americans. As a result, some segregated school systems in the South began immediately to integrate their schools. Others moved slowly or even resisted integration. However, today there are few schools, if any, in the South or elsewhere that are deliberately segregated.

6. Why was the Brown versus Board of Education case important? _____

_____

    Lawyers and lawmakers alone did not win victories for African-Americans. Civil rights organizations' initiation of and participation in such activities as sit-ins, marches, and boycotts had much to do with getting the courts and legislative bodies to act in favor of complete equality for African-Americans.

    Perhaps the most famous demonstration was the March on Washington on August 28, 1963. At that time some 225,000 Americans, white and African-American together, met at the Lincoln Memorial in Washington, D.C. Millions of other Americans watched the exciting but peaceful proceedings on the television as speaker after speaker spoke against discrimination in any form.

    In the year following the March on Washington, Congress passed the Civil Rights Act of 1964. Under the terms of this act, discrimination in public places was declared illegal. The act also helped African-Americans in matters of voting, employment, and education. The direct action tactics of civil rights groups were once again important in the passage of this and other laws.

    Since 1964 there have been some important gains by African-Americans. Following are only a few of the positive happenings:

1967—Thurgood Marshall was sworn in as the first African-American Supreme Court Justice.

1971—The Supreme Court ruled that bus transportation must be provided by school districts as necessary to achieve the racial integration of schools.

1978—The Supreme Court ruled that African-Americans and other minorities may be given some preference with regard to college admissions.

1989—General Colin Powell, an African-American, was chosen to be the highest ranking military officer in the United States: Chairman of the Joint Chiefs of Staff.

1992—Ronald Brown, an African-American and former Chairman of the Democratic National Committee, was appointed Secretary of Commerce by President Clinton.

7. What were four kinds of actions taken by civil rights groups to help the African-American cause? _____

_____

_____

_____

_____

8. Try to think of reasons why the March on Washington (1963) action was held at the Lincoln Memorial in Washington. _____

_____

_____

_____

_____

9. Why is it especially important to have African-Americans as justices on the United States Supreme Court? _____

_____

_____

_____

_____

MARTIN LUTHER KING: CIVIL RIGHTS LEADER

Procedure

The short biography of Martin Luther King may be utilized in either of two ways, as follows:

1. Read the story to your students as they take notes in the spaces below the illustrations on the facing page. Encourage them to keep their notes brief; complete sentences are not necessary.

2. The story can be photocopied and distributed. Have your students read the story and then write two or three questions, including brief answers, beneath each illustration. The questions can be asked of other students in the class. *Note*: The advantage of this procedure is that in order to write questions and answers it is necessary to study and understand the material. Also, it fosters the whole language approach.

Regardless of which strategy you use, have your students respond in writing (on the reverse side of their papers) to the following:

✎ How would you feel if you were required to sit in the back of a bus?

✎ Suppose you were denied the right to eat in a restaurant because of the color of your skin. What would be your reaction?

✎ Why did Martin Luther King deserve the Nobel Peace Prize?

✎ What do you think Dr. King was referring to when he spoke of the "promised land" the evening before his death?

✎ Think of a caption for each of the illustrations 1–6.

1. There were two main sources of learning in Martin's young life: books, and his father, who was a Baptist minister. His father knew that in Atlanta, Georgia, where the family lived, Martin, as an African-American, would be treated by most of the city's white population as an inferior person. His father wanted to make sure that Martin didn't come to believe that he was inferior. So, he reminded his son again and again, "You are as good as anyone else."

2. As a young man, Martin had some question as to what he wanted to do with his life. Should he be a doctor, or perhaps a lawyer? In either profession he would be in a position to help people. However, he came to realize that he could best serve God and his people by becoming a minister. He studied hard. He gave his first sermon to his father's congregation when he was only seventeen years old. Martin became ordained as a Baptist minister when he was eighteen years old.

3. Martin realized that even though he had been ordained, he needed further education. He enrolled in the Crozer Theological Seminary, Pennsylvania. While there he learned of the work of Mahatma Ghandi. Ghandi had done much to help India's poor people, who were treated badly by upper-class Indians and the British who ruled India. Mahatma's success was due, in part, to *non-violent resistance* to unjust laws. It occurred to Martin that he could use Ghandi's approach to help African-Americans gain their just (equal) position in American society.

4. After graduating from Crozer, Martin continued his education and earned a Doctor of Theology degree from Boston University. Between his time at Crozer and Boston University, Martin married Coretta Scott, who was studying to become a singer and performer. The newly married couple moved to Montgomery, Alabama, where the now Dr. Martin Luther King became Pastor of the Dexter Avenue Baptist Church.

5. In Montgomery, Dr. King became a respected leader in the struggle to help African-Americans achieve the full and equal citizenship to which they were entitled. Among other things, he participated in organizing successful boycotts against public bus transportation, which required that African-Americans sit at the back of busses. From that time on the list of non-violent protests that were led by Dr. King goes on and on including lunch counter sit-ins to do away with the practice of not allowing African-Americans to eat in "white only" restaurants, and the famous peaceful march in Selma, Alabama, to gain voting rights for his people. For his work in bringing about changes in a peaceful manner, Dr. King was awarded the Nobel Prize for Peace—one of the greatest honors that can be given to a person.

6. Many millions of people—African-American and white—respected and loved Dr. King for his work, but there were others who feared and hated him. His home was bombed, as was his church. He was often threatened and beaten. None of this stopped him from doing the work he had to do, and, most of all, he never returned violence with violence. But one night, April 3, 1968, he had a premonition that his life might be taken. He said, "I've seen the promised land. I may not get there with you, but we as a people will get to the promised land." The very next day he was gunned down in Memphis, Tennessee, where he had gone to help African-Americans earn the same amount of money as whites for doing the same work.

MARTIN LUTHER KING: CIVIL RIGHTS LEADER

25-4

243

THE PEACE CORPS

The information on this page will help your students appreciate the fact that the government and people of the United States have always been ready to help those who are less fortunate. The Peace Corps is but one of many such efforts.

Background Information

☞ The Peace Corps had its beginning in 1961 in President John F. Kennedy's administration. In its first year of existence more than 13,000 men and women joined the Peace Corps. During the Corps first thirty-three years more than 120,000 Americans served. At least 80 countries have been helped. It may come as a surprise to some that the Peace Corps has also helped people in the United States who were or are in need.

☞ What does the Peace Corps hope to accomplish?

(1) Help people to meet their immediate needs for food, clothing, and shelter.

(2) Help people to better provide for themselves by teaching them skills in, among other things, carpentry, masonry, plumbing, roofing, farming, forestry, cooking, sewing, motor repair, and child care. Some volunteers specialize in teaching reading, writing, and arithmetic to children and adults.

It is not possible to give an accurate figure, but it is a certainty that thousands, if not millions, of people are healthier today—and even alive—as a result of the work of Peace Corps health care specialists such as doctors, nurses, and medical technicians.

(3) Help foreigners better understand Americans, and help Americans better understand foreigners, in the interest of world peace. For example, knowing the language, customs, and religions of others helps eliminate misunderstandings that may escalate into war.

Questions and Answers about the Peace Corps

☞ Who may join the Peace Corps? *Any American citizen over 18 of any race, religion, ethnic background, or sex (female volunteers comprise almost 50%) who has specified skills and knowledge that can be taught to others; college-educated individuals particularly desirable;* *married couples, provided they both have skills to teach, have no dependents, and serve in the same country.*

☞ How long do volunteers serve? *An initial two years, plus three months of preparatory training in special technologies, language, customs, history, geography, etc., of the host country; extension of service possible (about 33% re-enlist).*

☞ Do volunteers receive pay? *Allowances for food, clothing, and shelter, averaging about $300 per month; upon return to the United States: $175 for each month served to help in readjustment.*

☞ What are some of the specific accomplishments of the Peace Corps? *A reforestation program in Thailand; increased rice production in Sierra Leone; polio vaccine for children in Brazil; increased poultry and egg production in India; an aqueduct bringing clear, pure mountain water to a village in Columbia. The list could go on and on easily filling a hundred pages of a book.*

Extension Questions

☞ In terms of material things what would Peace Corps volunteers from a large city find different and need to adjust to in a rain forest community in Southeast Asia, equatorial Africa or some other remote place? *In most cases absence of the following: running water, indoor toilets, bathtubs or showers, washing/drying machines, air conditioning, electric lights, television, libraries, public transportation, daily newspapers, packaged food, dentists, doctors, barber shops, banks, book stores, ice cream parlors, restaurants, hardware stores, and so on.*

☞ Suppose you were a person in a poor country such as Uganda. What reactions and feelings might you experience when some Peace Corps volunteers first came to your village? *Uneducated persons might wonder about differences in skin color and clothing, strange customs such as shaking hands, and unfamiliar eating habits; they might also wonder why "rich" Americans would come to their village, and whether those Americans would "look down" on them.*

Name: _____ Date: _____

HISTORY AND GEOGRAPHY IN EASTERN ASIA

This activity will help you better understand the locations of places in East Asia, all of which have been associated with our history in some way.

Label your map as follows. At

- Ⓐ China
- Ⓑ North Korea
- Ⓒ South Korea
- Ⓓ Japan
- Ⓔ Taiwan
- Ⓕ Vietnam
- Ⓖ Laos
- Ⓗ Cambodia
- Ⓘ Myanmar
- Ⓙ Thailand
- Ⓚ Malaysia
- Ⓛ Philippine Islands

2. Name the capital city, indicated on the map, of each of the following countries:

China_____ Laos_____

No. Korea _____ Cambodia _____

So. Korea _____ Myanmar _____

Japan _____ Thailand_____

Taiwan_____ Malaysia _____

Vietnam_____ Philippine_____
                      Islands

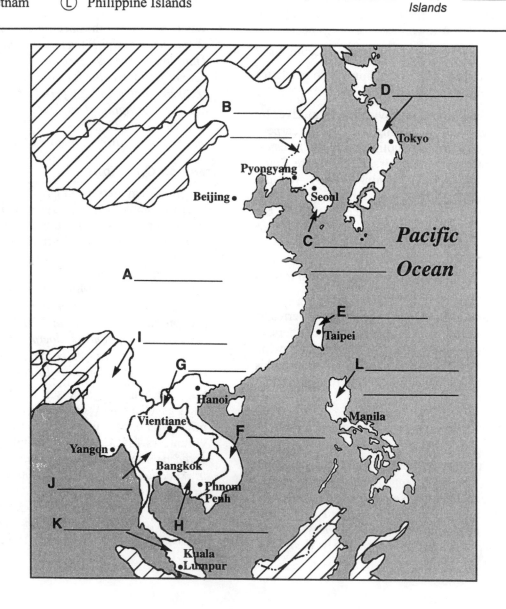

WAR IN KOREA

1. *Before reading the material below, add labels to the map as follows:*

❶ **Soviet Union** (now Russia)   ❹ **Pacific Ocean**

❷ **Mongolia**   ❺ **Japan**

❸ **China**   ❻ **Formosa** (now Taiwan)

During World War II, the Allies (United States, Soviet Union, etc.) had discussed what was to be done with the Japanese empire after its defeat. One of the most important parts of that empire was Korea.

2. *On the large map circle the peninsula of Korea.*

The Allies agreed that Korea should become an independent country. Temporarily, however, the peninsula was to be divided into two parts separated by the 38th parallel. The Soviet Union was to occupy North Korea, and the United States was to occupy South Korea.

3. *Find the dots labeled A and B on the small inset map. Connect the dots. Write 38th P (P for parallel) on the line.*

On June 25, 1950, North Korea, aided by the Russians, shocked the world by launching a sneak attack on South Korea. The United Nations was asked to come to the aid of South Korea. The Security Council agreed to help and asked the United States to take the lead in stopping the North Koreans.

Battles raged back and forth across the peninsula. North Korea was not successful in forcing the United Nations troops to leave South Korea. In fact, the United Nations' troops drove the North Koreans north to the Yalu River.

4. *Circle the Yalu River on the small map.*

At that point, China entered the war to support North Korea, which was going down to defeat. Chinese Communist troops crossed the Yalu River and drove the UN troops back to the 38th parallel.

5. *Draw arrows across the Yalu to show the direction of the Chinese attacks.*

At the 38th parallel neither side could move the other side very far from the line. The war almost came to a stop. The two sides began negotiating a peace settlement. After months of bickering the two sides reached an agreement: The war would end, and the 38th parallel was to be the dividing line between two new independent countries—South Korea and North Korea.

The cost of the war to the United States was very great. More than 54,000 of our men died, and more than $20 billion was spent. But there were some good results. For one thing, the Communists were kept from taking over all of Korea. The United States showed that it would live up to its responsibilities no matter what the cost. This encouraged free people throughout the world. The United Nations, too, showed that it could do more than just talk about preserving world peace. Fifteen nations besides the United States actually sent troops to Korea to fight the Communists.

6. *On the reverse side write the answers to the following questions.*

✍   What kept the UN and South Korea from scoring a complete victory over North Korea?

✍   In what way did the Soviet Union fail to keep its promise to the Allies?

THE UNITED STATES FIGHTS A WAR IN VIETNAM

The Vietnam War, as it is frequently called—although Congress never actually declared war in Vietnam—was the longest war in American history. America's involvement in Vietnam caused much costly and complex conflict at home and throughout the world: many civilians and soldiers were killed and wounded in Vietnam; many political actions were taken to pursue or withdraw from the conflict that was causing such dissatisfaction in the United States; many countries became directly or indirectly involved.

The account that follows is, of necessity, simplified, but it may have the virtue of helping your students understand, at the least, the chronology of the affair. The misery that the war engendered is probably incomprehensible, especially to young minds.

Extension Questions

❑ Thousands of men who disagreed with the war evaded the draft in various ways, including leaving the country. At the end of the war, President Carter granted pardons to most of those men. Do you agree or disagree with his action? Why or why not?

❑ Should the United States involve itself in wars or disturbances in other countries as we have done in recent years in Korea, Vietnam, the Persian Gulf, Somalia, Rwanda, and Haiti?

Chronology of the Vietnam Affair

❑ Starting about 1858 Vietnam became one of France's colonies. However, in 1940 after France had been defeated by Germany in WWII, the Japanese, as allies of Germany, took possession of Vietnam. Japan remained in control until its own defeat by the Allies in 1945.

❑ There was a power vacuum in Vietnam after the Japanese withdrawal. Then, the former rulers of Vietnam, the French, returned and regained control. But, many of the Vietnamese opposed the return of France; they were no longer willing to remain a colony. So, a rebellion known as the Indo-China war began. Western nations such as the United States supported the French. Communist nations such as Russia and China supported the revolutionaries. As can be realized, Vietnam's troubles were involving more and more nations beyond its borders.

❑ In the spring of 1954, the French suffered a great defeat by the Communists in the Battle of Dien Bien Phu. This defeat ended French control and resulted in a peace conference held in Geneva, Switzerland in 1954. In attendance at the conference were various nations including the United States, France, Russia, and China. Because most of northern Vietnam was Communist, and southern Vietnam was not, there was considerable disagreement. The result was a compromise: Vietnam was to be divided into two parts—North Vietnam and South Vietnam.

❑ Because there was still considerable hostility between the two parts, and South Vietnam feared North Vietnam, the United States was asked by the South Vietnamese to send advisors to help train a South Vietnam army. We agreed to the request.

❑ In 1957, Communists in South Vietnam, known as Viet Cong, and aided by North Vietnam, began a rebellion against the government of South Vietnam. Things were going badly for the government, especially since the Viet Cong were being supported by troops and supplies from the north. What had started as a rebellion in South Vietnam soon became a war between north and south. Then, at the request of the South Vietnamese government, the United States took a more active part by sending troops.

❑ As early as 1960 Americans at home were becoming increasingly critical of our involvement in Vietnam. Opposition to the war increased as news of American casualties—some 56,000 before the war ended—was broadcast over radio, printed in newspapers, and, vividly depicted on daily television. Riots took place throughout the country, especially in colleges and large cities. So great was the feeling against the war—which had in one way and another been part of the administration of five presidents—that the United States actively sought a cease-fire agreement. This was finally achieved in 1973. The war was over as far as United States involvement was concerned, and all of our armed forces were withdrawn.

❑ Soon after the United States withdrawal, North Vietnam went on the attack against South Vietnam. This time they were successful. The two parts of Vietnam were combined into one nation which took the new name: Socialist Republic of Vietnam.

THE PERSIAN GULF WAR AND GEOGRAPHY

To fully understand the Persian Gulf War it is necessary to know the geography of the region where the war was fought. This activity will help you locate and remember the places that were important to the war.

1. On the lines below write the names of the countries lettered and labeled on the map.

A _____

B _____

C _____

D _____

E _____

F _____

G _____

H _____

I _____

J _____

K _____

L _____

M _____

N _____

O _____

_____

P _____

Q _____

2. Next to the numbers on the map write the names of the waters as listed below:

①   Black Sea

②   Caspian Sea

③   Mediterranean Sea

④   Red Sea

⑤   Gulf of Aden

⑥   Persian Gulf

⑦   Gulf of Oman

⑧   Arabian Sea

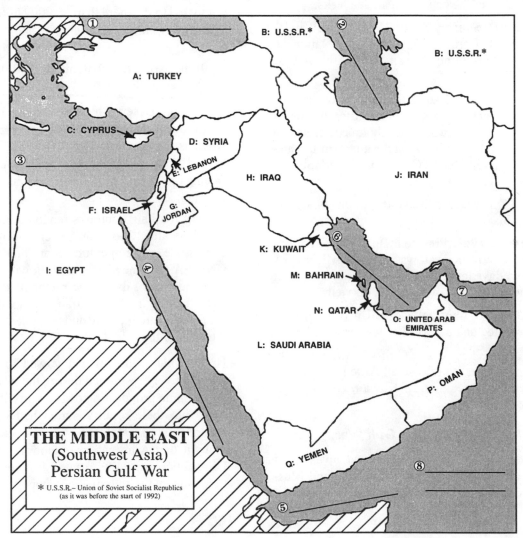

① _____

B: U.S.S.R.*

②

B: U.S.S.R.*

A: TURKEY

C: CYPRUS

D: SYRIA

E: LEBANON

③ _____

H: IRAQ

J: IRAN

F: ISRAEL

G: JORDAN

K: KUWAIT   ⑥

I: EGYPT   ④

M: BAHRAIN

⑦ _____

N: QATAR

O: UNITED ARAB EMIRATES

L: SAUDI ARABIA

P: OMAN

THE MIDDLE EAST
(Southwest Asia)
Persian Gulf War

Q: YEMEN   ⑧ _____

⑤

* U.S.S.R.– Union of Soviet Socialist Republics
(as it was before the start of 1992)

248

THE PERSIAN GULF WAR: SIDELIGHTS

A Brief Chronology

August 2, 1990: Iraq invaded Kuwait, annexed it as part of Iraq, and seized its oil fields.

August 6, 1990: The United Nations Security Council reacted to Iraq's invasion by authorizing economic sanctions and, if necessary, military action against Iraq. President Bush acted upon the belief that Saudi Arabia would be Iraq's next target (Iraq had already made forays into Saudi Arabian territory) and began to mobilize American military forces. This was the beginning of "Operation Desert Shield."

November, 1990: The United Nations dispatched more than 400,000 troops to Saudi Arabia (eventually, 18 nations sent ground troops, and 14 sent ships) to protect the country against attacks.

November–December, 1990: Unsuccessful diplomatic attempts were made by the United Nations to bring a halt to the Iraq-Kuwait-Saudi Arabian hostilities.

January 16, 1991: Iraq defied a United Nations' ultimatum to get out of Kuwait or suffer the consequences. United States planes bombed targets in Kuwait and Iraq, the heaviest air attack in the history of warfare. Thus, "Operation Desert Storm" began.

January 17, 1991: Iraq fired missiles into Israel and Saudi Arabia.

February 24, 1991: President Bush ordered an invasion of Kuwait. Kuwait was secured by UN/USA troops two days later. In its retreat, Iraqi troops set fire to more than 500 of Kuwait's oil wells.

March 3, 1991: Iraq realized that it had been severely defeated and a cease-fire was arranged.

April 11, 1991: The Persian Gulf War was officially ended. Iraq agreed to release all Allied war prisoners, repeal its annexation of Kuwait, and pay war damages.

Sidelights of the Persian Gulf War

➢ Opposition to Iraq's unwarranted invasion of Kuwait was widespread. Even Arab and Muslim countries joined in the condemnation of Iraq's (Saddat Hussein's) actions. These nations did more than just condemn. They sent troops and ships to help defeat the Iraqi's. Included in the Arab and Muslim nations that went to Kuwait's rescue were Bahrein, Qatar, United Arab Emirates, Oman, Morocco, Syria, Egypt, Pakistan, Senegal, Niger, and Bangladesh.

"Western" countries that joined the "Coalition," as it was called, included NATO nations and New Zealand, Australia, and Argentina.

➢ During the Persian gulf War, some 500,000 members of the United States military were in the Persian Gulf region at one time or another. 148 of these individuals were killed in combat—a relatively small number of casualties compared to the more than 58,000 United States military casualties in Vietnam, and 54,000 in Korea.

It is estimated that about 100,000 Iraqi troops were killed.

➢ "Operation Desert Shield" was the UN/USA effort to protect Saudi Arabia from Iraqi attack, whereas, "Operation Desert Storm" was the United Nations war against Iraq, including the freeing of Kuwait and the bombing and entering of Iraq itself.

The Iraqi air force was rendered impotent a few days after Operation Desert Storm began. During the entire operation more than 100,000 UN/USA airplane sorties were flown over Iraq. Iraq sought to salvage the remnants of its 700 aircraft by flying 137 to Iran but, upon arrival, the planes were interned and remained so for the duration of the war.

➢ Israel, which Hussein had vowed to destroy, was relatively restrained during the war despite the extreme provocation of Iraqi missiles being fired into their country. Israel had been persuaded not to enter the war because it was thought that Arab nations supporting the UN/USA action would be resentful of Jewish participation and withdraw their support.

THE UNITED STATES AND THE SPACE AGE

Notable "Firsts" in American Space History:

➡ 1962 (Feb. 20): Lt. Col. John H. Glenn became the first American to orbit the earth. The length of time for the three orbits he made was 4 hrs., 55 min.

➡ 1965 (June 3): Edward H. White was the first American to "walk" in space.

➡ 1969 (July 20): The first human to set foot on the moon was astronaut Neil Armstrong who was accompanied on the mission by Edwin E. Aldrin and Michael Collins. The crew was on the moon for 21 hrs., 36 min.

➡ 1975 (July 15–21): The first space link-up of an international nature took place. The United States space craft *Apollo 18* connected with the Soviet Union's *Soyuz 19*. The crews cooperated in space experiments, shared meals, and took part in a news conference.

➡ 1983 (June 18): Astronaut Sally Ride became the first American woman to travel in space.

➡ 1983 (August 30): The first African-American in space was Guion Bluford, a crew member of the space shuttle *Challenger*.

➡ 1986 (January 12): William Nelson was the first Congressman to experience space travel.

➡ 1992 (June 25–July 9): The longest amount of time spent in a space shuttle flight was set by the crew of the shuttle *Columbia*.

➡ 1992 (September 12): Astronaut Mae Carol Jemison became the first African-American woman in space.

➡ 1993 (April 8): Ellen Ochoa, astronaut, aboard the space shuttle *Discovery*, was the first Hispanic woman to experience space flight.

Planting the American Flag on the Moon

Neil Armstrong, Michael Collins, and Edwin Aldrin were part of a post-moon flight press conference. One of their interesting anecdotes had to do with the planting of the American flag on the moon's surface. Because there is no wind on the moon to cause a flag to wave, they attached some wire to the top hem to make the flag stick out straight from its pole.

During the conference Aldrin said, "We had some difficulty getting the pole of the flag to remain in the surface. In penetrating the surface we found that most objects would go down about 5, maybe 6, inches and then meet with gradual resistance. At the same time there was not much of a support force on either side (*Note*: the surface was mostly dust), so we had to lean the flag back slightly in order for it to maintain this (upright) position. So many people had done so much to give us this opportunity to place the American flag on the surface. To me it was one of the prouder moments of my life, to be able to stand there and quickly salute the flag."

Discussion Questions:

Should the United States be spending billions of dollars ($4 billion in 1970, $8 billion in 1986, $14 billion in 1993) to explore space?

The chief argument against the space program is that the money that is being spent, the man/woman power that is being deployed, and the resources that are being consumed could be better used in helping the millions in the country who are ill-fed, ill-clothed, ill-housed, ill-educated, and lacking in proper medical care. For example, if the money used for the space program were used for medical research, it might be possible to find a cure for cancer and heart disease relatively quickly. Critics also say that money is being spent and lives are being endangered without significant tangible returns.

*The chief arguments in support of the program follow: (1) The space program itself creates jobs; (2) in terms of military strategy, the nations that command space may be in the position to command the earth; (3) the earth's population is expanding so rapidly that in the not-so-distant future it may be necessary to colonize outer space; (4) the earth's resources are being so rapidly depleted that we may have to find new resources on distant planets or the moon; (5) the prestige of the United States is at stake; (6) space satellites are paying dividends in that they enable us to relay radio messages and TV programs, and they gather information that helps forecast the weather, and they can be used to provide surveillance of enemy installations; and (7) methods and materials developed for space travel are being put to consumer use, as, for example, a **sight switch** that through the movement of the eyes turns a switch on and off thus enabling handicapped people to turn on TV, lights, etc.*

CHRISTA McAULIFFE: SCHOOL TEACHER, ASTRONAUT

On May 5, 1961 Christa Corrigan's eyes and those of her classmates in Framingham (Massachusetts) Junior High School were glued to a black-and-white television set. They were watching Alan Shepard, United States astronaut, lifted into space on spacecraft *Freedom 7*. Christa was thrilled; it may have been then that she first got the idea that some day she, too, might fly in space.

The years flew by; Christa graduated from Marian High School after a busy, happy, and satisfying four years of hard study and activities. She even met the boy—Steven McAuliffe—she was to marry after they both completed college. But, Christa never lost her dream of space flight.

From high school she went on to Framingham State College, where she majored in history and earned a teaching certificate. Even in college, as busy as she was, she still thought about space travel. The continued success of the American space program heightened her interest, especially when she watched Neil Armstrong walk on the moon's surface.

After college, just as they said they would, Christa and Steve were married. Then, while Steve was studying for his law degree in Washington, D.C., Christa began her teaching career and earned a master's degree in education.

Soon after Steve earned his law degree, the young family—with the addition of a baby boy, Scott—moved to Concord, New Hampshire. Christa and Steve then had another child, Caroline. Christa, who had wanted to get back into teaching, which she loved, applied for a position, and was appointed social studies teacher in the local high school. As was typical of Christa, she became active in school matters and even found time to be involved in community affairs. She was universally respected and liked.

Then, one day Christa learned that NASA (National Aeronautics and Space Program) was searching for a school teacher to be the first "ordinary" citizen to travel in space. Here was an opportunity to realize her dream! She lost no time in making an application—along with 13,000 other teachers. When she told the students in her classes what she was doing, they were thrilled.

Months went by. Then, in April 1985, Christa was notified that she was one of the 113 finalists in the search, and that if she was still interested she should report to Washington, D.C. Christa was interested—very interested. She reported to Washington, was interviewed, observed and tested. Imagine her joy when she was chosen to be one of the final ten applicants. She was told to report to Houston, Texas, for more training and tests.

It was at the Houston center that the teacher applicant—the one who would actually travel in space—would be chosen. After more weeks of training to see if she was "right" for the rigors of space travel, NASA announced over the air waves, that Christa McAuliffe, Concord High School teacher, would be the one who would travel into space on the *Challenger* shuttle.

The rest of the story is hard to tell—it is so sad. After more training for Christa and the other six participants, lift-off day arrived—January 2, 1986. It was a cold and windy day, so cold that it posed a risk for the flight. However, after much debate among the scientists, it was decided to proceed. Then, 73 seconds after lift-off and 50,000 feet into the atmosphere, *Challenger* burst into flames, exploded, and all seven brave Americans aboard were killed. Christa McAuliffe had achieved her dream of space flight that, in the end, had turned into a nightmare.

Christa has not been forgotten. Her life remains an inspiration for others who dare to try. Today, those who visit the Christa McAuliffe Center in Concord or the Christa McAuliffe Library in Framingham are reminded of her determination to realize a dream and that it is other Americans such as Christa who, at great risk, have helped make our country great.

---

1. In the illustration *Challenger* is shown on the launching pad just before lift-off. Write a suitable caption—sentence form—on the lines beside the illustration.

Note: Respond to the next three directives on the reverse side of this page.

2. Think of five adjectives that describe Christa's character and personality.

3. What might have been Christa's thoughts upon learning that she was to travel on the *Challenger*?

4. Write what you think Steve McAuliffe might have said to Scott (10) and Caroline (6) when they learned that their mother had been killed.

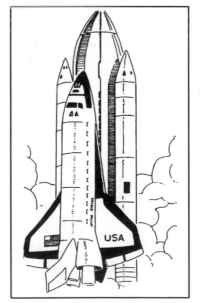

Cape Canaveral, January 2, 1986

_____

_____

_____

_____

_____

_____

_____

ENVIRONMENTAL PROBLEMS

The *Statistical Abstract of the United States* is an invaluable source of information. It is used by corporations; writers of history, geography, sociology, and economics; governmental organizations; and the general public—to name a few—for accurate, up-to-date, reliable, and unbiased information. It is published annually by the United States Bureau of the Census. The range of subjects it treats is tremendous and is included in some 1400 tables. If one wants to know, for example, how many bicycles were stolen or how many million of tons of corn were sold in a given year, the answer can be found in the *Statistical Abstract*, as it is called. It would be a rare library that does not have this valuable resource on its reference shelves.

The three tables copied (slightly enlarged) from the 1993 Statistical Abstract will offer your students opportunities to become familiar with the kinds of tables found in the book, and, concomitantly, help them come to a better realization of significant environmental problems.

Procedure

1. Photocopy the facing page and distribute, or you may want to make a transparency for projection.

2. Obtain a *Statistical Abstract* and explain its organization.

3. Have your students respond to the following short-answer questions.

4. An alternative approach: Photocopy the bottom part of this page and the accompanying page for distribution. Students may answer the questions on their own, writing their responses on the reverse side of the page.

Table 380

1. From what source did the *Statistical Abstract* obtain its information?

2. Explain the difference between endangered and threatened as related to wild animals.

3. How many United States mammals are classified as endangered? Threatened?

4. In the United States what is the total number of threatened species of all kinds?

5. In the United States what is the total number of endangered plants?

Table 366

6. What organization furnished the information for the table?

7. In what year did the greatest number of oil spills occur?

9. Does the number of incidents of oil spills from 1973 to 1992 seem to be getting smaller or greater?

10. How many oil spill incidents in 1992 did not occur on tank ships, tank barges, or "other vessels"?

11. In 1992, what was the greatest single source of oil spills—vessels or non-vessels? How many gallons?

Table 372

12. Is waste that comes from *junked autos* included in the report?

13. How many pounds of waste were generated on the average by each person every day in 1990?

14. What is the source of the greatest producer of waste in the United States: food, glass, or paper and paper board?

15. How many percent lower was food waste in 1990 than in 1960?

16. For the years reported, was there any decrease in the daily amount of waste per person?

17. Have your students "round-off" the figures for "Waste generated," 1960–1990. Then, construct a bar graph that compares the years. A suggested design follows:

SOLID WASTE GENERATED: 1960–1990

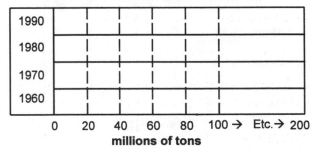

ENVIRONMENTAL PROBLEMS

No. 380. Threatened and Endangered Wildlife and Plant Species—Number: 1992

[As of October 19. Endangered species: One in danger of becoming extinct throughout all or a significant part of its natural range. Threatened species: One likely to become endangered in the foreseeable future.]

ITEM	Mam-mals	Birds	Rep-tiles	Amphib-ians	Fishes	Snails	Clams	Crusta-tions	Insects	Arach-nids	Plants
Endangered species, total	305	226	80	14	66	8	42	8	15	3	282
U.S. only	37	57	8	6	52	7	40	8	13	3	274
U.S. and foreign	19	16	8	•	3	•	•	•	1	•	7
Foreign only	249	153	64	8	11	1	2	•	1	•	1
Threatened species, total	32	12	32	5	36	6	2	2	9	•	73
U.S. only	6	7	14	4	30	6	2	2	9	•	62
U.S. and foreign	3	5	4	1	6	•	•	•	•	•	9
Foreign only	23	•	14	•	•	•	•	•	•	•	2

• Represents zero. 1 Species outside United States and outlying areas as determined by Fish and Wildlife Service.
Source U.S. Fish and Wildlife Service, *Endangered Species Technical Bulletin*, monthly.

No. 366. Oil Polluting Incidents Reported in and Around U.S. Waters: 1973 to 1992

YEAR	Incidents	Gallons	YEAR	Incidents	Gallons
1973	11,054	15,289,188	1986	6,330	4,427,544
1974	12,083	15,739,792	1987	6,083	3,759,983
1975	10,998	21,528,444	1988	6,155	6,617,278
1976	11,066	18,517,384	1989	7,923	13,506,643
1977	10,979	8,188,398	1990	9,600	11,375,576
1978	12,174	11,035,890	1991	9,850	1,452,103
1979	11,556	10,051,271			
1980	9,886	12,638,848	**1992**	**8,790**	**1,503,862**
1981	9,589	8,919,789	Tankships	198	117,899
1982	9,416	10,404,648	Tank barges	328	73,559
1983	10,530	8,378,719	Other vessels	4,893	400,296
1984	10,089	19,007,332	Non-vessels	3,371	912,108
1985	7,740	8,465,055			

Source U.S. Coast Guard. Based on unpublished data from the *Marine Safety Information System*.

No. 372. Municipal Solid Waste Generation, Recovery, and Disposal: 1960 to 1990

[In millions of tons, except as indicated. Covers post-consumer residential and commercial solid waste which comprises the major portion of typical municipal collections. Excludes mining, agriculture and industrial processing, demolition and construction wastes, sewage sludge, and junked autos and obsolete equipment wastes. Based on material-flows estimating procedure and wet weight as generated. NA Not available]

ITEM AND MATERIAL	1960	1970	1980	1985	1986	1987	1988	1989	1990
Waste generated	87.8	121.9	151.5	164.4	170.7	178.1	184.2	191.4	195.7
Per person per day (lb.)	2.66	3.27	3.65	3.77	3.88	4.01	4.12	4.2	4.3
Materials recovered	5.9	8.6	14.5	16.4	18.3	20.1	23.5	29.9	33.4
Per person per day (lb.)	0.18	0.23	0.35	0.38	0.42	0.45	0.52	0.7	0.7
Combustion for energy recovery	(NA)	0.4	2.7	7.6	9.6	16	24.5	27.1	29.7
Per person per day (lb.)	(NA)	0.02	0.06	0.17	0.22	0.36	0.59	0.6	0.7
Combustion without energy recovery .	27	24.7	11	4.1	3	2	1	2	2.2
Per person per day (lb.)	0.82	0.66	0.27	0.1	0.07	0.05	0.02	0.4	0.5
Landfill, other disposal	54.9	88.2	123.3	136.4	139.8	140	135.1	132.4	130.4
Per person per day (lb.)	1.67	2.37	2.97	3.13	3.18	3.15	3.02	2.9	2.9
Percent distribution of generation:									
Paper and paperboard	34.1	36.3	36.1	37.4	38.4	39.1	38.9	37.6	37.5
Glass	7.6	10.4	9.9	8	7.6	6.9	6.8	6.7	6.7
Metals	12	11.6	9.6	8.6	8.5	8.3	8.3	8.2	8.3
Plastics	0.5	2.5	5.2	7.1	7.2	7.5	7.8	8	8.3
Rubber and leather	2.3	2.6	2.8	2.3	2.5	2.5	2.5	2.4	2.4
Textiles	1.9	1.6	1.7	1.7	1.6	2.1	2.1	2.9	2.9
Wood	3.4	3.3	4.47	5	5.3	5.5	6.1	6.1	6.3
Food wastes	13.9	10.5	8.7	8	7.7	7.4	7.2	6.9	6.7
Yard wastes	22.8	19	18.2	18.2	17.7	17.4	17.2	18.1	17.9
Other wastes	1.6	2.2	3.4	3.6	3.4	3.3	3.1	3.1	3.1

Answer Key

North America: The Setting for American History

Major Rivers

1. Mississippi	4. Rio Grande	7. St. Lawrence
2. Missouri	5. Columbia	8. Hudson
3. Yukon	6. Ohio	

Major Mountain Chains

9. Brooks Range	12. Sierra Nevada	15. Sierra Madre Oriental
10. Alaska Range	13. Rocky Mountains	16. Sierra Madre Occidental
11. Cascade Range	14. Appalachian Mts.	

Major Islands/Groups

17. Greenland	19. Bahamas	21. Cuba
18. Baffin Island	20. Santo Domingo	

Major Surrounding Waters

22. Arctic Ocean	26. Chesapeake Bay	30. Pacific Ocean
23. Davis Strait	27. Gulf of Mexico	31. Gulf of Alaska
24. Hudson Bay	28. Caribbean Sea	32. Bering Strait
25. Atlantic Ocean	29. Gulf of California	33. Bering Sea

Major Lakes

34. Great Lakes	36. Great Slave Lake
35. Lake Winnipeg	37. Great Bear Lake

The Earliest Americans

Text Questions

1. No	3. Yes	5. Yes	7. No
2. No	4. No	6. No	

Map Questions

1. Yukon, Mackenzie
2. Missouri
3. Ohio, southwest
4. Cuba, Santo Domingo
5. Aztec, Mayan, Carib, Arawak (Seminole acceptable)

Matching

9, 8, 2, 7, 6, 1, 3, 4, 5

The Ten States with the Greatest Indian Populations

OK: 12½	NM: 6½	TX: 3	SD: 2½
CA: 12	NC: 4	NY: 3	
AZ: 10	WA: 4	MI: 3	

Indian Ruins of Old Mexico

1. Mayans and Toltecs, wells, 180′, 1500 peninsula of Yucatan
2. El Salvador, Honduras, Belize, Mexico, Guatemala
3. 212′, 692′, 11 acres
4. Northeast, about 30–35 miles

Pages 7–8   The Mayan Indians and Corn

1. Suggestions: "What is this? Could it be a better kind of corn? It has lots of kernels! I'm going to show it to the others."
2. The positions of the heavenly bodies would help people know when to plant their crops.
3. They could fertilize, rotate their crops from year to year, plow more deeply.
5. Seems certain, may have had the idea, perhaps, probable beginning, most likely, almost all, may have starved

Page 9   The New World and the Old World—Five Hundred Years Ago

1.

ITEM	INDIANS	EUROPEANS
Weapons	bows and arrows	guns, swords
Boats	canoes	sailing ships
Homes	covered with bark, skins	stone, storied, windows, gabled roofs
Ways of transporting goods	back packs, dogs with travois	carts and oxen
Roads	dirt trails	cobblestones
Clothing of men	skins, moccasins	hats, coats, cloaks, helmets, shoes, boots
Clothing of women	skins, moccasins, wrap-around skirts	cloth dresses, bonnets or hoods
Ways of transporting people	walking, canoe	horses, carts

2. Dogs, birds
3. Harvesting, pounding corn, caring for children, transporting (dog), preparing weapons, hunting (return of hunter)
4. Man (muscle) power
5. Fringed skins
6. Autumn (harvesting, bare trees)
7. Leaving (goods being taken from the cart, men carrying sacks on to the ship)
8. He is armed with a gun, and he is wearing a helmet and upper-body armor.

Page 14   Indians and Horses

I. Important discoveries and inventions
  A. Incandescent lamp
  B. Gun powder
  C. Guns
  D. Automobile
  E. Airplane

II. The development of horses
  A. Length of time in North America and how known
    1. 50 million years before first humans in North America
    2. Fossilized remains
  B. Changes in horses
    1. From 11" tall to present size
    2. Toes to hooves
    3. Breeding
      a. For strength
      b. For speed

III. Disappearance of horses in North America
  A. Explanations
    1. Died as a result of climate changes
    2. Travelled to Asia

IV. Pre-horse Indian transportation
  A. Humans
  B. Dogs pulling travois
    1. Description of travois
      a. Stretcher appearance
      b. Skins laid between poles
      c. Poles attached to dogs

255

C. Items transported
1. Possessions
2. Children

V. Cortes in Mexico
A. Indians astonished
B. Horse and rider one thing?
C. Fear of horses

VI. Indians and horses
A. Leaning about horses
B. Obtaining horses
1. Through trade
2. Capturing or stealing

VII. Locating buffalo with horses
A. Indian scouts
B. Signals to camp
C. Riding to herds

VIII. Hunting buffalo
A. Organized by leader
B. Rules of hunt
1. Strict
2. Special tasks

IX. Processing buffalo
A. Items obtained
1. Meat for food
2. Skins
a. Robes
b. Blankets
c. Tent coverings
3. Bones
a. Needles
b. Arrow heads
c. Knives
4. Sinew for thread
5. Rawhide
a. Cord in bows
b. Snowshoes
6. Horns for containers
7. Stomachs for bags
8. Skins for boats

X. Advantages of horses for hunting buffalo
A. Follow buffalo swiftly
B. Follow buffalo further

XI. Advantages of horses for transportation
A. Carry people
B. Carry/pull heavy loads

Page 16   Eastern Woodlands Indians

1. True (A fire is observable.)
2. May be true (Indians hunted wild animals.)
3. May be true (This is a reasonable inference: a lake is shown.)
4. May be true (The canoe is made of either bark or skins.)
5. Probably not true (The house is a sign of stability.)
6. Probably not true (The house doesn't appear large enough; only three people are shown.)
7. True (There are stakes along the canoe's sides, drying racks, and a pole over the fire.)
8. May be true (An Indian is dipping into a pot that is most likely filled with pine pitch.)
9. Probably not true (There are leaves on the trees and the men's upper bodies are not covered.)
10. Probably not true (At least one person could fit within the span of each pair of stakes.)
11. May be true (There is no indication of agriculture, so the Indians' food most likely was obtained from fish or wild animals.)
12. May be true (The woman appears to be carrying water pails and is walking toward the lake.)

Page 17 **Viking Ships**

1. Up to 90´, Suggestion: approx. 1/3 the length of a football field; 17´
2. 3´; Ships easy to enter or exit, could sail in shallow water
3. At least 34
4. Muscle (oars) or wind when available
5. Easier steering, stability, increased speed
6. Lapped boards
7. To frighten the enemy
8. Sacks

Page 18 **Vikings in North America**

1. (1) Faeroes Islands (4) Vinland   (7) Cape Cod
   (2) Iceland   (5) Newfoundland
   (3) Greenland   (6) Nova Scotia
2. Newfoundland
3. Unfriendly Indians, sickness, hunger

Page 19 **Portugal Finds an All Water Route to East Asia**

1st column: Congo, 1488, 1498
2nd column:
1. a. No   c. Yes
   b. Yes   d. No

2. Canary Islands, Cape Verde Islands, Equator, Cape of Good Hope

Page 21 **Columbus Discovers a New World**

2. 5 - Cuba   2 - Palos
   7 - Azores   8 - Lisbon
   1 - Spain   6 - Hispaniola
   4 - San Salvador 3 - Canary Islands
3. La Navidad
4. North America or , possibly, Bahamas
5. The *Santa Maria* was wrecked.

Page 23 **The Voyage of Magellan**

Order of sentences: 5, 6, 7, 2, 3, 1, 4

Page 24 **The Voyage of Magellan**

2. 1. Portugal   5. Straits of Magellan   9. Philippine Islands
   2. Spain   6. Tierra Del Fuego   10. Cape of Good Hope
   3. San Lucar   7. Pacific Ocean   11. Africa
   4. South America   8. Guam
3. a. Is the world round?
   b. Can the East Indies be reached by sailing west?
   c. Is there a water passage between North America and South America?
4. Juan Sebastian del Cano

Page 27   **Explorations of the USA'S South and Southwest**

Ponce de Leon: Puerto Rico, Bahama, Florida, Tampa
Hernando Cortes: Cuba, Yucatan, Gulf of Campeche, Veracruz, Tenochtitlan, Mexico City, Gulf of California
Hernando De Soto: Savannah, Appalachian, Mississippi, Natchez, Brazos
Francisco Coronado: Grand Canyon, Rocky, Canadian, Arkansas

Page 29   **A Village in Spanish America**

Spanish	English	Spanish	English	Spanish	English
sombrero	hat	cielo	sky	tejado	roof
caballo	horse	gente	people	pared	wall
mujer	woman	carro	cart	camino	road
cacto	cactus	ganado	cattle	árboles	trees
hombre	man	rueda	wheel	carpintero	carpenter
montaña	mountain	templo	church	herrero	blacksmith
casa	house	niños	children	hierba	grass

Page 37   **Frenchmen at Work in the New World**

1. A: Fishing off Newfoundland   D: Exploring Lake Champlain
   B: Meeting the Indians   E: Farming along the St. Lawrence
   C: Trading with the Indians   F: Cooking for the Family
2. A: Four men, ropes, mast, casks
   B: Arrows, quiver, canoe, trees
   C: Furs, quivers, feathers in hair, fringed shirt
   D: Islands, mountains, plumed hat, feathered Indian
   E: Oxen, plow, hat waving, harness
   F: Fireplace, bucket, kettle, floor-length dress

Page 38   **Viking/Spanish/French Explorers Crossword Puzzle**

¹P	A	C	²I	F	I	C		³V	I	N	L	A	N	⁴D
			U			⁵G								E
⁶G	⁷A	S	P	E		⁸I	R	O	Q	U	O	I	S	⁹I
	L		G			A								C
	G		O			¹⁰N	I	A	G	A	R	A		E
	O				¹¹C	O	D							L
¹²N	I	N	A			B			¹³L					A
	Q			¹⁴C	H	A	M	¹⁵P	L	A	I	N		N
	U					N		A	S					D
¹⁶P	I					K		N	A		¹⁷P			
	N		¹⁸P	¹⁹A	L	O	S		A		²⁰L	E	I	F
				Z				M			E		N	
²¹M	O	N	T	E	Z	U	M	A			E		T	
	R			E						²²B	A	²³N	K	
		²⁴O	C	T	O	B	E	R				O		

258

Page 40   **Settlers from Many Countries**

1. "But, they had suffered from wars and heavy taxes. Some had been punished because they wanted to worship in a way that was different from their rulers ways of worship."
2. Hard-working, expert woodsmen, excellent farmers
3. Manufacturing, cloth weaving

Page 42   **Roanoke Island: Site of the "Lost Colony"**

1. ". . . the settlers did not have the knowledge, skills, and willingness to work."
2. Reachable by water, easily defended, protected from storms by the eastward islands
Reading a Map: 36°N, Outer Banks, Albemarle, Atlantic Ocean, 22-25, Hatteras, Chowan

Page 52   **Minority Explorers and Builders**

1. *Indigo:* Moses Lindo
   Arizona, New Mexico: Estevanico
   Astronomy: Benjamin Banneker
   Trading: Aaron Lopez
   Huguenots: Paul Revere
   Exporter of colonial products: Aaron Lopez
2. "Five or six of his crew members were Jews by birth."
3. "More than one million French Huguenots . . . were not allowed to settle in French colonies."
4. Knowledge of Indian language and customs; scouting abilities
5. Dogs
6. Work in fields, shops, homes
7. Royal blue dye
8. Trade brought widely separated colonists together in mutual endeavors.
9. Surveyor, mathematician
10. Africans settled in lands claimed by the French (Louisiana).

Page 53   **Working in a Colonial Home**

1. | *Family Member* | *Task* |
   | --- | --- |
   | Grandmother | Baking (kneading dough) |
   | Young boy | Carrying wood |
   | Mother | Weaving cloth |
   | Father | Cleaning gun (preparing for hunting) |
   | Girl | Dipping candles |
   | Grandfather | Repairing/making shoes |
2. Gun powder, wax
3. Baking
4. Fire, lantern
5. Oil, coal, gas; electricity; factories (mills); store (bakery); shoemaker

Page 60   **Symbol of America: The Kentucky Rifle**

1. a. Heavy   b. Not accurate   c. Limited effective range
2. A grooved barrel that spiraled the bullet toward its target
3. The bullet fitted tightly into the barrel of the rifle; thus, none of the force of the exploding powder was wasted.
4. Musket
5. The rifle used smaller bullets and less powder; consequently, hunters and pioneers could make longer journeys with less weight to carry.
7. 3, 4, 2, 6, 5, 1

Page 62   **Freedom of the Press: The Peter Zenger Case**

1. Zenger was imprisoned.
2. Munday, goal, citty
3. See or speak with people
4. Wife, servants, hole
5. To keep on writing and printing ("entertaining"}

Page 64   **Multi-Cultural Additions to Standard English: Pennsylvania Dutch**

1. Stomach
2. String
3. Little, little while
4. Scratch
5. Hungry
6. Tired
7. Bark
8. Kiss
9. Sick
10. Silly
11. Crawl
12. Quick, quickly
13. Slippery, village or town
14. Funny
15. Ridiculous
16. Angry
17. Nosey, snoopy, curious

Page 66   **Ben Franklin: Inventor, Patriot, Statesman**

1st column: 5, 8, 7, 6, 1, 7, 4, 6, 2, 4, 2, 2, 3, 2
Poor Richard's Almanac: 3, 5, 6, 1, 2, 4

Page 67   **Map Locations in Eastern North America: 1492–1775**

A, I, G, I, B, A, G, F, B, D, G, D or C, D, D, D, F, B, H, G, A, C, H, E

Page 68   **Sequences in Early American History**

1. John Cabot
    Sir Francis Drake
    Massachusetts Bay Colony
    Growing tobacco
    House of Burgesses
    Pennsylvania Colony
    John Smith
    Dutch Colony
    Christopher Columbus
    Spanish horses
    Viking settlements in Iceland
2. 6, 2, 7, 3, 1, 5, 4, 8
3. 3, 1, 2, 5, 4
4. 1, 2

Page 70   **French and English Interests Begin to Clash**

g. France, France

Page 73 **How the British Captured Quebec**

1. 1st column of pictures from top to bottom: 3, 4, 6
   2nd column of pictures from top to bottom: 5, 1, 2
2. a. • The deserters told Wolfe of the expected French ships.
   • The darkness of the night made it difficult for the French to recognize the British ships.
   • The French-speaking English soldier fooled the French guard.
   b. *Pictures:* 3. The English ships approach Quebec under the cover of darkness.
   4. A French guard is fooled by a French-speaking English soldier.
   6. General Montcalm is surprised to see the English troops.
   5. The English climb the path to the plains of Quebec.
   1. Quebec has a lower town and an upper town.
   2. Two French deserters reveal secrets to the English.

Page 78 **Paul Revere: Patriot, Silversmith**

1. 3, 5, 1, 4, 6, 9, 8, 7, 2
2. 8, 4, 1, 7, 2, 3, 9, 6, 5
3. Guns are not all held the same way, the soldiers are not in step, no two uniforms are alike
4. "A voice in the darkness, a knock at the door."
5. 40 years
6. To prevent denting
7. The direction from which the British would come
   Suggestions: "I can't believe it!" "What will we do?"
   "I'd better warn the neighbors."

Page 82 **The British Plan to Win the War**

Completion: Champlain, George, Hudson, St. Lawrence, Ontario, Mohawk, New York City, Hudson

Page 83 **A Secret Message to General Burgoyne**

1. His force was too small.
2. "I own to you I think Sir W's move just at this time the worst he could take."
3. Message in 2nd column: *Note*—Secret words are at the ends of the lines. "General Clinton left New York to capture American forts on the Hudson River. He was sure that this would force the Americans to send some troops to the South. He was successful. But instead of marching north to join Burgoyne, he decided to return to New York."
4. (1) He sent troops to capture American supplies.
   (2) His raid was not successful.

Page 87 **Washington's Victory at Yorktown Ends the War**

1. British ships could help in any land battles he might fight; if a retreat were necessary, British troops could help his troops to escape.
2. This was his chance to trap the British.
3. Cornwallis could not escape by sea because the French fleet at the entrance of Chesapeake Bay kept the British ships from escaping.
4. French troops under the command of General Rochambeau were available to help Washington.
5. a. British   b. British soldiers carrying a white flag. c. He's indicating, "Hold fire!"

Page 90   **Crossword Puzzle: From Colonies to Independence**

Page 92   **Organizing and Governing the Northwest Territory**

2. New York, Massachusetts, New Hampshire; Vermont
3. Great Britain and the United States

Page 94   **Understanding the Constitution**

1. F	4. F	7. F	10. F
2. T	5. F	8. F	
3. F	6. T	9. F	

Page 95   **Alexander Hamilton: Patriot, Statesman**

Paragraph #'s: 5, 1, 4, 3, 8, 2, 7, 6

	Suggested Nouns	*Suggested Verbs*
3.	Dock, ship	Waving (goodbye), leaving
4.	Gate, wall (brick)	Helping, comforting, demonstrating (background)
5.	Soldiers, horse	Marching, training
6.	Window, minister	Marrying, reading (book)
7.	Banner, podium	Speaking, listening
8.	Pistols, observers	Dueling, observing

Page 97   **Sequoia: Indian Scholar**

1. a. Cherokee   f. Twelve years
    b. Tennessee   g. (1) Sequoia National Park (and trees)
    c. Northern Mexico   bear his name.
    d. Seventy-three   (2) Statue in Statuary Hall, Capital
    e. Wife burned work;   Building, Washington, D.C..
        Indians burned his
        cabin.
2. "He gave up this method becuase he realized that a person would have to remember thou
    sands of symbols."
3. R, P, M, B, A, J, Y, Z, E, T

Page 98   **Thomas Jefferson: Statesman, Patriot**

1. *1st column of illustrations*: 28, 19 or 31, 3, 22
    2nd column of illustrations: 9, 4, 32, 6
2. 17, 20, 15, 5, 18

Page 99   **Three African-Americans in the Far West**

1. 15 years
2. *Suggested:* How many beaver furs for the rifle? How far does a bullet go? How long does it
    take to load? Is it powerful enough to kill a deer?
3. He's riding a horse, carrying a gun, wearing a hat, and he has a knife on his belt. He has a
    pack on his saddle.
4. He actually occupied the land.
5. He could raise his family in freedom.
6. *Suggested:* Top picture: York explains a rifle.
                 Middle picture: Beckwourth rides to a trading session.
                 Bottom picture: Bush and family migrate to Oregon.

Page 103   **Sacajawea and the Lewis and Clark Expedition**

1. a. 12; b. 12; c. Shoshonis; d. Jean Baptiste, "Pomp"; e. 100; f. Wyoming
2. Guide, interpreter
3. *Suggested:* Sacajawea and her husband meet Lewis and Clark at a Mandan village in North
    Dakota
4. "As belongings of the expedition floated past her, she fished them out of the water."
5. *Suggested:* "At last I have returned home. My brother is here to welcome me. Soon, I shall
    see the friends of my childhood."
6. "She and her husband walked hundreds of miles along the river bank, assisting Lewis, who
    was taking notes on the land, plants, and animals. *Note*: Also acceptable: "She continued to
    carry her young son in a papoose on her back, a load that even the men would have found
    difficult."
7. *Suggested:* hardy, uncomplaining, brave, resourceful, helpful, intelligent
8. Various answers

1. Food, guns, ammunition, horses (in those times), clothing—almost anything that could be useful to soldiers and civilians.
3. The ships are covered with cobwebs, which are symbolic of people and events standing still and undisturbed.
4. "The British actually fired upon our battleships. They often impressed, or forced, sailors from American ships to work in the British navy."
5. Final paragraph, 2nd and 3rd sentences
7. They thought that if the British won the war, it would bring a halt to American settlement in their lands.
10. "The British burned the White House and soon other public buildings in revenge for the United States capture and burning of Toronto, Canada."

Page 107   Word Search: People and Events —1775 to 1860

W	A	S	H	I	N	G	T	O	N	F	U	L	T	O	N	S
G	A	A	S	T	E	A	M	B	O	A	T	X	V	K	N	T
E	T	R	E	N	T	O	N	F	R	A	N	C	E	O	C	L
R	C	A	W	F	R	A	N	K	L	I	N	B	S	L	O	A
I	A	T	Y	I	Z	G	A	G	E	K	C	R	A	A	N	W
E	L	O	O	W	T	R	E	V	E	R	E	A	C	F	S	R
A	I	G	R	H	M	H	D	H	X	F	Y	D	A	A	T	E
L	F	A	K	I	O	A	M	N	F	O	W	D	J	Y	I	N
W	O	B	T	T	R	M	T	E	X	A	S	O	A	E	T	C
O	R	O	O	M	S	I	J	K	X	L	M	C	W	T	U	E
L	N	S	W	A	E	L	N	P	Q	I	R	K	E	T	T	R
F	I	T	N	N	S	T	G	O	L	D	C	T	A	E	I	I
E	A	O	U	V	A	O	B	C	O	N	C	O	R	D	O	V
C	D	N	G	H	I	N	Q	U	E	B	E	C	E	J	N	E
O	R	E	G	O	N	K	M	O	N	T	C	A	L	M	L	R

Page 109   Narcissa Whitman and Crossing the Rockies

Suggested captions:

Picture 1: Narcissa and Marcus are making plans for their mission. They are thinking of ways to teach the Indians.
Picture 2: Marcus is pointing to the place where he will establish the mission. He is explaining that it is a good site because two rivers meet there, and transportation would be facilitated.
Picture 3: There were many rivers to cross. Often, Marcus had to help turn the wheels of the wagon.
Picture 4: Narcissa is hoping that her child is still alive. Marcus does not want to tell her the sad news.

Page 110 **Narcissa Whitman and Crossing the Rockies**

Suggested outline:
1. Narcissa's early life
   a. Birth place: New York State
   b. Graduated Franklin Academy
   c. Ambition: Missionary to Indians

2. Narcissa's ambition made possible
   a. Meets Marcus Whitman
   b. Marcus and Narcissa engaged
   c. Will establish a mission together

3. Narcissa's marriage delayed
   a. Marcus to survey mission possibilities
   b. Marcus returns with good news
   c. Marcus and Narcissa marry

4. The journey west
   a. Other missionaries accompany
   b. Difficult journey
   c. Narcissa strong and determined

5. The journey's end
   a. Six months on trail
   b. Arrival at Ft. Vancouver
   c. Narcissa rests and teaches

6. The search for a mission site
   a. Marcus travels back up the Columbia
   b. Suitable site found: Waiilatpu
   c. Close to present day Walla Walla, WA

7. At home in the mission
   a. Mission established
   b. Indians cared for and taught
   c. Alice Clarissa drowns and dies

8. A family of eleven
   a. Narcissa grieves, work continues
   b. Narcissa adopts 11 children
   c. Raises children as her own

9. Death at the mission
   a. Indians misunderstand teachings
   b. Pioneers taking Indian land
   c. Disease strikes Indians
   d. Indians attack Waiilatpu
   e. Narcissa, Marcus, 11 others killed

10. Emigration grows
    a. Other pioneers follow the Whitmans
    b. 1843: great migration of settlers
    c. Each year more and more settlers

11. Winning the Oregon Territory
    a. Ownership of Oregon questioned
    b. Presence of American settlers important
    c. Oregon Country becomes U.S. possession

Page 114 **The Erie Canal: A Water Highway in the West**

1. 2,500,000
2. $250
3. Mohawk River
4. Albany
5. Lake Erie
6. *Acceptable:* 400–450 miles
7. $25, $225
8. 13 days
9. Animal power (mules, horses)
10. The bridges that crossed the canals were low.

Page 118   **The Beginning of Railroads in the United States**

1. *Peter Cooper*: railroad pioneer; worked to develop steam locomotives
   Baltimore and Ohio: Early railroad company, tried to put sails on trains as means of locomotion
   The Tom Thumb: America's first steam locomotive
   August, 1830: Tom Thumb successfully pulls railroad cars
2. a. Tracks could be laid along rivers
   b. Tracks could be laid anywhere
   c. Railroads provided faster transportation
3. **Bull**: stubborn, belligerent, determined
   Engineer: angry, impatient
   Farmer: aggravated, angry, embarrassed (possibly)
4. *Suggested*:
   Bull: No way you're going to get by me!
   Engineer: Get that darn bull off the tracks before I run him over!
   Farmer: Get off those tracks you crazy bull!
   Passenger: If they don't get that bull off the tracks, we will all die from smoke inhalation!

Page 120   **Transportation by Land and Water**

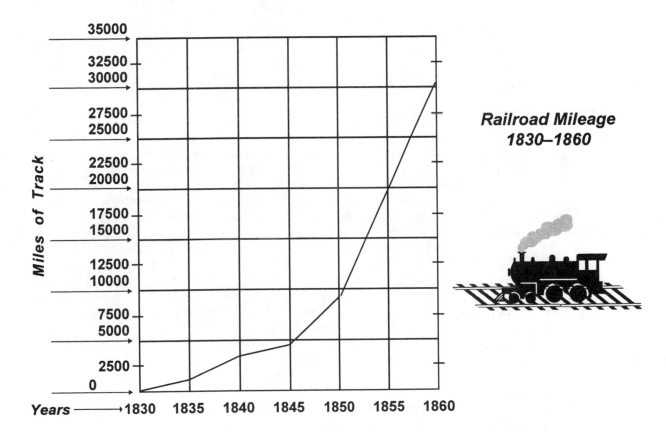

266

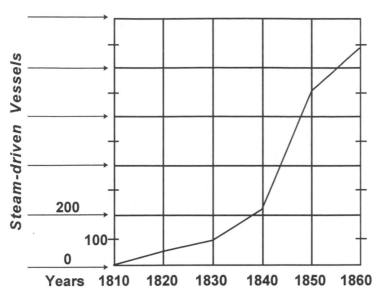

Steam-driven Vessels

200
100
0

Years 1810 1820 1830 1840 1850 1860

Title:

Steamboat/Steam Ship Growth

1810–1860

Page 121   **Robert Fulton, Inventor**

1. 3, 2, 1, 4, 6, 5
2. 4, 5, 3, 1, 6, 2, 5, 4
3. 5, 2, 3, 6, 4, 1

Page 122   **The Conestoga Wagon**

1. Conestoga, Pennsylvania (1750)
2. 24 ft., 60 ft.
3. Driver's place to guide animals, operate brake, rest
4. Wrenches, hammers, awls, pliers (mostly items for repairing the wagon or horses' harnesses, as compared to farming tools, which would have been carried inside the wagon)
5. The rims were broad and, therefore, had greater surface area than narrow rims would; this helped to prevent sinkage.
6. Loads would not fall out the front or the back when the wagon was going up or down steep hills.
7. Joints were stuffed with tar or pitch.
8. Privacy, shelter from storms, shelter from heat
9. High wheels would clear stumps and road ruts (The high wheels also gave more clearance when crossing shallow streams or deep puddles.)
10. The white covers called sailing ships to mind, especially when the wagons were seen at a distance as they moved through high grass.
11. Curtains, clothing, bed sheets, sacks, covers for harvested crops
12. **Wood:** for buildings, furniture
    Wheels: as a windlass for hauling pails of water from wells
    Spokes: for fences, stakes
    Iron rims: could be heated or melted down to fashion other tools
    Body: Corn crib; boards for sides and roofing of cabins

Page 124   **Cyrus McCormick: Agricultural Inventor**

1. a. Cyrus McCormick
    b. McCormick's invention of the reaper
    c. Virginia
    d. July, 1831; July, 1832
    e. To demonstrate the effectiveness of the reaper
2. About 100 people
3. July, 1831
4. Steele's Tavern, Virginia
5. Six acres
6. 24 men chopping with sickles
7. Improve how it cut wet grain; find way to prevent the reel from knocking grain to the ground
8. Modestly (modest)
9. Not mentioned: The price of wheat would come down.

Page 125   **Life on the Plains**

Pictures
Pictures numbered, as follows:
1st column: 2, 9, 8, 3, 1   2nd column: 5, 10, 4, 7, 6
Words
1. Travelling by <u>Conestoga</u> wagon (e)
2. Building a <u>sod</u> house (f)
3. Digging for <u>fresh</u> water (g)
4. Farming with a <u>steel</u> plow (b)
5. Trying to stop a <u>grass</u> fire (d)
6. Clouds of <u>hungry</u> grasshoppers (j)
7. Fighting a <u>blinding</u> blizzard (h)
8. Fleeing a <u>frightening</u> tornado (a)
9. Erecting a <u>barbed-wire</u> fence (i)
10. Stuck on the <u>muddy</u> road (c)
To go ahead: Build cabin, dig for water, plant crops (Accept other reasonable sequences)

Pages 127–128   **Improvement in Industry: Making Cloth**

1. Grinding wheat, spinning yarn, and weaving cloth
2. *Possibilities:* Quality of health care; ways of preserving foods; means of communication and transportation
3. "More food, more clothing, more houses, better tools, and better means of transportation were needed."
4. Watt was able to use his own ideas in conjunction with the ideas and developments of others to develop his invention.
5. Water power, steam power
6. It was necessary to develop a faster way to weave yarn into cloth.
7. A power loom (weaving machine) was developed.
8. "The British would not allow the Americans to buy the British textile machines or the plans to make them. So strictly did the British guard their secret that textile workers were not allowed to leave the country."
9. In Lowell's factory both spinning and weaving were done in one building.
10. Slavery would increase as the need for and use of cotton increased (and this actually happened).

Page 129   **Revolution in Communications: Samuel Morse**

Message at bottom of page: MORSE WAS A GREAT PAINTER. HE ALSO TOOK THE FIRST PHOTOGRAPHS MADE IN AMERICA.

Page 134   **The Union Grows: Texas, California, and Lands Between**

The Annexation of Texas

1. James Bowie, David Crockett
2. Santa Anna
3. San Jacinto
4. 1836 (March 2)
5. Republic of Texas

6. Sam Houston
7. 9 years
8. 1845
9. Austin
10. 266,807 sq. miles

The War with Mexico

1. Nueces River, Rio Grande
2. General Winfield Scott, Old Fuss and Feathers, Zachary Taylor, Old Rough and Ready, Monterrey
3. Treaty of Guadalupe Hidalgo (1848)
4. California, Texas, Arizona, New Mexico, Nevada, Utah *Note*: Parts of other states were also made from former Mexican territory: Oklahoma, Kansas, Wyoming, and Colorado (3/4ths of Colorado was formerly Mexican)
5. Stephen W. Kearny, Bear Flag Republic
6. 1853, $10 million (The original agreement called for $15 million), Arizona and New Mexico

Page 136   **Gold in California**

2. a. 3000 miles, 6–8 months
   b. 7400 miles, 2–3 months
   c. 13,000 miles, 3–4 months
3. Transcontinental, Isthmus of Panama

Page 137   **Diary of a Forty-niner**

Special terms (in order of appearance)
7-claim; 11-claim jumper; 4-color; 2-diggings; 1-grubstake; 5-nugget; 3-pan; 8-pay dirt; 9-rocker; 6-salt pork; 10-strike
Questions

1. March 27
2. April 4

3. April 13
4. He buried the gold.

5. $15,000

Page 138   **Historic Conversations**

1st column: 9, 3, 4, 5, 6
2nd column: 8, 7, 1, 13
3rd column: 2, 10, 11, 12

Page 140   **The Oregon Country is Peacefully Divided**

1. Ship *Columbia*: Carried Captain Gray from Boston to Oregon
   Willamette River: Oregon stream running through a fertile valley in which many Americans settled
   1846: Date of treaty between Americans and British that settled the Oregon Country dispute
   49th parallel: Line of latitude that became the boundary between the United States and Canada from the Pacific coast east, almost to the Great Lakes
2. Third item: Washington, Oregon, Idaho
   Last item: Spain

Page 142 **Harriet Tubman: Liberator, Army Scout, and Spy**

Facts about Harriet Tubman

1st picture: 1, 4, 12   4th picture: 3, 7, 9, 13, 15
2nd picture: 5, 11, 16   5th picture: 2, 8, 14
3rd picture: 6, 10, 17

Page 144 **Population Statistics Through 1860**

Graph

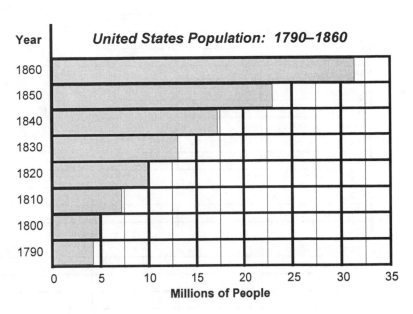

United States Population: 1790–1860

Population Centers Change and Move

1. 9, 4
2. Charleston, Salem, Providence, Norfolk, Richmond
3. 60,000; 500,000
4. 70,000

Page 145 **Frederick Douglass: Abolitionist, Writer**

1. Narrative paragraph sequences: 2, 8, 7, 4, 3, 9,. 6, 5, 1
2. Sentence additions to paragraphs: 2, 8, 9, 7, 4, 6, 5, 1, 3

Page 149 **The Fugitive Slave Act of 1850**

1. "All citizens were to aid in carrying out the law; for example, citizens had to assist in the capture of slaves."
2. A fine of $9,000, a jail sentence of 54 months (4 years, 6 months)
3. *Suggested*:
    Officer with badge and stick: "I don't like to be a part of this, but it's the law and I am sworn to enforce it."
    Man holding warrant: "I have a legal right to capture that runaway and return him to his owner."
    Man standing in front of runaway: "This man is in a free state; if you try to take him we will resist you."
    Boy with hoop and stick: "It's not fair. Some day I'm going to become a lawyer and help runaways."
    The runaway: "They can put me in chains, take me back and beat me, but at the first chance I'll run away again or die trying."

6. 11, 23   7. Oregon, California   8. Texas

9.

State	Free	Slave	Date of Secession
Virginia		✓	April 17, 1861
Tennessee		✓	May 7, 1861
North Carolina		✓	May 20, 1861
South Carolina		✓	December 20, 1860
Georgia		✓	January 19, 1861
Florida		✓	January 10, 1861
Alabama		✓	January 11, 1861
Mississippi		✓	January 9, 1861
Louisiana		✓	January 26, 1861
Arkansas		✓	May 6, 1861
Texas		✓	February 1, 1861
West Virginia		✓	
Oregon	✓		
California	✓		
Kansas	✓		
Minnesota	✓		
Iowa	✓		
Missouri		✓	
Wisconsin	✓		
Illinois	✓		
Indiana	✓		
Kentucky		✓	
Ohio	✓		
Pennsylvania	✓		
New York	✓		
Vermont	✓		
New Hampshire	✓		
Maine	✓		
Massachusetts	✓		
Rhode Island	✓		
Connecticut	✓		
New Jersey	✓		
Delaware		✓	
Maryland		✓	

271

American History to 1860 Trivia Challenge

1. *My Bondage and My Freedom*
2. Pennsylvania
3. *Half Moon*
4. *Poor Richard's Almanac*
5. 4
6. Jacques Cartier
7. *The North Star*
8. John Chapman
9. *Sarah Constant, Goodspeed, Discovery*
10. 1st
11. Sir Wm. Berkeley
12. 1729
13. Bear, Star
14. 1777
15. 3rd 4th
16. *Bonhomme Richard*
17. March 5, 1770
18. East India Company
19. 1847
20. Gentleman Johnny
21. Samuel Adams, John Adams, Robert Treat Paine, Elbridge Gerry
22. December 26, 1776
23. James Lawrence
24. *Golden Hind*
25. Mad Anthony Wayne
26. Donald McKay
27. Henry
28. Carpenter
29. Grand
30. Mountain
31. James K. Polk
32. Nathan Hale
33. 1636
34. Louis Joliet, Jacques Marquette
35. Lapwai Mission
36. Murder
37. Potomac
38. Meriwether Lewis, William Clark
39. Liberty, Land
40. Tories
41. William
42. Andrew Jackson
43. Boston News-Letter
44. Virginia Dare
45. Old Hickory
46. 1847
47. 15
48. Princeton
49. Society of Friends
50. Honest Abe or Rail Splitter
51. Alamo
52. St. Augustine
53. Concord, MA
54. Cherokee
55. 1648
56. Molly Pitcher
57. Aaron Burr
58. American River
59. Texas, California
60. Swedes
61. Paterson, NJ
62. Captain Robert Gray
63. Tom Payne
64. John Quincy Adams
65. Kentucky
66. Maize
67. 1775
68. Francis Scott Key
69. Lowell Mason
70. Annapolis
71. Out of Many—One
72. Montezuma
73. 1848
74. John Jay
75. Monticello
76. Trenton
77. Shoshoni
78. Morristown, NJ
79. James Madison
80. Georgia

Two Great Sections Fight A Civil War

1st column: It was the final event that brought about the Civil War.

Understanding

1. 2nd paragraph: forts, army camps, post offices, arsenals
2. "The Confederates had demanded the surrender of the fort several times."
3. "President Lincoln had sworn to 'preserve, protect, and defend the Constitution of the United States.'..."
4. 2nd column, 1st paragraph: "He had refused the appointment because he did not wish to fight against the people of his own state."
5. Richmond was the capital of the Confederacy.
6. A civil war may cause members of the same family or friends to fight against each other.

Two Great Sections Fight a Civil War

2. Texas, Arkansas, Louisiana

1. "These two forts guarded the northern approaches to the Mississippi River."
2. Tennessee; Mississippi
3. "This split the Confederacy into an eastern and western section."
4. Lee invaded the North.
5. "Sherman's idea was that the South would stop fighting only if it could no longer make war."
6. Lee realized that there was no way the South could win the war, that many lives would be needlessly lost, so he surrendered.

John Ericcson

1. Thirty-six years old
2. 2nd paragraph: "He hated slavery."
3. "With their new weapon, the Confederates hoped to break the Union's blockade of the Confederate coast."
4. 4th paragraph: "It was destroyed by the Confederates themselves to keep the Union from capturing it."
6. *Suggested:* If the South had been able to break the Union blockade by using ironclad ships they would have been able to export cotton and use the money earned to buy war supplies. At the least, this would have prolonged the war. Perhaps a stalemate would have occured. In such a case, the South would have been an equal partner at the peace table.

Carl Schurz

1. He took part in a revolution against the government of Germany. The revolution failed; Schurz had to leave the country.
2. He had to leave Germany secretly. He is hiding beneath a bridge while soldiers search.
3. Army officer, Secretary of the Interior, senator, newspaper writer

Robert Smalls

1. Smalls's family was smuggled aboard the *Planter*.
2. 1st paragraph, last sentence
3. Smalls became a member of the US Navy, a pilot on the *Planter*, then Captain of the *Planter*.
4. 3rd paragraph, last sentence

Questions answered in story: 2, 3, 5, 6, 9, 10, 11, 12

1.   Abraham Lincoln, as President; figuratively, a "Captain"
        The Civil War
        The United States
        Saving the Union
        Peace
        The United States is in no danger of being "wrecked."
        The nation reunited
2.   "It is some dream that on the deck,
               You've fallen cold and dead."

The Census: Counting the People in the Country

Population Growth of the United States: 1790–1860

Year of Census	Population of the Country	Population Living in Farm Areas	Population Living in Towns and Cities	African-American Population
1790	4,000,000	3,800,000	200,000	757,000
1830	13,000,000	12,000,000	1,000,000	2,300,000
1860	31,000,000	25,000,000	6,000,000	4,500,000

Page 170   **Soldiers of the Plains**

1. 1st paragraph, 4th and 5th sentences
2. 1st paragraph, 6th sentence
3. Veterans of the Civil War were experienced fighters who were used to living in difficult situations.
4. 3rd paragraph, last sentence
5. The words of praise from General Merritt and many others; nine African-American soldiers were awarded the Congressional Medal of Honor.
6. The cattlemen wanted unfenced grazing land for their cattle; also, fenced land would be a hindrance and an obstacle when they drove their cattle to markets and railroad stations.
7. The blizzard is so fierce that the soldier must lead the horse and break trail.

Pages 173–174   **Plains Settlers, Indians, and Buffalo**

1. b. Black Hills, Ozark Mountains, Ouachita Mountains
   c. Missouri River
   d. Rocky Mountains
2. Light rainfall, shallow rivers, few lakes
3. There was very little wood available for houses, barns, furniture, fuel, or fences.
4. Telephone, telegraph, mail delivery; railroads, roads
5. *Suggested:* You are taking our land, killing our buffalo, spreading your diseases, and not keeping the treaties we have made together.
6. The Indians saw the Union as the greatest danger to their way of life. A split within the country would make each part weaker, so they worked to encourage the split. Then, if they helped the Confederacy gain its objectives, the Confederacy might be more reasonable with them after winning the war.
7. a. Stampeding herd, train stopped, people shooting, dead buffalo, helpless calves, flat land, poles and wires.
   b. *Suggested*: The train has stopped to allow passengers to get off and shoot buffalo. The buffalo are stampeding and splitting into two herds.
8. With the demise of the buffalo the Indians lost their major source of food, clothing and shelter (skins), and other necessities such as pieces of bone for needles, sinews for snow-shoes, and so on. Without the buffalo, the only way that Indians could continue to live was to go to reservations.
9. The government is trying to compensate for past wrongs and injustices against the Indians by hearing their grievances and awarding compensation when justified.

1. Norway
2. A wind mill pumps it up from the ground; rain barrel
3. Leaks
4. Tree trunk (branch)
5. Warning, hunting, herding
6. Rifle

Page 177 **The American Cowboys During 1865–1890**

1. a. T; b. F; (**True** not justified because the text says **some**); c. F; d. T; e. T; f. F
2. Statements to be underlined: a, b, d
3. *Suggested*: Cowboys driving cattle to stockyards and/or a railroad shipping point. (The foreground cowboy is looking for strays; the three background cowboys are keeping the cattle in a herd and keeping them moving.)

Page 178 **Cowboys: Clothes and Equipment**

2. Additional uses of the items listed in the diagram:
   A: Carry water; wave as in a signal
   B: Wave as in a signal; use as a bandage
   C: Identification; wallet
   D: Keep hands warm; help prevent blisters
   E: Additional warmth; prevent chafing of thighs when riding a horse; protection from rain
   F: Prevent shoes from slipping *through* stirrups; "high" to prevent snake bites
   G: A "hand grip" for more stability when horse is galloping or bucking
   H: "Sleep mat" on ground; quick tent

Page 179 **Identifying Cattle**

1. Three: cutting, clipping ears; tattooing; branding
2. By registering the brand in a government office
3. If a cattle brand is too simple, cattle rustlers could easily alter it.
4. From left to right; c, l, a, f, h, j, b, d, e, g, i, k

Page 180 **The Heroic Retreat of the Nez Perce Indians**

1. The Nez Perce contended that the land was their land, that they had been there first.
2. 1st paragraph, 5th sentence: "However, the Nez Perce could not accept the only solution that was acceptable to the United States government—removal to a reservation in Idaho."
3. The Nez Perce thought they could live in freedom in Canada.
4. Chief Joseph; 1700 miles; 75 days; 200 warriors; fewer than 87 warriors; 2000 troopers
5. They stopped too soon, only thirty miles from Canada.
6. Caption of picture: "My people, some of them, have run away to the hills. . . ."

Pages 181–182 **The First Transcontinental Railroad**

1. 600 sq. miles, 500 sq. miles
2. $1920 (640 acres x $3.00); $19,200 (6400 acres x $3.00)
3. Central Pacific, Union Pacific, Omaha, Sacramento, Platte, Promontory, Nevada
4. Salt Lake
5. Five
6. 1775 miles
7. Europeans entered the United States on the east; Asians entered the United States on the west.

The Spanish-American War: Fighting on Land and Sea

Fighting the War

1. Spain
2. The Spanish fleet was destroyed
3. Luzon
4. South China Sea
5. Acceptable: 725-800 miles
6. West
7. July 17, 1898
8. "They met very little resistance."
9. Cuba gained independence, and was helped by the United States to get started as a nation. Puerto Rico became an United States possession.

Helping Cuba

1. After independence from Spain, Cuba had no established government.
2. Paragraph 3, sentences 2 and 3
3. After May 20, 1902, the United States ended its participation in Cuba's governance.

Facts About Puerto Rico

1st column, in sequence: H, GP, IT, IT, H, GP, E, GC, H, H, P, GP
2nd column in sequence: H, GC, H, H, E, GC, E, GP, P, IT, P, GC, E, IT, GC, IT, GC, GP

The Early Hawaiians

2. North
3. Polynesians populated most of the islands (The Polynesian Triangle).
5. Outrigger
6 They carried live pigs (pork) and live chickens (eggs, chicken).
7. Hollow bamboo logs held water.
8. The Polynesians caught birds that landed on their crafts, and fish from the ocean.

Challenge question: The Polynesians charted the movements of the stars and used the stars as navigational aids.

The United States Acquires Alaska

Fill in the blanks: 50, Bering Strait, Kodiak

Understanding

3. Furbearing animals were becoming scarce.
4. (1) Alaska has many natural resources; (2) If we don't acquire Alaska some other nation, perhaps unfriendly, will; (3) We set a precedent for purchasing land with the Louisiana Purchase (and the Gadsden Purchase);
5. *Suggested*: If an unfriendly nation in Asia, for example, possessed Alaska, then that nation would be in a good position to invade Canada and/or the United States.

George Washington Goethals: Canal Builder

1. Dutch
2. 1858
3. Imagination, stubbornness, faithfulness
4. Barges
5. Corps of Engineers

6. He felt it was his duty and responsibility to oversee the construction of the canal through to the end.
7. Goethals was a Major-General in World War I.
8. Experience
9. The water may be too rough or too shallow.
10. (1) Unload the big ship, (2) transport the materials to the dock by small boat, (3) unload the materials onto the docks, (4) manually carry the materials up the slope to dry land and storage or further transportation by other means.

Page 195   Matthew Henson: Polar Explorer

1. 1999
2. 2, 3, 4, 1
3. "He was cheerful. . . ."
4. Peary's dream: 3rd paragraph, last sentence
   Peary's character: 4th paragraph, 5th sentence
   Polar cold and Peary: 4th paragraph, 3rd sentence
5. Four Eskimo
6. *Suggested*: Peary and Henson were walking over treacherous ice and snow. Peary was in the lead. Suddenly, a fierce and angry musk-ox charged from behind a snow bank. Peary was unarmed. Henson, who carried a rifle, saw the danger Peary was in and quickly reacted. He aimed his rifle, pulled the trigger and shot the musk-ox dead in its tracks.

Page 199   Immigration Facts: 1820–1992

Bar graph

1. 2,300,000; 4,900,000; 21,500,000; 10,100,000; 1931 to 1950; 1,600,000; 11,900,000
2. a. 8,500,000; b. 23,600,000; c. 58,200,000

Circle graph

3. *Suggested*: About 62% of all the people who have emigrated to the United States came from Europe. The rest of the emigrants are made up of 25% from the "Americas," 11% from Asia, and only 2% from other parts of the world.

Completing a Bar Graph

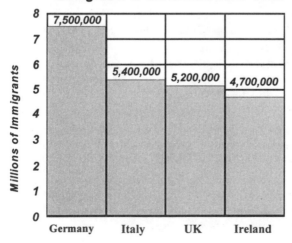

European Countries Sending the Most Immigrants to the U.S.A.: 1820–1992

Page 201   **Emigration: The Voyage to a New Home**

1. *Sentences in sequence:*
   1st paragraph: "Some emigrants had never seen an ocean."
   2nd paragraph: "The days passed very slowly."
   3rd paragraph: "Then, other emigrants. . . ."
   4th paragraph: "The long nights were not quiet. . . ."
   5th paragraph: "Sometimes, adult emigrants taught. . . ."
   6th paragraph: "The friends they had made. . . ."

2. *Suggested*: As the ship passed the Statue of Liberty the small family was deep in thought. The father was thinking that he could raise his child in a free country; no longer would he have to obey laws he had no part in making. The mother had other, quite different thoughts: she would have her own house and garden, and maybe she could find work as a seamstress because she was skilled in sewing. The little girl? She was wondering what school would be like, and would the other children like her.

Page 202   **Americans: Out of Many–One**

1. Eight
2. Two, two
3. Judith Chung
4. Anthony Lazzaro, Robert LaCrosse
5. Elsi Rothacker, Anna Rostovich
6. Helena Chung, Katherine Blackhawk

Page 205   **The Wright Brother Fly an Airplane at Kitty Hawk**

Weight: 600 lbs
Wing Span: 40½ feet
Number of Propellers: 2
Type of Motor: gas
Gas Tank Capacity: 1 gal.
Type of Landing Gear: skids
Where Displayed: Smithsonian Institute, Washington, DC

Cost: $1000
Place First Flown: Kitty Hawk, North Carolina
Date of First Flight: December 17, 1903
Length of First Flight: 120 feet
Duration of First Flight: 12 seconds
Pilot's Position During Flight: prone

Page 206   **First Solo Atlantic Flight**

True-False in sequence: T, F, T, F, F, T, T, F, T, T, F, T, T

Page 207   **European Nations Choose Sides in World War I**

1. Ireland, Great Britain, Belgium, France, Luxembourg, Portugal, Italy, Montenegro, Albania, Serbia, Greece, Romania, Russia
2. Germany, Austria-Hungary, Bulgaria, Turkey
3. Norway, Sweden, Netherlands, Denmark, Switzerland, Spain
4. Serbia, Greece, Romania
5. Ireland, Great Britain, Portugal, Albania

Page 210   **World War I Changes the Map of Europe**

1. Austria, Estonia
   Czechoslovakia, Latvia
   Yugoslavia, Lithuania
   Poland, Finland
   Hungary

   Note: Soviet Union could be included because of name change and significant boundary changes.

2. Estonia, Latvia, Lithuania, Poland, Finland
3. Russia
4. Soviet Union (Union of Soviet Socialist Republics)
5. Romania

278

The 1920's: Years of Growth

1. Population: 14,000,000
   Newspaper circulation: 10,200,000
   Telephones: 6,000,000
   Automobiles, trucks, and busses: 15,500,000
   Tractors on farms (thousands): 536,000
   Airplanes produced: 4,018
2. 5,000,000; the great increase in motor vehicles and tractors made horses less necessary
3. Motor vehicles need oil and gasoline (made from oil). It was important to move oil swiftly and inexpensively to all parts of the country; pipelines filled that need.
4. Lumbering (Cutting lumber and hauling it to the mills where it was made into boards or processed into pulp for papermaking may be considered as part of the lumber industry.)
5. The lumber industry would grow significantly; concomitantly, forests would become depleted, resulting in loss of habitat for wildlife.

Page 214 **From the Civil War to the Great Depression: Crossword Puzzle**

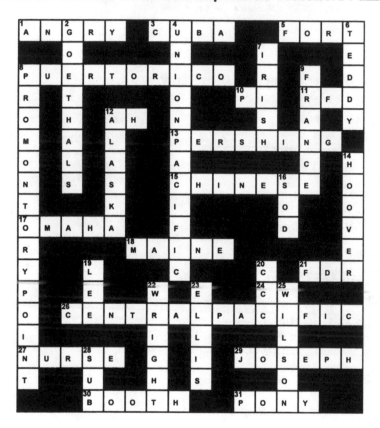

Jim Thorpe: All-around Athlete

T	N	A	S	S	O	C	I	A	T	E	D
V	E	F	J	B	R	O	W	N	G	E	O
J	W	O	A	I	S	T	A	R	I	T	L
A	A	O	K	L	A	H	O	M	A	E	Y
V	T	T	S	O	C	O	S	X	N	D	M
E	H	B	F	A	T	H	L	E	T	E	P
L	O	A	D	S	N	I	R	I	S	H	I
I	H	L	X	N	S	W	E	D	E	N	C
N	A	L	R	F	E	D	I	S	C	U	S
T	C	A	R	L	I	S	L	E	F	O	X
U	K	E	I	S	E	N	H	O	W	E	R
E	D	E	C	A	T	H	L	O	N	A	Q

Jesse Owens: Olympic Champion

1. *Paragraphs and related pictures:* 5, 4, 2, 1, 3
2. *Paragraphs and related sentences:*
    1st paragraph: F, D, B, G
    2nd paragraph: A
    3rd paragraph: E, J
    4th paragraph: H, K
    5th paragraph: C, I
3. *Captions (Suggested):*
    Picture 1: Winning for OSU
    Picture 2: Scholarship Offers in the Mail
    Picture 3: Jesse Wins in the Olympics
    Picture 4: Jesse Is Coached by Mr. Riley
    Picture 5: Young Jesse Goes to Work in the Cotton Fields

Althea Gibson: World Champion Tennis Player

1. Paragraph 1: Picture 2
    Paragraph 2: Picture 3
    Paragraph 3: Picture 1
    Paragraph 4: Picture 5
    Paragraph 5: Picture 6
    Paragraph 6: Picture 4
2. *Suggested*:
    1. Althea defends herself and her friends
    2. Althea drops out of high school
    3. Althea's talent is recognized
    4. Winning the girls' singles in the New York State Open
    5. Enjoying the peak of her career
    6. Scoring an academic victory

Pages 223–
224   **Dictators Take Over Russia, Italy, and Germany**

A Dictator for Russia
1. 1st paragraph, 4th sentence
2. Dishonest, cruel
3. Nicholas was forced from his throne; later, he and his family were killed.
4. 4th paragraph, 1st sentence
5. 5th paragraph, 1st sentence

A Dictator for Italy
1. 1st paragraph, 5th sentence
2. Mussolini opposed the Communists and met force with force to end the Communist threat.
3. Mussolini's force began a "march on Rome."

A Dictator for Germany
1. a. Germans were a master race.
    b. Germany was poor because it was not large enough.
    c. Germany was surrounded by enemies.
    d. Jews were responsible for Germany's troubles.
2. a. Opposing newspapers were shut down.
    b. Opposing parties could not have meetings.
    c. Opposing people could not use radios for broadcasting.
3. Hitler had them jailed, and/or beaten, and/or killed.

Page 226   **Dwight D. Eisenhower: World War II General, President**

Column 1	*Column 2*
5: January, 1933	1: October 14, 1890
8: June 7, 1948	10: March 28, 1969
4: March, 1918	3: June 14, 1911
7: June, 1942	9: Summer, 1952
6: December 7, 1941	2: Spring, 1909

Page 228   **Japanese-Americans During World War II**

1. 1, 7, 3, 19 or 20
2. Sentence 6, 12, or 13
3. Sentence 14 or 15
4. Sentences 19 and 20
5. Soldiers, spies, and translators
6. *Suggested:*

Japanese soldier: Halt! Who are you?

Terry Doi: I am a Japanese-American soldier.

Japanese soldier: We could kill you. What do you want? Are you here to surrender?

Terry Doi: No. I am not here to surrender. I am here to ask you to surrender. You are completely surrounded. We know you are brave fighters, but we do not want to kill you. If you surrender you will be well treated.

Japanese soldier: How do we know what you say is true? We have heard that you Americans torture and kill prisoners.

Terry Doi: That is not true. We follow the rules of war that say prisoners will not be harmed and that they will receive decent food, clothing, and shelter. I would not lie to you. We don't want you or our own soldiers needlessly killed or wounded. You are brave soldiers fighting for what you think is right, but believe me, your deaths would serve no purpose. There is no way you can win. We are much too strong.

Page 229   **Albert Einstein: Winning the Race to Develop the Atom Bomb**

1. 1st paragraph: last sentence
2. 2nd paragraph: 2nd sentence
3. 3rd paragraph: 5th sentence
4. 4th paragraph: 2nd sentence
5. 3rd paragraph: 3rd sentence
6. 1933
   1940
   Princeton, NJ
   Mathematical formula
7. He drove Einstein (and other Jews) from Germany. Einstein then used his genus to help the United States.

Pages 230–231   **Winning the War in the Pacific**

1. To be checked: Burma, Thailand, Malaya, Manchuria, Borneo, French Indochina, New Guinea, Sumatra, Java, Korea
3. 5 months
6. Column 2, 1st paragraph, last two sentences
9. Page 230, last paragraph, 3rd sentence
10. Page 231, column 1, 2nd paragraph, 2nd sentence

Page 232   **Jack Kennedy and PT-109**

1. *Suggested:*

    CREW OF UNITED STATES TORPEDO BOAT RESCUED
    Sank in Collision with Japanese Destroyer
    11 Crew Members Saved, Two Dead
    Heroic Rescue by Lt. Jack Kennedy

    Solomon Islands, August 1943

2. *Suggested:*
    "This is station WXYZ: A report just in. The crew of PT-109, feared lost in a collision with a Japanese destroyer, has been rescued. Eleven men were saved, but two were killed in the crash. The crew abandoned the sinking PT and, led by Lt. Jack Kennedy, swam through shark infested waters and Japanese-dominated islands to an uninhabited island. Near death after three days of little food and water, the survivors were discovered by native members of a spy network, who notified American authorities. PT-109's crew is making a good recovery.
3. Sentence: "The crew swims back to the wreck and clings to its sides during the long night."

Page 240-241 African-Americans and Others Fight Discrimination

1. *Suggested:* All people regardless of race, religion, ethnic background, or political beliefs would be equal in every respect. There would be no discrimination in employment, voting, housing, education, and utilization of public and private facilities.
2. The NAACP sued in the courts for equal rights and worked to have laws passed that helped African-Americans.
3. The National Urban League worked to help African-Americans obtain equal opportunity and equal pay employment.
4. By being promoted to Brigadier General, Davis was a fine example for all Americans, especially African-Americans.
5. Executive Order 9981 ended segregation in the armed forces.
6. It ended segregation in the public schools.

7. Boycotts, sit-ins, marches, demonstrations
8. The Lincoln Memorial and Abraham Lincoln were symbols of freedom for all; the site was near the seat of the United States government (White House, Congress, Supreme Court); the site was easily accessible and could accommodate large crowds.
9. An African-American justice would understand and be sympathetic to African-American problems.

Page 245 **History and Geography in Eastern Asia**

2.

Country	*Capital*	*Country*	*Capital*
China	Beijing	Laos	Vientiane
No. Korea	Pyongyang	Cambodia	Phnom Penh
So. Korea	Seoul	Myanmar	Yangon
Japan	Tokyo	Thailand	Bangkok
Taiwan	Taipei	Maylasia	Kuala Lumpur
Vietnam	Hanoi	Philippine Islands	Manila

Page 246 **War in Korea**

6. • China entered the war in support of North Korea.
   • The Soviet Union had agreed to the temporary divisiion of the Korean peninsula into two parts: North Korea and South Korea. Then, the Soviet Union broke this agreement by supporting North Korea in its invasion of South Korea.

Page 248 **The Persian Gulf War and Geography**

A: Turkey	G: Jordan	M: Bahrein
B: USSR	H: Iraq	N: Qatar
C: Cyprus	I: Egypt	O: United Arab Emirates
D: Syria	J: Iran	P: Oman
E: Lebanon	K: Kuwait	Q: Yemen
F: Israel	L: Saudi Arabia	

Page 251 Christa McAuliffe: School Teacher, Astronaut

1. *Suggested:* The space shuttle *Challenger* rests on the launching pad just before blast-off, January 2, 1986
2. *Suggested:* Persistent, intelligent, determined, brave, hard-working
3. *Suggested:* I've dreamed of this, worked for it, and now I've got it. It scares me a little, but everything is going to be all right.
4. *Suggested:* "Children, you saw the *Challenger* blow up, and I know you feel sad and broken-hearted. Your mom is gone, and she is not coming back. You can be very proud of her, though, because she followed a dream as far as she could. She is a hero, and she'll never be forgotten for her bravery and daring. It's people such as your mother who have made our country great through courage and sacrifice."